Many books have been written on the 'Second Russian Revolution'. This masterful account by Jonathan Steele, the *Guardian*'s long-serving Moscow correspondent, is different. It looks at Russia in the round – before, during and after Communism – and unravels the key issues troubling outside observers and the Russians themselves. Why hasn't the end of the Soviet system produced democracy? How great is the danger of Russian nationalism?

Eternal Russia draws directly on interviews with the leading figures, including Gorbachev and the former Communist party Politburo, as well as senior members of the Yeltsin team. As the extraordinary changes unfold from 1987 to the present day, we follow the citizens' movements and the protest marches, the 1991 coup, Yeltsin's dramatic showdown with parliament, the elections of December 1993 and the return of Solzhenitsyn to his native land.

In this timely and provocative book, Gorbachev's *perestroika* and the Yeltsin reforms are placed in the broad sweep of Russian history, vividly highlighting the difficulties facing those attempting to build democracy and the rule of law in Russia's changing yet changeless conditions.

Jonathan Steele has twice won the International Reporter of the Year title in the British Press Awards for his coverage of the Soviet Union and Russia. In 1991 he also received the London Press Club's 'Scoop of the Year' award for getting to Gorbachev's prison villa on the Crimea and talking to the President during the coup.

Born in 1941, he read classics at King's College, Cambridge, and received a Master's Degree in Economics from Yale University. He joined the *Guardian* in 1965, and has worked as a correspondent in Eastern Europe and Washington, as joint Foreign News Editor and Chief Foreign Correspondent. He was Moscow bureau chief from 1988 to 1994. He is married with two children.

By the Same Author

WORLD POWER
THE LIMITS OF SOVIET POWER
SOCIALISM WITH A GERMAN FACE
EASTERN EUROPE SINCE STALIN
ANDROPOV IN POWER (*co-author*)
SUPERPOWERS IN COLLISION (*co-author*)
THE SOUTH AFRICAN CONNECTION (*co-author*)

ETERNAL RUSSIA

Yeltsin, Gorbachev
and the Mirage of Democracy

JONATHAN STEELE

faber and faber
LONDON · BOSTON

To Ruth, Paul and Ben

First published in 1994
by Faber and Faber Limited
3 Queen Square London WCIN 3AU
This paperback edition first published in 1995

Photoset in Ehrhardt by Datix International Limited, Bungay, Suffolk
Printed in England by Clays Ltd, St Ives plc

A CIP record for this book is available from the British Library.

ISBN 0-571-17338-1

2 4 6 8 10 9 7 5 3 1

Contents

CONTENTS

Acknowledgements

Scores of people who were in the thick of the events discussed in this book gave up their time to talk to me, both while perestroika was underway and when it was over. I particularly want to thank Yuri Afanasyev, Vadim Bakatin, Oleg Bogomolov, Anatoly Chernyayev, Igor Chubais, Ivan Frolov, Mikhail Gorbachev, Andrei Grachev, Vladimir Ivashko, Alexander Kabakov, Boris Kagarlitsky, Otto Lacis, Ivan Laptev, Alexander Lebedev, Yegor Ligachev, Alexander Likhotal, Anatoly Lukyanov, Arkady Maslennikov, Arkady Murashev, Pavel Palazhchenko, Alexander Prokhanov, Grigory Revenko, Oleg Rumyantsev, Nikolai Ryzhkov, Georgy Shakhnazarov, Viktor Sheinis, Sergei Stankevich, Lev Sukhanov, Pavel Voshchanov, Alexander Yakovlev and Nikolai Yefimov.

I also owe a debt to those who read parts of the draft and made helpful comments. They include Michael Emerson, Nirupam Sen, and Kyle Wilson. Perry Anderson, Margot Light, Nodari Simonia, and Nikita Vvedenskaya were kind enough to read virtually the entire manuscript. Their detailed remarks and corrections were invaluable. Ben, Paul, and Ruth Steele also read the draft with critical eyes. Julian Loose and David Watson, my editors at Faber, were always active with ideas for improvements. John Rettie, my *Guardian* colleague in Moscow while most of this book's story unfolded, was a cheerful foil and fort-holder. Peter Preston, the Editor of the *Guardian*, and Paul Webster, the Foreign Editor, accepted my taking time off to write this book. David Hearst, my other colleague in Moscow, plugged the gap in the last months of its completion. I am grateful to them all.

vii

Dramatis Personae

Afanasyev, Yuri Radical reformer. Academic historian. Co-chair of Inter-regional Group in Soviet Congress of People's Deputies.

Bakatin, Viktor Soviet Interior Minister (1988–90); chair of KGB (1991). Close ally of Gorbachev.

Barannikov, Viktor Army General. Russian Interior Minister (1990–91); Russian Security Minister (1992–93). Arrested during storming of White House.

Bragin, Vyacheslav Pro-Yeltsin MP. Appointed head of Ostankino TV station in January 1993. Dismissed in December 1993.

Burbulis, Gennady Close adviser to Yeltsin. Mastermind of 'Russia First' strategy, which led to declaration in December 1991 that USSR was dead. State secretary of Russia (1992). Broke with Yeltsin in late 1993. Elected to Parliament in December 1993.

Chernomyrdin, Viktor Prime Minister of Russia since December 1992. Representative of old Soviet nomenklatura, converted to market economy with strong role for state. Was Soviet Minister of Gas Industry (1985–89).

Gaidar, Yegor Leading monetarist, and architect of economic 'shock' therapy. Former economics editor of Communist party organ, *Pravda*. Russian Minister of Economics (1991–92). Acting Prime Minister (June to December 1992).

Gerasimov, Gennady Spokesman of Soviet Foreign Ministry (1986–91).

Gorbachev, Mikhail General Secretary of Communist Party of Soviet Union (1985–91). First and last executive President of USSR.

Grachev, Pavel Commander of Soviet Air Force, who switched to Yeltsin's side during failed 1991 coup by hard-liners. Russian Defence Minister 1992. Reluctantly agreed to send tanks against Parliament in October 1993.

Khasbulatov, Ruslan Law professor who became speaker of Russian Parliament in 1991, when his then patron, Yeltsin, became executive President. Broke with him on issue of shock therapy, and Yeltsin's wish to rule by decree. Arrested after storming of White House.

Kozyrev, Andrei Russian Foreign Minister since 1990. Radical advocate of pro-Western strategy, who later moved towards a more centrist definition of Russia's national interest.

Kravchuk, Leonid First President of Ukraine. Signed pact with Yeltsin ending USSR in December 1991.

Kryuchkov, Vladimir Chair of KGB (1988–91), and leader of 1991 coup.

Ligachev, Yegor Member of Soviet Politburo (1985–90). Main conservative critic of Gorbachev reforms.

Lukyanov, Anatoly Former ally of Gorbachev, who was speaker of Soviet Parliament (1990–91). Arrested for role in 1991 coup.

Luzhkov, Yuri Mayor of Moscow from June 1992.

Makashov, Albert Hard-line former army general. Brought armed men to defend White House in September 1993.

Nazarbayev, Nursultan President of Kazakhstan.

Pavlov, Valentin Soviet Prime Minister (1991). Arrested for role in 1991 coup.

Polozkov, Ivan Hard-line first secretary of Russian Communist Party. Fierce critic of Gorbachev in party struggles.

Pugo, Boris Soviet Interior Minister (1990–91). Committed suicide to avoid arrest for his role in 1991 coup.

Rutskoi, Alexander Major General who became Hero of Soviet Union for his role in air force in Afghan war. Elected as Vice-President with Yeltsin in June 1991. Broke with Yeltsin over shock therapy. Arrested after storming of White House. Leader of patriotic movement.

Ryzhkov, Nikolai Soviet Prime Minister under Gorbachev (1985–91).

Shevardnadze, Eduard Soviet Foreign Minister (1985–91). President of Georgia since 1992.

Shushkevich, Stanislav Chair of Byelarus parliament (1991–94). Joined Yeltsin and Kravchuk in ending USSR in December 1991.

Silayev, Ivan Russian Prime Minister (1990–91).

Sobchak, Anatoly Law professor and leading liberal in Soviet Parliament, who was elected Mayor of St Petersburg in 1991. Ruled city with firm hand, alienating former supporters.

Solzhenitsyn, Alexander Author of *Gulag Archipelago* and many other powerful denunciations of Stalin's camps. Forcibly deported in 1974. Lived in USA and returned to Russia in 1994.

Stepankov, Valentin Russian prosecutor-general (1991–3), responsible for investigating 1991 coup. Wrote highly controversial book about the coup.

Volsky, Arkady President of Russian Union of Industrialists and Entrepreneurs. Representative of old nomenklatura and former Central Committee adviser.

DRAMATIS PERSONAE

Yakovlev, Alexander Main liberal ally of Gorbachev in Politburo, but resigned from party before 1991 coup. Switched to Yeltsin's team.

Yakovlev, Yegor Liberal editor of *Moscow News*. Leading supporter of Gorbachev during glasnost period.

Yanayev, Gennady Soviet Vice-President (1990–91). Arrested for role in 1991 coup.

Yavlinsky, Grigory Radical economist, who advised Gorbachev in first effort to switch economy to market principles. Rival of Gaidar, and critic of his shock therapy. Elected to Parliament in December 1993 at head of Yabloko ticket which he founded.

Yerin, Viktor Russian Interior Minister since 1992. Strong supporter of Yeltsin during storming of White House.

Zhirinovsky, Vladimir Extreme chauvinist leader of ill-named Liberal Democratic Party of Russia. Advocates restoration of Russian empire.

Zorkin, Valery Chair of Russian Constitutional Court (1991–3).

Zyuganov, Gennady Leader of revived Russian Communist Party. Supports alliance with moderate nationalists, but not with Zhirinovsky.

Yeltsin, Boris Russian President from 1991.

Introduction

Pale midday sunlight caught Alexander Solzhenitsyn's lined face as he paused on the aircraft steps and looked towards the hills of eastern Siberia before setting foot on home ground again. Russia's most famous writer was back after twenty years of exile. The date: 27 May 1994. The place: Magadan, sometimes known as the Gateway to the Gulag, that fearful system of camps dotted around Stalin's Soviet Union like a secret archipelago and immortalized in Solzhenitsyn's books. Magadan was the reception centre for prisoners sent to the lumber camps and gold mines of the nearby Kolyma peninsula.

The returning Solzhenitsyn had not chosen the place of his first landfall deliberately. It happened to be a scheduled stop on Alaska Airlines flight 201 from Anchorage to Vladivostok, and until the plane taxied to the bleak-looking terminal, it was not clear whether the border guards, still dressed in the uniforms of the KGB, would allow him to alight. Normally, transit passengers are required to stay on board.

But the Russia to which the writer was coming home was a new place. The order went out to let him and his wife, Natalya, come down the gangway to talk to the small group of well-wishers who had gathered on the tarmac with bouquets of flowers and presents in their hands. Regrettably, the same liberalism did not extend to me or the handful of other reporters travelling on the historic flight. We were permitted to stand on the plane's steps since this was 'American soil', but not to descend fully. From our elevated vantage point we watched Solzhenitsyn stoop and touch the ground with one hand. 'With reverence I pay my respects to the soil of Kolyma, in which are buried many hundreds of thousands, even millions, of our murdered countrymen,' he told the two dozen greeters in a short prepared speech.

He looked sombre when he returned to his back-row seat in the plane's first-class compartment ten minutes later. There was still no joy on his face when he reached his main destination, Vladivostok, that evening, nor when he addressed three thousand people at the Pacific coast city's waterfront at nightfall. 'I know I am returning to a Russia tortured, stunned, altered beyond recognition, convulsively searching for itself and its true identity,' he confided. 'My heart longs for the day when our country's long-suffering people might finally find a ray of light ahead.'

Three years after the fall of Communism, Solzhenitsyn's gloom was justified. As a non-Russian who had visited the country regularly for about twenty years and lived in it for six, I shared it. I had seen Red Square for the first time as a student in July 1961, when Stalin lay alongside Lenin in the mausoleum. The dictator's body was removed a short time later. In the 1970s and 1980s the *Guardian* sent me on several reporting assignments to the Soviet Union. The paper's last correspondent had left in 1948, and I was meant to add on-the-spot coverage to what our resident Kremlinologist, Victor Zorza, was gleaning from meticulous study of the Soviet press.

Although even then it was clear that inside the monolithic system cracks of dissent and dissatisfaction were growing, nothing like Gorbachev's perestroika was predicted. When I returned to live in Moscow, change was everywhere. The potential for huge transformations seemed enormous. Yet there were also indications that the process of democratizing a country which had always laboured under one kind of authoritarian rule or another would be measured in generations rather than years.

Many analysts and reporters saw the great climax of 1991 as the end of totalitarianism and the dawn of democracy. That was how Boris Yeltsin in all sincerity presented it, and Western governments were happy to hear him. I was not so sure. The more time elapsed since the August coup, the more I became convinced that the story which I began with in 1961 was the same one that Russians had lived under for the whole of this century, and further back than that. The events of 1991 had not produced answers to the key questions of Russian history, nor launched the country unequivocally on the path to democracy. Clearly the summer of 1991 was a turning point, a moment of discontinuity, but was it sufficient?

Russia has had many 'revolutions from above' which ended in failure. Before Communism, under Communism and after Communism, the key issues remained. How would Russia develop a civil society? When, if ever, would this conglomerate of individuals scattered across the world's largest landmass build a functioning and cohesive system of self-government, with the network of political parties, civic associations, clubs, professional societies, trade unions and pressure groups that give people a sense of belonging? When would they feel they had something to work for, a future that they as citizens could plan.

It is not just a matter of the institutions of democracy – an independent press, a system of law, regular elections, a code of ethics for public servants, a full-time parliament, an accountable executive and well-organized political parties. It is the fabric of consensus, the notion of solidarity, the feeling that the individual's opinion matters, or, to put it at its most basic, self-confidence and social optimism.

Even before the August coup, part of the Russian media had started a love affair with the era before the Revolution of October 1917. It was as though the Bolsheviks were foreign invaders, who had come in and destroyed a peaceful idyll. A film by Stanislav Govorukhin with the title *The Russia We Lost* perfectly captured this mood of self-deception, with happy snaps of the last Tsar and his family and old newsreels of eager peasants and workers happily toiling in fields and factories or building railways across a country bursting with the energy of early capitalism. After the decades of Stalinist propaganda, people were easily taken in by the new distortions. They liked the pessimistic racism, inherent in Govorukhin's claim that Communist terror had permanently damaged the Russian nation's genetic pool and that seventy-four years of Bolshevism had resulted in the survival of the least fit. Few Russians wanted to admit that their country before the 1917 revolution was a poor, underdeveloped place, with much of its industry in foreign hands, no universal suffrage, mass illiteracy, no widespread tradition of entrepreneurship, a tiny bourgeoisie, and only a few peasants with farms that made a living. The principle of private property was weakly established and there was precious little sense of nationhood.

With the collapse of Communism and the emergence of Vladimir Zhirinovsky anxious voices warned of a new danger, a revival of Russian 'nationalism'. But one of the features of pre-1917 Russia had been its inability to become a nation or develop a shared sense of what being a Russian means. In the nineteenth century a long-running debate emerged between what were called the Slavophiles and the Westernizers. The Slavophiles emphasized Russia's special destiny, its semi-Asiatic traditions and Orthodox religious heritage which would always, they argued, set Russia apart from the materialist culture of the West. The Westernizers acknowledged the correctness of much of the Slavophiles' analysis, but claimed that Russia must become more like the rest of Europe if it wanted to prosper. Yet Slavophilia was not nationalism in the usual sense of the word. It was wider than the concept of Russianness, since it took in other peoples who spoke Slavonic languages, and through its links to Orthodoxy was a way of describing a spiritual and intellectual identity rather than a political one.

Russia's failure to develop the constructive nationalism which usually goes hand in hand with the growth of a civil society was highlighted in the first intellectual onslaught on the October revolution by Russian liberals, a collection called *Iz Glubiny* (From the Depths) edited by Pyotr Struve in 1918. They accused the Tsars of having laid the groundwork for Bolshevism to grow. The Tsars, they complained, had created a state, but not a nation.

The Bolsheviks for their part had no interest in developing nationalist feeling among Russians. With their goal of fostering 'proletarian internationalism' through the creation of the world's first multi-ethnic state, Russia's new rulers consciously built on the Tsars' omission. They were happy to leapfrog over the issue of Russian nation-building. Only briefly during the Second World War did Stalin attempt to raise the Russian national banner in a bid to rally people against the Nazi invaders. How then, I wondered, could there be a return to Russian nationalism if there never had been any such strong feeling before?

Today's reformers emphasize the massive and destructive changes which the Bolsheviks undoubtedly brought about, yet there were significant anti-Bolshevik thinkers at the time who wondered how much of a revolution, if any, the changes of October 1917 really amounted to. 'In Russia there has been no revolution,' Nikolai Berdyayev concluded. 'All of the past is repeating itself and acts only behind new masks,' he wrote a few days after the seizure of the Winter Palace and the collapse of the provisional government. 'These turbulent processes are occurring only on the surface. These processes are only the rotting of the ragged clothes of unregenerated Russia. We are living out the consequences of our old sins.'[1]

Was the same gloomy conclusion feasible after August 1991? Was the Yeltsin 'revolution' no more than another surface stirring, a dramatic-looking upheaval which changed the country's governing institutions but left Russia's fundamental problems and underlying qualities untouched? Look how hard it was to build a multi-party system. The ending of the Communist party's monopoly saw the birth of scores of groups which called themselves parties. Without exception, they had little organization, low membership, and only minimal structures outside Moscow and St Petersburg. Gorbachev's effort at creating a law-based state appeared only to lead to rising crime in the streets, large-scale corruption in the process of privatizing industry, and widespread withholding of taxes by enterprises and individuals.

As Russia moved into the market economy era under Yeltsin,

and the West slowly began to learn how hard it was to graft a different system on to its defeated enemy, the need for an historic perspective became more urgent. Those of us with the luck to witness the extraordinary events of 1988 to 1994 at close hand sometimes had to pinch ourselves to appreciate their seismic quality.

But when the dust settled, what was really new in Russia? This is the main question which runs through this book. Institutions and practices enshrined in the Soviet system had certainly disappeared. The Communist party was forced out of power and marginalized. The state planning mechanism had collapsed. The KGB was dismantled. The great weight of fear which had paralysed the older generation and left its mark even on those brought up in the softer years of Brezhnev had been lifted. But were these changes, however momentous and rapid, enough to create a revolution of behaviour, let alone a major break in Russian history towards democracy and the rule of law?

True revolutions are about power and property. They break the authority and wealth of an existing élite, and distribute it among new players, as indeed did that of October 1917. Yet even that revolution, as Berdyayev indicated, was in line with Russian tradition and failed to make a decisive break from the past. By comparison with 1917, the Yeltsin 'revolution' was less of a change. Many of his political team, including Yeltsin himself, as well as many of the new entrepreneurs who emerged in the transition to a market economy were members of the old élite. There was no great redistribution of wealth and power.

Moreover, Soviet society had already begun to evolve away from totalitarianism after Stalin's death. Gorbachev's perestroika accelerated the process of democratization and destroyed the totalitarian system. Yeltsin's period in office has done little to build new structures of democracy in their place. Only in the economic field did Yeltsin launch a major change, with his programme of 'shock therapy', aimed at a rapid shift from central planning and resource allocation to free market principles. But progress turned out to be slower and more difficult than he and his team of reformers originally hoped, precisely because of special Russian factors.

This book's longest section deals with Russia's search for new democratic institutions on the road to a market economy and a law-based state. It starts with the Soviet parliament, which began work in 1989, moves on to the first freely elected Russian Congress of People's Deputies and the establishment of a Constitutional Court, and finally looks at the 1993 elections. It also examines the faltering effort to import market concepts from the West.

Gorbachev's role in this hesitant process is as important as Yeltsin's. A key theme of this book is why the founder of perestroika failed. This may sound a harsh judgement, since Gorbachev succeeded beyond his expectations in removing the institutions of repression and central control over Soviet society. His place in history would be assured for this alone, even without the changes he countenanced in Eastern Europe and in ending the Cold War. But Gorbachev failed in his project for reforming Soviet society through a reformed Communist party. Were there occasions when, if he had taken different decisions, the party's apparatchiks could have wholeheartedly accepted perestroika rather than quietly sabotaging and later openly trying to block it? Or was the logic of the developments which perestroika set in motion bound to sweep the party away?

Gorbachev also failed in a second task, the preservation of the Soviet Union. This task, it must be said, was not one of the goals of perestroika, since no one in 1985 imagined the USSR was under threat of falling apart. But how far was Gorbachev responsible for putting its implosion on the agenda, either by his own mistakes or because his policies led in that direction? At least, the process happened with remarkable smoothness. Compared with other European empires, the Soviet empire fell apart with almost no bloodshed. Eastern Europe was given up without a shot being fired. The 'inner empire', the republics of the Soviet Union itself, broke away with only minimal resistance from Moscow. Where there was conflict, it was not between Russians and non-Russians, but between other ethnic groups. How Russians adjusted to the loss of empire and why, against expectations, they reacted to the transition non-violently and without turning to xenophobia is the good news in this book.

Russia always was different from the rest of Europe, and it remains so. In the years of the Cold War, when the Soviet Union was perceived as an enemy, outside interest in what happened in Moscow was largely based on considerations of foreign policy. What was the other super-power planning to do next? Now that the Cold War is over, our 'need to know' has in no way lessened. Today the key questions centre on Russia's internal development. What factors make this country different from its neighbours, and how will Russia change in the years ahead?

I have tried to answer the riddle from a thematic rather than a chronological point of view. Part One looks at two key episodes in the Gorbachev era, the rise of glasnost and the August coup, and relates them to Russian history. In a country where individual leaders have always played a disproportionate role, it also briefly assesses the Gorbachev and Yeltsin legacies. The central part of the book develops the arguments in greater detail. Part Two examines the fall of Communism. In Part Three I analyse the way the Soviet empire collapsed and Yeltsin came to power. Part Four is devoted to Russia's new institutions.

This book is in part a memoir of the most tumultuous years in Russia's recent history, but it also looks far beyond them: backwards to the period before the October revolution, and forwards to the current struggle to create a democratic society in Russia, this time in post-Communist conditions.

The problem is as eternal as Russia itself.

1

A Special Society

1

First Shoots of a Civil Society

How openly people have begun to talk

MIKHAIL GORBACHEV, IN SIBERIA, SEPTEMBER 1988

By May 1987, two years after Gorbachev took office, the weekly journal *Moscow News* had become the flagship of glasnost, the paper which more than any other was willing to break the taboos of Stalinist censorship. It reported on crime and corruption. It discussed drug abuse, prostitution, and police brutality. It reopened the controversies of Soviet history for a new generation, revealing details of the Gulag's prison camps and publishing, for the first time since Khrushchev's period, the fierce warning about Stalin which Lenin wrote before his death.

On my earlier visits to the Soviet Union the paper had been a dull tabloid, translated into several languages and normally found lying around in the foreigners' section of airports. For a time its editor was Gennady Gerasimov, from the Novosti press agency. Under perestroika, like many other orthodox Soviet officials, Gerasimov was to change dramatically. He left *Moscow News* in August 1986 and was promoted to press spokesman for the Foreign Ministry, where he became renowned for his dead-pan quips. 'It certainly wasn't the Prize for Economics,' he commented at an official briefing in 1990 when Gorbachev's Nobel Peace Prize was announced.

Gerasimov's paper changed even more starkly than he did. The new editor, Yegor Yakovlev, quickly won a reputation for being bold at a time when boldness was risky. Crowds pressed against the glass cases outside the paper's editorial offices every Wednesday to read pages from the latest issue pinned up inside. When a friend and I detached ourselves from the scrum and walked into the paper's shabby front hall off Pushkin Square, we were eager to meet this champion of unorthodox thinking. What we found was some way short of fearless radicalism. Yakovlev's answers revealed how far the changes still had to go.

'There should be no blank spots in Soviet history,' he told us, but when we asked about the Soviet intervention in Czechoslovakia in 1968 he replied with chilling conservatism: 'I went to work in Czechoslovakia in 1971, when the wounds were still fresh. My sincere conclusion is that by August 1968 anti-socialist forces were preparing for civil war. I heard from many people, in Prague and the provinces, that if Soviet troops had not entered, there would have been bloodshed.'

What about civil society developing under glasnost? we continued. Yakovlev was not familiar with the concept and asked for an explanation. If democracy was to have any meaning, there had to be a dense network of civic activity between the only two spheres which the Communist party had allowed, the family and the state's mass organizations. Instead of the state and Communist party maintaining their top-down control over an atomized society, individuals must develop horizontal links. Yakovlev accused us of imposing Western notions of grassroots political activity on the Soviet Union. When we pointed out that in Eastern Europe, in particular in Hungary and Poland, a new generation was busy discussing the possibility of a revolution from below, he seemed unmoved. As a Russian official, there was no reason why Yakovlev should have been thinking about independent political movements which might change his society. The concepts were alien. He saw reform as a matter for élites.

Nevertheless, compared with any discussion with a Soviet editor in the past, Yakovlev's willingness to criticize the reality of Soviet life was unusual. The next evening he took us to a public meeting called to establish a 'Discussion Club for Friends of Science'. The hall was packed with about 500 people, tense, energetic and eager. Many took notes. Others were recording the discussion, apparently for friends who had not dared to come. Or perhaps they wanted to keep the tapes as a souvenir. Several Russians had already warned us that glasnost might be reversed.

The audience was composed of the intelligentsia, academics, officials and journalists. They were predominantly middle-aged, most of them representatives of the so-called 'shestidesyatniki' (people of the 1960s), the generation which came to political maturity around the time of Khrushchev's brief thaw. Their leading figure was of course Gorbachev himself. The platform was entirely male. Yakovlev sat beside Yuri Afanasyev, a leading historian, Abel Aganbegyan, a top economist, and three other academics. There were printed invitations from the Komsomol, the Young Communist League, with a quotation from Gorbachev saying, 'We need dialogue with the people. We need a broad spectrum of advice'.

The invitation said the club would give people an opportunity to exchange views on politics, economics, science, art, sport and literature. Excerpts from the speeches give the flavour of cautious reformism: 'This is a social struggle, not a class struggle'; 'We are living in an agony of the Stalinist administration. Khrushchev did not distance himself from the Stalinist system and was crushed by it as a result'; 'Our Institute is sometimes known as the Institute for Public Opinion, but as someone said, "How can you have an Institute for Public Opinion when there is no public opinion?"'

Yakovlev made a short speech. He told two anecdotes, showing how old attitudes died hard. A fire at a seminary in Zagorsk, the headquarters of the Russian Orthodox Patriarch, had killed two priests. When he rang the seminary to check the details for *Moscow News*, a monk asked him, 'Have you got authorization for these questions from the central committee?' In Leningrad protesters wanted to demonstrate against the demolition of the Hotel Angleterre, an historic landmark where the poet Sergei Yesenin had

5

been found dead in the 1920s, ostensibly a case of suicide. They went from one party and city committee to another asking for permission. No official wanted to take responsibility. Finally, in despair, they asked the junior officer at the front desk of the local police station.

After the speeches, questions came thick and fast. Isn't it time to publish George Orwell? Why can't we have an objective history of Trotsky? Will Bukharin be rehabilitated? Why do newspapers only cover demonstrations abroad? Why isn't the KGB under the control of the central committee? We wrote out a question in Russian and passed it to the front. Why was there no public debate over nuclear power in the Soviet Union? The scientist's answer was disappointing. The press had begun to discuss it but there was no alternative to nuclear power at the moment. This drew some applause but we thought we also detected some submerged dissent. A few minutes later a woman with a black shawl draped round her shoulders rose to her feet. She claimed that in the United States no new nuclear reactors had been commissioned since the Three Mile Island accident. Of course there were alternatives, she went on. One of them was energy conservation. The audience received her remarks enthusiastically and some people shouted for her to go on. But the chairman was already calling out with some menace, 'Spasibo, spasibo' (Thank you, thank you).

Afterwards, we went up to her. She explained she was active in another of the new clubs. Known as the Club for the Year 2050, it aimed to develop a new ecological system by that date. When we inquired whether there was any restriction on these clubs, she said limitations were mainly self-imposed. You could start a club for energy conservation but not a club against nuclear power. A club against nuclear weapons? That would be unnecessary, she said, since everyone was against them. A club arguing for alternatives to conscription? There were a few informal pacifist groups, she explained.

The protest over the Hotel Angleterre which Yakovlev had mentioned was one of the first unsanctioned public demonstrations for many years which was not severely repressed. A few participants were detained but quickly released. It was not surprising that environmental issues sparked the first grassroots activity. In those early days of perestroika it was safer to be green than anti-red. In Armenia, before the demonstrations over Nagorno-Karabakh, there was a public campaign against the highly-polluting Nairit synthetic rubber plant in Yerevan. In Lithuania demonstrators marched to the Ignolina nuclear power plant, demanding better safety standards.

Throughout 1987 the clubs and interest groups grew rapidly, giving rise to a new Russian word, 'nyeformaly' (the 'informals'), which even appeared in *Pravda*, the staid organ of the central committee. The paper admitted that the first informal groups began as long ago as the mid-1960s, but the real growth began with glasnost. Initially they brought together young people interested in rock and pop music, computer games, sport and karate, which had been banned until the late 1970s. In some cities self-styled vigilantes and Afghan veterans formed groups to fight against corruption. Although Yegor Yakovlev did not recognize the phrase 'civil society', they were the first shoots of a new and independent phenomenon. After decades of tight control by the party, people were beginning to form their own groups, separate from the mass organizations of a centralized society, the Communist party, the Young Communist League, the Union of Soviet Women and the like.

In the long years of Stalinism no public space was permitted outside these vast top-down institutions. People were forced to retreat into the narrow circle of their family and a few trusted friends. They lived in what came to be called 'kitchen society', saying what they felt only in the safety of their cramped state flats. Even this escape into privacy was not available for everyone. Millions of Soviet families lived in communal apartments, sharing with strangers who might denounce them. Sometimes the whole Soviet Union was described as a giant 'kommunalka'. The apathy and despair which often led to drunkenness was exacerbated by these grim conditions. Under Gorbachev's perestroika the fear lifted, making it possible for people to seek a wider group of friends again, and share views and interests with casual acquaintances.

In the summer of 1987 I ran into the next stage in the development of these clubs. This time the focus was openly political, and the tone was increasingly directed to action, not just discussion. About 500 representatives of 47 political, cultural and ecological groups met for a three-day conference in a factory's 'House of Culture' to draft a ringing manifesto for change. Boris Yeltsin, the Communist party chief in Moscow, was already showing signs of being more of a populist than Gorbachev, and had adopted a policy of being more tolerant towards the 'informals'. Although his officials authorized the conference, its organizers played safe and did not inform any Western journalists in advance. It was the first conference of independent left-wing reformers to have been officially sanctioned for more than fifty years. Publicity was obviously a sensitive matter.

The conference organizers let me break the story only after the first guarded but supportive report appeared in the Soviet press in the journal *Ogonyok* more than a fortnight after the event. The *Ogonyok* piece did not report the proposal by the most radical group, known as Democracy and Humanism, for an end to the one-party system (which was rejected by a majority of participants). It suppressed the call for a monument to be built to the victims of Stalin and did not mention that two of the organizers had been imprisoned under Brezhnev. Gleb Pavlovsky was arrested in 1982 for editing the first seven issues of a left-wing samizdat journal, *Poiski* (Searches). Boris Kagarlitsky published a samizdat paper, *Levi Povorot* (Left Turn) and spent thirteen months in prison.

One purpose of the conference, which was organized by the 'Club of Social Initiatives', was to unite the new informal groups round a common platform. The most contentious issue was whether it would be explicitly labelled 'socialist'. The conference split on the point. One group, led by Oleg Rumyantsev (who later went on to found the Social-Democratic party of Russia and, as a member

8

of the Russian Supreme Soviet, was in charge of rewriting Russia's constitution) favoured a relatively loose 'Circle of Social Initiatives'. The other group, led by Kagarlitsky (who later became a member of the Moscow city council and founded the Party of Labour) formed a Federation of Socialist Clubs.

Both groups agreed on what they called the 'Three Nyets': No to violence and the propagation of violence; no to ideas of racial or national exclusiveness; and no to claims to a monopoly on the truth in detriment to people's right to search for it independently themselves. The manifesto of the Federation of Socialist Clubs, adopted at the conference, acknowledged the constitutional role of the Communist party of the Soviet Union, but said the party was not united: 'Its ranks include people who bear responsibility for the abuses and miscalculations of the past, and who formed that mass of bureaucrats and officials who cut themselves off from the hopes and needs of their people. Our aim is to support the healthy and progressive forces in the party's leadership and the rank and file'.[1]

Many of the manifesto's proposals echoed what dissidents had been saying in underground bulletins and appeals in the 1960s and 1970s. Now, amazingly, they were being outlined at an officially permitted conference. But this was still 1987, and glasnost – what some critics called 'a licence to speak' – had some way to go. The Soviet press's failure to publish the manifesto suggested it was still considered too radical, and that the party leadership was not willing to be overtaken by independent groups 'from below'. But these first political 'informals' would soon infiltrate their ideas into the mainstream, via the democratic reform groups which were to emerge inside the Communist party. The Komsomol, the Young Communist League, was the first official organization to be infected with the spirit of change. One Soviet paper reported that 60 per cent of the informals were members of the Young Communist League.[2] Some of their ideas were later to be adopted by Gorbachev, whose speeches in 1988 and 1989 often sounded like the dissident tracts of the 1970s.

The summer of 1987 saw the first public demonstrations in

Moscow. Street protests were allowed provided the organizers advised the authorities in advance of the number of participants and the venue, but even some illegal demonstrations were tolerated. Ecologists took to the streets outside Moscow's town hall. A group of rabid nationalists and anti-Semites, called Pamyat (Memory) held a meeting in October Square, and were invited by Communist officials to meet Boris Yeltsin, to explain their case. Several hundred Crimean Tatars repeatedly gathered at one end of Red Square itself. In a sitdown protest calling for rehabilitation and the right to return to their homeland from which Stalin had expelled them, they demanded to speak to the party leadership. Andrei Gromyko, then the chairman of the presidium of the Supreme Soviet, agreed to receive them. This was unprecedented. For more than half a century demonstrations had only been permitted if they were under direct Communist party auspices. Any spontaneous protest was quickly dealt with. It was one measure of the difference between Khrushchev's thaw and the changes brought about by Gorbachev that even in Khrushchev's day demonstrations were forbidden. Under Brezhnev they were ruthlessly stamped on.

A rare outburst of public emotion took place in July 1980 during the Olympic games. The authorities had cleared the city of dissidents to prevent them having contact with foreign correspondents and other visitors. They could not foresee that Vladimir Vysotsky, the country's most popular singer, would die at the young age of forty-two in July. Sometimes described as the 'dissident of song', Vysotsky's Christian philosophy, husky voice and despair at the stifling inertia of Soviet life struck a chord in many sectors of society. His use of prison slang alluded to a criminal but also a political underworld that had never previously been allowed to go public. Pirate recordings and cassettes of his songs sold vigorously on the black market, until the official company Melodia brought out the first long-playing record two years after his death. His family timed the funeral for St Vladimir's Day, 28 July. Tens of thousands of mourners gathered outside the Taganka theatre where he had often performed. I watched in amazement as mounted police tried to control the throng which spilled into the road, halting traffic. The crowd was spontaneous and too large for the police to round up. Vysotsky's ballads about the hopelessness of life in the present system made him enormously popular in the middle ranks of the party and the ruling élite as well as among the disaffected. Even Brezhnev was known to listen to him. It was hardly surprising that the authorities did not dare to penalize people for taking part in his funeral.

Organized protest was a different story. Thanks to the constant tapping of dissidents' telephones by the KGB, it was almost impossible to plan any demonstration without the security organs knowing. When eight people unfurled a banner in Red Square on 21 August 1968 to denounce the Soviet-led invasion of Czechoslovakia, they were arrested within seconds. One of the few demonstrations which lasted more than an hour took place in September 1974. It was the high point of détente with the United States. Richard Nixon had finished his second visit to Moscow as president three months earlier, a trip he visibly enjoyed since the Soviet Union was remarkably free of any hostile press articles that mentioned the word 'Watergate'. The warmth of official US-Soviet relations encouraged a group of avant-garde artists to hope that the authorities would not be too rough on an open-air exhibition they were planning. The artists, who were not members of the official unions, telephoned as many Western correspondents as they could find to invite us to the bleakest outskirts of the capital. Since our phones were tapped, even if theirs were not, it was obvious that the KGB would know of the protest. The artists were undeterred. Their work was not explicitly political. What made it different was that many of the canvases were abstracts, much of it derivative of Western styles. As long as they exhibited in their own flats or badly-lit basement studios, they were tolerated. They could even sell their work to foreigners without difficulty. Among the diplomatic and journalists' community, owning so-called 'dissident' art was much in vogue.

But public exhibitions of unofficial art were still banned. We

assembled in an open field at the edge of a housing estate at about
10 a.m. on a Sunday morning. The artists' aim was to hold an
open-air show on a piece of waste-ground in order to dramatize the
fact that they were unable to exhibit in any indoor hall, since all
halls belonged to the state. The aim was to create a 'scandal', and
with the KGB's help, they did. About two dozen painters turned
up, a scruffy group carrying mainly unframed canvases under
plastic wraps. Almost simultaneously we spotted the arrival of two
bulldozers which came along the road, mounted the pavement, and
headed towards the corner of the field where we were standing.
Without any explanation they started to accelerate and reverse in
our midst, forcing people to scatter, and making it impossible for
any of the artists to stand for long in the same place and hold up a
picture for correspondents to admire. The bulldozers were helped
by a gang of about a dozen well-built young men in casual clothes
who continually elbowed us out of the way. They tore some
canvases, and told us not to interfere with the bulldozers' work. When
we asked 'What work?' one of them said the local council was
constructing a playground for the children of the nearby housing
estate. On a Sunday morning?

The foolish pretence that this was not a police action angered many
of us. A light drizzle was falling and as artists fell in the mud which the
charging bulldozers were churning up, I asked one driver his name.
'Ivan Ivanovich Ivanov,' he sneered. 'Lenin would have been
ashamed of you,' I shouted with more effect than sense. Ivan Ivanov
looked stunned and briefly stopped his vehicle. The incident lasted
about an hour and a half and as the artists left with the remains of their
pictures, a lorry used for street cleaning came down the road to deliver
the *coup de grâce*. Its jeering driver shot jets of water at us. Back in our
offices, we wrote enraged reports on the affair. They caused a world-
wide storm. Within two weeks the artists were given permission to
hold an open-air exhibition in a section of Izmailovo Park in north-
west Moscow. It was a rare and short-lived victory. Many of the
painters later emigrated to the West – some had always intended to –
and the site was not used regularly in the years which followed.

It was not until glasnost that it had a major revival and expansion. Izmailovo Park became Moscow's main artistic flea market, full of Gorby dolls, gently mocking the supreme leader, the ultimate symbol of the new Soviet openness. Most of the paintings in the park were aimed at the casual tourist market, but by then every aspect of good Russian and foreign art could be freely exhibited in official studios and galleries. The basements of the Pushkin gallery and St Petersburg's Hermitage were unlocked, revealing long-hidden canvases by Kandinsky, Malevich, Picasso and others.

In the first year of Gorbachev's rule party tolerance of dissent was no wider than it had been in those grim days of 1974. The big change came in 1986 after the Chernobyl nuclear disaster. For the first forty-eight hours there was silence, but as the West increasingly insisted on having information to determine the extent of the radiation Gorbachev realized that the accident could not be covered up. This was the turning-point of glasnost. The opening-up on Chernobyl led to demands for information and action on the whole spectrum of environmental pollution in the Soviet Union. The press began to report other accidents. Crime and prison statistics, a long-held secret in the Soviet media, were published. Soon Soviet journalists were writing about all the seamy aspects of Soviet life, concentrating with relish on everything which had long been forbidden.

Between 1986 and 1988 every remaining taboo was broken. A non-Communist press emerged from the underground. Instead of the old typewritten dissident bulletins, like the 'Chronicle of Current Events', which were secretly passed from hand to hand, often landing their compilers in gaol, lap-top computers produced unofficial newspapers. The small gravel plaza at the end of Moscow's inner boulevard by Kropotkinskaya metro station became a hive of activity on Saturday mornings with a range of amateur newspapers on sale, representing every conceivable group from monarchists to nationalists to anarchists.

Sometimes more than one taboo fell in the same week. I was

invited one evening in November 1988 to the Vasilyev theatre to see a small drama school put on what was billed as Moscow's first erotic art show. A thousand people, jammed into the stuffy basement, watched an actress carried shoulder-high, sitting statuesquely on a wooden board and wearing nothing but a white tulle veil and a sequin-studded mask. To the notes of a mournful saxophone, two men lifted the veil which covered her and slowly daubed her with paint. Two nights earlier, 300 people packed into Moscow's Aviation Institute for a discussion devoted to Trotsky. In the audience were the sons and daughters of other convicted 'enemies of the people'. The meeting ended with a call for Trotsky's rehabilitation and the publication of his books.

Journalists and editors in the official as well as the 'informal' media enjoyed their new freedom to write and publish whatever they liked. Long-banned Russian books which had been published years earlier in the West appeared at home at last, although many of their authors had emigrated or been forced to leave Russia in the Brezhnev years. Most came out first in the thick monthly literary journals, pushing up their circulations to unprecedented levels. No author of serious literature was left unbanned.

Once the taboos were broken, officials in the Communist party took commercial advantage of the changes. Publishing was one of the first areas where market forces overcame ideology. During a visit in 1990 to the Red Proletariat publishing house, the central committee's main printing press, I saw an ancient conveyor belt carrying hundreds of identical book-covers for binding. At the end of the room a picture of Lenin looked down from the wall, beside red banners exhorting printers to overfulfil the plan. Examining the moving covers closely, I saw the book was Solzhenitsyn's *Gulag Archipelago*. 'It is one of our most profitable titles,' beamed the manager proudly.

The voluntary association, Memorial, revealed the secrets of Stalin's years of terror even more dramatically than Solzhenitsyn. Set up by former camp inmates to document the details of the dictator's murders and help victims' families, Memorial organized branches in every major Russian city. Their first exhibition in Moscow was a 'Wall of Conscience', mounted in the House of Culture in an electric light-bulb factory in the autumn of 1988. The factory was chosen because many of its own staff were arrested in the 1930s. Anyone could pin up mementoes and photographs, either just to honour the dead, or to ask for help in tracing how, when and where their loved ones died. 'Who knows my father?' asked a handwritten sign with a telephone number. 'Sergei Alexeyevich Zaitsev, born in 1893, worked in Moscow as a printer until May 1937, spent May to June in the cells of the Lubyanka and Butyrki. From July to December and later, he was in exile, then on a state farm in the Aktyubinski district, then in the camps . . . If you have any information, please phone.'

A middle-aged lady told me how her father was the main engineer who helped to build the road from Minsk to Moscow. After his arrest on trumped-up charges of being a saboteur he was sentenced, like thousands of others, to ten years in camps 'without the right of correspondence'. Families knew there was no point in trying to find out which camp their men were in. Gradually they learnt it was outright deception. The phrase meant the prisoner had been shot immediately. Standing before the Wall of Conscience with its snapshots, poems, and messages, Russians found it hard to hold back their tears. Foreigners hung back in respectful awe, as though we were intruding on massive private grief, a Russian family mourning which we could never comprehend.

Khrushchev brought millions back from the camps in the first wave of rehabilitations, but did nothing to turn the memory of Stalin's crimes into a civic event. People celebrated the return of relatives or mourned their dead at home with friends. Under Gorbachev, they could gather in public and warn a new generation about what had happened. A year later Memorial was able to go further. A thousand people gathered outside the KGB headquarters at the Lubyanka itself. Holding lighted candles they formed a ring around the gaunt building in memory of the hundreds of thousands shot in its basement. Passers-by watched with interest, but no sense of shock. It was hard to imagine that as recently as two years earlier such a demonstration and the authorities' calm response to it would have been unthinkable.

Yet if these early demonstrations and political meetings were taking place within the established system, what was to happen from 1989 onwards was nothing less than the transformation of that system. The politics of protest became the politics of seeking alternatives. Two new parliaments came into being, pushing the Communist party aside. The mainstream press became as free as the unofficial press. A host of political parties were formed and officially registered. Workers broke from the Communist-dominated trade unions and formed their own. Strikes rocked the economy. In the fourteen non-Russian republics nationalist movements sprang into existence and pressed for greater rights or complete independence. Long-suppressed arguments and conflicts mingled with new struggles. Perestroika – 'restructuring' – started to seem an old-fashioned word. The whole system was being destroyed, not re-built.

At first there was something exhilarating about it. To see public life awaken and people discard their fear was moving and impressive. Only a few ultra-conservatives resisted it. But as the destruction continued it became clear that the country lacked architects with a blueprint for the structure which should follow. There were grandiose hopes for a new and effective multi-party pluralism, but no one with a clear view of how to build it, and very few builders able and willing to do the work. The politics of alternatives did not turn into the politics of creating a social consensus and institutions which could resolve conflicts peacefully.

The end of Soviet control over Eastern Europe and the collapse of Comecon, the old trading system, caused a sharp contraction of mutual deliveries between the member states. Within the Soviet Union the drive for autonomy in the republics and later for full political independence produced more cracks in traditional economic links. The abandonment of the old system of state orders to factories and state allocation of raw materials created a free-for-all in which managers reverted to barter. The economic reformers embraced the notion of a market but found it hard to introduce in conditions of declining output and a monopolized economy where a few enterprises controlled key sectors. Privatization turned into the redistribution of state assets without any mechanism for improving efficiency or increasing production.

Some analysts argued that this did not matter. The old system was so terrible that anything would be better. It was also so unnatural that there could be no transition to a new system, except on its ruins. Others said the difficulties Russia faced were the inevitable birthpangs of democracy. The country was passing through a stage of development which had taken most industrial countries decades to achieve, and none of them had done it smoothly. Britain's relatively calm progress to democracy since 1688 was the exception, not the rule. Most Western countries had suffered enormous upheavals and bloodshed. Chaos, uncertainty and a large measure of residual authoritarianism were only to be expected in Russia. Yet both sets of responses begged the question of where Russia was moving and whether it was advancing to democracy at all.

2

The Leaders' Legacy

*It was like being in the front line of a war. I lived
through several lives, and I don't know how I survived.*

MIKHAIL GORBACHEV, DECEMBER 1992[1]

*That's how my fate turned out. I'm always
fighting. For several years it's been a constant
struggle.*

BORIS YELTSIN, APRIL 1993[2]

Mikhail Gorbachev's six-and-a-half years in power were a triumph
of reform and a tragedy of errors. A man who meant so well for his
country and did more to change it than any previous Russian ruler,
either before or since the October Revolution, ended up defeated
by mistakes. Some were caused by his own short-sightedness and
indecision. Some arose from factors which he did not foresee or
could not surmount. Some were inherent in the reform process
which he had unleashed.

Gorbachev was far and away more democratic than the Communist leaders who went before him, yet not democratic enough to
accept that the party in which he had spent his life had to step
aside. When the party failed to reform itself he could not understand
that it was finished. Gorbachev was also more willing than his
Soviet predecessors to contemplate a loose form of state structure,

yet when demands by the non-Russian peoples for greater
sovereignty started to call the Soviet Union's survival into question,
he tried to resist. His strategy only hastened what he was trying to
avoid.

Gorbachev's main achievement was to allow things to happen.
He opened the windows of a house whose inhabitants were slowly
suffocating and let in air. If Ronald Reagan, who shared the
pinnacle of world power with him in his first three years, was the
Great Communicator, a consummate master of the skills of
American media politics, Mikhail Gorbachev was the Great Facilita-
tor. He deliberately started an open-ended process, and even when
it went beyond the limits he had expected, in the main he permitted
it to continue. He presided over the non-violent break-up of the
Soviet empire in Eastern Europe. When it came to the disintegration
of the Soviet Union his instinct was to prevent it, but even here he
largely avoided the use of force. His intellect told him that he had
to try to resolve the conflicts by political means.

Gorbachev was supreme at manoeuvring. He was often criticized
for hesitating between two points of view or looking for uneasy
compromises, but he felt he had to take both the conservatives and
the reformers with him. This tactic, which served him well at the
beginning of perestroika, became a disadvantage when the process
of change accelerated. Instead of taking decisive action and going
with the reformers, he temporized and lost support.

He came to power without a plan. When the magnitude of the
changes he was presiding over began to dawn on people two or
three years after perestroika started, supporters and enemies
speculated that he must have intended them from the beginning.
He concealed his radical designs, they assumed, because he would
never have been allowed to continue in office if his Politburo
colleagues had realized he intended to end the Communist party's
monopoly on power and switch the Soviet command economy to a
market system. Gorbachev refused to accept this analysis. 'I must
tell you frankly,' he told the Polish parliament in 1988: 'In the
beginning we did not understand the need, or rather the inevitability

of reforming the political system. Our experience during the first stages of perestroika brought us to it.'[3] Like most other Russians, he changed his view of the world between 1985 and 1991. Anatoly Chernyayev, one of his closest aides, described it as Gorbachev's 'internal revolution'.[4]

The image of the Soviet system as a totalitarian structure often conceals more than it reveals. No system is hermetic, and there will always be places where different currents of thought develop and eventually break through. All depends on what institutions operate in any given society. In the USSR the principal legal organization was the Communist party, so it was not surprising that it should become the nest-bed of various political tendencies. By 1985 several currents of thought in the party were visible to party insiders, if not yet to the public at large, in front of whom the façade of unity had to be maintained. Georgy Shakhnazarov, a professor of political science, who served as one of Gorbachev's closest advisers from February 1988 until the end, quoted Gorbachev as saying: 'our party was never one where everyone agreed. It was a political organization with the most varied tendencies and currents, Christian Democrats, social democrats, nationalists, hardline Marxists and orthodox Marxists.'[5] Gorbachev was a member of the social-democratic current from at least 1985, if not earlier, Shakhnazarov said. By that he meant the group 'which stood for socialism, not communism – normal, healthy socialism'.

Gorbachev's commitment to change was the culmination of a long process. During his years in the Politburo, which he joined as its youngest member in 1978, Gorbachev saw enough to become convinced that reform was needed. Access to KGB reports on the true state of the economy helped to open his eyes. He was not the only man near the pinnacle of the Soviet system who saw the reality, and by the time he was chosen to lead the party, the coalition for reform at the middle and senior levels of the apparatus, though not in the Politburo itself, was overwhelming. This meant that Gorbachev had the advantage of working at the head of a team of party insiders who shared his views.

The image of a crusader or lone reformer is wide of the mark. The economy's growth rate was slowing down. Labour productivity was falling. Corruption was still rampant, in spite of some effort at a clean-up under Andropov. After years of massive investment in agriculture, output was low and consumer goods production was not high enough to give people, particularly those who had travelled abroad, what they felt they had a right to expect. The underlying consensus was summed up in the phrase, 'We can't go on living like this,' as Gorbachev told his wife, Raisa, the day he was elected. He disclosed the conversation in a talk to former class-mates at the Law Faculty of Moscow University in June 1990.[6]

In 1985 everyone knew what they were against. They disagreed on what they were for. There were three broad currents in the party, though with some overlap between them. A Stalinist strain wanted to maintain the existing economic system of central planning but make industry more efficient through capital-intensive technologies and greater use of computers. A Leninist strain favoured more radical economic changes and some political reforms as well. It harked back before the era of Stalin's five-year plans to the 'New Economic Policy' of 1921, when the economy was not run by administrative decree and managers had some leeway to take their own decisions on investment and the disposal of profits. A variety of forms of socialist ownership was allowed, including co-operatives and lease holding. Though they called themselves Leninists, this group contained the social democrats. Finally, there was a small school of thought, mainly among party intellectuals, which was groping towards Western liberal economics, concentrating on cutting the government's budget deficit, reducing subsidies on prices, turning services and small-scale trade over to private hands and making the rouble convertible in the hope of moving towards a more open economy and export-led growth.

Initially Gorbachev hovered between the first two currents. Later when they did not produce the results he wanted he flirted with the third. Although his inconsistency exasperated friends and opponents alike, his mistakes in this field were forgivable. No country had switched from central planning to the market and there was no experience to guide him. Gorbachev was surrounded by economists who knew only one system, and when he looked to the West for advice after 1990 he found economists with equally narrow expertise. Perestroika's failure to improve the Soviet standard of living gradually eroded Gorbachev's popular support, but he drew back from launching a switch to market conditions for fear that the upheaval would make things worse. By the end of 1989 many people were openly complaining that 'all that perestroika has given us is the right to speak out on how bad things are', or as one joke put it, 'Perestroika is the truth, the whole truth, and nothing but the truth'.

Gorbachev's main mistakes were in the political field. He launched a programme of political reform, including a reform of the Communist party, but was never sufficiently consistent. He missed several chances to enlist democratic allies into a broad coalition of forces in favour of perestroika, yet turned a blind eye to its conservative enemies. He knew there was strong resistance to change within the party, but refused to confront the saboteurs or make an open alliance with the reformers. He kept trying to balance between them, partly because of indecision but partly because he refused to contemplate splitting the party.

While these turbulent discussions were going on, Gorbachev would sometimes dip into history to remind himself how Lenin behaved during crises. It seemed an extraordinary diversion for a man so busy. 'Not only Lenin', he told me during an interview, when I expressed some surprise that he had found the time. 'I went back to the transcripts of the party congresses which went on in his time just to see the live discussion. It was good training for me. Lenin could speak pretty directly, and sometimes he was subjected to annihilating criticism. I observed how he behaved. That was also a lesson for me, seeing the intellectual disputes, the quarrels. It gave me a boost. But even though those were cruel times and Lenin was drawn into bloody things like the Red Terror, he never put his opponents in discussion up against the wall.'[7]

Some analysts have argued that Gorbachev began with economic reform and only when he became frustrated switched to political reform. This was the exact opposite of the Chinese experience, where economic reform moved ahead while political reform was blocked. The distinction is only correct in part. Gorbachev did start with economic reform but he never gave up. He advanced on both the economic and political fronts. The difficulty was that he faced powerful and organized resistance, which he compounded by his own wavering. A majority of party officials were dubious about political reform, if not directly hostile. They saw a direct threat to their own positions. Industrial managers felt similarly about economic change.

Alexander Yakovlev, in reflections after the collapse of the Communist party, argued that Soviet society under Stalin had been a triumvirate of powers: the party apparatus, the economic apparatus and the apparatus of repression. The dictator and his immediate entourage sat above them. Even under Stalin, however, autonomous processes developed within the triumvirate which led them to prevent a new dictator emerging after his death. They had suffered from Stalin's unpredictability themselves. For a time the party apparatus retained the primary role, based on its control of ideology, the glue which attempted to legitimize the system, but in the 1960s and 1970s the apparatus's separation from ordinary people, their alienation from the intelligentsia, and their narrow-mindedness and dogmatism lowered the party's reputation. Although the outward rituals continued, local economic managers, particularly the directors of plants in the military-industrial complex, increasingly gained influence over government in the regions. 'From the beginning of the 1970s the central committee reigned, but did not rule,' according to Yakovlev.[8]

The party depended on the industrial managers for information before it took decisions and for support in implementing them. Party apparatchiks had to listen to technocrats. This tendency had always been endemic in the system, and it was partly in order to counter it that Stalin turned to repression. In the first years of

23

Brezhnev's time there were frequent shifts of industrial personnel as the party tried to maintain control. Brezhnev later gave up, and ambitious specialists saw their careers depend less on the views of the party apparatus in the centre and more on those of the industrial managers. In the republics careers depended on loyalty to the local leadership rather than on Moscow. Perestroika was welcomed initially by party officials, Yakovlev argued, because they hoped it would restore the party's primacy over the economic managers, the so-called 'khozyaistvenniki'. It failed to do that and was soon perceived to be a threat, as calls grew for competitive elections within the party while new political forces were emerging outside the party. Meanwhile, the economic managers also felt threatened, not by perestroika's first steps since its attack on central planning helped them, but by the subsequent talk of 'new forms' of socialist ownership and the emergence of leaseholders, and co-operatives.

As he struggled to achieve his goals within a declining consensus, Gorbachev was doomed to a perpetual contradiction. On the one hand, he would reason, argue and try to convince the apparatus. On the other hand, he would plot, intrigue and manoeuvre, knowing that he could not take it with him willingly. Sometimes he would use the party's old hierarchical traditions to enforce loyalty and obedience. In the later years he would frighten them by threatening to resign. Gorbachev's emotional behaviour reflected this constant tactical struggle. 'Even as late as 1991,' says Anatoly Chernyayev, 'he could get irritated and lose all his "new political thinking". He would then behave like a classic regional party secretary.'[9]

His decision to release Andrei Sakharov from exile in Gorky in 1986 was a typical case of avoiding discussion. The Politburo had no prior warning. Gorbachev made the move after repeated pressure from the Western leaders he met in his first year and a half in power. The first official to hear that Sakharov was to be allowed to return to Moscow was Mikhail Zimyanin, the ideological chief in the central committee secretariat. Chernyayev was with Gorbachev when he told Zimyanin and some other officials. 'Their eyes went square and Zimyanin turned green,' Chernyayev recounted. The main reason was not the release as such, but that Gorbachev had acted on an issue in Zimyanin's competence without consulting him. The Politburo also learnt about it after the event. No one voiced any objection, according to Chernyayev, when Gorbachev told them. The problem was what to say in the 'explanation' that would have to be sent down the party ladder to the lower ranks. For years Sakharov had been branded as a traitor. What had changed now?

Gorbachev had most of his policy ideas and reforms prepared for him outside the Politburo or the central committee secretariat by 'creative groups' of senior advisers. The leaders were men who had all worked at one time or another in the 1960s in Prague on the journal *Problems of Peace and Socialism*. Surrounded there by other Marxist idealists and intellectuals from Europe and the Third World, they hoped for a third way between capitalism and Stalinism – a form of humane and democratic socialism. Most were inwardly shocked by the Kremlin's reaction to the Prague spring in 1968 which had been trying to put into practice the ideas they had worked on. Almost twenty years later, as advisers to Gorbachev, these classic 'shestidesyatniki' (1960s men) had a new chance. Anatoly Chernyayev specialized in foreign affairs. Georgy Shakhnazarov was an expert on judicial and constitutional matters. Ivan Frolov handled culture, education and party history.

Even when issues were put before the Politburo, Gorbachev often pre-empted discussion with the rambling but authoritarian style that he later showed publicly when he presided over the Supreme Soviet. Behind his professorial manner Frolov was an excellent mimic. Safe in retirement at his dacha, he later gave a mischievous performance of Gorbachev's presentation at the Politburo, introducing the analysis of the October Revolution which he was to make public on its seventieth anniversary. It was typical of Gorbachev's style. The general secretary asked for comment on the document but, before anyone could speak, said that it was not necessary to mention 'points of detail', since these could be written down and handed to his staff. All he wanted to know was whether the Politburo accepted the main lines of the document. Of course, he continued, a great deal of work had already been put into it. He had sacrificed a good chunk of his holiday in preparing it, and it would be a pity to have to re-do everything. In other words, people were being asked not to comment but merely approve what had been done already.

The relations between a general secretary and the Politburo had always been difficult. In a Western system of government the president or prime minister chooses his cabinet. In the Soviet Union they chose him and then put the matter to the central committee to ratify. There was no tradition of a clean sweep at the top when a new administration came in. General secretaries spent the first two or three years of their power trying to remove opponents they inherited. Gorbachev proved adept at doing this initially but his use of advisers and brains trusts meant that even potential allies in the Politburo felt excluded. By running his reform campaign like a conspiracy behind the Politburo's back he inevitably built up a reservoir of mistrust. It would later encourage his opponents to plot against him.

Gorbachev's growing troubles at home in trying to reform the Soviet system increased sympathy for him abroad. Here was a man who had taken on one of the hardest challenges in the world and, in spite of resistance, was not giving up. In the rest of the Communist block his prestige was enormous. At a speech before the United Nations in December 1988 he had enunciated the new principles of his emerging foreign policy. He wanted to take the ideological struggle out of international relations and put universal human values above class interests. This was not confined to relations between states with different social systems, that is, between the capitalist and socialist worlds. It applied to relations among states of the same social system. In effect Gorbachev was saying that he would not intervene in Eastern Europe. The message was overwhelming. It frightened the old rulers and encouraged the reformers. 'To deny a nation the freedom of choice, regardless of the pretext or the verbal guise in which it is cloaked, is to upset the unstable balance that has been achieved so far. Freedom of choice is a universal principle. It knows no exceptions,' he told the United Nations.

The West was impressed by Gorbachev's argument that the world was 'interdependent' and that threats to the planet's survival meant nuclear confrontation had to be diminished. His words were coupled with unilateral cuts and far-reaching offers of disarmament. In Germany, in particular, at the front line of the Cold War, where people knew they would be the first victims of an East-West confrontation, Gorbachev's new approach was received with enthusiasm.

The year 1989 was the high-point of his time in office. After four years in power Gorbachev's ability to appear fresh, innovative and exciting were astonishing. The world rightly sensed that this was a man with unusual qualities for a contemporary politician. He learnt as he went along, which was the authentic mark of the non-dogmatist. He was not cynical. He had a vision and a set of values which went beyond the mere business of staying in power and trying to make things marginally better than he found them. His strategy for a new and better world was based on a humbler and more open-minded approach to international relations than leaders of great powers usually adopted. Gone was the chauvinism of arguing that his country had an historic mission to help others become civilized. In his United Nations speech he relegated the Russian Revolution to the past and suggested countries should learn from each other and the common fund of human achievement which transcended national boundaries.

'Nowadays it is virtually impossible for any society to be "closed",' he told the world body in New York. 'Two great revolutions – the French Revolution of 1789 and the Russian Revolution of 1917 – exercised a powerful impact on the very nature of the historical process – but today a new world is emerging. Further global progress is possible only through a quest for universal consensus . . . as the multi-faceted nature of the world asserts itself, it undermines arrogant efforts to teach one's democratic patterns to others – to say nothing of the fact that democracy, when exported, often loses its value . . . What we need is unity through diversity . . . This new stage requires that international relations be freed from ideology.' Several months before the peaceful revolutions in Eastern Europe and the breaching of the Berlin Wall, Gorbachev was pronouncing the end of the Cold War. He was hoping it would involve a mutual truce and a search for ways of sharing experience, what he called 'co-creativity and co-development', rather than one-sided triumphalism.

People abroad responded to his hopeful message with gratitude and two foreign visits which Gorbachev made in 1989 produced unprecedented outbursts of 'Gorbymania'. In May he travelled to Beijing to end a quarter-century of Sino-Soviet Cold War. His impending arrival was the signal for thousands of students to start a sit-in at Tienanmen Square in protest at their government's resistance to reform. By the time he flew in, virtually the entire square was occupied by students, grouped round a series of tents where hunger-strikers were lying. At first Gorbachev's Chinese hosts did not risk dispersing the crowd. Instead, they tried to pretend it was not there. Although the Great Hall of the People, the government headquarters, was virtually surrounded by demonstrators, the Chinese authorities refused to change the venue of Gorbachev's first meeting and he was forced to drive in via a back door. They accepted reality two days later and asked him to hold his eve-of-departure press conference at his residence in a distant villa. The decision was taken at the last minute and some 200 journalists as well as the Soviet press spokesman were already waiting in the Great Hall when the venue was switched. Reporters forced their way through the throng and rushed in search of taxis and rickshaws where the streets were clearer a quarter of a mile away.

I had rented a bicycle which was conveniently propped up by the steps of the Great Hall. People were packed shoulder to shoulder round the building in the hope of seeing Gorbachev. There was no

alternative but to ride down the single traffic lane kept clear for
ambulances taking fainting hunger strikers to hospital. Angry
marshals shouted and waved me back until I pulled from my
pocket a postcard-sized photograph of Gorbachev. It had been
given to me by a Soviet official who said they stuck it on their car's
windscreen to show the police who they were. It turned out to be a
magic credential. As I held the picture aloft, the mood changed.
Tens of thousands of people cheered, clapped and gave the V-sign
as I frantically pedalled by.

In Germany three weeks later the enthusiasm was similar.
Outside Bonn's town hall crowds assembled two hours before
Gorbachev and his wife were due. George Bush had been in the
square a few days before with only a few passers-by bothering to
greet him. In the giant hall of a steel plant in Dortmund 8,000
workers waited to hear Gorbachev speak. 'Gorby, Gorby', the sea
of hard-hats roared as he mounted the platform. Gorbachev put
aside his prepared text and for a few moments became a revivalist
preacher: 'If you ask me what my greatest impression has been over
these last few days, I would say this: what we have experienced on
your soil has moved us very much. We saw many faces and we
looked into many eyes, and we felt the movement of people's souls.
The desire to come towards each other, to trust each other, to fight
together for a better world – that is the most important thing.' No
other politician could dare to say such unscripted things, one felt.
The steel-workers knew they were in the presence of a star, an
emotional man of enormous idealism. Their hands beat together in
appreciation for several minutes. Three Turkish immigrant workers
in sweatshirts standing near me clapped as loudly as the rest. His
was a message which went beyond nations.

For all his personal charm and in spite of his repeated diplomatic
surrenders, Gorbachev never broke through the barrier of anti-
Sovietism among Western leaders, whatever ordinary people felt.
He might be a 'good' Communist but he was still the incarnation of
the enemy state, and it was not until Boris Yeltsin replaced
Gorbachev, burying both the Soviet Union and Communism in

Russia, that Western leaders relaxed. This is not to say that Gorbachev's initial strategy of unilateral moves towards arms control and sweeping offers of a non-nuclear world were naïve. By undermining the Soviet Union's 'enemy image' he hoped in part to appeal to Western public opinion and the peace movements to put pressure on their governments for an end to the arms race and for cuts in military spending. His strategy worked to an extent. The 1987 treaty eliminating the Soviet SS20 missiles and the American medium-range nuclear weapons which NATO had managed to deploy in Europe only after massive public protests gave both sides an equally balanced success.

After a year of painful reflection in retirement, Gorbachev strenuously denied that his concessions to the West had been excessive. In an interview in the office of his Foundation on the eve of his first anniversary out of power, he told me his arms control initiatives expressed a world-wide hunger for change. He rejected the charge that the West had made him buckle under pressure. 'That's absolutely not true. There are notes in the presidential archives which can be read. There you'll see that in all these talks Gorbachev was at least on an equal footing or was in the dominant position.'[10] Smiling, he added, 'because behind us were all these initiatives. This led a lot of politicians to anxiety and alarm. These changes in the world were connected to Gorbachev and perestroika, so they were saying, "We had better lay siege to this fellow and corner him". I knew. I got information from people who were in the inner circle. But they failed. Gorbachev never felt overwhelmed. He was in the saddle, because we were expressing what had ripened in the world.'

At home his popularity continued to slip. The fact that he was fêted abroad and visibly enjoyed the applause seemed to increase his negative image in the Soviet Union. Some of his Politburo colleagues saw it as an escapist dereliction of duty. On his return from a trip to Italy at the end of 1989, Ligachev went to the airport in the normal way of Party protocol to meet Gorbachev. 'The whole of Milan, the whole of Rome came out to see me,' Gorbachev enthused as the two men walked to their cars. 'You should go to

Sverdlovsk and Nizhni Novgorod and talk to people there,' Ligachev replied coldly.[11] 'Huh, Yegor,' snapped Gorbachev, 'you're playing the same old gramophone record again.'

Gorbachev often said he wanted a revolution 'from below' but when it happened he could not accept it. He never seemed to want to be outflanked on the progressive wing, as though only he, as the leader of perestroika, could decide at what pace it should go. The reformers in the informal political clubs had proposed a broad-based alliance for reform. They said this would replace 'authoritarian perestroika' with 'democratic perestroika'. Later they were matched by reformers in the new Soviet parliament and in the Communist party itself. But Gorbachev would not agree to a coalition for reform which would align non-Communist reformers with progressive forces in the party. It was as though after giving the green light to grassroots activity he did not dare to accept its advocates as his political equals, let alone as allies. His old instincts as a party apparatchik proved to be too strong. When hostile placards appeared at the May Day parade in 1990, he lost his temper and walked off the reviewing stand above the Lenin mausoleum. In 1991 he referred to demonstrators who assembled outside the Kremlin as 'mobs'.

Gorbachev's failure to understand the nationalism of non-Russians stemmed from the same lack of democratic instincts. He had not spent enough time listening to non-Russians. He could not grasp that Baltic peoples had a different conception of Russia from his. He believed the Soviet Union was indeed a new kind of state which made nationalism out of date. Even when his fellow Slavs, the Ukrainians, were preparing to vote for independence in December 1991, Gorbachev was unable to believe it. The result shocked him, and even after the vote he continued to argue that Ukrainians had not opted to leave the Union. One problem was that he hardly ever travelled to the other republics, even after nationalist pressures burst into the open. When he visited Lithuania in January 1990 it was the first time he had been there for ten years. (In 1980 he was there as the Politburo's representative to 'celebrate' forty years of Soviet power, the anniversary of what most Lithuanians saw as their annexation). His only trip to the Caucasus as leader was a day trip to Armenia after the earthquake. He even had his enormous Zil limousines flown down to Yerevan for the tour, but Nikolai Ryzhkov, the prime minister, persuaded him to leave them at the airport and use a bus. He lost much of the sympathy his visit was meant to arouse when he addressed a crowd with an attack on the Armenian nationalists who were raising the issue of Nagorno-Karabakh. In Kiev in 1985 he referred to being 'in Russia'.

Nevertheless, Gorbachev might have avoided the break-up of the Soviet Union if he had taken different decisions. His main mistake was not to treat the three Baltic republics as a separate case. They were the last republics to be incorporated into the Soviet Union, and the deed was done by force. As soon as their populations voted for pro-independence governments in the spring of 1990, Gorbachev should have accepted the verdict. Gorbachev acted as though the Baltics were a test case. If they were allowed to leave, his fear was that the other republics would want to go too. It was a misreading of history. But this is not to say that he should have let the Baltics go and then tried to maintain the Soviet Union as it was. He should have made changes in the USSR too.

In the autumn of 1989 the Inter-regional Group of Deputies, the main democratic faction in the newly elected Congress of People's Deputies, proposed that the USSR become a confederation instead of the tight federation it had been since 1922. Their plan, which would have given individual republics greater economic and political rights, chimed in with the spirit of decentralization and greater democracy which Gorbachev's perestroika was aiming to develop. Gorbachev rejected it. Later in April 1991 under pressure from Yeltsin, by then Russia's parliamentary leader, Gorbachev came round to the confederative view. It was the underlying principle in the long series of negotiations over a new Union treaty which he conducted with other republican leaders at his country house at Novo-Ogaryevo. But the loss of a year and a half was a vital factor in increasing the political polarization which eventually spelled Gorbachev's doom. It allowed the pro-empire forces in the army and party who mounted the August coup to grow stronger. They saw his confederalism as at best weakness, at worst treachery. On the opposite flank it pushed the anti-party democrats in the Russian parliament more firmly into the Yeltsin camp and against Gorbachev. The president was left with minimal support.

After his mistakes with the party and the future of the Union, Gorbachev's third major error was his mishandling of Boris Yeltsin. It was the most conspicuous example of one of Gorbachev's key weaknesses, his poor judgement of individuals and his inability to make close friends. Gorbachev was the direct opposite of Brezhnev, the ultimate 'clubbable' Soviet politician who loved nothing better than to drink with friends. Socially, Gorbachev was a loner. Interviewed on Russian television a year after his resignation, he revealed that he had invited no friends to his flat in that time. 'Our home is our castle,' he said. Lukyanov, his colleague from university days, said he had not once been asked to the Gorbachev home throughout the years of perestroika.[12]

Gorbachev could be remarkably insensitive to colleagues. When Eduard Shevardnadze, the Foreign Minister, announced his resignation at the Congress of People's Deputies in December 1990, Gorbachev publicly accused him of disloyalty and hinted he was a coward. Admittedly, Gorbachev was shocked and upset, but in expressing out loud the feelings that other politicians would have kept for their closed circle of advisers Gorbachev confirmed the impression that he was a man with no confidants. Similarly, when Prime Minister Ryzhkov unexpectedly came under vicious and unfair attack in parliament over a never-substantiated allegation of corruption, Gorbachev did nothing to defend him. This coldness to those he worked with closely was a matter of character, but his rapid promotion to the country's ruling body appears to have reinforced it. His elevation to an unusually elderly Politburo at the age of forty-eight put him in an awkward position, too young for his new colleagues, too important to be convivial with his contemporaries.

Gorbachev always addressed his colleagues as 'ty', the pronoun for family friends, intimates, and – in this case – juniors. He expected everyone to reply with the formal 'vy', including men who were regularly around him, and even his senior in age such as Alexander Yakovlev. This was partly a relic of Communist party norms, a phoney comradeship carried over from Gorbachev's 'obkom' days when first secretaries at any level often used 'ty' but expected their subordinates to say 'vy'. Yeltsin, to his credit, never did this as president.

Gorbachev's disastrous relations with Yeltsin were based mainly on excessive mistrust, a strange factor since it was clear after the coup that Gorbachev's mistake *vis-à-vis* the plotters had been the opposite. Every conspirator was a man Gorbachev had promoted and trusted. Yeltsin was the exception to this general rule. His very first signs of disagreement with Gorbachev's policy in the summer of 1987 seemed to make Gorbachev unusually angry. For the next four years the two men never patched up their quarrel.

One of Yeltsin's initial charges against Gorbachev in 1987, which he repeated publicly at the nineteenth party conference in June 1988, was that Gorbachev was allowing a cult of 'vozhdism' (praise for the supreme leader) to grow around him. The charge seemed wild, and there was certainly no genuine basis for comparison between Gorbachev and Russia's earlier autocrats like Ivan the Terrible, Peter the Great and Stalin. But Yeltsin had put his finger on something. Gorbachev did have a serious character flaw. He could not brook equals. In his memoirs Nikolai Ryzhkov recalled agreeing with Yeltsin's criticisms at the party conference. 'The outward trappings of power always delighted Gorbachev. He loved being the top man,' he wrote in 1991.[13] Ryzhkov complained of Gorbachev's constant amendments to the Soviet constitution, and his continual creation of new bodies of power – the council of the federation, the presidential council, the security council and so on. 'It was a typical Russian characteristic – the drive towards autocracy.'[14]

*

34

Gorbachev's excessive trust of subordinates and his excessive mistrust of Yeltsin were not in contradiction. They were part of the same syndrome. As long as a man was in a definite position below him in the hierarchy, Gorbachev was willing to overlook almost any amount of disobedience. If a man was in an undefined role, especially if he was also pretending to rivalry, Gorbachev was jealous. Yeltsin had his own ambitions. He too was a proud and prickly man. But Gorbachev was the man with the initial position of strength. He should have taken the first step to reconciliation with Yeltsin. There were many opportunities, but he could never bring himself to offer Yeltsin a post of genuine responsibility or a political alliance. On the contrary, he repeatedly tried to block Yeltsin's advance, including in all three elections – first to the leadership of the Soviet parliament, then to the Russian parliament and finally to the Presidency of Russia. Even when it was clear that his attacks on Yeltsin were used by Yeltsin to gain yet more support, Gorbachev could not stop himself. It was not just that he hated a rival. He particularly seemed to hate a rival who presented himself as more progressive than himself.

He had awkward moments with the once dissident physicist, Andrei Sakharov, after he became a member of the Congress of People's Deputies, for the same reason. Like Yeltsin, Sakharov was outside the established hierarchy of power yet somehow on a par with Gorbachev, both in the eyes of his countrymen and abroad. Sakharov was the moral conscience of Russia. Gorbachev found this hard to handle. Three days before Sakharov's death, we witnessed a painful scene in the Congress of People's Deputies. The frail, stooping physicist came to the rostrum and called for the Congress to discuss the removal of every article in the Soviet constitution which obstructed perestroika, including Article Six which enshrined the leading role of the Communist party. Gorbachev was visibly unhappy. He also wanted to remove Article Six but in his own time. From his position on the platform above the rostrum he said that Sakharov's formula was too vague. It was one of Gorbachev's typical interventions, unfairly exploiting his use of the chair to give commentaries on other speakers. Sakharov pottered off, then turned back so as to hand Gorbachev a sheaf of supporting telegrams from the public. A testy Gorbachev said he could give Sakharov three files of opposing telegrams. 'No need to put pressure on us by trying to manipulate public opinion,' we heard him snap.

It was an undemocratic remark in an undemocratic context, but revealing. Gorbachev was the most democratically-minded man who had ever ruled Russia, but he was still not democratic enough to see what was happening beneath him. And there were times when he seemed to want to be the only democrat around.

The irony of Gorbachev's place in history is that a man who wanted to build ended up at the head of a process of destruction. The irony of Yeltsin's is that a man who had shown great energy in destroying came to power when building was needed. Although Yeltsin delivered the death blows to the Soviet Communist party and the Soviet Union, they were already moribund when he struck. The new Russian republic of which he was the first president started at ground level. Russians had emerged from the autocracy of a single party and a single ideology. In a very short space of time, they had lost an empire and the last remnants of faith in a bright and imminent future.

Yeltsin had an unparalleled opportunity to move Russia towards building democratic new institutions. In many ways he has squandered it. He has not set up his own political party to create a lasting basis of support. He did not introduce a new constitution for Russia early in his term, when he still had majority backing in parliament. He started to undermine the Russian Congress of People's Deputies which he had inherited, even though it was the body which first introduced a democratic separation of powers, with an executive presidency and a constitutional court. He fell under the influence of the most radical of the anti-Communists in his entourage, many of whom did not understand the complexities of the Russian economy. They advised him to move to the market by the fastest possible means via 'shock therapy'. The result was a catastrophic increase in inflation, the destruction of people's savings, and an acceleration in the fall of output.

Yeltsin was lucky that his mistakes and miscalculations did not undermine his own popularity as fast as earlier similar ones had undermined Gorbachev. In the April 1993 referendum on whether voters had confidence in him Yeltsin managed to win the support of 58 per cent, only six million fewer than had voted for him in 1991. Voters saw no real alternative. While Gorbachev had Yeltsin as a potential rival, at least from 1989 onwards, Yeltsin's only challenger was Ruslan Khasbulatov, a man with none of Yeltsin's personal appeal and one insuperable flaw. He was a Chechen from the North Caucasus, who would never be chosen by the Russian electorate for high office. The results of the referendum on the other questions were less good. A narrow majority voted for new presidential elections, and only 53 per cent supported Yeltsin's economic policies. In more than half the regions and republics, majorities rejected them.

Yeltsin won largely because of his personality, which was well projected on state-controlled television, and because of his reputation. People remembered him as the man who had stood up against the coup plot in 1991. Reformers recalled his sensational resignation from the Communist party in 1990. While Gorbachev appealed to the intelligentsia, Yeltsin came across as an authentic Russian man of the people, bluff, hearty, moody, but also courageous when necessary. His heavy drinking did not worry people at first. When he appeared drunk, with his normally carefully sprayed hair flopping over his left forehead, at one evening session of the Congress of People's Deputies in March 1993, most Russians I talked to forgave him. His mother had just died, and parliament was giving him a difficult time. Only later, after several drunken episodes abroad, did the public mood change. He was harming Russia's prestige.

Yeltsin came to power by brilliant and at times bold use of the democratic space which perestroika created. He ran for election when other senior ex-Communists shied away. But Yeltsin was not a committed democrat. Had he been, he would have used his time to strengthen the country's fledgling institutions, an independent press, an effective parliament, the constitutional court. He would have tried to create a culture of consensus. He would have consulted regularly with the leaders of the parliamentary factions. He would have tried to find compromise. Instead, from the autumn of 1992 onwards, he chose the path of confrontation. He exaggerated the danger of a Communist return and, like many other Russian leaders before him, convinced himself that his policies were being sabotaged in the provinces. He polarized the political scene, forcing the centrists in parliament to take sides. Most of them chose to oppose him, not because they disagreed with his strategy of reform but because of his tactics. He then treated them, including his vice-president, Alexander Rutskoi, as irreconcilable opponents.

Yeltsin is not a team player. A former 'obkom' secretary like Gorbachev, he expects obedience and finds it hard to work with people who disagree with him on issues he understands. He is not a man who is able to listen to argument and try to win people over by persuasion. When he sacked Viktor Barannikov, the security minister, in August 1993, he lost the last survivor of his original cabinet apart from Andrei Kozyrev, the Foreign Minister. In less than two years, everyone had gone. On subjects such as economics where he feels out of his depth, he adopts a 'hands off' approach, tolerating an extraordinary disparity of view. For most of 1992 and 1993 he allowed rows to rage within his government over the speed of reform. Monetarists and state interventionists operated independently, causing confusion and uncertainty in Russia and abroad. In 1994 he allowed Viktor Chernomyrdin, the prime minister, to choose a new government which excluded the best-known monetarists, but then followed most of their policies.

The Gorbachev era freed Russian society politically. The Yeltsin reforms, following the break-up of the state planning system, freed Russia's economic 'estates'. Alexander Yakovlev, in the analysis described earlier in this chapter, explained how party officials and state enterprise managers were often in conflict in the Communist period. After Communism these enterprises, which were often monopolies, were able to operate freely. So too was the president. He was the freest ruler in modern Russian history, as free as any Tsar. In the Communist system the general secretary, although nominally the supreme ruler, was accountable to the Politburo. Below them was the central committee in which the economic managers were well represented. The Communist system was not democratic, but it was an effective administrative machine which worked and where the 'estates', whether they were industrial sectors, the collective farm lobby or regional politicians, had a framework for presenting their interests.

When Yeltsin came to power, the machine had broken down, and he did little to put a new one in its place. Politics at the top became a battle for Yeltsin's ear. He was surrounded by advisers, many of them cronies from earlier times. There were no clear structures with lines of command. Yeltsin wanted to be above politics. He despised the Congress of People's Deputies where the élites had some representation. This was one reason why they began to oppose him. His entourage resembled a feudal court. When people misbehaved, he punished them by taking away their privileges, such as the Zil limousine which vice-president Rutskoi lost when he criticized the president.

Yeltsin's great service is that he has not reverted to repression. His style is autocratic, his manner authoritarian. When in September 1993 he dissolved the Supreme Soviet, he also called elections for a new two-chamber parliament. His action in closing parliament was not that of a dictator, but rather of a man who finds it hard to negotiate with other people and hopes that by changing the rules he can eliminate them.

The shock results of the December 1993 election showed this strategy had failed. Yeltsin was depressed. In the months that followed he frequently appeared exhausted, and his concentration span narrowed. But he accepted the new political reality. He did not use hardline methods again. He also began to shift towards the centre of the spectrum, although this meant abandoning the radical reformers with whom he had earlier allied himself.

He strengthened his links with the old industrial and economic nomenklatura, the same élite which had run the Soviet Union. They had been carefully preserving their positions by taking advantage of privatization to retain control of the enterprises which they managed, but now with the added benefit of being able to enrich themselves. Indeed, it became increasingly clear in the years after the August 1991 coup that it had done little more than eliminate the ideological apparatus of the old Soviet establishment. Those who earned salaries from mouthing the party line from Moscow lost out because the Communist party no longer ruled. The economic managers were still in place. Most welcomed the shift to a market economy since they could make easy money, and no longer had to hide it.

In the patchy and generally unrevealing book he wrote after the storming of Parliament, Yeltsin commented: 'We must finally admit that Russia comprehends democracy poorly.'[15] It sounded as though the man who had been wrongly touted by Western governments as a great reformer was excusing his own mistakes and seeking to justify a return to a more authoritarian regime. There should be no surprise in that. Yeltsin had served the old Soviet system, and benefited from it, for most of his career. By the time he started to rise, after Stalin's death, Soviet Communism was no longer a regime of random and widespread terror. It was an authoritarian, centralized and repressive system which fitted Russian traditions and the Russian character, or it would not have lasted so long.

Yeltsin understood the system's growing inefficiency and the disadvantages of repression no earlier than Gorbachev. His break with the Communist party in July 1990 was motivated by political expediency more than moral principle. Yeltsin's main belief is that Russia needs strong central rule to bring in democracy. He is not the first Russian leader to think so: Russia will be lucky if he is the last.

3

The Roots of Failure

There is noise in the capitals
The prophets thunder
A furious war of words is waged
But in the depths, in the heart of Russia,
There all is still, there is ancient peace.

NIKOLAI NEKRASOV, C. 1850

Worse than poverty, more bitter than hunger is the suppression
of the people by absolute powerlessness in the face of arbitrary
officialdom.

FROM A RESOLUTION BY A VILLAGE ASSEMBLY
IN KAZAN PROVINCE, 1907[1]

In the summer of 1988, three years into perestroika, the Moscow intelligentsia was buzzing over an article in *Novy Mir*, the most prestigious of the literary monthlies. Written by an economic journalist, Vasily Selyunin, the article strongly criticized Lenin. Taking issue with the Gorbachevian view that socialism began to be distorted under Stalin, Selyunin argued that Stalin had merely revived repressive practices which Lenin brought in a year after the Revolution during the time of 'War Communism'. Lenin used terror against counter-revolutionaries, herding thousands of people into camps and shooting others. Lenin confiscated land from rich peasants. Lenin destroyed the market economy.

The Selyunin article was the first scholarly polemic against the founder of the Soviet state to be published in the Soviet Union. While his criticism of Lenin created a sensation since it broke a seventy-year-old taboo, the largest part of his article dealt with a wider issue. It analysed pre-revolutionary Russian history in order to identify the foundations of the authoritarianism which the Bolsheviks later enlarged. Selyunin focused on the reigns of Ivan the Terrible and Peter the Great, the two Tsars who were treated relatively favourably by Stalinist historians. Their role as builders of a powerful Russian state appealed to Stalin. Selyunin recorded that Ivan turned free peasants into serfs, while Peter used serf labour in manufacturing, a move which helped to prevent a bourgeoisie and a capitalist economy developing in Russia.

The *Novy Mir* piece reopened an important issue which the distortions of Soviet historiography had long suppressed. The progressive character of the October Revolution was taken for granted, and history-writing by Soviet authors consisted in stressing the gap between what followed 1917 and what had gone before. But as the Communist party's grip on ideology loosened under glasnost, a new contrast between the pre- and post-revolutionary periods emerged – with the roles reversed. The line was that before 1917 Russia had been developing into a democratic state. A nascent bourgeoisie was coming to prominence, and the country was casting off its Asiatic heritage. Then came the First World War, and the ensuing chaos which the Bolsheviks were able to exploit in order to seize power. Under this analysis the October Revolution destroyed the emerging capitalist structures, stifled a budding democracy, and took the country backwards again.

The argument was not new to Western analysts, but the excesses of Stalinist history-writing had banned it from Russia. Unfortunately, instead of being debated, it became a new orthodoxy, accepted in the Russian media almost without challenge, and leading to dangerous simplification. Without it, public euphoria after August 1991 would not have been so great, and the subsequent disappointment so damaging. Russian publicists might have done better to examine those features of their society which make any attempt at democratization difficult. What was it which undermined the progress made during the 'discontinuities' in Russian history so that the country's political development was forced back into the traditional mould?

The answer to this question illuminates the deeper reasons for Gorbachev's failure, apart from his mistakes. It also shows why Yeltsin's reforms took so long to bear fruit, and in some cases failed too. Russia had never developed a civil society, and there was no way that the removal of the Communist party would immediately usher in democracy. Many of those who called themselves democrats in the early 1990s were merely anti-Communists. They knew what they were against. They did not know what they were for. Some were 'neo-Bolsheviks' (the phrase coined by the liberal perestroika press) in that they used authoritarian methods to try to bring in democracy – which was not entirely surprising since most of the anti-Communists were former Communists.

In his study, *Russia under the Old Regime*, Richard Pipes traced the long authoritarian tradition in Russian history. One element was the status of the serfs, though Pipes attacked what he called the mistake of confusing Russian serfdom with slavery. Unlike the slaves of North and South America and the Caribbean, the Russian serf lived in his own house, not in slave quarters, and could keep most of the product of his labour. The worst feature was the serf's permanent subjection to the will of others. 'Totally lacking in legally recognized personal rights, the peasant regarded all authority as by its very nature alien and hostile,' Pipes wrote.[2]

Russian history is punctuated by a series of spectacular peasant revolts, first under the leadership of Stepan Razin in the 1670s, a century later in the time of Catherine the Great under Yemelian Pugachev, and during the 1905–7 Revolution. The risings of the seventeenth and eighteenth centuries were led by Cossacks, the communities of runaway serfs who had escaped to the southern and eastern boundaries of Tsarist power. The expansion of the Tsarist empire involved constant efforts to penetrate and take over these communities, and then use them as the guardians of Russian power against other ethnic groups.

Pipes regards these revolts as exceptions. For the most part, serfs were passive. The tyranny of nature – the harsh climate and the vast countryside – weighed them down. Serfs abandoned the land, if they could, taking up handicrafts, peddling goods, and performing casual labour in the towns and cities. Nineteenth-century romantics among the gentry, who only saw serfs during pleasant summers on their estates, imagined they loved the land. In reality peasants wanted to be free of toil on the land. Another escape was through alcohol. According to legend, when the Muslims tried to persuade Prince Vladimir of Kiev in the tenth century to take up Islam, he replied with a jocular rhyme: 'Rusi est' vesel piti, ne mozhet bez nego byti' (Russians are merrier when drinking, they cannot live without it). Patriarch Nikon tried to enforce prohibition in the seventeenth century on the grounds that drunkenness had become so widespread. His campaign failed and at the end of the nineteenth century income from alcohol sales was the largest item in the Imperial budget. Three hundred years later Gorbachev tried almost the same thing, launching a nationwide anti-alcohol campaign. It was one of his first mistakes, and did much damage to his image among ordinary Russians. Instead of trying to handle alcoholism as a social problem with a variety of causes, he fell back on old-style disciplinarian methods. Intellectuals and government officials tended to laugh off the ban on alcohol sales as a mild inconvenience but male manual workers saw it as a new blow in their already difficult lives. It undermined Gorbachev's effort to portray himself as a man in touch with the popular mood, and created the impression that he was more concerned with discipline than incentives.

It would be wrong to give the impression that there was no organization in Russian villages. The potential elements of a civil society were in place in the form of the village commune, the 'obshchina' or 'mir', in which most peasants lived. These existed in Russia from the Middle Ages. After the emancipation of the serfs in 1861 they played a larger role as a self-governing territorial community and the main legal owner of the land. Power resided in the communal assembly made up of the heads of households or their representatives. Decisions in a communal assembly were usually by consensus rather than majority vote. Typically, the more active members, often the wealthier ones, took the lead. Landless peasants and non-peasant families, including the priest, were excluded from the assembly. The chief executive was an elder elected for three years. A peasant would only keep and be able to pass on to younger family members the land round his house, not the land he farmed. Most arable land was held as temporary allotments granted by the commune. It was periodically reassigned. Pasture and forest land were reserved for collective use. As a result, Pipes concluded, Russian peasants had great difficulty comprehending the notion of property, confusing it with usage or possession. This was a key factor which Stalin's policy of collectivizing agriculture consciously built on. When Yeltsin later tried to encourage the private ownership of land, he found few people ready to take it. Russian peasants were attached to the gardens round their homes, and urban Russians wanted allotments but this was not the same as making a living out of agriculture, let alone a switch to capitalist farming. In the nineteenth century peasants could also buy private land from non-commune sources, but few bothered to do so. In the late twentieth century under Yeltsin little had changed.

Theodore Shanin, another leading historian of pre-revolutionary Russia, emphasizes the political turbulence rather than the passivity of the Russian countryside. In his view peasant revolts were a constant feature, rather than the exception. They were always ruthlessly suppressed by the Tsar's autocracy with the use of troops. By the nineteenth century the Cossacks had been fully bought off and set apart from the peasants as a military caste. As a result the countryside became quiet. After emancipation, the peasant commune served two functions, which benefited the state as well as

45

the peasants, according to Shanin in *Russia as a 'Developing Society'*.[3] The commune assured economic services and some collective welfare and security for its members. It helped the state by providing an administrative device for tax collection and local policing. But the commune also helped peasants organize in self-defence against the state. 'In the 1905–7 revolution, the Russian peasant commune was dramatically to reveal its characteristics as a generator of egalitarian ideology, and a school for collective action, capable of turning into well-organized revolt overnight,' Shanin wrote.

The 1905–7 uprising was marked by a variety of seditious actions, including incursions into private and state forests to cut timber illegally, sending peasant cattle on to private grazing land, and the mass robbery of stores and warehouses. Manor houses were burned down; squires were murdered. There were collective demands for lower rent and a refusal to supply wage-labour to private estates and to pay tax. The disturbances covered most of the rich, black-earth zone of Ukraine and southern Russia as well as some of the more densely populated areas nearer Moscow. In many areas peasants expelled every manifestation of Tsarist authority and set up small islands of self-rule.

With the Tsar in temporary retreat in 1905, and the establishment of the first Duma, or consultative assembly, the peasants even formed a nationwide organization, the All-Russian Peasants' Union. It called for a Russia 'in which the land belonged to the peasants, held in a roughly egalitarian division and worked by family labour without the use of wage-workers . . . All farming land would be assigned to the village communes . . . Trading in land was to be abolished and private ownership of land brought to an end . . . Free education for all was particularly emphasized.'[4] The All-Russian Peasants' Union was an important building-block on which a civil society could have been constructed, but it came to nothing as a result of internal divisions and official repression.

A key aspect of Russia before the Bolsheviks was the absence of a politically active entrepreneurial class. This does not mean

46

Russians were never interested in trade or manufacturing. Pipes pointed out that the natural poverty of the soil and the climate compelled them to become craftsmen in order to supplement their incomes. Throughout the eighteenth and nineteenth centuries a cottage industry developed 'whose enterprising leaders differed little from self-made enterpreneurs of the Americas'. By 1914 Russia's industrial output was fifth in the world and a small group of rich merchants and manufacturers had developed, whose mansions are still visible throughout Moscow and St Petersburg.

Why did they not form a bourgeoisie and acquire political ambitions? One reason was the banning of political parties or any kind of nationwide organization until the beginning of the twentieth century. Another was the Russian Tsars' attitude to property. They operated on the basis that the Tsar owned his realm. The medieval Western European distinction between ownership ('dominium') and authority ('imperium') did not apply. Russian Tsars, moving out from their original territory in Kiev, acquired their land by conquest. The Tsar was both proprietor and sovereign, unlike kings in Western Europe who were bound to respect their subjects' property. Initially the Tsars only owned the land, but as trade and small-scale industry developed in the sixteenth and seventeenth centuries they used their power of decree to impose royal monopolies, expropriate private businessmen and eliminate competition. Later they took over the mines. Ivan the Terrible in a letter to the English Queen, Elizabeth I, jeered because English merchants, unlike Russians, 'seek their own merchant profit'.[5] Only in north-west Russia, close to the German city-states, did medieval cities develop on the Western European pattern as a body of men with rights not shared by the rural population. Muscovite cities did not differ from country settlements. There was no private property in urban land. It was all held conditionally.

For centuries Russian commerce was mainly carried out by barter. A person's capital was goods and merchandise, and money was principally used for small-scale transactions. It was not until the mid-nineteenth century that the first successful commercial banks were founded. Peter the Great had tried to encourage industrial development by abolishing the royal monopolies on everything but grain, salt, tobacco and vodka. He wanted to build up a group of domestic manufacturers to resist the intrusion of foreigners. But after his death the monopolies were restored. The Tsarist government owned the means of production, set the prices and took most of the output. Only the surplus could be sold at free prices. Peter's grandson, Peter the Third, made a new attempt to stimulate the economy by revoking the decree which permitted merchants to purchase serfs. From then on they could only hire labour for wages. Serf ownership was restricted to the gentry. The move had the opposite effect to what Peter intended. Instead of promoting efficiency, it deprived the incipient middle class of access to the main and cheapest source of labour.

The Russian state system was run by a hierarchical bureaucracy with considerable powers. The legal system was rudimentary. The government did not start judicial proceedings to defend citizens, but only to protect its own interests. It was up to the injured party to initiate criminal and civil trials. Moreover, most of the laws covering Russia's system of government were never formally promulgated. Whether it was serfdom and the authority of landlords over peasants or the requirement that Jews live within a restricted area, the so-called Pale of Settlement, the Tsar's subjects had to accept official statements of the law as unchallengeable. The parallels with the system after 1917 are obvious.

The Selyunin article with which this chapter began accepted the special nature of Russian history but argued that there were two periods when Russia could have developed a progressive form of capitalism and a system of political democracy. The first came with Alexander II's reforms in the 1860s. These included the emancipation of the serfs and the judicial decree which laid down that all criminal offences be tried publicly in ordinary courts. The reforms were short-lived. In 1880, after one of several assassination attempts against him, Alexander II reverted to repression. He set up a new department of state police and a special 'protective section', the 'okhrana', which later became the basis for the Bolsheviks' police.

Alexander's cycle of reform and repression was a classic case of change 'from above' which was aborted 'from above'. Nevertheless, in spite of the political stagnation, Russia did advance on the path of capitalism between 1860 and 1914. But progress was uneven and the social changes which went with it did not presage a liberal form of government or produce a civil society able to defend political democracy. There was a two-year famine from 1891 to 1893, an industrial leap forward, a financial crash in 1899, war with Japan, revolution and repression, and then a final economic boom from 1910 to 1913. While the growth of industrial output seemed impressive, most of it was due to an increase in the work force rather than to greater efficiency. But the country's population remained predominantly peasant. At the end of the century only 5 per cent of the labour force was involved in manufacturing compared to 57 per cent in Britain.

The boom in the 1890s did less than expected to produce a Russian entrepreneurial class. It was promoted by state-generated railway building, and protectionist policies which encouraged industrialization, yet by 1900 most of Russia's 932 towns still had no factories or railway station. Much of the expansion was financed by foreign rather than Russian capital. By 1913 41 per cent of the capital in joint-stock companies in manufacturing, mining and banking was foreign. While this helped to accelerate Russia's industrial development, it did not produce a sufficient political counter-weight to the power of the Tsar. Russia's big businessmen numbered fewer than 100,000. Between them and the five million industrial workers were a larger group of middle and poor tradesmen, craftsmen, shop assistants and pedlars. The main features of the Russian bourgeoisie, in Shanin's words, were 'its relatively small size; the supremacy of traders over industrialists within it; provincial, narrow-minded and backward business practices and extreme despotism towards employees'.[6] Most businessmen were politically indifferent. The few who were prepared to commit themselves were usually monarchist, xenophobic, and anti-liberal.

The pre-war boom was not led by private enterprise but by a

huge growth in the state-owned sector of the economy. It quadrupled between 1890 and 1913. The state was directly engaged in manufacturing, mining and the liquor monopoly, and through the court, the bureaucracy and the army was also the country's biggest consumer, giving it the power to influence markets, prices, and profits, and thus dominate private business. Russia's officials were not suited to run, let alone encourage an entrepreneurial economy. They were untrained and corrupt in their contacts with the private sector. Promotion was secured by blind loyalty to superiors or by bribing the Tsar's courtiers. Again, the parallels between this system and that which prevailed under Communist party rule are obvious. It would require more than the abolition of the Communist party for a spirit of entrepreneurship to develop in Russia.

The second moment when, according to Selyunin, reforms had a chance to bear fruit was when the last Tsar's Prime Minister, Pyotr Stolypin, tried to break the peasant communes and encourage private farming. Peasants would be awarded title to the land so as to give them a stake in property and encourage extra production. Ironically this was much the same motivation for the Yeltsin attempts at land reform. Stolypin was highly praised by several of the new post-Communist 'democrats' who also hoped that peasants would produce more if they had title to the land.

But like the reforms of Alexander II, Stolypin's did not get far. This was not because they were cut short by the October Revolution and the Bolsheviks, as Selyunin argued. They had run adrift before that as a result of Tsarist government policy which continued to favour industry. Promoting industry by government subsidies in a mainly agricultural society meant squeezing the peasants. In the years after the start of the Stolypin reforms the terms of trade between town and country worsened for peasants, who were also hit hard by taxes. As the majority of the population grew poorer, the internal consumer market was reduced and industry was deprived of customers. The political result was dangerous. Growing inequality led to the social explosion of 1917, after the system suffered a general crisis with the onset of the First World War.

It is true there was a large increase in grain production, much of it for export, but as with the rise in industrial output it was not matched by a significant increase in productivity. The growth was mainly a result of bringing virgin land under cultivation, particularly in Asiatic Russia, and to the natural increase in the rural population. Unlike Western Europe, relatively few peasants migrated to the towns. In the central regions of Russia there was an actual decline in farm output between 1890 and 1913. The amount of land per peasant was decreasing, and even on the large estates little capital investment took place. These were the same areas where agriculture continued to be in crisis throughout the Soviet period. The slump started well before the Bolshevik take-over or collectivization.

On the eve of the First World War industrialization had brought a significant rise in production, but had not created either a politically active entrepreneurial class or a noticeable rise in the living standards of the urban proletariat working in the new factories. On the contrary, as a result of industrialization enough of an exodus of the peasants to the towns had occurred to make the Bolshevik Revolution possible, though not inevitable. Without the upheaval caused by the war Russia's authoritarian form of capitalism might eventually have transformed itself into something more democratic. But a series of defeats, coupled with Tsar Nicholas II's narrow-mindedness, created the final stage in the crisis of authority which destroyed his regime. By the time of the February 1917 upheaval which led to his abdication, what little chance there was for a gradual evolution of the regime into a parliamentary system was already lost. The fact that the October Revolution in Petrograd was an almost bloodless *coup d'état* (in Moscow there were several days of street fighting) suggests the degree of acquiescence, if not support, it had.

Selyunin's critical discussion of the October Revolution and the degree to which it was a break in Russian history or a continuation of earlier trends revived a debate which broke out among intellectuals within days of the Revolution itself. The arguments were suppressed by the Bolsheviks and were unknown to a later generation of Russians. Pavel Milyukov, foreign minister in the first provisional government, and a leader of the Constitutional Democrats, wrote his *History of the Second Russian Revolution* within weeks of October 1917. He blamed the collapse of Tsarism and the overthrow of the provisional government on the 'weakness of the principle of statehood in Russia and the predominance of elements who were alien to the state or as anarchists hostile to it'.[7] This was a result of Russia's special, non-Western development. There were other factors: the absence of a bourgeoisie; the 'utopianism' of the Russian intelligentsia; the anarchism of the masses; and the autocracy's refusal to reform. The liberal philosopher P.I. Novgorodtsev saw the old regime's failure in its inability to unite the state and nation. Its 'dogmatic and isolating' ideology of autocracy and Russian Orthodoxy prevented the growth of nationhood. A peasant, when asked to give his nationality, was more likely to say 'Orthodox' than 'Russian'. If he wanted to be more precise geographically, he might say 'Orthodox, from Novgorod' or whatever the province was in which he lived.

One of the first contemporary critics of the October Revolution to be published in Russia after glasnost lifted censorship was Nikolai Berdyayev. His brand of political pessimism enjoyed a burst of popularity among many of the Moscow intelligentsia as Communism declined. They felt the country had been so damaged by the Communists that it would be hard to revive. An earlier exponent of this form of Russian gloom, Berdyayev, rejected any belief in progress. His concerns were culture, Christianity and individual freedom, which he was sure Russians did not care about. He praised the writer Nikolai Gogol for identifying the elemental defects in the Russian character, their pomposity, greed, deceit, malice and despotism. 'I see the sickness of the Russian moral consciousness above all in the denial of personal moral responsibility and personal moral discipline, in the weak development of a sense of duty and honour . . . The Russian does not feel morally accountable to a sufficient degree and he inadequately respects the qualities of an individual.'[8] Russian models were martyrs, not heroes. They learned patience, not enterprise. But Russians could also break out into violence. The failure to find a balance and the constant oscillation between passivity and violence was due, Berdyayev thought, to a fundamental lack of self-confidence.

In spite of the country's many Orthodox churches Berdyayev felt Russians remained pagan. He shared this view with the mid-nineteenth century writer Vissarion Belinsky who described Russians as a profoundly atheistic people. They were not well acquainted with the Bible or the Lord's Prayer, and usually despised the village priest. In his *Open Letter to Gogol* Belinsky wrote that Russians 'retain a good deal of superstition but not a trace of religiousness. Superstition passes with the advance of civilization, but religiousness often keeps company with it. We have a living example in France where even today there are many sincere Catholics among enlightened and educated men ... The Russian people is different.'[9]

His point is well illustrated by the revival of all kinds of mysticism, anthroposophy, and Eastern cults which developed under perestroika. There was great popular interest in astrology and horoscopes, as well as in homeopathic medicine and faith-healing. At the end of the 1980s Anatoly Kashpirovsky, a television hypnotist, was eagerly watched by millions. The shallowness of Russians' religious belief helps to explain the relative ease with which the Bolsheviks eliminated Christianity in the 1920s and 1930s. The Muslims of Soviet Central Asia retained their ceremonial customs, circumcision, religious weddings and burials after the mosques were closed or destroyed by the Bolsheviks. In Russia most Christian families gave up all forms of observance. The trend was enhanced by the murder of hundreds of priests and the destruction of churches, as well as by industrialization and the mass movement of peasants to the towns. The revival of Orthodoxy under Gorbachev permitted churches to be restored and reopened. People of all ages attended church services. But it was often out of curiosity or to join the fashion rather than from belief. State rather than church weddings remained the norm, and by 1993 church-going was not a widespread process in a Russian population of 150 million.

Whatever hold the Orthodox church had in the nineteenth and earlier centuries over Russians, it was never a democratic church. It was always closely associated with the Tsarist state, and discouraged the peasants from any form of self-organization. Its style was feudal and autocratic; the form of its services tended to debase the human being. The absence of pews or seats, requiring worshippers, including the old and infirm, to stand or kneel on an uncarpeted stone floor set the Orthodox church apart from the Catholic and Protestant churches of Central and Western Europe.

Taking a very different perspective from Russia's other publicists, Leon Trotsky also regretted the crudeness of Russia's feudal tradition and the low level of its bourgeois democracy. 'The Russian people was not less heavily oppressed by nobility and Church than the peoples of the West. But that complex and rounded-off way of life which, on the basis of feudal rule, grew up in Europe – that Gothic lace-work of feudalism – has not grown on our soil . . . We lacked the life-matter for it. We could not afford it . . . A thousand years we have lived in a humble log cabin and filled its crevices with moss – could we dream of vaulting arches and Gothic spires? How miserable was our gentry! Where were its castles, its tournaments? Its crusades, its minstrels, its chivalrous love?' [10]

Antonio Gramsci, the Italian revolutionary and intellectual, first formulated a distinction between 'domination' and 'hegemony' as types of political rule. In Western Europe, he argued, the bourgeoisie exercised its power by controlling and manipulating people's cognition. The bourgeoisie's view of the world held sway in the media, in the education system, and in general public discourse. This 'hegemony' of ideas went largely unchallenged, and had the explicit consent of most of the governed, since their interests were partly met. By contrast, Gramsci wrote, Russia's political organization was marked by 'domination'. Before and after the October Revolution Russia's rulers held sway by coercion.

There was no network of independent and voluntary associations in which mutually shared ideas could gain support and eventually become 'hegemonic'. For new ideas to replace the old ones there had to be a long march through the institutions of civil society. Socialist revolutions had not taken hold in Western Europe in the 1920s because society was not yet ready to accept them. In Russia the situation was different. After centuries of state domination and repression of independent institutions there was only a weak civil society. New ideas could take control quickly, though they might then find it hard to put down roots. This was one reason why the October Revolution succeeded in establishing itself as a system of power. For it to gain popular or intellectual acceptance was another matter.

A crucial component of civil society is its best educated members. In pre-1917 Russia this group was relatively small. It was split between those who were willing to serve the state and those who wanted to stand apart. Peter the Great tried to encourage Western-style education in Russia, but while the state needed educated and therefore Europeanized people, it was afraid of them. It made it hard for them to exercise any political rights or freely use the knowledge they had acquired. The educated had three choices: to keep quiet and take a job in the Imperial administration; emigrate; or become an 'internal exile', retiring to some Chekhovian Cherry Orchard in the country. It was this last group which became known as the intelligentsia.

The word is not a generic term for all intellectuals. The Russian intelligentsia defined itself by virtue of its capacity for critical, independent and therefore seditious thought, which put it in permanent opposition to the state's values. As such it has no parallels in other European societies. University-trained administrators of the state machine were excluded, and excluded themselves, from the intelligentsia. Most priests and army officers were similarly not counted. The intelligentsia covered the liberal professions, the writers, poets and political journalists, plus some engineers and agronomists, and of course Russia's active dissidents, its revolutionaries. As Isaiah Berlin put it, 'The Russian intelligentsia, because it was small and consumed by a sense of responsibility for its brothers who lived in darkness, grew to be a dedicated order, bound by solidarity and kinship. Isolated and divided by the tangled forest of society which was impenetrable to rational organization, they called out to each other in order to preserve contact. They were citizens of a state within a state, soldiers in an army dedicated to progress, surrounded on all sides by reaction.' [11]

If the intelligentsia was united in opposition to the state, it was fiercely divided over tactics and goals. Arguments were all the more passionate in that the participants were few. Intellectual disagreement was often seen as emotional betrayal. Groups formed, divided and re-formed into new but temporary coalitions with such rapidity that it was usually psychologically safer to be alone. The intelligentsia were cut off from ordinary people, the 'narod', but most felt they understood them and could speak in their name. It was a long historical phenomenon which Trotsky called 'substitutism'. In 1825 the aristocratic officers known as the Decembrists, who rebelled against the Tsar, tried to represent the ideas of a middle class not yet born. Half a century later the Narodniks claimed to speak for a silent peasantry. Finally, as Trotsky put it shortly after the abortive 1905 Revolution, Marxist intellectuals set themselves up as the voice of a weak but newly awakening working class. The intelligentsia's isolation from the narod, particularly the peasantry, combined with its inability to take political action, led some Russian intellectuals to believe Russians had a special 'soul'. It was based on the notion that society was deeply unjust, that change was hopeless and that Russians were uniquely patient. They were a 'much-suffering' people.

The Revolution split the intelligentsia as nothing had ever done before. While Mensheviks and social-democrats criticized it as an historically premature and therefore doomed seizure of power, they would not support the intervention of the anti-Bolshevik Whites in the civil war. Russia's nationalists were also divided. The liberal Pyotr Struve, who vigorously supported the anti-Bolshevik side in the civil war, believed that Russia could have found a social consensus. 'Russia', he complained, 'was killed by the intelligentsia's lack of nationality, the only instance in world history of the brain of the nation being oblivious to the national idea.'[12] Nikolai Ustryalov, a leading Constitutional Democrat (Cadet), took the unusual line of supporting the Bolsheviks, though from a nationalist rather than socialist position. They were the only force able to restore Russian national power and hold the country together. Although he considered their economic materialism and their advocacy of humanism and a paradise on earth to be false, the Bolsheviks belonged to Russian culture. Russian patriots should not oppose the Revolution but 'sound other strings in the national lyre', he wrote. The Revolution rose from the traditional anarchy of the Russian masses and the romanticism of the intelligentsia and was therefore part of the national genius. 'It is ours,' he claimed. 'It is authentically Russian, it is entirely in our psychology, in our past, and nothing similar can or will be in the West.'[13]

Seventy years later, after the long experience of Communist party rule, much had changed in Russian society. The country had industrialized. Literacy had spread. The size of the educated élite had grown. Emigration from the countryside to the cities, plus famine, forcible collectivization and repression had reduced the numbers of peasants and increased the industrial working class. Traditional property-holders had been destroyed. Private merchants and businessmen no longer existed. Social inequalities were substantially reduced, with the exception of a small stratum of party officials at the top. Russia, in short, became *déclassé*.

This massive and often brutal transformation of the social structure destroyed the few shoots of a civil society as well as the incipient growth of capitalism which had developed under Tsarism. But it also created a potential new basis for democracy. Paradoxically, as a result of urbanization and the state's huge investment in literacy, higher education and mass communications, Russia under Soviet rule gained more of the infrastructure for democracy than it had ever had. By 1980 there was a large, educated middle stratum and a technically skilled layer of industrial workers. With the ending of the totalitarian system under Gorbachev, the opportunity for change was made available. But Russian practice in operating democracy was low. A society which had always been run on vertical lines could not quickly develop the horizontal links and the self-organization which are the essence of civil society.

In the post-totalitarian dawn there was much bitter talk among Russia's reformers of 'Homo Sovieticus', a new breed which the seventy years of Communism had allegedly created. It was often shortened to 'sovok' from 'sovietsky chelovyek' (Soviet Man). The legacy of 'sovok' would make democracy hard to introduce, the reformers claimed. Gorbachev and the other Communist party architects of perestroika joined in describing the new breed's negative qualities, though they did not use the anti-Soviet term themselves. They saw it as a relic of the Stalinist system. One character flaw was egalitarianism, defined as a desire to pull everyone down to the same level. Another was dependency, which combined an unwillingness to take decisions or show initiative, with an attitude of passively waiting for the state to provide everything. A third defect was the almost universal willingness to steal public property on the grounds that it belonged to no one. A fourth vice was the irresponsibility of the intelligentsia, its unwillingness to compromise and engage in political organization as opposed to the speech-making and apocalyptic journalism which it so much preferred.

It was a formidable indictment, yet all these qualities had already been commented on by pre-revolutionary critics. Communist party rule reinforced tendencies which had been part of Russian life for centuries. Homo Sovieticus was Homo Russicus. As Gorbachev's perestroika merged into the Yeltsin reform era, the lesson was not that Russians were inherently incapable of forming a democratic society, either because of their pre-revolutionary history or because of Communist excesses. The point was that the burden of the past was extremely heavy. Institutions could be changed relatively quickly. Changing habits and attitudes would take a long time.

4

A Very Russian Coup

Dubček. Allende. Gorbachev? Be Careful.

LAPEL BUTTON, SEEN IN MOSCOW'S METRO, NOVEMBER 1988

Tanned but tired, his body visibly trembling with excitement, his face expressing relief at being free, President Gorbachev received a small group of correspondents in his Crimean dacha less than an hour after learning that the August coup was over. He had been held prisoner for three days in the luxury villa at Foros, unable to communicate with the outside world.

Now he was able to talk. 'Complete rubbish, the crudest pretext,' he answered unhesitatingly when asked if there was any validity in the coup leaders' assertion that he had fallen ill and been unable to run the country. No physical intimidation had been used against him, but he had been under constant pressure to make a deal, he said. He would have committed suicide if they had forced him to give in.

Gorbachev is a highly emotional man, who finds it hard to conceal his mood. He is not impulsive like Yeltsin, and Russians never use the word for that quality – 'emotsional'ny' – about him. He also rarely talks about his private life and feelings. In spite of this reticence, Gorbachev felt his politics. He did not just think them. His lively eyes always conveyed what was going on inside him but I had never seen him so animated as on this occasion at Foros. 'I made no deals. I maintained a firm position, demanding

59

the immediate summoning of the Congress of People's Deputies. Only they could decide the issue. Otherwise,' he told the plotters, trying to find the most delicate way of expressing the point, 'after any other step, I would have had to finish myself off. There could be no other way out.'

In the days after the coup some Russians wondered whether Gorbachev had been involved in planning it. Conspiracy theories are popular in Moscow. In a society where so much used to be controlled from above, people find it hard to accept unorthodox political moves at face value. The coup's fumbling incompetence also aroused suspicions. It was an elaborate charade in which Gorbachev must have been involved, so the theory went. His motive was to revoke the Union treaty and reverse Russia's growing independence under Yeltsin, but pretend he was having to do it as the price for ending a mutiny by powerful conservative forces.

For me the most convincing proof that Gorbachev knew nothing of the coup in advance was Gorbachev himself. No one who saw him at Foros, pouring out his fury at the plotters and glowing with delight at being set free, could credit for a minute that his imprisonment was a sham. Gorbachev is not an actor and his happiness was obvious. His twenty-nine-year-old daughter, Irina, was equally genuine, though she still seemed to be in a state of shock. Wearing a blue denim mini-skirt, she was standing in the ornate wood-panelled hall of the villa when we came in. To get to the sitting room where her father was we walked right past her. She seemed not to see us. It was not that she was avoiding eye contact. Her blank gaze was focused somewhere in the distance.

The plot theory emerged partly because some local people claimed they had seen nothing special near the villa during the Gorbachev imprisonment. Gorbachev told us there were troops all round it. It was later confirmed that they consisted of a regiment of KGB troops. Gorbachev's personal security chief Yuri Plekhanov sided with the plotters, and this allowed them to reach and enter the villa unannounced and leave again for Moscow. In the days which followed, Gorbachev's bodyguards stayed loyal to the president. Together with them, 'we held a front line,' he said. 'My guards were given orders to open fire and defend us against anyone who tried to break in.'

Perhaps this was somewhat melodramatic, since the plotters' only clear plan was to isolate Gorbachev and cut telephone communication with the outside world. This they indisputably did. *Pravda* later published a report and photograph of the log book of the KGB department which runs the government telephone system.[1] The log book was leaked by someone in the KGB or the prosecutor's office handling the case against the plotters. It shows a handwriten note from the duty officer, recording an order from Lieut-General A. Beda, the head of the government telephone system: '18 August. 17.50. Switch all connections from Moscow, Kiev, Sevastopol and Simferopol to Yalta and Foros to hand service.' This meant that all calls had to go through an operator. They were told not to provide connections. The log book also records that on 19 August at 10.08 p.m. Washington asked for President Bush to be connected to Gorbachev. The coup leadership was informed. They authorized the answer: 'Suggest connecting to Acting President Yanayev.' The Americans countered: 'We only want Gorbachev.'

At the beginning of the coup the plotters presumably also wanted to forestall any rescue bid. By the end they were losing support and may have thought of taking action against their prisoner. In the plane which took us to the Crimea on the mission to rescue Gorbachev that was a major fear. Before he raced up the steps of the civilian Aeroflot TU-134 at Moscow's Vnukovo airport, Alexander Rutskoi, Russia's vice-president, gave a chilling guess at the coup leaders' intentions. Marshal Dmitri Yazov, the defence minister, and General Kryuchkov, the KGB chief, had left Moscow by air an hour earlier for an unknown destination. 'They have three options,' Rutskoi conjectured. 'They may flee the country. They will bring Gorbachev here. Or they may try to conduct medical experiments on him to change him into a different man. Our job is to prevent it.'

I was the only English-speaking reporter on the plane. As with most scoops, it was 90 per cent luck, and 10 per cent intuition which got me on to it. Earlier in the morning, scores of us had been sitting in the gallery of the Russian parliament. It is part of the sprawling complex of the so-called White House, a giant concrete structure faced with marble, which was built for the government of the Russian Federation in the days when it was little more than a post office for the Kremlin. After Yeltsin's election as president of Russia it became his headquarters and a constant challenge to Gorbachev. During the coup it became a combination of armed camp, doss-house and grandstand for Yeltsin's team and hundreds of defenders. Cossacks in riding boots, with a weird array of leather belts and woollen hats tipped at improbable angles, prowled the endless corridors or flopped on sofas. Outside, the building was protected by barricades of buses, wooden planks and scrap metal as well as a human wall of volunteers.

Parliament was due to hold its first session on Wednesday 21 August, the third morning of the coup. The chamber was packed well before 10 a.m. Most people had slept little for the last two nights, keeping going on a combination of excitement and tension. Fears that the coup plotters would try to storm the building on Tuesday night had evaporated and a mood of elation was dominant now that it was clear the army had split. Yeltsin came to the rostrum and announced that he had been in contact with Kryuchkov, the KGB chief, and was proposing to fly with him to the Crimea to bring Gorbachev back to Moscow. 'No,' shouted several deputies. 'Don't go.' 'It's too dangerous,' other voices called out. Ivan Silayev, the prime minister of the Russian Federation, suggested he go instead, so as to remove any risk of Yeltsin's being arrested or taken hostage. Silayev proposed that Rutskoi should come too, plus a few deputies, a small team of Russian and foreign press and a doctor who could check Gorbachev's health. Georgy Shakhnazarov, one of Gorbachev's close advisers, asked for the floor. He had been staying at a sanatorium near Foros and was one of the last people to talk to the president on Sunday. He had sounded fine and there was no possibility that he was really ill.

After a brief break Yeltsin had a new bombshell. He had been informed the plotters were fleeing to Vnukovo airport. A huge cheer erupted. Would deputies give him a mandate to have them arrested? Another cheer, and cries of 'Yes'. The deputies looked delighted and several journalists headed for the door. This would be the high-point of the coup. I desperately wanted to watch the plotters being arrested so as to be sure that this crazy adventure was over.

My car was beyond the barricades about 100 yards from the White House. The direct route towards Vnukovo was blocked by a further set of barricades and, rather than trying to find side roads which might by then also be sealed, a colleague and I decided to drive up Leningradskoye Shosse and take the long route to the outer ring road. The ring road was jammed with traffic bypassing the centre and we drove on the verge or down the central reservation to get past. The Vnukovo turn-off was guarded by a policeman who was preventing traffic coming by. We told him we were reporters and were allowed to pass.

Suddenly we seemed to be in a war zone. Planes were still flying from Vnukovo, even if airport buses and private cars were not being allowed through. Strung out along the road were sweating people carrying suitcases. At first we thought we had stumbled on a group of refugees until we realized they were passengers, embarked on a five-mile walk to the airport. We took pity on one man and gave him a lift, but after barely fifty yards he gesticulated frantically at two women and some children tramping along the grass verge. 'My wife and mother and family,' he shouted. 'They must come too.' This was too much. We said we were in a hurry and had no room. Anyway we were going to the VIP airfield. Disappointed, he got out.

The right-hand lane of the road was clogged with a long column of tanks. The hatches were open in the heat and crew members' heads were visible. They were driving away from Moscow, a heartening sign. From the cakes of mud which were spattered along the asphalt from their treads, it was obvious that they had camped in fields.

At the closed black gates of Vnukovo Two, a minibus from Russian TV was parked. There were three reporters, but no sign of any coup plotters. A red Zhiguli police car drove up and a lieutenant told us a plane with some of the plotters had left Vnukovo at 2.30 p.m. By then it was 3.20 p.m. Other correspondents had arrived, and one told us that on the car radio he had heard an unconfirmed report that some of the plotters were arrested on the way to the airport. Now I was doubly disappointed, having missed some escape and the others being arrested.

There seemed nothing to do but return to Moscow. On the way back we saw a group of Volgas turning at high speed into the approach road to the civilian airport, Vnukovo One. It was strange but it could not be the plotters, I thought. We carried on back to Moscow until, a few minutes later, a second group of Volgas came by. This had to be investigated, so we turned the car and followed the motorcade. Only when Silayev stepped out of the middle Volga did I realize what we were following. In the excitement over chasing the get-away plotters, I had forgotten the Silayev mission.

The prime minister strode to the steps of a waiting TU-134, waved at a small crowd of cheering airport staff and disappeared into the plane. A large group of heavily armed police troops were standing at the foot of the steps, waiting to get on. It looked pointless to queue behind them. There was a small running board over the wheels of the steps. I walked round the police, jumped on to the running board and caught the attention of Valentin Sergeyev, an official from the Russian parliament's press service, who was half-way up the gangway. Reminding him of Silayev's earlier suggestion that reporters should join the trip, I urged him to let me on. He pondered and then said, 'Get on. Quick.' A French reporter and a Spaniard followed me as I ducked under the handrail and raced up the steps. In the plane I walked as far back as I could, just in case there was an official change of mind. In the third section we found a two-man Russian television team, a reporter from *Izvestiya* and a photographer.

The section filled up with several of the police officers. Some sat three to a two-seat row. The plane's doors were shut, the steps were wheeled back and we thought we were on our way, when someone rushed up outside, grabbed one of the ground crew's earphones to talk to the captain in the cockpit and pleaded with him to open the doors again. It was Vadim Bakatin, a member of Gorbachev's presidential council who had been late getting to Vnukovo. Sacked as interior minister under pressure from the conservatives some months earlier, he would be appointed to head the KGB after the coup. He was let on to the plane. The delay had cost us about twenty minutes. In the air at last, we learnt that no one knew where we would land. The naval airfield at Belbek nearest to Foros where presidential planes usually came down was not secure. The group of twenty-eight policemen were a crack squad from the Ministry of the Interior's academy at Ryazan. Specially trained for hostage releases and other emergencies, they had been summoned to Moscow that morning. They might be needed to secure our landing, we were told, or to help to get Gorbachev out.

During the two-hour flight to the Crimea, Yeltsin phoned the armed forces general staff and asked for everything to be done to allow the plane to land at Belbek. At 6.35 p.m. Boris Panyukov, the minister of civil aviation, was astounded to receive a phone call from Gorbachev himself, asking about the situation.[2] On hearing about the approaching Silayev mission, Gorbachev gave instructions to let the plane land safely. It was one of the first signs that Gorbachev was free. The coup plotters had already reached Foros, and Gorbachev demanded that his communications be restored before he would even contemplate seeing them. It took some time for the two sets of instructions to be forwarded to Belbek. Officers at Belbek later disclosed that it was only at 7 p.m., a few minutes before our plane landed, that the order was given to clear the runway.

Lieut-Colonel I.A. Shulga, the head of intelligence of the Black Sea fleet's coastal forces, told a Moscow newspaper that the plotters' first invitation to Yeltsin to fly to the Crimea was indeed a trick.[3]

He reported that early on Wednesday Major-General V. Romanenko, the commander of the coastal forces and a fierce critic of Yeltsin, gave orders for 300 naval infantry and twelve armoured personnel carriers to take control of Belbek and its runways. Admiral Khronopulo, the commander of the Black Sea fleet, arrived with Romanenko at the airfield. The troops were told an unauthorized plane would try to land. The orders were to seize it on the ground, and in the case of resistance, destroy it.

During the afternoon General Romanenko was informed that a plane carrying Marshal Yazov was approaching Belbek. He gave orders that this one should be allowed to land. The troops blocked the runway again and remained on the alert for the next plane, although officers watching the Russian parliament's proceedings on television realized that Yeltsin would not be one of the passengers. Anxious deputies had refused to let him fly. At 7 p.m. the airport commandant announced he had received a phone call from the commander of the eighth army in Kiev to free the runway. Admiral Khronopulo was informed and gave orders to remove the troops and armoured equipment. Bakatin's late arrival at Vnukovo turned out to be fortunate. 'If we had been twenty minutes earlier, we'd have been fired at, so you can say we had a narrow escape,' Rutskoi commented later.[4]

Although we landed safely, the situation was still confused. The plane was directed to a secluded part of the airfield. There were only a few vehicles for the Silayev delegation and people piled in, eight to a car. The police who had flown down with us stayed at the airfield. Local police guarded the side road leading down off the corniche to the Foros compound and took their time to allow the rescue motorcade through. At the villa itself a heavy lorry was drawn up across the drive to prevent the gates of the compound being rammed. By the time we arrived night had fallen. The cicadas were throbbing relentlessly in the trees. You could smell the peaches in the orchard that stretched out on the semi-circular bay near the villa. It may have been one of the most luxurious prisons in the world but the isolation, the uncertainty and fear that

it could all go horribly wrong must have been intense. Gorbachev's
wife, Raisa, had a nervous attack and lost her power of speech for a
time.

After our interview with the liberated president, no one saw fit to
provide us with communications. They seemed to forget that the
point of the exercise was to tell the world that Gorbachev was safe.
We were escorted to a three-storey hotel at the back gate of the
compound where the security personnel and staff lived. They told
us there were no phone lines to Moscow. Anxious that Gorbachev
and the Silayev team might leave without us, we asked to be taken
back to Belbek. They drove us to the top of the main drive and
then to the corner of the corniche. Abandoned without transport in
the dark, we began to give way to panic. We were sitting on one of
the world's great scoops and had no one to tell. After ten minutes a
convoy of Zils sped up the side road and whooshed off down the
corniche. Gorbachev was on his way back to Moscow, and now we
were prisoners at Foros.

After fifteen minutes which seemed more like fifteen hours, the
police produced a mini-bus which slowly trundled back to Belbek.
To our relief, the TU-134 and Gorbachev's presidential Il-62,
marked Sovietsky Soyuz (Soviet Union), were still on the ground.
Rutskoi, who took charge of the security precautions, insisted that
Gorbachev fly on the TU-134 which was still parked some way off.
We were not allowed on to the TU-134 this time. It turned out
that General Kryuchkov, the KGB boss, by then virtually a
prisoner, had been put in our seats.

Asked once again to wait, our patience snapped. Along with the
Russian TV crew we stormed up the steps of the Sovietsky Soyuz
and burst into the first section. In a small eight-seat compartment,
with seats facing each other and a table in between, I saw Lukyanov,
the chairman of the Soviet parliament, opposite Vladimir Ivashko,
deputy general secretary of the Communist party. It was a double
shock, since we had not known they were in Foros. 'Anatoly
Ivanovich, we have a small problem,' I blurted out. 'We need to
return to Moscow as fast as possible.' He gestured to me to sit next

to him. But the chance of a two-hour interview with one of the more mysterious figures in the coup – some called him the grey cardinal – was whisked away. A group of bodyguards rushed in and told us we would be going on a separate plane. In the third plane, another Il-62, two air hostesses told us they had flown down from Moscow with Lukyanov, Ivashko, Yazov and Kryuchkov earlier that day. 'They all sat together and were smiling some of the time. Their mood seemed good,' she reported. 'They ate well,' she added damningly.

When the men had arrived at Foros, it turned out that Yazov and Kryuchkov did not have as menacing a purpose as Rutskoi and Silayev had feared. Realizing the coup had crumbled, they wanted to try to convince Gorbachev their intentions had always been honourable, merely an attempt to save the Union. By going to Foros at the end perhaps they hoped to persuade Gorbachev to find a compromise which could legitimize their behaviour. But Gorbachev refused to talk to any of them except Lukyanov. He was the only one allowed into the villa. The others were held in a separate building, not yet visibly under arrest but by now at the mercy of the president. On the flight back to Moscow Gorbachev separated the two main plotters. Kryuchkov flew with him. Yazov was on the Il-62. On arrival in Moscow both men were taken into custody.

In the Kremlin, meanwhile, Venyamin Yarin, a deputy in the Supreme Soviet, was quietly arresting Vice-President Gennady Yanayev, the titular head of the coup. As a member of Gorbachev's presidential council, Yarin had an office in the same building as Yanayev. A worker from a huge metal plant in the Urals town of Nizhni Tagil, Yarin was chosen for the council because of his connections with the working class. Straight-talking and open, Yarin was always ready to chat to correspondents in the parliamentary lobby. A few days after the coup collapsed I found him on a bench in the corridor outside the canteen, where the smokers liked to congregate. He was still full of his exploit. During the coup he had come regularly to the Kremlin, where he worked with two other council members, Yevgeni Primakov and Vadim

Bakatin, in phoning members of the Supreme Soviet, finding out about the mood of deputies and the situation in their areas and reporting to Yeltsin. It was extraordinary that they had been able to carry on their subversive work only a few yards from Yanayev.

At around noon on the third morning of the coup Yarin made contact with the military commandant of the Kremlin, Major General Gennady Bashkin. The general assured him he was subordinate only to President Gorbachev and not to Yanayev. Emboldened by this assurance, Yarin and some of the other deputies still in the Kremlin decided the time was approaching to arrest Yanayev. They heard from the White House that the plotters were fleeing to Vnukovo. When word came through from another presidential adviser that phone links to Gorbachev had been re-established, Yarin decided to hesitate no longer. 'I went into Yanayev's office and explained that the president's power had been restored. I told him I was fulfilling a mission. His freedom would be limited to the walls of his office,' Yarin recalled. 'There was fear in his eyes. I told him not to do anything stupid, or lay hands on himself.' A single guard was posted outside the door. Next morning, when Yarin came to wake him, he found the room in a mess. Yanayev had apparently been drinking heavily and was asleep on a small divan. He took a long time to rouse himself and work out where he was. At 10 a.m. the Russian prosecutor arrived and read out the formal arrest warrant. Yanayev was led away. 'There was no need for handcuffs,' Yarin concluded.

If the coup ended with a whimper, it had hardly started with a bang. At the key meeting in the Kremlin which set up the coup leadership, the so-called state committee for the state of emergency, Gennady Yanayev, the titular head, was also under the influence of alcohol. (Next day, at his press conference, television pictures showed how Yanayev's hands were shaking.) The driving forces behind the coup were Kryuchkov, Dmitry Yazov, the defence minister, Valery Boldin, Gorbachev's Kremlin chief of staff, and Valentin Pavlov, the prime minister. The four men took their final decision on Saturday evening, 17 August.

On Sunday afternoon they despatched Oleg Baklanov, the deputy head of the defence council and a former central committee secretary in charge of the military-industrial complex, to Foros, together with Oleg Shenin, another central committee secretary, and General Valentin Varennikov, commander-in-chief of land forces. Boldin, as an old friend of Gorbachev, went with them. Baklanov began the encounter with Gorbachev but Varennikov did most of the talking. A tall, erect man with a small, well-clipped moustache, Varennikov was always courteous when we used to go up to him in the Congress of People's Deputies or at the last Communist party Congress. He made it clear he was unhappy with the way NATO, as he saw it, had taken advantage of the collapse of Eastern Europe and the reunification of Germany to strengthen its positions. In Foros he urged Gorbachev either to hand his powers to Yanayev and accept a state of emergency or to resign from the presidency. Gorbachev addressed him with elaborate politeness. 'Excuse me, Comrade Varennikov, I don't know your first name and patronymic.' Varennikov replied, 'Valentin Ivanovich.' 'Well then, Valentin Ivanovich, society is not a battalion. Left, right, left, right. Quick march. Your adventure will end with a fearful tragedy. Everything will be destroyed'.[5]

Empty-handed, the four-man team returned to Moscow with Gorbachev's security chief Yuri Plekhanov, leaving Gorbachev cut off. Now the plotters decided to form their committee, presenting the rest with a *fait accompli*. Kryuchkov, Baklanov, Pugo (the interior minister), Shenin, Boldin, Plekhanov, Yanayev and Pavlov met in the Kremlin on Sunday evening. Anatoly Lukyanov, the chairman of the Supreme Soviet, attended for part of the time. Alexander Bessmertnykh, the foreign minister, was brought in at around midnight but refused to take part and left. Prime minister Pavlov told his deputy Vladimir Shcherbakov about the meeting the following day. According to Shcherbakov, Pavlov said he spent Sunday afternoon at his dacha, drinking with his son who was about to leave Moscow on a trip.[6] By the time he received a phone call from Kryuchkov, summoning him to the Kremlin, he was already the worse for wear. He found Yanayev in a similar condition.

He had also had friends round. 'You and I are the two clowns,' Pavlov recalled Yanayev saying to him.

The coup continued in a similar vein. It was more a catalogue of accidents than a well-planned or well-executed venture. Neither the plotters nor their chief opponents, the Yeltsin team in the White House, were distinguished for their efficiency. The Yeltsin side at least had the excuse that they were reacting spontaneously, and no one can accuse them of a lack of determination. Yeltsin never wavered in his hostility to the coup, and his series of decrees warning officials that they risked prosecution for treachery and putting the armed forces under his control must have helped to split the army and reduce the temptation they would support the coup. But the defence of the White House and the placing of the barricades was a haphazard, disorganized affair. Yeltsin's call for a general strike was not followed up by visits by activists to factories to persuade workers to come out.

This was as nothing compared to the floundering on the putschists' side. They did not cut communications for the world's press to report on the affair, nor did they close the airports. Sitting in my flat in Moscow in the first two hours of the coup early on Monday morning watching the junta's decrees come over the television, I wondered how I could simultaneously be taking phone calls from radio stations around the world. Why were they getting through? When we set off at about 9 a.m. to drive to the Kremlin, we were amazed to see tourist buses disgorging passengers for the usual walkabout in the Kremlin grounds. On the way to the White House, we passed a long column of lorries laden with soldiers driving *away* from the Russian parliament towards the centre. When they stopped outside the Bolshoi theatre, I dutifully asked the driver of the first lorry where they were going, not expecting he would speak to a foreign correspondent. 'We have orders to stay here for a while and then move on. I'm not sure where to,' he replied. An officer hurried up and told him he should not speak to anyone. But it was already clear that if discipline was so slack this coup was not very serious. Other columns of tanks stopped obediently when traffic lights turned red.

Why did the troops fail to surround and seal off the White House before any supporters arrived? Why did they not arrest Yeltsin? On the morning of the coup Yeltsin and all his close colleagues were at their usual set of government villas at Arkhangelskoye, on the western outskirts of Moscow. It was here that they drafted the first emergency decrees repudiating the coup and calling for defiance. To arrest them or at least to have sealed off the compound would have been easy. Pavel Voshchanov, Yeltsin's press secretary, believes the plotters may have thought Yeltsin would collaborate with them, if Gorbachev refused.[7] The idea would have been to count on the two men's hostility and to offer Yeltsin a key position in the post-Gorbachev arrangements. Voshchanov says there was no basis for such expectations, but he finds it significant that the day after Yeltsin first publicly called for Gorbachev's resignation in February 1991, vice-president Yanayev secretly despatched a close aide to talk to Voshchanov about possible collaboration. Yeltsin refused to authorize any contacts. The incident suggests the anti-Gorbachev forces were already thinking of some sort of unconstitutional action.

Other accounts suggest the plotters did want to arrest Yeltsin. In his short book on the coup, Gorbachev quoted Baklanov, one of the plotters, as telling him at Foros that Yeltsin was going to be arrested.[8] Vadim Bakatin, who became KGB chief shortly after the coup, said he was told by a member of the KGB's crack 'Alpha' team of marksmen and counter-terrorist forces that the plotters ordered Yeltsin's arrest but the team's leaders did not agree.[9] This version is denied by Vladimir Ivanenko, one of Kryuchkov's deputies, who switched to Yeltsin's side before the coup. 'The Alpha group always obeys orders,' he told me.[10] He believed the plotters made no arrest order.

After their own arrest several of the plotters claimed they had good grounds for thinking that Gorbachev would go along with their aim of declaring a state of emergency and blocking the signing of the new Union treaty. Yanayev claimed Gorbachev had already authorized plans for introducing a state of emergency. It was hard to put much credibility on these accounts since it was clearly the plotters' best defence against the charge of treason. In a pre-trial interview another of the defendants, Lukyanov, took a different line. He rejected the version that Gorbachev had prior knowledge of the coup preparations. His line was that Gorbachev 'isolated himself'.[11] When the plotters left Foros, Gorbachev was free to return to Moscow himself, according to this version, but did not do so. He wanted to see which way events would go. If the plot succeeded, then Gorbachev would return to Moscow 'on a red horse' and take charge of the state of emergency and the clamp-down on liberal forces. If it failed, he would ride in 'on a white horse' and join with Yeltsin in conducting the market reforms.

Apart from their failure to neutralize Yeltsin, the plotters' main weakness was that they had no programme of action and no convincing explanations for Gorbachev's absence. At their press conference they could give no detailed information on Gorbachev's ill health or even provide a statement from a Kremlin doctor. They wavered between hinting at the use of repression to counter the country's crisis and suggesting that Gorbachev's reforms would continue and that the president might soon return to power. Most viewers came away with two impressions – relief that Gorbachev was obviously still alive, and contempt at the sight of Yanayev's shaking hands.

A key feature of the coup was how relatively few people actively opposed it. As we followed that first army column down Kalinin Prospect we saw almost no one give it a second glance. People did not stop and stare. No one waved their fists. Near the Bolshoi theatre an old lady fiercely shouted at one soldier who got out of the cab of a lorry, 'Are you going to shoot at your own people?' It was a rare piece of defiance. The soldier looked sheepish. When Yeltsin came out of the White House to climb on to a tank, it was a brilliant piece of symbolism, aimed for television. Apart from about thirty of us reporters, the actual crowd numbered under 200. News of the coup was by then five hours old, so there was time for thousands to have gathered. A few climbed on to another tank near

Yeltsin's, but alighted when the police asked them to. Although he urged people to stand firm and defend the White House, some of those who were there drifted off. A heavy-set woman said, 'I will be here until the tanks withdraw.' She looked as though she meant it but others viewed the coup with fatalistic despair. Two passers-by in civilian clothes who said they were off-duty policemen were unsure how it would turn out. 'Whoever wins, we are all losers. We always lurch from one extreme to another. It is so hard here to create a society based on law,' they told me. Then they too walked away.

Many of my Russian acquaintances reacted to the coup with panic. Some admitted later they wept when they saw the announcements on television. They were sure perestroika and its democratic reforms were over. Others who were on holiday in dachas outside Moscow refused to come into the city. Even young people said they were convinced the country would go back to repression. Although they opposed the coup, some confessed they were afraid to demonstrate against it for fear that if it succeeded they would be imprisoned or sent to camps. Those who had had contact with foreigners during the years of perestroika were sure they were doomed.

The crowd by the White House grew later in the afternoon, helped partly by contingents from the Moscow city hall on Gorky Street. The council was in emergency session but when deputies realized how few people were protecting the building, Mayor Gavriil Popov asked them to go to the Russian parliament instead. It was pointless to try to defend two places, he explained later. By nightfall there were barely 20,000 people round the building. A light rain was falling, and hundreds of umbrellas shielded people crouching round bonfires. Some fifty tanks and armoured personnel carriers which had switched to the Yeltsin side were drawn up near the building. Two rows of buses and concrete slabs blocked the access roads. The crowd was brave and determined, but thin. Even at the height of the siege of the White House on the second night, the crowd did not exceed 50,000. They were not a cross-section of a new firebrand generation eager to change the rotten world inherited from their parents. A survey by the newspaper *Nezavisimaya Gazeta* of 141 members of self-defence groups created by the Russian parliament's defence headquarters found that 55 per cent were aged over 30. Their social basis was relatively narrow. Blue-collar workers formed only 19 per cent of the contingent. The dominant group, 69 per cent, had higher education.[12]

Indeed, on the second morning of the coup I began to wonder whether it might not succeed. On the Monday it had all seemed so half-baked. The coup-plotters' rambling press conference must have lost them any support they had, one thought. They clearly had no programme of action short of taking power, so what would allow them to gain authority where Gorbachev had failed? Even if the crowd at the White House was small, there was Yeltsin's call for a strike. Censorship of the press would not stop it getting out, because it was being beamed in by (still unjammed) foreign radio stations. Some papers even reported it on Tuesday morning.

A visit to two large factories near our home in southern Moscow on Tuesday changed my mood to one of alarm. 'They are all working,' said a young man in a denim outfit as he emerged from the Ordzhonikidze machine-tool plant. 'People are afraid of losing their jobs and we don't have proper unemployment benefits here.' Gloomily he added, 'Everyone's for themselves, unfortunately.' Three more workers emerged. 'I support Yeltsin, but I don't know if we'll strike. It depends on the director. If he says we should, we'll come out,' said an elderly worker. Asking for the director's permission seemed an odd way to start a strike, but I phoned the director from the factory gate to check. He refused to let me come and see him, but said down the line, 'I don't think Yeltsin's appeals are really correct in this situation. The most important thing is to maintain stability, and not give way to emotions.'

At the Zil plant, where 100,000 workers make the Politburo's limousines as well as thousands of lorries a month, the mood was equally passive. Two apprentices by the main gate said they were on a training course. With relief, they explained this meant they did not have to strike. One of them said everything depended on the army, 'or rather the officers,' he corrected himself. 'Ordinary soldiers have no rights.' His friend was even more pessimistic. 'I think the coup will succeed. People are tired and beaten down.' Throughout the country the response to Yeltsin's strike call was minimal. Boris Gusev, the head of the state committee for chemistry and biotechnology, cheerfully told a cabinet meeting convened by Pavlov on the first evening of the coup, 'We have phoned 100 enterprises. They all support the emergency committee.'[13] Even allowing for some exaggeration, his report sounded correct.

A poll taken on the second day by the all-union Centre for Studying Public Opinion found only half the population were willing to condemn the coup in two of three Russian cities they surveyed.[14] In Leningrad 23 per cent and in Voronezh 28 per cent considered the junta lawful. Another 23 per cent in each city were not able to say one way or the other. In Krasnoyarsk in Siberia the junta faced more opposition, with only 12 per cent believing it to be lawful. But this city is more remote from central Russia and perhaps less typical.

After the coup, Yeltsin and Gorbachev each had an interest in magnifying the popular resistance. Yeltsin wanted to justify his moves to outlaw the Communist party and bring in a market economy as soon as possible by saying that the August events showed the public was overwhelmingly against the old command-administrative system. Gorbachev wanted to share the credit for the coup's failure, and take some of the gloss off Yeltsin's contribution, by saying it was doomed from the start. 'Our work over these last six years hasn't been in vain. Our society is different,' he told us at Foros.

Gorbachev knew this was an exaggeration. At the press conference in November 1991, launching his book on the coup, he avoided a straight answer to a question whether the country's passivity did not mean that the plotters might have held on if they had not made the mistake of ordering troops into Moscow. This obliged the security forces to decide quickly whose side they were on. When I tackled him on the point at a reception afterwards, he answered, 'I know the crowds were small, but I couldn't say that'.

A similar putsch against Khrushchev had succeeded in 1964. Like Gorbachev, he was on holiday in the Crimea when a group of his Politburo colleagues organized their move to oust him. They did not even have to pretend he was ill. They merely summoned him back to Moscow and presented him with their decision to replace him, and asked the central committee in Moscow to endorse it. There was no public reaction in the streets. This time, Dmitri Yazov, the defence minister, told the prosecution's interrogators, after his arrest that he had hoped the 1991 coup would be similar: 'We thought we just had to make a declaration and the people would say "Carry on".'[15]

In that sense, Gorbachev was right that the country had changed since 1985. Public opinion was a force which the plotters had to reckon with, though neither they nor anyone else could be sure how it would react. Even if ordinary people were passive, the Soviet Union had new institutions. One reason for the plotters' feebleness and confusion was their desire to respect the forms of legality as far as possible because they could not rely on automatic obedience from the armed forces and the bureaucracy. Although Gorbachev was not a popularly elected president, he had been chosen by the Congress of People's Deputies. It was not a rubber-stamp like the central committee in Khrushchev's day. Nevertheless, in spite of the progress, the Soviet Union had not yet become so democratic by 1991 that the coup was doomed. It had become anarchic, even ungovernable, because Gorbachev had broken the old lines of-command. What was still missing was a powerful and demo-cratically-minded public, willing to stand up for its rights.

The other difference from Khrushchev's time was that there were two sources of authority, the Soviet president and the Russian president. This created a crisis of loyalty at the top. Faced with orders to obey either a virtually unknown vice-president and a dubiously constituted emergency committee claiming to represent Soviet power, or Boris Yeltsin, the directly elected president of

77

Russia, most senior officers chose the latter. The coup failed, not because of mass resistance, but because the plotters ran out of steam and lost their nerve, and because the army commanders split. The other branches of the security services took no offensive action. On 20 August, the second day of the coup, the KGB's Alpha group reconnoitred the White House on Kryuchkov's orders but reported that it could not be captured. As a result, according to Vladimir Ivanenko, the head of Russia's KGB who was a key figure in the White House at the time, no order to storm it was ever given.[16] Interior ministry troops were not deployed throughout the coup, largely thanks to the deputy minister, General Boris Gromov. On holiday when the coup started, he was summoned back to Moscow on Monday by his boss, Boris Pugo. He told the minister he rejected the coup and for the next two days managed to delay or ignore his boss's orders.

The only troops mobilized were from the army and air force, but key officers refused to obey Marshal Yazov's orders to move on Moscow, in particular Marshal Yevgeni Shaposhnikov, the air force commander (who later became the senior commander of the forces of the Commonwealth of Independent States) and General Pavel Grachev, commander of the airborne troops. Yeltsin's firm stand in declaring Yazov a criminal and ordering the forces to support the elected president of Russia convinced most officers.

Even before the army made its position known the coup was collapsing because of divisions and hesitation among the plotters. They had no contingency plan of action in case Gorbachev refused to accept their demands. They only formed their emergency committee afterwards. The documents they published on television and radio early on Monday morning had been drafted in advance, but that was all that they had prepared. Marshal Yazov did not start briefing army commanders until 6 a.m. The plotters censored the press for a few hours, but this quickly began to break down. On the Monday evening TASS and the central television news were already reporting Yeltsin's defiance, albeit in a low-key and careful way. When, on the second day, the presidents of Kazakhstan and the Ukraine, the two largest republics, condemned the coup after having taken a wait-and-see position on 19 August, it was all over. The plotters' hope of saving the Union had clearly failed. The adverse reaction of Leonid Kravchuk in Kiev and Nursultan Nazarbayev in Alma Ata on 20 August may have been as decisive in breaking the plotters' already failing nerves as was Yeltsin's resistance. Even though it was Yeltsin's resistance which encouraged the two men to act, it was their move which doomed the coup. What was the point in taking control of Russia if the other republics were leaving the Union anyway?

The fact that most Russians were too afraid and cautious to confront the coup did not make a difference. The coup was an adventure from the top which collapsed from the top. In this it was similar to the botched putsch against the Tsar mounted by aristocratic officers in December 1825. The Decembrists' motives were very different from those of the plotters of August 1991. They were young progressives who wanted to free the serfs, safeguard civil liberties with an independent legal system and replace the Tsar's autocracy with a constitutional monarchy. Their defeat was caused, just as in August 1991, by lack of planning and a collapse of morale in their own ranks. They intended to act on the day the army was to swear allegiance to the new Tsar, Nicholas I, but some officers defected at the last minute. Others led their troops on to the square in St Petersburg where the ceremony was due to take place, then lost their nerve and did not give the order to rise. For six hours loyal and mutinous units faced each other until the Tsar brought up reinforcements. At dusk the rebels gave up.

The Decembrists' revolt was a pure palace coup, as was the plot against Khrushchev. In 1991, by contrast, a few thousand Russians took to the streets, and this played a role in encouraging the army to split. But it was not the determining factor. Only when the coup was safely over did huge crowds emerge. The funeral procession through the streets of Moscow on Saturday 24 August for the three young men killed on the second night produced a mass outpouring of relief and gratitude, estimated at a quarter of a million people. Where were these Russians when the coup hung in the balance?

2

The Fall of Communism

5

Challenge to the Party

*To reform a party which is used to giving commands and
having a single ideology, and does not know what
political struggle and theoretical creativity mean,
is pure Utopia.*

VADIM BAKATIN, FORMER INTERIOR MINISTER, 1992[1]

The foreign ministry's press centre had rarely been so packed. The press corps had rarely been so bored. It was the closing evening of the nineteenth Communist party conference in June 1988, and the daily summary of events which was due to be provided by a senior official was late starting. Although the main issue of the conference was 'democratization', the old Kremlin rules still applied. Foreign journalists were barred from the conference hall and would only be fed selected information by official briefers.

Suddenly the large screen at the end of the room lit up. Recorded excerpts from some of the day's speeches were about to be shown on national television. This was better than nothing, and reporters relaxed. What we saw was extraordinary, and for the next hour or so we watched spellbound, as did millions of Soviet viewers. The elaborately formal and staid tone of normal party meetings was discarded. We were spectators at a verbal boxing-match between two members of the central committee, Boris Yeltsin and Yegor Ligachev. First they showed Boris Yeltsin, the Moscow party chief who had resigned from the Politburo eight months earlier. To

Gorbachev's fury, Yeltsin had used a central committee meeting devoted to the seventieth anniversary of the October Revolution to make a series of criticisms of perestroika. Yeltsin had subsequently been replaced as Moscow party chief and been given a job as a junior minister.

Yeltsin's speech began sensationally. The foreign media were buzzing with an interview he had given the BBC during President Reagan's Moscow summit in May, in which he said Ligachev was obstructing perestroika and should resign. No mention had appeared in the Soviet press but many delegates had heard about it from foreign radio broadcasts. One delegate took the floor and asked what Yeltsin had said and why the Soviet press had suppressed it. On the rostrum at last, Yeltsin confirmed that he believed it was time for Ligachev to go. This was unprecedented behaviour for a Communist party gathering where unity was supposed to be preserved. Then Yeltsin gave his views on party democracy. He demanded the publication of leaders' salaries and the party's accounts. He called for the dismissal of Politburo members left over from Brezhnev's time because they shared the old leader's guilt. He attacked the privileges of the élite. 'In my opinion, the principle should be this: if there is a shortage of something in our socialist society, then that shortage should be felt in equal degree by everyone without exception,' he thundered as many delegates heckled him. Finally he turned his fire on Gorbachev's policies. In a point which was to become a favourite theme, Yeltsin said perestroika had not solved any real problems for ordinary people. He urged the party to concentrate on one or two specific tasks in the next two or three years rather than trying to change everything.

The next speech the television showed was Ligachev's angry reply. It won him widespread ridicule in the streets, though in the hall the delegates listened respectfully. Ligachev claimed unconvincingly that there were no differences in the Politburo over perestroika. 'There are neither conservatives nor reformers in the leadership,' he argued. Party officials lived modestly and had no privileges other than being 'in the front line' and serving the people 'with their faith and truth'. He accused Yeltsin of having managed the party badly in Sverdlovsk, unlike his own tenure in Tomsk. Recently Yeltsin had broken party rules by giving interviews to the 'bourgeois press'. Ligachev called Yeltsin by the condescending pronoun 'ty' and used his first name, Boris, instead of the polite form Boris Nikolayevich. 'Boris, you are wrong,' he snapped, a phrase which became a favourite quote in the liberal press, delighted that the dignity of the Politburo had collapsed and given way to playground name-calling.

Ligachev appeared to agree with Yeltsin on one thing – the flimsy nature of perestroika. While Yeltsin criticized it for not improving people's standard of living or getting goods into the shops, Ligachev suggested it was a dangerously open-ended policy which had not been thought through. He picked up a comment made earlier in the conference by the writer Yuri Bondarev, who compared perestroika to a plane taken up by a pilot without knowing where he would land. 'Wisdom tells you that before going in somewhere, you should think about how to get out,' Ligachev warned. It was the first time the public had seen such arguments aired by top party politicians in public. They were to become the two main criticisms of perestroika from then onwards: its lack of results and lack of direction.

For Soviet television viewers it was amazing stuff, and when Pravda appeared next morning with the texts of the speeches, there were long queues to buy it. This too was a first. Every delegate's speech was published the next day, and the conference had already seen some unusually outspoken criticisms before the Yeltsin-Ligachev bout. In Pushkin Square, about 200 yards from the Kremlin, strangers eagerly discussed the conference. Pushkin Square, one of Moscow's favourite small parks, split down the middle by Gorky Street, had become an unofficial centre for spontaneous political discussion. Like Speakers' Corner in Hyde Park, it had a number of cranks but the main feature was a kaleidoscope of intense conversations in which anyone could join in. The police did not know how to handle it. On one occasion I watched a policeman snatch a computer print-out from a woman's hand. (The old days of typewritten dissident statements had given way to computer technology.) It turned out that the woman represented nothing more subversive than a temperance group. 'It's only a manifesto against alcohol,' she laughed. The crowd jeered at the policeman. On other occasions the police would arrest people, fine them a few roubles, then let them out.

The drama of the Yeltsin-Ligachev clash obscured Gorbachev's main aim in calling the party conference. Anatoly Chernyayev, a close political aide, described it thus: 'He wanted the party to declare publicly that it would give up its role as an arm of the state.' This dual system, in which the party ruled over the government, made some sense in the 1920s when the Bolsheviks relied on officials and technocrats from the former Tsarist regime. Political commissars were supposed to ensure that party directives were carried out and that government officials remained loyal. Later, when every senior local government official and economic manager was a party member, dual administration was unnecessary and inefficient.

Inside the party there was no democracy. In the early years of its power the Bolshevik party had been a forum for competing ideas and furious debate. Even after Lenin's prohibition of factions in 1921, arguments continued to range over strategy and tactics. But as Stalin gradually tightened control over the party, it increasingly turned into a mechanism for implementing policy and a transmission belt taking orders from the top to the bottom. The principle of 'democratic centralism' was abused so as to structure the party on rigidly hierarchical or militaristic lines, with each level subordinate to the one above. Since the 1920s there had been no public debate, no licence for members to criticize the leadership, no secret balloting. At the lower levels members were allowed to criticize each other, but more often they were expected to criticize themselves. 'Denounce' would be a better word. One man would accuse another at a party meeting of being a bad official, of treating his staff badly or discrediting the party because of a spectacular divorce. There was no discussion of the main lines of party policy.

Only a few people joined the party because they were interested in ideas. Most did so for the sake of their careers. Party membership was a requirement for promotion in almost every profession, from the army to medicine, from industrial management to publishing, from journalism to education. The ambitious joined because they wanted power, since the party itself had close to a million paid positions on offer. Others identified the party as the body which had rallied the country against the Nazi invasion, just as it had won the civil war, since, however narrowly based the October Revolution was, the Bolsheviks had managed to widen their appeal from 1918 to 1921. They could not have won the civil war without this. The war against the foreign enemy in 1941 was an even greater challenge, and men like Chernyayev and Alexander Yakovlev joined the party during it, seeing it as the mainstay of Russia's resistance.

Whatever their reasons for joining, ordinary members had no say over party policy. Gorbachev was a child of this system of conformism, which even in the less vicious period after Stalin's death was backed by the ultimate sanction of expulsion from the party, which could cost a person whatever job they held in a collective farm, a factory or a government institution. Gorbachev joined the ladder after university, bent not just on party membership as the key to a good job, but on a career within its ranks. He worked for eighteen years in the party administration of the Stavropol territory in southern Russia, the area where he was born and grew up. At first he headed its Young Communist League and from 1970 to 1978 he was the first secretary of the party.

Stavropol was a territory or 'krai', but it was equivalent in the party structure to a region or 'oblast'. The boss of its leading organ, the krai committee or kraikom, was like an appointed state governor. In his vast area the secretary was the supreme leader, not accountable to any local parliament or electorate. Since there were no politics in the usual sense of the word, a kraikom or obkom secretary was the equivalent of the director of an important subsidiary of a huge corporation, accustomed to lobbying in the centre, i.e. Moscow, for money and then allocating the funds and checking how they were spent. He gave orders and expected to be obeyed. Although there was a local soviet or council, it was not elected in a contested ballot and had no independent source of funds. Nevertheless, even a regional secretary's power was limited, and he was not a genuine manager. He had little say over the largest factories, as they were subordinate to Moscow, or over the police and security organs.

Gorbachev and Yeltsin both spent the main part of their careers at this level. Gorbachev was kraikom secretary of Stavropol. Yeltsin was obkom secretary of Sverdlovsk. The job provided almost automatic membership in the central committee. While Stavropol was primarily agricultural, Sverdlovsk was a major industrial centre in the Urals with a larger population. Some analysts have suggested this was one reason why Yeltsin found it hard to work under Gorbachev. Yeltsin always felt he was the senior figure.

Although it was obvious by 1980 that the system was not giving adequate results, to decide to change it required enormous determination. Gorbachev had the courage to undertake the task, but he was faced with a fundamental paradox. Perestroika was a process of democratization, a policy of bringing people into the political arena and allowing them to take their own decisions. It was a strategy of giving society the freedom to develop according to its own natural laws. Logically, therefore, no guiding body was needed. This in itself obliged the Communist party to give up its monopoly of power and change itself radically, becoming a normal parliamentary party which would compete alongside other parties. Another major problem was that Gorbachev hoped to persuade a majority of the party's full-time officials, its apparatus, to work with him in dismantling the party's power. He was asking an élite voluntarily to relinquish its role, a task which has few historic examples of success.

Gorbachev originally intended to use the nineteenth party conference as a further device to outsmart the Politburo. It was the first such conference the party had held since 1941. Normally delegates from all over the country met once every five years at a party Congress. Their job was to elect a new central committee, sum up the previous period and approve guidelines for the next one. The last Congress had taken place only two years before in 1986, but Gorbachev was coming up against opposition to his reforms from party officials and local managers. He wanted to bypass the conservatives by going to the party as a whole with a series of radical changes. He assumed that the party's nineteen million members were more progressive and in touch with daily life than the professional apparatus. The aim was to use them to elect a new central committee. In any case, he assumed that delegates would follow the tradition of voting to approve whatever the general secretary proposed.

His plans were frustrated by the party apparatus, which took advantage of the rules for electing delegates which the old central committee had laid down a year before the conference. Candidates had to be nominated at grassroots level by ordinary party branches. Since this might help the reformers, the names would then be passed up for approval to a series of party committees before being voted on at regional and republican level. This made it easy for the apparatus to reject radicals. Faced with a conservative majority among the delegates, a disappointed Gorbachev decided in advance of the conference not to ask it to elect a new central committee. The perverted delegate selection process confirmed Gorbachev in his view that he must press on with the reforms. He developed a new proposal, this time to reduce the role of the entire party apparatus by creating a new elected legislative chamber, the Congress of People's Deputies, and a full-time parliament. He decided to spring it on the delegates without advance notice or discussion in the press, though he did put it to the Politburo on the eve of the conference.

It was a typical example of Gorbachev's style. When they arrived in Moscow, delegates thought they knew what they would be discussing. A month before the meeting opened, Gorbachev had published the 'Theses' or main proposals for the conference. They called for a transfer of power from party committees to local elected councils so as to end the Communist party's and the state apparatus's duplication of power. Party members were to use their influence in the councils to promote party policy rather than have party committees issue directives which duplicated the work of the councils. Party posts would have to be filled through competitive elections.

The theses were radical, but Gorbachev surprised delegates by going further in his opening speech to the conference. It contained three notes not heard before. He came out for 'socialist pluralism', meaning that there should be a wide exchange of views and organizations, provided they all accepted socialism. He also called for the Soviet Union to become a 'law-based state'. It was the first hint that basic human rights rather than class interests should be the foundation of Soviet law. Gorbachev's third and most dramatic proposal was for a full-time parliament or Supreme Soviet in place of the old one, which used to meet twice a year for a mere two days at a time.

The parliament would have two tiers. There would be a larger chamber, known as the Congress of People's Deputies, with 2,250 members, which would meet for about two weeks in the spring and autumn and have a five-year mandate. It would choose around 450 of its members to serve in the Supreme Soviet. This would work full-time and have considerably wider powers and responsibilities than the old rubber-stamp parliament. Two-thirds of the 2,250 members would be directly elected by voters on a competitive basis in which any number of candidates could be nominated.

Gorbachev assured delegates that the proposals did not dispense with the party. He argued that the party would dominate the new parliament by virtue of the large number of its members represented there. To loud applause he told the conference there would not be a multi-party system or opposition parties. Privately he hoped the party members elected to parliament by the public at large would be different from those who had been chosen for the conference. In order to try to persuade the party to accept it Gorbachev inserted a sweetener. One-third of the new parliament would not be elected by direct popular ballot. They would be chosen by 'public organizations' such as the Communist party, the trade unions, the Young Communist League, the women's organization, the academy of sciences, and so on. This was partly a device to ensure guaranteed seats for members of the 'nomenklatura', the party's carefully vetted list of people permitted to hold the state's best jobs. Without such a safety-valve the proposals might not have got past the conference.

A second apparent compromise concerned local government. Gorbachev contradicted his stated aim of separating the party from government by saying that the first secretary of the party in a district or region would as a rule be recommended for the chairmanship of the local council. The aim was to persuade local party leaders that they would not lose control of events if power shifted from the party organization. The move was criticized by several delegates and Gorbachev was forced to explain his logic halfway through the conference. He wanted to ensure the party's guiding role was maintained.

If this sounded comforting for anxious party leaders who feared they were being excluded from power, Gorbachev added another surprise point which was to turn out to be the party's undoing. Party leaders would first have to be elected by the people to the councils. Only then would they be expected to be chosen as chairman by the other elected members. If local party bosses thought they would be guaranteed election from 'safe' seats, like those arranged for one-third of the national parliament, they were cruelly disappointed. If they failed to be elected, Gorbachev told them, they would have to draw the appropriates conclusions.

At the end of four days delegates were understandably tired. The Ligachev-Yeltsin clash was uppermost in many minds. But Gorbachev pressed his case home. In his closing address he proposed that the elections to the new-style Soviet parliament take place in April 1989. Elections to the parliaments of the republics should take place in the autumn of that year. Gorbachev got what he wanted. There was no tradition of voting against the leadership, let alone a secret ballot. In a massive show of hands, the delegates unanimously endorsed Gorbachev's package. It amounted to the biggest change in Soviet politics for sixty years.

The package was the product not just of the liberals in the Politburo. It had the strong support of Anatoly Lukyanov, who was to turn against Gorbachev's reforms two years later. While still a law student, Lukyanov had done his university thesis on Lenin's original notion of a congress of deputies. He was very attached to the idea of a specific Soviet-type of parliament, different from the West's. Gorbachev sent Lukyanov and Yakovlev off to his official country estate, Novo–Ogaryevo, with a small group of advisers to work on the project. According to Lukyanov, they actively discussed the idea of a multi-party system, and put it to the Politburo three times, though not as a proposal for immediate decision. The idea of a Congress of People's Deputies was intended as the substitute for this, a broad representative body which would reflect the spectrum of opinion in the country, a kind of 'people's park', in Lukyanov's phrase.[2] The notion that one-third of the seats be assigned to social organizations was not just a way of appeasing conservatives. It was intended to guarantee wide representation. Leading liberals like Gavrill Popov, later the mayor of Moscow, and Daniel Granin and Chingiz Aitmatov, well-known writers, were selected on this basis, as was Andrei Sakharov, who insisted on being chosen by the Academy of Sciences rather than by a local constituency.

Criticism of the Congress idea came from Ligachev, who later described it as 'political shock therapy'. He saw it as part of a double blow, the second aspect of which was Gorbachev's virtual abolition of the central committee secretariat in September 1988. The secretariat was the party's administrative arm, which turned Politburo decisions into directives and sent them down the line. Gorbachev suspected the secretariat of distorting or blocking his policy, as a result of Ligachev's influence. Now the central apparatus lost its ability to direct party affairs, which were left to individual regional and local branches on their own. Nikolai Ryzhkov, the prime minister, also attacked the plan. He warned the Politburo that by making the new Congress of People's Deputies the supreme organ of power in the land they were dangerously blurring the necessary division between the legislative and executive. It was an argument which was to be raised later by Yeltsin in his battles with the Russian parliament. 'The state may lose its governability,' Ryzkhov told his colleagues.[3] In the past, the Soviet government had been able to get on with its work. The duplication of party and state might have been wasteful, but at least, as far as Ryzhkov was concerned, there was a clear chain of command. Making the government answerable to a legislature which would be constantly swayed by 'populist pressures' was dangerous. Ryzhkov accepted that the idea had good Bolshevik credentials in the famous revolutionary slogan 'All Power to the Soviets', which helped Lenin and his colleagues win public support in 1917. But what was good tactics in gaining power was not necessarily wise once power had been established. Ryzhkov concluded, correctly as it turned out, that the creation of the Congress would 'accelerate' events.

For Gorbachev the main aim of the changes was to bring new blood into the system. He was disappointed with the results of his efforts over the previous three years to put a new generation of leaders in charge of local party committees. 'After two or three rounds of replacement, the basic corps of people remained very much the same,' he told me.[4] Statistically, the changes looked impressive. On the eve of the nineteenth party conference ten of the fourteen republican party leaders and ninety-three of the 157 obkom leaders were new in their jobs.[5] But, as Gorbachev explained, there was little change in their stance. 'One part of the nomenklatura went out and another came in,' he said. 'The leadership's reformist stance and the desire for support from the bottom could not link up because of these structures.' Sensing what he called 'a cry from the soul from below,' Gorbachev decided there had to be a major addition to his revolution from above. This was the new Congress of People's Deputies. The only way to prevent the reforms from running into the sand, as those of Khrushchev and Kosygin had done two decades earlier, was to widen their scope.

With the advantage of hindsight, it has been suggested that those who wanted a gradual reform of the system rather than the breakneck dismantling which actually happened could have tried two other possible approaches. One was not to go outside the party but keep the reforms within its framework while making them more radical. This might have been done if Gorbachev had tried to mobilize the nineteen million members of the rank and file against the 300,000 full-time officials. Gorbachev briefly flirted with the idea at one point, though it appeared to be out of frustration rather than as part of a considered campaign. On a tour of Siberia he urged workers in Norilsk to put pressure on their local party officials while he as general secretary would do it from above. According to Ryzhkov, 'there was a strong reaction both in the Politburo and the country'. As prime minister, he regularly met enterprise directors. 'They couldn't understand. "Why should we be between the anvil and the hammer?", they complained.' Ryzhkov advised Gorbachev to be more specific. If he unleashed a general revolt against full-time officials and the administrative nomenklatura it could get out of control. Ryzhkov's anxiety was understandable, and Gorbachev did not repeat his action.

The other potential approach went to the opposite extreme. According to this argument, instead of launching any political reform at all Gorbachev and the Politburo should have followed the Chinese model and concentrated on rapid changes in the economy. In a sense this was what Andropov had been trying to do during his short period of power from 1982 to 1984, although he never intended to go as far as the Chinese had done in permitting private agriculture. But he was willing to make a major push to attract foreign capital by offering them unlimited scope for repatriating profits, as the Chinese were doing with their 'free economic zones'. Gorbachev followed no part of the Chinese model – a block on political change but widespread privatization of small business and market incentives in agriculture. Oleg Bogomolov, the director of the Institute of the Economy of the World Socialist System, made a brief effort to recommend private agriculture in 1987. Invited to Beijing by Oleg Troyanovsky, the Soviet ambassador, he spent almost a month studying China's experience. On his return he wrote a memorandum to Gorbachev, who invited him to be one of the speakers at a seminar of senior party and government officials in June. But Gorbachev soon made it clear he was uninterested, apparently thinking the ideas were too radical. He interrupted Bogomolov in the middle of his presentation and cut it short. A few months later Abel Aganbegyan, a leading economist who frequently advised Gorbachev, told a conference in Washington that the Soviet Union did not intend to emulate China and introduce a broad array of market mechanisms.[6] While not advocating private farming as the solution, Ryzhkov later commented that the Politburo made a strategic mistake in not concentrating on agriculture at the start of perestroika. 'I understand why Gorbachev didn't want to,' he commented. 'He had been in charge of agriculture for seven years before becoming general secretary. If in 1985 we had put everything into agriculture, it would have raised the question what he had been doing all that time before.'[7]

The nineteenth conference highlighted two important problems for Gorbachev, as he struggled to control the reform process. First, the party hierarchy might be manipulated into giving formal approval to radical changes but this did not mean it accepted them or would willingly put them into practice. If the first three years of perestroika had shown that the Soviet Union could not be reformed with the support of the party apparatus, the questions changed in 1988. Could there be reform in spite of the apparatus? In other words, could it be neutralized? Second, the conference showed that on the opposite flank the democratic press was beginning to cross the limits Gorbachev hoped it would set itself voluntarily. Fired by glasnost, some journalists were already straying beyond 'socialist pluralism' in their reports and comments on the conference.

The press's boldness was a marked change from their behaviour only a few months earlier during the so-called Nina Andreyeva affair. A sensational letter, written by Nina Andreyeva, a Leningrad chemistry lecturer, appeared in the paper *Sovietskaya Rossiya* on 13 March. It caused an immediate scandal because of its lengthy criticism of Gorbachev's policies, though without mentioning his name. It said glasnost was causing ideological confusion and leading students to a 'loss of political bearings'. It pointedly asked 'which class or stratum of society is the leading and mobilizing force of perestroika?' and hinted that the reformers' loyalty to socialism was in doubt. 'They eschew proletarian collectivism in favour of the notion of the intrinsic value of the individual, refusing to recognize the leading role of the party and the working class in building socialism and perestroika. The champions of "left-wing liberal socialism" are shaping the tendency which leads towards falsifying the history of socialism. They try to make us believe that the country's past was nothing but mistakes and crimes, and keep silent on the greatest achievements of the past and present,' she wrote.

If published a year later, let alone two, Nina Andreyeva's ideas would not have caused even a minor stir. They represented the views of a significant though unquantifiable number of party conservatives. But in 1988, three years after Gorbachev came to power, glasnost had not yet reached the point where conservative views which broke ranks with Gorbachev's position could be published. It was immediately assumed the article had the backing of Ligachev, still the secretary for ideology. The extraordinary aspect of the affair was not the letter, but the way both Gorbachev and the liberal press and intelligentsia reacted. Editors assumed it represented a change of policy at the top. They thought it was either an attempted putsch against Gorbachev – and the longer Gorbachev took to criticize it the more alarming this seemed – or, more conspiratorially, Gorbachev had himself changed his line and given up on perestroika. Adding to the mystery was the fact that Gorbachev had left for Yugoslavia on the day the article appeared, but even on his return he said nothing about it publicly. No one in Moscow dared to criticize the letter. The intelligentsia were in despair, as though perestroika had come to an end. Mikhail Ulyanov, the head of the union of theatre workers, described the mood when he addressed the nineteenth party conference three months later, 'Many people – not all, but many jumped to attention and awaited their next orders . . . We were scared by her letter. That is what is terrifying. Had those instructions appeared, people would have rushed to obey them, without thinking or hesitating . . . They realized this was wrong but they waited, they trembled and waited patiently, obediently, and with a sense of foreboding.' Their supine reaction was a reminder that almost every member of the new 'glasnost élite' was a party member, usually in their fifties or older. They were used to party norms and remembered the collapse of the Khrushchev thaw. Ulyanov gloomily asked, 'Is it again that accursed fear which sits in our genes?'

Gorbachev's reaction was mixed. Although he said nothing publicly, he talked about it repeatedly on his trip to Yugoslavia. 'He saw it as a gauntlet thrown to us,' his close aide Georgy Shakhnazarov recalled.[8] On his return he summoned the Politburo which discussed the issue for two days. Afterwards he authorized Yakovlev to draft a long article attacking Nina Andreyeva's points, which was published in *Pravda*. But he did not sack Ligachev or any of the others he suspected of supporting the letter. He even told Ligachev that he did not believe he had been behind it, though his private view was different, according to Anatoly Chernyayev, one of his close aides.[9] Reinforcing this impression, Yakovlev reported that from then on Gorbachev 'stopped believing Ligachev'.[10]

Gorbachev was not yet ready for an all-out clash with Ligachev, which would have been inevitable if he had accused him of deception. The concept of a split in the party was still taboo. Yakovlev had written him a memo as early as 1985, urging him to split the party. His idea was academic, almost naïve. The aim was not to create a multi-party system, but to improve the quality of debate. 'The two parties would create a field for competition. They would renew themselves, and alternate in power as a result of elections.

Society would get a powerful charge of dynamism.'[11] Gorbachev rejected the idea out of hand. In 1988 the argument against a split was that the conservatives might turn out to be the major force.

Gorbachev knew Ligachev represented a substantial body of opinion in the party. Ligachev was not a defender of Stalin. His wife's father, a General in the Red Army, was shot in 1937 after a typical ten-minute trial in which he was accused of the unlikely crime of being an 'Anglo-Japanese-German spy'. His own father, a peasant, was expelled from the party. But Ligachev was a Stalinist in that he accepted the basic parameters of the prevailing system; central planning, state ownership of the means of production, a one-party state, and tight party control of the media. His view of perestroika was confined to modernizing the economic system by giving managers more incentives and cleaning up corruption.

Another former 'obkom' secretary, Ligachev comes across in his autobiography as a bluff believer in discipline but also naïve. He recalled how in 1949, as the first secretary of the Young Communist League in Novosibiirsk, he was accused of Trotskyism for setting up youth brigades in local factories and collective farms.[12] They charged him with trying to separate young people from the party. Stalin was still in power, and one of Ligachev's friends, the first secretary of the YCL's Leningrad branch, had already been tried, convicted and shot for similar offences. Ligachev was lucky that he was only sacked. Instead of accepting his fate, he wrote a letter to the central committee, complaining of unfair treatment. Within three days he was summoned to Moscow. There he was escorted to a room where two officials, a man and a woman, were sitting. In a firm but leisurely way, the man asked the young Ligachev about his work in Novosibiirsk. After a few moments the woman went out. The man's tone changed. 'Comrade Ligachev, I advise you not to make any more appeals. Go home as fast as you can. Do you know who this woman is? Comrade Mishakova . . .' Comrade Mishakova was notorious as a vigilant 'sniffer-out of "disloyal"' party cadres, Ligachev recalled. He promptly left the room and went home to Siberia.

The Nina Andreyeva affair showed Gorbachev's unwillingness to deal with the conservatives either by forcing them out of the party or by debate. It was a far cry from the 'comradely polemics' which he advocated. 'We still lack political culture, we lack the culture to conduct debate and respect the viewpoint even of a friend, a comrade,' he had said a year earlier.[13] The conservatives began to feel there was a double standard and that perestroika could only be publicly criticized from the liberal flank. Gorbachev had never reacted so sharply to a controversial article in the liberal press, even though it was clear he was not happy with the liberals. Realizing the importance of the media, he regularly met editors, most of whom were keen supporters of glasnost. With censorship in abeyance, he wanted to persuade them to behave with restraint. They should not question the principles of socialism. In July 1987 at a meeting with editors he accused some of them of 'social demagoguery'. He told them it was undemocratic when nationally circulated papers were 'usurped by Moscow authors' and the same three or five people dominated their opinion columns. At the nineteenth party conference a year later, he complained: 'In the past some people monopolized the mass media, and we all know how that ended. Now we can see how another group of people are trying by stealth to monopolize the press as the tribune of all the people. We want a pluralism of opinions.'

The issue Gorbachev was touching on was ultimately insoluble. Confident again after the *Pravda* article attacking Nina Andreyeva, the liberal press went from strength to strength. Glasnost was exhilarating and heady, and editors – even more than Gorbachev – felt the party was an obstacle to reform. Few of them were willing to make tactical concessions in the rare atmosphere of a free press. Readership was rising. Paper was subsidized and there were no financial problems. Liberal editors were eagerly sought out by Western journalists and invited to conferences abroad, which they took as flattering confirmation of the correctness of their views. Had the editors been willing to give space to the conservatives they might have reduced some of the growing tensions, but this was to expect the improbable. Before the 1917 Revolution, the Russian media was already more interested in polemics than reporting. Journals were there to propagate a point of view rather than provide a forum for debate. After the Revolution one-sidedness became a way of life. In the famous slogan by Lenin, which used to flash out in neon near Moscow's Byelorussian railway station, 'A journalist should be an agitator, propagandist, and organizer'.

Glasnost did not change editors' approaches. A struggle for power was going on throughout Soviet society, and the press was one of the most important weapons in it. It was unrealistic to imagine that Russian editors would be tolerant to other points of view as though they were living in a placid, harmonious community. To restore party or government control over the media was no answer either, and when Gorbachev briefly suggested it in 1991 the outcry forced him to back down.

Surrender at the Polls

*The biggest party in the Soviet Union
is the party of non-party people.*

YEVGENI YEVTUSHENKO, OCTOBER 1988

Yegor Ligachev was right to describe Gorbachev's decision to allow contested elections for a new Soviet parliament as 'political shock therapy'. It was therapy for Soviet society, and a shock for the Communist party. The election campaign for the new democratic Congress of People's Deputies was the signal for full-scale independent political activity on a wide scale. Residents of housing estates were able to get together and hold meetings to nominate candidates. Political clubs could issue leaflets on street corners without fear of arrest. Speakers could criticize the Communist party from public platforms. It was a learning process for everyone, party officials, the election commission, political activists and the public. As we tramped up the ice-covered steps of local Houses of Culture and factory halls during that winter we felt we were watching a once-stagnant society shake off its last covering of fear.

Towards the end of the campaign the star candidate in Moscow, Boris Yeltsin, was being mobbed at huge meetings attended by thousands of voters. I preferred the smaller, rough-and-ready occasions and the street-corner discussions away from the television cameras, where people were beginning to flex their political muscles for the first time. It was what Gorbachev called a 'school for democracy', though when the results came out the main lesson was for the Communist party apparatus. For the first time for seventy years the mass of people in the country, who were not party members, were able to pass a verdict on party officials by secret ballot. The results were not a blow to the party as such, since 87 per cent of the elected deputies were Communists. The big loser was the party apparatus.

One of the first nomination meetings took place in early January at the Red Proletariat machine-tool plant, in the Oktyabrsky borough of Moscow, where we lived. It was a strange, hybrid occasion, a traditional set-up but with tentative shoots of something more radical trying to break through. A stocky, grey-haired figure with a ruddy complexion came to the platform and introduced himself as Nikolai Blinikov, a member of the factory's council of workers' collectives. 'This is all spontaneous. Nothing's been prepared in advance,' he began. In the seats in front of him sat just over 300 employees. Red Proletariat had rented a House of Culture for the meeting, a hall like a cinema with banks of seats in faded red plush and a wooden platform. With 6,000 workers at the factory, there was no room for them all to take part. Various workshops delegated colleagues to speak on their behalf.

The new election law was complicated. Candidates could be nominated at local meetings, provided at least 500 people turned up and voted, or directly from large factories and institutes. A successful nominee had to be supported by more than half the people at the meeting. There was no limit on the number of nominees in each borough, but after the initial selection they had to be screened by a special constituency committee before being registered as official contestants on the ballot. The reformers suspected this was a device for disqualifying radicals.

Blinikov had been given the honour of making the first nomination at Red Proletariat's meeting. 'In the past so many mistakes were made when candidates were chosen. That's why we feel so much responsibility,' he announced timidly. Then he came to the point. 'I have been asked to nominate Yuri Kirillov, our general manager.' It was hardly a radical choice, and when Blinikov described the general manager as 'a simple Soviet worker, who has not been spoilt by success', a few people laughed. A man in the hall rose. 'Are there going to be any other candidates?', he inquired in what sounded like a critical tone. The chairman of the meeting, the head of the factory's council of workers' collectives, replied sternly, 'I was told there were no other names. Do you object?' 'No, no. We don't object,' the questioner hastened to assure him. 'We didn't have any explanation of the system in our small workshop, that's all.' In the past, a mildly sceptical question would have been unthinkable. Even to ask one in 1989 took some courage.

Two workers came to the platform to support Kirillov's nomination. He was described in glowing terms as a good organizer, who knew every employee's name. 'His parents are collective farm workers, so he knows what work is all about,' said one man. 'On public holidays he attends parades as an ordinary person, not as the general manager. When he first became deputy general manager he visited one of the workshops which has no heating or water supply, and quickly solved its problems. Thanks to him, we have a rest home in the Crimea, and we have carried out perestroika without closing a single workshop.' The deputy secretary of the Communist party in the factory came up to praise Kirillov. She was followed by a younger woman in glasses, the Young Communist League organizer. 'Young people in the factory are all for Kirillov, and will vote for him,' she asserted. Next in line was the trade union chairman, with another unswerving speech of support.

It looked as though the meeting was about to come to a prompt and smooth close, when a bald man, with his tie loosened at the collar, asked to speak. He introduced himself as Viktor Oskin, an engineer. 'Kirillov has so many commitments. I don't know how he'll stick to them all,' he said sceptically. 'Anyway, if everything's been decided in advance, why are we having this meeting?' Some people in the audience did not like that. 'Why are you talking?' a voice shouted. Oskin ploughed on. 'Once again we've only got one candidate.' Now the heckling grew louder. 'Who elected you as a delegate?' 'What are you doing here?' It sounded like a relic of old-style intimidation, like the barracking Yeltsin had had to put up with at the party conference the year before. But as I attended more of these meetings, it appeared to be something else as well, a general Russian unwillingness to listen to points of view one did not agree with on the principle that 'if you're not with me, you're against me'. Even the so-called democrats were quick to give the slow handclap to unpopular comments.

Undeterred by the heckling, Oskin continued his criticisms. 'They talk of democracy, and we've only got one candidate. When we leave here, people will ask us what we were doing.' His speech struck a chord with some workers in the hall. 'Of course, he's right,' shouted a man behind me. A young delegate said his collective did not support the general manager. 'We don't know his programme, or what he stands for. We'll need him here as general manager more than as a deputy. Why do we have to nominate anyone? There'll be candidates from other places.' Now the man behind me was shouting, 'Why doesn't Kirillov speak, and tell us what his programme is?' Sensing danger, the chairman tried to head that idea off. He quickly asked for a vote on the original proposal to nominate Kirillov. A voice muttered, 'We spend our whole life just raising our hands.'

Judging by the interruptions, the sceptics in the hall were few, but Kirillov had the sense to realize that in the new conditions of competitive democracy he could not allow a vote to go forward without even making a speech. He asked the chairman for permission to come up to the platform. 'We've heard criticism, and we must listen to it,' he began diplomatically. 'It would not be right to deny people who oppose me the chance to speak.' He had only learnt two days earlier that he was going to be nominated, he disclosed. The proposal was quite unexpected, but after consulting a former manager who was a member of the Supreme Soviet, 'I realized that it's easier to be a general manager if you're also a deputy. It's easier to get land to expand the factory or build a club.' He promised, if elected, to get a new block of flats built for Red Proletariat's workers within two years. There was also a plan to build a children's pioneer camp outside Moscow.

A voice complained that Kirillov had outlined a programme for the factory, not for the people of the borough as a whole. There was 'no big thinking'. Kirillov looked embarrassed. 'Let's work it out together,' he suggested. On this weak note, the chairman abruptly ended the discussion. Should the vote be done by an open show of hands or by secret ballot, he asked. There was a chorus of shouts in favour of open voting. People seemed anxious not to waste more time. The vote was taken for Kirillov. Ten hands went up against him. Seven abstained. He was elected by a huge margin. After the hostile interruptions, Kirillov's landslide vote of support seemed an anti-climax. The opposition was obviously unprepared, and had not found their own candidate.

If Kirillov's ride was easy enough, the same could not be said of the meetings held by local residents rather than in factories. Here the crowd came from a larger catchment area, was more anonymous and usually more independent. A worker in a factory needed courage to propose a rival candidate against a manager. At a constituency meeting the range of options was often broad, as I discovered when some of the voters of the Ramenki ward in the borough of Gagarin made their choice. It was a Saturday afternoon when most Muscovites wander round the shops or relax at home. The borough's main landmark is a monstrous statue of the first man in space, a gleaming silvery giant on top of a tower, looking as though he is being propelled into orbit by nothing more than the

CHALLENGE TO THE PARTY

energy of his rather grim smile. Otherwise the area is similar to
most central Moscow boroughs, a collection of housing blocks on
either side of streets lined with birch trees.

The meeting was in a House of Culture, easily identifiable by the
tall portico with yellow pillars and a pediment, the standard design
for this sort of building. Several groups had asked for a chance to
nominate candidates. The hall had only 600 seats, so the local
executive committee gave out tickets. Every staircase in the blocks
of flats (eighty in all) was allocated seven tickets, which the house
committee would distribute. The mayor handed out the other forty.
Hundreds arrived without tickets but were promised that if they
did not mind standing in the cold a loudspeaker would broadcast
the proceedings. Yeltsin represented the borough of Gagarin in the
Moscow city council, and word was going round the crowd that he
was one of the nominees.

Still a member of the central committee, Yeltsin had already
been proposed by a number of branches for one of the 100 seats
reserved for the Communist party. A list of 312 names was sent up
to the Politburo by party branches, but when the Politburo
discussed the matter before submitting it to the central committee
for the vote they slimmed the number down to exactly 100. As a
result, even members of the central committee would not be able to
take a decision, since the number of candidates equalled the number
of seats. It was a cowardly move, which not only set a bad example
to other public organizations but gave the impression – correct, of
course – that the Politburo was afraid of competition. But central
committee members were given a small margin to express a prefer-
ence. They could mark 'yes' or 'no' against each of the 100 names.
Twelve votes out of 641 were cast against Gorbachev, 59 against
Yakovlev, and 78 – the highest number of negative votes – against
Ligachev.[14]

Another curiosity of the Politburo decision was that Yeltsin's
name was dropped from the list. This was a major mistake by
Gorbachev, since it forced Yeltsin to turn to the people to get
elected. Perhaps he would have done so anyway, since even if he

had been chosen for one of the party's 100 seats he need not have accepted the offer. Yeltsin's friends were already discussing whether he should try to become chairman of the Russian parliament, a position which would be better reached through direct popular ballot.[15] By excluding him from a reserved Communist party seat, the Politburo left him no alternative.

Yeltsin's exclusion was announced a few days before the Gagarin meeting. His supporters suspected that the authorities' next step would be to keep him off the public ballot. There was a loophole which might disqualify him. As first deputy chairman of the state building committee, Yeltsin had the rank of a Soviet minister. The law said ministers were not allowed to be members of the Congress of People's Deputies, but it did not specify clearly whether they could be candidates. Upstairs in the Ramenski House of Culture the suspicion of rigging hung heavy in the air. The pro-Yeltsin people feared all the tickets had been allocated to his opponents. On the platform under a bust of Lenin and beside a grand piano an elderly figure was sitting alone. Introducing himself as Vladimir Mikhailov, chairman of the local veterans' organization, he said the election committee had asked him to run the meeting. Yeltsin's supporters were not reassured since veterans are often active party loyalists. 'Eight local groups called for this meeting,' Mikhailov announced. 'Two party branches, residents' committees in two blocks of flats, two veterans' groups, and two women's councils. As candidate, they have all proposed Boris Nikolayevich Yeltsin.' The tension evaporated, and there was prolonged applause.

When Mikhailov asked if there were any more candidates, another pensioner, proudly wearing his medals, put himself forward. He was allowed to make a brief speech. He attacked Yeltsin for 'having no programme and not coming to this meeting'. Several people in the crowded hall whistled angrily until a woman shouted, 'What a disgrace that we don't listen to the other candidates. I support Yeltsin but let's at least hear the others.' A Yeltsin adviser came forward and apologized for his absence, but announced that if elected the candidate would resign as a government minister. A young man, who identified himself as a local councillor, proposed the mayor, on the grounds that the candidate ought to live in the borough. This brought knowing looks from some of the Yeltsin supporters. Three more people offered themselves before the list was closed.

'How shall we vote?', the chairman asked. 'Why not vote for them as a list? We are not limited to one,' a member of the audience called out. Again the Yeltsinites were suspicious. Names from every election meeting were to be forwarded to a special constituency committee for screening. If Yeltsin's name was just one of many, he would have more risk of being rejected. 'Let's vote for each candidate separately,' someone shouted. This procedure was adopted. Second victory to the Yeltsinites. The whiff of a landslide was going round the hall. The mayor rose and withdrew his candidacy. 'I see you want Yeltsin,' he commented. When the names were put to the vote one by one, Yeltsin received 510 votes. Three voted against and five abstained. No one else got more than token support. Like the Red Proletariat meeting, it was another landslide, but at least there was a contest.

Four days later I sat in on the screening committee's meeting for the borough of Gagarin. Perhaps it was because a foreign reporter was there, but the proceedings had the same quality of good intentions and earnest experimentation which marked the public meetings. One of the defeated candidates from Ramenki complained that the crowd had been excessively partisan and had whistled during his speech. He wanted to have another meeting in another hall. The committee spent some time discussing whether people could have a second chance, then decided to telephone the central election commission to get advice. They were told one chance was enough. Three students from an institute where four candidates had been nominated, including Yeltsin and Sakharov, were asked why they had not stuck with one. But the committee agreed that it was legal to propose any number provided each one had the support of at least half the meeting.

Outside Moscow the nomination process was less democratic. In

384 of the 1500 seats only one name was put on the ballot, and most of these candidates were full-time party officials or local administrators, hoping for safe seats. Under the rules army officers could run for office, and there were complaints that some of these men came under strong pressure from senior officers not to stand. Eventually, however, seventy-nine officers won, in some cases by defeating other military candidates. General Boris Snetkov, the commander of Soviet forces in East Germany, was defeated by a colonel who campaigned for radical reform of the military, including the abolition of conscription.

Radical groups complained of leaflets being torn off walls and obstacles put in the way of nomination meetings. Since halls had to be large enough to take 500 people, and every such building belonged to the state, it was easy for officials to claim they were over-booked or closed for repairs. The nomination procedure in the public organizations which had reserved seats was also easy to manipulate. The presidium of the Academy of Sciences initially refused to select Andrei Sakharov even though he was put forward by several institutes. After protests by hundreds of scientists outside the building the presidium reconsidered the matter and put him on the ballot. The Writers' Union took two days and several rounds of secret balloting to bring eighty-eight names down to twelve.

When the campaign proper began, the tentative meetings we had seen at the beginning turned into full-blooded confrontations between candidates. Television and radio played a surprisingly minor role. In most Moscow constituencies debates between all the candidates were the norm, and voters who wanted to take part crammed into Houses of Culture, cinemas and other public halls. Usually the format was scrupulously fair, with each candidate required to answer the same question so that voters could compare their replies. But once again the audience was quick to hiss those who waffled, said unpopular things or exceeded their time. Star candidates like Yeltsin would hold meetings of their own.

One curiosity of the poll was that more candidates were party members than at the previous no-contest elections, where the tradition had always been to appoint a number of hand-picked non-party people to give an image of broad-mindedness. Since members of the old Supreme Soviet had little power, this was no concession. Under the new system people outside the narrow party nomenklatura had a real chance of being elected. It was no accident that many reformist members of the intelligentsia and other white-collar professionals with an interest in politics who were long-time party members for career reasons decided to run. While the proportion of candidates from the creative and scientific intelligentsia went up, there were negative features. Fewer women ran, and there were fewer workers and collective farmers. It was a further sign that perestroika had not yet inspired large sections of the Soviet population to take advantage of the new opportunities. Perestroika might just be replacing one élite by another.

The elections dealt the final blow to the notion of a Communist party monolith. Although the Communist party published an election manifesto, it was not binding on candidates. Few mentioned it in their campaigns, and some even argued against it. Party members stood against each other in many areas and the central committee's only instructions to local branches were not to interfere. Candidates ran as free individuals, unbound by party loyalty or discipline and able to put forward whatever programme they liked. Ligachev later complained that this was a disastrous mistake, a clear sign that Gorbachev had already begun to betray the Communist party. In his view, Gorbachev should have used the campaign to promote his view of perestroika rather than leave the party rudderless. But this was a misreading of Gorbachev's intention. He deliberately took a passive line, both to force candidates from the party apparatus to show some genuine initiative themselves and so as to separate the wheat from the chaff.

As a result, the campaign of 1989 was a non-party one, an unusual phenomenon in any developed country. There was one major exception to this point. Candidates who were closely identified with the Communist party apparatus, as opposed to being merely party members, usually had a hard time. From the politics of silence under Brezhnev the country had moved by 1989 to the politics of protest. The election gave voters their first chance to say what they thought of individual officials. Many of them took it with relish. Faced with the onslaught, most party officials gave up, or took refuge in manipulation to get elected. Far from 'learning democracy' they fell back on the party's long practice of authoritarian behaviour, the only strategy they knew. Even before the campaign began, there were clear signs that the party was not able or willing to engage in dialogue. In November *Pravda* published a long piece urging officials to listen to the informals, get into discussion with them, and be able to stand up for the party's views and ideals. 'But the trouble is that many party workers and Soviet officials, even if they go to political clubs, keep quiet and abandon the ideological field,' it complained.[16]

The election campaign magnified the problem. The scores of senior officials who had managed to get themselves on the ballot without any rival candidate barely bothered to look for votes. They assumed they would be elected automatically. But as polling day grew closer, it began to dawn on people that the electoral law required successful candidates, even those who were unopposed, to get at least half the ballots cast. Voters were allowed to cross out a candidate's name if they did not like him or her. If the candidate failed to get over half, there would have to be a new election. There also had to be a turn-out of at least 50 per cent for the election to be valid in each constituency. These tough rules were the brainchild of Anatoly Lukyanov, as he proudly told me later.[17] They were not entirely novel, since even under the old Soviet single-list system, when voters had no choice of alternative candidates they could cross out individual names. This had defeated senior party figures, including Andrei Kirilenko, a member of the Politburo, in the not so distant past. Lukyanov transferred the idea to the new-style elections as 'a risky, but necessary system for democracy'.

Of all Russia's major cities Leningrad stood out by the high number of party officials who were running unopposed. Four of the city's twenty-one constituencies had a lone candidate, and in each case it was a senior official. One of them was the region's party boss, Yuri Solovyev, who was an alternate member of the Politburo. To his credit, it must be said that at least he was up for election whereas, with one exception, every other Politburo member, including Gorbachev, had been given one of the 100 reserved Communist party seats. Why they were afraid became apparent when I visited Leningrad's Lomonossovskaya metro station two weeks before the poll. 'Cross out Solovyev's name', demanded handwritten banners which pickets were brandishing as hundreds of commuters poured out of the escalators. The pickets were from a coalition of informal groups, called Election 89, which had been set up in January with the aim of agreeing on a list of candidates progressive enough to support. They also organized a panel of lawyers and poll-watchers to advise candidates and check the ballots and counting procedures on the day. Solovyev's supporters had managed to block any other candidate from getting on the ballot in his Nevsky constituency. Workers' collectives which wanted to hold nomination meetings were told this was 'unproductive'. This caused considerable anger around the city and even the party paper, *Leningradskaya Pravda*, had to report calls for Solovyev's withdrawal. *Izvestiya's* local correspondent ridiculed it in the paper as 'an election without a choice'.

Realizing how the tide in the constituencies was running, Solovyev attempted to win support through a leaflet campaign. His people passed out printed handbills, but from what I saw it looked a thankless task. 'At least Comrade Gorbachev is not afraid to come out and meet people,' an angry woman in a brown raincoat shouted at one of the leafleters by the metro station. 'We never see Solovyev.' 'I suppose you're paid for this, and you probably already have a car and a dacha,' a man sneered at another Solovyev canvasser. 'Why do we live worse in Leningrad than any other Soviet city?' When the results were announced two weeks later, it became clear that the city which had led the 1917 Revolution had also led the uprising of 1989. Some 55 per cent of voters struck Solovyev out. The three other unopposed party officials, including the mayor and his deputy, received less than 50 per cent of the poll. Anatoly Gerasimov, the city party boss and the only senior official with an opponent, was defeated by a twenty-eight-year-old engineer (and party member) supported by Election 89.

In cities around the Soviet Union party officials suffered defeats. More than thirty senior figures failed to gain election, including the mayors of Moscow and Kiev. Sometimes the very fact that officials had not dared to face an opponent alienated voters. 'I lost because I was unopposed,' complained Valentin Zgursky, Kiev's mayor, in the best quotation of the election campaign.

While the results were a shock to party conservatives, they also seemed to dismay Gorbachev. At the nineteenth party conference the previous summer he had implied that senior officials who failed to win a public vote of confidence should resign their party posts. His proposal for elections was partly meant as a device for removing opponents of perestroika. But when the results came in Gorbachev backed off, as though frightened by the extent of the party apparatus's unpopularity. At the next Politburo meeting he tried to put a brave face on it, even claiming that the results were a victory for the party, since so many Communists were elected.[18] But he made no call for the losers to resign and instructed the media to play down the results.

Lukyanov, who made the main report to the Politburo after the elections, argued that he had predicted some senior heads would roll. It was no tragedy and the party would have to expect to lose officials who had little public support.[19] Lukyanov later defended the decision not to insist on the defeated candidates' resigning their party posts since the leadership wanted to drive home the lesson that loss in elections was not automatically the end of a person's career. In spite of this argument, the decision was a retreat from Gorbachev's earlier line and another example of his vacillation. He would launch reforms but then try to delay or prevent them proceeding to their logical conclusion.

Gorbachev was also patently upset by Boris Yeltsin's triumph, with 90 per cent of the vote in Moscow. He failed to congratulate him. No national newspaper mentioned Solovyev's defeat the next morning, and Yeltsin's victory was buried in *Pravda* in a general round-up which did not report the scale of his support. The newspaper produced the condescending explanation that 'not all the electorate had enough political sophistication', a line which was echoed by Vladimir Khodyrev, the mayor of Leningrad, with his comment: 'Some leaders lost because the people had poor information about their activities, and therefore had to be content with rumours and the grapevine.' After seventy years of monopoly control by the party over the media, this was rich.

When he broke his public silence three days after the poll at a meeting with editors, Gorbachev tried to take a measured line. He described the results as a victory for perestroika because 'the people felt their strength'. He criticized the losers for turning their offices into 'unapproachable fortresses and losing contact with ordinary citizens'. But he also urged the media not to dramatize the results. Once again there was nothing about immediate resignations.

Gorbachev may have delayed because he had already made other plans for reforming the party apparatus. At a plenary meeting of the central committee in late April he engineered the resignation of seventy-four full members, a quarter of its voting strength, and twenty-four alternate members in the biggest overhaul it had known for years. The changes were not connected to the election results. The retirees included Andrei Gromyko, the former foreign minister and head of state, and several survivors from the Brezhnev Politburo. In their place, twenty-four other members were promoted to full voting status. Gorbachev's aim was to reduce the danger of a revolt in the central committee of the kind which overthrew Khrushchev a quarter of a century earlier.

At the time most commentators analysed the plenum's results as another Gorbachev triumph. Yeltsin might be the master of crowd-pulling but Gorbachev was still the wizard in the Kremlin, able to manipulate the central committee at will. It took only a week for the truth to emerge. Gorbachev's victory at the plenum was Pyrrhic. When *Pravda* published the full transcript of the meeting in early

May, readers could see the extent of the apparatus's reactionary defeatism. Even after the resignation of the ninety-eight, the mood of conservatism among the remainder was overwhelming. Apart from Gorbachev, fourteen members spoke and everyone was worried about something, whether it were too much glasnost, the iconoclastic tone of the media, the licence allowed to informal groups, the decline in the party's authority or the collapse of ideological certainties. Abdul Rahman Vezirov, the party boss of Azerbaijan, even coined the lurid phrase 'ideological AIDS' to describe the independent magazines which, he felt, were seeping into circulation unchecked.

The message in the two events, the March elections and the April plenum, ought to have been clear to Gorbachev. The party apparatus was unable to compete publicly for support or even accept the necessity for change. To go on believing it could be reformed without more determined leadership from the top or more pressure from the grass-roots was surely an illusion.

6

The Failure of Reform

*In every Western country parties try to become the
government. Here we pride ourselves on getting the party
out of government.*

COMMUNIST INTELLECTUAL IN TV DISCUSSION, OCTOBER 1989

The elections to the Congress of People's Deputies were the
watershed, and from then on the Communist party's old position in
Soviet society was doomed. Alexander Yakovlev's comment that the
party reigned but from the early 1970s had ceased to rule was taken
a step further. Like the emperor with no clothes, the party no
longer even reigned. Between 1989 and 1991 the last remaining
aura of its authority was stripped away, as more and more groups
spotted its nakedness. Individual membership declined because of
resignations, and the number of new applicants dropped away,
particularly among the working-class whose interests the party
claimed to represent. The liberal intelligentsia, which initially supported the party because Gorbachev promoted glasnost, lost interest. Even the conservatives gave up on the party, and when they
mounted their coup against Gorbachev in 1991, they barred the
party's official leadership, including Vladimir Ivashko, Gorbachev's
deputy, and most of the central committee secretaries, from their
planning. This was the party's final humiliation. The coup plotters,
all life-long Communists, were primarily trying to save the Soviet
Union rather than the party.

Had they succeeded, no doubt they would have tried to revive the party. They would have overturned the ban which Yeltsin, by then the elected president of Russia, had put on party activity in the KGB, the army, the police and industrial enterprises. Gorbachev's failure to block it was one of their complaints against him. They would probably have rewritten the relatively progressive party programme which Gorbachev had persuaded the central committee to adopt in July 1991. But these were not the plotters' main concerns. The coup's goal was to stop the new Union treaty from being signed.

Though enormously weakened after the 1989 election, the party did not succumb smoothly. There were paroxysms, temporary recoveries and relapses, and no one saw the process clearly at the time. Gorbachev himself was caught in contradictions. He had announced at the nineteenth party conference that the party should move out of government, but he still did not accept that there had to be a multi-party system. For the reformers this was the key issue throughout 1989. In order to bring it in the constitution had to be changed, with the removal of Article Six which enshrined the Communist party's leading role in Soviet society and sanctioned the one-party system. Andrei Sakharov and Anatoly Sobchak, the eloquent lawyer who became Leningrad's first democratically elected mayor, mentioned it in their election manifestos. Reformers raised the issue at the first session of the Congress of People's Deputies and made a strong, though unsuccessful, push for a constitutional amendment at the second session in December. Gorbachev was not yet ready to support them.

By then there were three broad divisions of opinion. A minority of people wanted to remove the Communist party from power altogether. To them it was a criminal organization, the symbol and instrument of a totalitarian system. It was not just a question of forcing the Communist party to accept the right of other political parties to exist. Soviet society had to be 'de-ideologized'. The Communist party must give up its branches in the army, police and KGB as well as in factories and institutes, and should be organized geographically, like parliamentary parties in Western countries, in the places where people live, not where they work. Andrei Sakharov, by then prominent as a member of the Supreme Soviet, advocated this line, and it was taken up actively by his supporters. At his lying-in-state and funeral in December 1989, which prompted a huge outpouring of public grief, hundreds of mourners wore lapel buttons with the number six and a line through it – shorthand for the constitutional change they wanted.

A second group wanted to reform the party so that it could compete in elections with some chance of success. They also supported a constitutional change to remove the Communist party's monopoly, but were not anti-Communists. Many were party members themselves. They did not support the view that the whole party was to blame for its past mistakes. If it reformed, it had a chance, indeed a duty, to maintain a social-democratic option in Soviet society. The third group was resistant to change. Some of these were against it on principle, believing that the party was the only bulwark against a market economy and a restoration of capitalism. Others were more 'statist'. They felt the Soviet Union was under threat from internal economic disintegration and separatism in the republics, and that any weakening of the party would lead to a further weakening of the state. Their primary concerns were imperial rather than ideological. The events of 1989 produced a sharp polarization between the first and third groups.

The first session of the new Congress of People's Deputies, which was televised live and held the country spellbound for two weeks, lifted the last taboos on criticizing the Communist party and its most sacred institutions. The use of troops to break up a non-violent protest in Tbilisi led to demands for Politburo members to be brought to account. This was no longer one senior party member publicly attacking another at a party conference – the sensation of 1988. This was MPs calling for the party leadership to account to parliament. People who had long been opponents of the party, like Sakharov and the scores of former dissidents and political prisoners whose views were eagerly sought by the liberal press, found themselves being supported by hundreds of ordinary Russians. Every day they were bombarded with letters and telegrams. Perestroika's failure to bring any economic improvements drained away the party's support and pushed thousands into opposition. Coupled with the collapse of the Communist parties' authority in Eastern Europe, there was a growing feeling that the party had exhausted its last chance, and should step aside.

The reformers in the party had their eyes on the party congress, scheduled for later in 1990. They saw it as the last chance to turn the party into a normal parliamentary forum. The reformers took a softer line on the fate of the USSR. Most of them hoped to see it survive as a loose confederation rather than the federation which Gorbachev advocated, but they were not opposed to outright independence for the Baltics. It was this relaxed 'anti-imperial' line plus their suspicions of the army, KGB and other state security organs which led to the description of the reform movement as 'the left'. The party conservatives were dubbed 'the right'. The labels were simplistic and misleading since they ignored the economic policies which the various groups supported. It seemed strange to call reformers who wanted to minimize, if not eliminate, the state's role in running the economy, and advocated ending price subsidies and promoting wider income differentials in Soviet society 'the left'. The labels are best avoided. When I once asked Tatyana Zaslavskaya, one of Moscow's leading sociologists, to define them in the current Russian context, she threw up her hands and laughed, 'We're used to describing nice people as the left. That's all'.

Moscow's Aviation Institute was the scene of the party reformers' most important meeting. A large hall, in yet another House of Culture, was decked with provocative slogans – 'Against the political mafia, a United Democratic Block', 'Time for the Party to Repent before the People'. The crowd of roughly 500 people, mainly in their thirties and forties – once again almost entirely male – was not a group of fervent anti-Communists. This was the first all-union conference of party clubs and party organizations, and virtually everyone was a Communist party member. The very concept of such a conference was subversive, since under party rules members were forbidden from forming 'horizontal' links. The fear was that this could lead to factions, which would then start to organize against the official party line. By January 1990 when the all-union conference took place, this was already a ridiculous notion, since the elections in March 1989 had shown there was no longer any party line. The party was in a state of chaos, defeatism and fragmentation.

Most delegates at the conference still hoped they could correct this. They came from seventy-eight cities and represented about 100 clubs. They wanted to turn the party into a genuine supporter of perestroika and a parliamentary democracy. The conference was opened by Igor Chubais, a lecturer at an institute. He denounced the party in its present form as 'an army of ideological security' and urged Gorbachev to set up a round table on the pattern of Eastern Europe at which every political group could sit alongside the Communists and reach a consensus on reform. The aim was to give concrete and constructive form to the Revolution from below which Gorbachev claimed he wanted. 'We've invited Gorbachev to this conference. Maybe he's here. Please stand up,' Chubais joked. The next speaker, Vladimir Lysenko, broached the idea of a split in the party. He calculated that between 10 and 20 per cent of the party were neo-Stalinists, who only wanted cosmetic change but intended to keep its monopoly, 20 to 40 per cent were reformers who favoured a parliamentary party, and the rest were moderate centrists who wanted a more open party but still as the linchpin of a one-party system. The reformers should try to ensure they had a powerful block of delegates at the party Congress, directly elected by party branches through secret ballots rather than the old system of screening at the obkom level. If that failed, and the apparatus manipulated the choice of delegates, then they should hold an alternative Congress.

Gavriil Popov, who was later to become mayor of Moscow, said the reformers should prepare an alternative platform and insist that delegates to the Congress be elected on the basis of adherence to the official or the alternative platform. They should consider splitting from the party altogether if necessary. A dampening note was sounded by Vyacheslav Shostakovsky, the rector of the Higher Party School. 'Listening to you, I thought for a moment we were already living in a democratic society,' he told the delegates. 'Certain realities cannot be avoided. We don't have a democratic society, and glasnost inside the Communist party is strictly rationed.' Although he supported their aims, he warned that Soviet society was too atomized to support a functioning multi-party system. People were not ready to start building alternative structures of power. His analysis was correct, as events were to show once the Communist party collapsed.

Shostakovsky concluded that the best strategy was still to try to change the Communist party from within, but not be too optimistic even about this. In spite of Shostakovsky's caution, the two-day conference ended in an upbeat mood with the creation of a 'Democratic Platform'. The reformers' hopes of getting a good block of delegates to the Congress were strengthened over the next few days. The best news was a revolt by party members in three Russian cities, Sverdlovsk, Tyumen, and Volgograd (formerly Stalingrad), against the obkom leaders. It seemed symptomatic of a new mood of change, which could offer a real chance of the party's democratizing itself from within.

The steps up from the grey water of the Volga at its main frontage in Volgograd pass two pompous concrete porticoes, then give out on to a small square near one of the city's countless war memorials. The city's long and successful resistance to the Nazi onslaught was the turning-point in the Second World War. Whole sections near the river have been kept in ruins as a reminder, and on a hill stands a 150-foot statue of the 'Motherland', a giant female figure carrying a massive sword. But the smaller memorial by the main river landing has a more intimate, inviting quality. In early February 20,000 people gathered round it, demanding the resignation of the local party leadership. Revelations of misuse of state flats for their families, mismanagement of the local economy and a long record of deafness to popular wishes had culminated in an explosion of public anger.

Vladimir Kalashnikov, the obkom secretary, was a friend of Gorbachev's, but over the previous two years had become a tainted figure. His biggest blunder was what became known as the 'tomato war'. Plumbing depths of stupidity which are hard to believe in a country which had a food shortage, he went after private tomato growers on the grounds that they were 'speculators'. Housewives and pensioners, many of them veterans of the historic siege of Stalingrad, found their back-garden greenhouses being smashed by police. Plants were ripped out. Boxes of tomatoes were tipped up and run over by lorries.

The protests forced Kalashikov to resign, and when I visited the town it was run by a 'provisional committee' of twenty party members, pending a delegate conference which would elect a new leadership. A stormy meeting was going on at the Polytechnical Institute as faculty and students chose delegates. It was clear that the Democratic Platform was having an impact. 'Do you favour the Democratic Platform or the Gorbachev platform?', one nominee was asked as he stood at the rostrum in a large lecture theatre. 'That's a big issue. I would need forty minutes to answer it,' he began hopelessly. There were shouts of 'Take him off the list'. 'No, take him right out of the party,' joked a woman two rows behind me. It was a merciless occasion. Tolerance is not a Russian tradition and it did not take long for groups in the audience to sum up a man. This candidate was indecisive. That one came from the old guard. Several candidates failed to show up, wisely as it turned out. The audience was not unanimous. They shouted at each other as well as at the nominees.

Through the hubbub it emerged that the supporters of the Democratic Platform were in a minority. A young man, sitting with a group of students at the back, took the microphone and was the first to lift people's sights to a wider audience. 'I'm not a party member. But if people like Kiselev are elected to the party leadership, then I'll join,' he told them. Later the man explained that Alexander Kiselev was the local leader of the Young Communist League. The League had been collapsing even faster than the party. Membership in the YCL used to be virtually compulsory for anyone with ambition. People could not leave freely since their careers could suffer. The YCL was thinking of changing the rule so that people could go without having to have their branch's permission. In spite of the risk, as many as 80,000 young people in Volgograd had resigned from it over the past year.

Kiselev had won widespread support in the elections to the Congress of People's Deputies in 1989 when he trounced a nationally known conservative writer, Yuri Bondarev, after scores of students knocked on voters' doors and gave out leaflets. 'Until recently there was no real effort to involve young people in politics,' Kiselev told me later that day, pointing to one of the phenomena which distinguished Russia from Eastern Europe. Whereas in Czechoslovakia and East Germany the crowds which demonstrated for democracy were dominated by the young, in Russia the generation between thirty-five and fifty was the main force. The stagnation and hypocrisy of the Brezhnev years left young Russians cynical and bored with politics, and the Gorbachev changes had failed to shake them. The mobilization of students in 1989 turned out to be brief. In the Yeltsin years young people's alienation from politics became even more marked.

Lieut-Colonel Igor Lukashev, an engineering instructor at Volgograd's air force academy and a candidate in the elections for the Russian parliament, which were due that March, told me he hoped workers would become politically active. His expectations were not high. 'In Volgograd the workers are still quiet but you cannot get far without them in an industrial city like this.' One reason was the housing queue. Workers depended on the management and the party committees in the factories and were afraid to criticize conditions. 'Until people get flats, they are like serfs,' Colonel Lukashev commented gloomily. If the dominant mood at the Polytechnical Institute was conservative, how much more so was it in the region's rural areas where people tended to vote as the collective farm chairman advised them?

Even in the city, in spite of the meeting of 20,000, there was no sustained political activism. A memorial meeting for Andrei Sakharov attracted 250 people. On a Saturday afternoon I watched candidates campaigning for the Russian parliament. Only 200 stopped to listen at a meeting addressed by several candidates in the main shopping street. Many of the slogans warned of apathy. 'People, wake up. Our passivity helps the apparatus,' said one. The colonel feared that the revolt against the obkom leadership might turn out to have been a palace coup, in which the crowds in the street on that one day were just extras. 'The main thing is to break the power of the apparatus. Otherwise, we're just changing the names of the leaders.' He was right. The new obkom leader eventually appointed by the delegate conference was another senior apparatchik, Alexander Anipkin, the former head of the city party committee. Anipkin, who campaigned vigorously for public office by making regular attacks on his old colleague, the former party boss Kalashnikov, also won election to the Russian parliament.

Once again, the message was that Russians were unwilling to move from protest to a more sustained and fundamental process of change. If fear was removed and passions were roused, people would on occasion stand up and throw out the 'old rascals' but they were not ready to alter the entire system. More than in other European countries, there was a sense that politics were a spectator sport. If people took an active part in anything, it was an occasional march or public meeting.

People's apathy was hardly surprising in the light of Russia's history of authoritarianism. The corruption of the Brezhnev years had added cynicism to the general alienation from politics which Russians had long felt. In Moscow, however, leaders of the Democratic Platform were still hopeful. They were encouraged by the turn-out for a march in central Moscow which they organized along with other reformist groups, calling for the removal of the constitution's Article Six. Some 200,000 people ended up in Manezh

Square just below the walls of the Kremlin for the biggest protest rally since the 1917 Revolution. A few days later Gorbachev persuaded the central committee to remove the Article. His conversion to the notion of a multi-party system had taken a long time. A year earlier, in a rather testy two-hour meeting with a group of workers, Gorbachev had ridiculed the idea, arguing that dictatorships often had multi-party systems.[1] By itself the existence of several parties did not mean democracy. 'There is no basis for discussing it . . . two parties, three parties, it is all nonsense. If you have three or four parties, you can still have so much tyranny that nobody can open his mouth or speak freely . . . First, one or two parties on the basis of class . . . then 120 on the basis of nationality . . . all this is being foisted on us by irresponsible people.'

Gorbachev's change of mind was caused by several factors: the performance of the apparatus in the March 1989 elections and the feeling that reforms were needed in advance of the elections to the Russian parliament in March 1990; the collapse of Communist rule in Eastern Europe; pressure from the Democratic Platform and others in the party; and Gorbachev's self-image as a reformer. To have a constitution guaranteeing one party a monopoly looked like an anachronism. Like so many of his moves Gorbachev's decision included escape hatches and was not clear-cut. The escape hatch was the creation of an executive presidency. Gorbachev persuaded the central committee and subsequently the Congress of People's Deputies to adopt a constitutional change setting up the new post at the same time as they abolished the Communist party's monopoly. The move fitted logically with the spirit of the nineteenth party conference back in June 1988 and the aim of ending the party's duplication of the government's role. It succeeded in this only too well. Once the executive presidency was created, the party lost another of its props. The Politburo was pushed to the side-lines by the presidency and the new presidential council which Gorbachev created to go with it. Asking the party to accept the removal of Article Six was demanding less of it than to support an executive presidency, though most members of the central committee did not see that at the time.

In the Congress of People's Deputies Gorbachev had a harder job of persuasion to do than in the central committee. Many Russian deputies were jealous of their new role, while those from the republics, particularly Estonia, Latvia and Ukraine, were worried about the dangers of the reimposition of a strong central hand. (The Lithuanians had stopped attending the Congress.) Russian reformers did not like the way the president would be able to appoint the members of the constitutional review committee which was supposed to check the validity of legislation. Gorbachev backed off, and said the president would only appoint the chairman. Deputies from the republics objected to the president's powers to declare martial law or a state of emergency in any republic without first seeking approval from its parliament. Again, Gorbachev retreated.

Gorbachev's major mistake was in not submitting himself to election. The constitutional amendments said the president would be chosen by direct popular ballot for a five-year term but a Gorbachev ally, Vladimir Kudryavtsev, a lanky, Dickensian figure with the saddest smile in parliament, argued that this first time the Congress should choose the president. Even Gorbachev's liberal adviser, Alexander Yakovlev, claimed that the country's crisis was too severe to allow a presidential election. There were scenes of near farce when Gorbachev tried to organize a token alternative candidate for the vote in the Congress. Vadim Bakatin, the interior minister, was proposed but withdrew. When the chairman of the session continued to treat him as a candidate, the luckless Bakatin returned to the rostrum, pleading only half in jest, 'You seem to have lost my withdrawal statement. In no democratic country is a person forced to stand for president'.

Had Gorbachev run in a popular vote, he would almost certainly have won. Yeltsin had already made it clear he would not be a candidate, and there was no one else with national authority. But Gorbachev may have feared that Yeltsin's supporters would make him change his mind, or that many people would abstain or cross out Gorbachev's name, as they had done to senior party officials in the

1989 elections. This could have weakened his authority abroad as well as at home. However, these were worst-case assumptions. The more likely outcome was a victory at the polls, which would have given Gorbachev the legitimacy he still lacked. When I talked with Gorbachev a year after he lost power, he was beginning to concede the depth of his error. 'It was perhaps a mistake,' he said, then repeated the argument he had used at the time, that the country could not afford the luxury of a long electoral campaign. In 1991 Yeltsin ran for the new post of president of Russia and trounced five opponents. Without the same legitimacy Gorbachev looked weak in comparison.

Having failed to take the risk of elections to the presidency, Gorbachev failed either to insist on a drastic reform of the party or to dump it. He was like a man riding two horses, and both were lame. The presidency gave him power but insufficient authority. The Communist party was crumpling under him.

With the presidency established, the party made a final lurch to the conservative side. In early April it published an open letter to members condemning factionalism and urging branches to expel those who supported a split. Any doubt about whom the letter was aimed at was removed when Igor Chubais, one of the founders of the Democratic Platform, was sacked by his party branch. Other reformers in Byelorussia and Ukraine suffered the same fate. The letter provoked a wave of anger. Boris Yeltsin accused conservatives of trying 'to mount a coup against perestroika in the party'. He called for the creation of a new political party. Yuri Afanasyev, another reformer, urged members to leave the party but in an organized way to get maximum publicity. 'We need time to do as much harm as possible to this party which has done so much harm to us all these years,' he argued brutally.

In fact, the open letter was not a product of the party's conservatives. It was approved and accepted by Gorbachev. Like his reaction to the moves to remove Article Six of the constitution the previous autumn, it was as though he alone should decide when the time for changes was ripe. Rather than trying to urge reformers who were on his own wave-length to wait a while, he chose to alienate them by taking action against them. He still could not accept that a split in the party might be the best way to restore its authority and prestige.

Besides the Democratic Platform, a second group of reformers was hoping to influence the approaching Communist party Congress. This was the Marxist Platform. Led by Alexander Buzgalin, another university lecturer, the Platform was put together by members of the Federation of Marxist Party Clubs. They criticized the social-democratic drift of the Democratic Platform as well as the official one. The Platform's aim was 'to restore confidence in the party in that section of the working class for which the possibility of working freely and collectively and being masters rather than hired labour is one of the chief assets'.[2] Attacking the Democratic Platform for ignoring economic issues, the Marxist Platform called for a democratically regulated market in which consumer unions would determine prices and supervise the quality of goods, and workers would have strong material incentives. The totalitarian and bureaucratic system would be dismantled in favour of self-management at all levels. State property should be redistributed among workers' collectives and local authorities.

Support for the Marxist Platform was considerably smaller than for the Democratic Platform, but both were too late. When the party met for its Congress in July 1990, it was to all intents and purposes beyond any chance of reform. Party branches in the regions had successfully organized the selection of delegates so that the reformers were in a small minority, with 20 per cent of the support at most. Individuals were resigning in droves. Some four million were thought to have left over the previous year, although it was hard to quantify since branch secretaries were reported to be refusing to register the resignations so as to conceal the grim picture. For the first time correspondents were allowed to attend the Congress. We felt we were watching the end of an era. There was plenty of anger, but it had the smell of impotence. Delegates complained at the collapse of the party's authority, the continuing stagnation of the economy, the implosion of the Warsaw Pact and rising ethnic tensions. They had nothing specific to put forward to improve the situation. The Congress was like yet another protest meeting, a forum for emotional speeches and ill-prepared votes.

During one of the breaks I went in search of a 'typical' delegate. From his profile, Sergei Ushakov seemed as good as any; a Russian, thirty-nine years old, married, with two children, he came from Armavir, a town of 180,000 in the North Caucasus. He had spent the last five years as a full-time branch secretary in the building company where he used to work. The party helped him get further education, so he was loyal to it for that. But he was no diehard with blind faith in the party's future. He gave the party only two years to regain its declining support, or admit that the anti-Communists were right all along.

He denied being an apparatchik though he fitted statistically into the largest category of congress delegates, the 43 per cent who were full-time party officials. He took a drop in pay when he became branch secretary, serving the 150 party members in the 1000-person company. He was chosen as a delegate by ballot against three opponents. Like almost half the delegates, he was at a party Congress for the first time. He was not impressed by Gorbachev's speech to the Congress – 'no profound analysis of the situation and no programme for getting the party and the country out of the crisis'. His friends among the other delegates from his area shared his view, he said. He respected Ivan Polozkov, the new leader of the party conservatives, but did not agree with him on everything. 'He has a strong position in defence of the socialist ideal and the preservation of the party. We know all these attacks on the party, the army and the KGB are just the beginning. It's not long before people go on to attack Soviet power itself.' But he supported Gorbachev because he saw no alternative and did not want people to write the Congress off as a 'conservative Congress'.

Ushakov joined the party in 1976, when he was twenty-five. 'No one forced me. I am a worker. The socialist ideal was dear to me, and I knew that Marxism is the ideology of the working class,' he explained. But he believed the Soviet Union's mistake was that it had 'deviated from the market'. 'There is such a thing as a socialist market. Yet this scheme of nationalizing everything and creating the slogan that man is the master when we all knew it was not true in practice – this alienation made people indifferent and brought us to disaster,' he complained. The party must be honest. If it could not show the working class any improvement in two years' time, the whole socialist system and the Soviet Union itself would explode, just as it had done in Eastern Europe.

Ushakov did not expect the Congress to end with a formal split so much as with the resignation of thousands of members, particularly among the intelligentsia. He was right, though the resignations went beyond that. Next day an elderly pensioner to whom I gave a lift said he was leaving the party as soon as the Congress was over. He was a former fighter pilot who had flown in the Korean war, wearing a Chinese uniform, since Stalin refused to admit Soviet involvement. 'Many of my friends are leaving too. It has been a hard decision, but the party is not up to the task. Our ideal does not work'.

The sensation of the party Congress was Boris Yeltsin's announcement that he was suspending his membership. Although he did not resign completely, arguing that as long as he was chairman of the Russian parliament, he should be independent of all parties, it was a thunderbolt for most of the delegates. He was the first senior figure voluntarily to renounce membership. The press box in the balcony was close to where the party delegates from the army and navy sat. We watched the frisson of shock go through their ranks as Yeltsin strode out of the hall.

Yeltsin's departure should not have been a shock. His call for a new political party a few weeks earlier was a clear warning of his intentions. Two other leading reformers, Gavriil Popov and Anatoly Sobchak, the mayors of Moscow and Leningrad, also withdrew. The Democratic Platform made no formal announcement of a break, but many of their members slipped away over the next few weeks and months. Alexander Buzgalin, the leader of the Marxist

Platform, stayed in the party and was elected to the central committee.

The only remaining issue was whether the party would wither away or be driven out of existence by decree. The Democratic Platform had already called for society to be 'de-ideologized' (see page 116). There were a few local, non-workplace party branches, known as territorial branches, meant for pensioners and housewives, but most branches were in the workplace. In several of these a movement towards 'de-partyization' began spontaneously. The Baltic Shipping Company in Leningrad had led the way in February 1990 by reassigning the 200 political commissars on its ships to other jobs. Abolishing party branches became a key issue in the miners' strikes in the spring of 1991. At Uralmash, the huge machine-tool plant in Sverdlovsk, workers held a referendum on the party's future. Some 65 per cent of the workforce took part, and 87 per cent of these voted to expel the party branches from the premises. How far such moves would have gone on their own in other factories is hard to say, but during his campaign for the Russian presidency in the summer of 1991 Yeltsin promised to ban organized political activity at workplaces throughout the Russian federation. On 20 July he issued a decree to do so.

Ironically, the decree unintentionally gave some tactical help to Gorbachev, who was about to put a new draft party programme to the central committee. Members were so incensed with Yeltsin's move that they gave little time to the programme. Under the title 'Towards Humane, Democratic Socialism' it played down the role of Marxism, allowed religious believers to join the party and promised that the party would operate exclusively by parliamentary means and make coalitions with other parties. Although the central committee was still dominated by conservatives, they accepted the programme as a basis for discussion. This was not a sign of some road-to-Damascus conversion. Alexander Yakovlev described it a short time later as 'pure opportunism, extraordinary opportunism, typically Communist opportunism'.[3] Soon afterwards, during the August coup, the party leadership was to display an even greater example of opportunism. While its general secretary was a prisoner in the Crimea, it sat on its hands to wait and see whether the putsch would succeed.

The Party is Over

The Chinese president once said to me, 'If you want to wish your biggest enemy the worst possible thing, wish him to live in a time of reform.'

ANATOLY LUKYANOV, JANUARY 1993[4]

It was 3.30 p.m. on 23 August 1991, two days after the coup collapsed, and the party branch in the international department of the Communist party's central committee was about to hold the most extraordinary meeting in its history. Although the department worked full-time on party matters, its members regularly assembled for a 'party meeting', like any one of the tens of thousands of party branches around the Soviet Union.

When they entered the room that afternoon, few could have guessed what the priority item on the agenda would be. Point number one, they discovered to their astonishment, was baldly entitled 'The case of Comrade G. I. Yanayev'. The Communist party's general secretary, Mikhail Gorbachev, had been detained incommunicado for three days. The rest of the leadership was the target of massive criticism for failing to take a strong line during the coup. Outside the party's headquarters in Moscow's Staraya Ploshchad' angry crowds had gathered and were calling for it to be banned. Yet, in this atmosphere of turmoil and crisis, the main thing the international department's party organizer thought of doing was to discuss whether Comrade Yanayev, who had already been arrested for leading the coup, should remain a member of the party. It was an amazing triumph of formalism over common sense – this time the last.

'Don't call him comrade,' muttered one member, I was later told by Andrei Chuzhakin, a senior party official who attended the meeting. 'Just G. I. Yanayev.' Yanayev had become a member of the branch in the international department when he was promoted to the Politburo as the man in charge of the party's international links. Under new rules which Gorbachev had brought in to strengthen the rights of the rank and file, only a member's branch could recommend his or her expulsion, and not the apparatus as had happened in the past.

The mood of the meeting was firmly in favour of expelling Yanayev, but a debate raged for half an hour over what formula to use for justifying the deed. One suggestion was that he be expelled 'for attempting to interrupt the democratization process which the CPSU was conducting'. 'He didn't interrupt it. He speeded it up,' someone objected. When the vote was taken, the decision was unanimous, though only sixty of the branch's 200 members had turned up.

Item two on the agenda was the wording of an appeal to the central committee and all party members to call an emergency plenary meeting and party congress. By then it was 4.15 p.m., and the crowd outside the building was becoming more excited. The central committee headquarters stands on a small hill. Its ground-floor windows are relatively high off the street and the tall doors of polished wood are curtained in green, making it impossible for outsiders to catch a glimpse of the interior. In the old days the road in front of the building was sealed off by police who blew the whistle on any unofficial car which tried to drive in. Pedestrians were able to hurry past, but no loitering was allowed. To guard against possible bombs, there were none of the little metal urns for cigarette butts and other rubbish which used to grace Moscow's other streets. That day the police had retreated and were watching nervously as a crowd stood outside the front of the building. Yet even here the numbers were relatively small, perhaps 2000 at most, and they were not taking any risks. This was not like the mass of people which had stormed through the state security police headquarters in Berlin, ransacked the party buildings in Sofia, or seized Ceausescu's palace in Bucharest two years earlier.

The crowd was pushing at an open door. Its wishes had already been met from on high, as the branch meeting of the international department was to discover. A colleague came into the room and announced, 'Comrades, listen. The intercom has just announced that by order of the mayor and with the consent of the president of the USSR we have to leave the building by 5 p.m. Anyone who remains after five will be arrested. You can take your personal items with you, but it is prohibited to remove any documents. On your way out you may be subjected to a body check.' The meeting quickly voted to support the appeal to the central committee and then adjourned. Chuzhakin gathered up his things and escaped by a side door. He and his boss crossed the road to the Hotel Rossiya and ordered a shot of vodka to calm their nerves.

Officials from the Russian prosecutor's office sealed the front doors of the building with lead-wire to prevent access and ensure nothing was tampered with. Some of the crowd moved round to the back of the building and jeered at party workers as they emerged. I watched as several women carrying plastic bags were stopped and told to show what they were taking home in case they were hiding papers. They looked frightened. 'Leave them alone,' someone in the crowd shouted. Once again, there was little passion in it.

The previous evening, when a crane worked for several hours to remove the huge statue of Felix Dzherzinsky, the founder of the Soviet security police, from its tall plinth outside the Lubyanka, the spectators had been more lively and animated, but they had dispersed quickly once the statue had gone. By 11 p.m., when only the pedestal was left like a fat shoulder stump from which the arm has been amputated, a few drunks were wandering through the square, looking more bleary than exultant. The symbol had gone, but the substance, the KGB headquarters, remained unsealed and intact. After the collapse of the Soviet Union five months later, it continued to house the Russian ministry of security, with a staff cut of no more than 30 per cent. This roughly compensated for the loss of the other republics, and left Russia with the same number of secret policemen as before.

The Communist party was less favoured. The performance of its leadership during the coup was a disgrace. Although formally it was not part of the coup, almost every figure in the state committee for the state of emergency was a senior party member. The party's official newspapers, including *Pravda*, published the texts of all the coup leader's pronouncements. More important, the Politburo failed to condemn the coup or take any action to save its general secretary Mikhail Gorbachev.

Ivashko was recovering from an operation at a sanatorium near Moscow when a friend rang early on the first morning of the coup and told him to turn on the radio. When he heard what was happening, Ivashko immediately drove to Staraya Ploshchad' and called a meeting of about eight members of the central committee secretariat and Politburo. Oleg Shenin, one of the plotters who had been to see Gorbachev the previous afternoon, read them a draft of a telegram which he suggested they send to party branches round the country, but according to Alexander Dzasokhov, a Politburo member who attended the meeting, Shenin hid his visit to the Crimea from them.[5] He behaved as though he knew as little about Gorbachev's state of health and the whole affair as they did. Accepting the state committee's line that Gorbachev was too ill to run the country, the meeting not only did not criticize the coup plotters' actions, it approved Shenin's text which called for support for the coup. The only addition it made to the draft was a sentence urging Communists to obey the constitution. The result was a cunningly worded telegram which allowed the party to look both ways at once. It went out in code at 10.50 a.m. on the first day, saying 'From the central committee to all republican, territorial and regional committees: in connection with the introduction of a state of emergency take measures for Communists to act in line with the state committee for the state of emergency. In practical actions be guided by the constitution of the USSR. We will inform you later about a plenary meeting of the central committee and other meetings.'

Dzasokhov later claimed that the party leadership could not have taken stronger action. 'There were very senior people on the state committee for the state of emergency. Moscow was quiet. There were no tanks on the street at the time,' he told me. Ivashko was even less repentant. A year after the coup I saw him by chance at the constitutional court during its hearings on whether Yeltsin had been right to ban the Communist party. 'It wasn't a putsch. They didn't arrest anyone,' he argued. 'It was an illegal action done by people who should have consulted the party.'[6] Ivashko conceded that 'it is hard to find any justification for cutting off the president's phone, but to call it a putsch would stretch the dictionary definition.' The deputy general secretary said he had not called an immediate plenary meeting of the central committee because the first question members would have asked him would have been about Gorbachev's health, and he had no information to give them.

Georgy Shakhnazarov, Gorbachev's close aide, arrived at Staraya Ploshchad' on Tuesday 20 August after managing to get back from the sanatorium where he was staying near Foros. He found Alexander Dzasokhov and urged him to take firm action. 'The party and its leadership had only one chance to save itself. It had to condemn the conspiracy immediately and resolutely, call on Communists to oppose it, and demand the president's release. Otherwise, it would be the end of the CPSU,' Shakhnazarov remembered telling him.[7] Dzasokhov was struck by the argument and claims he prepared a statement, announcing his resignation from the Politburo. But he did not yet hand it in. His colleagues also chose to wait and see. Later that day Dzasokhov talked with Ivashko and another central committee secretary, Yuri Stroyev. They decided to try to fly to Foros to see Gorbachev, but when they approached acting president Yanayev on Wednesday morning he said that only Ivashko could go. Yanayev urged Ivashko to fly with Lukyanov, Yazov and Kryuchkov that afternoon.

The party leadership's equivocation was repeated throughout the country. Most regional party committees obeyed the secret telegram sent from Moscow on Monday morning. Only on the second day did some of the republican party leaders, acting out of nationalism rather than loyalty to Gorbachev, start to condemn the coup. In Russia's cities the party was inactive. No senior party officials went to the White House to express their solidarity with Yeltsin. Alexander Yakovlev and Eduard Shevardnadze who crossed through the barricades and visited the headquarters of the resistance on the Tuesday night were no longer members of the party. They had resigned shortly before the putsch.

Given the leadership's unwillingness to recognize the gravity of the coup, the farce that was played out at the international department's meeting on Yanayev two days after the coup's collapse was understandable enough. At the very same moment, though, a tragedy was going on a mile away in the chamber of the Russian parliament in the White House. Gorbachev was answering questions from Russian deputies. What he no doubt thought would be a friendly session from a broadly sympathetic audience turned out to be a roasting, led by Boris Yeltsin. It was the nearest thing to a revenge match after the humiliation which Yeltsin had suffered when he was sacked as Moscow's party boss by the city party committee in 1987. Now the roles were reversed. Gorbachev was the victim, still not aware how much his authority had dwindled during the coup. Yeltsin was the supreme leader. There was one big difference between the two occasions – television. While Yeltsin's humiliation in 1987 took place behind closed doors in sight of some 300 party officials, Gorbachev's grilling was shown live around the world. It was Gorbachev's grimmest hour, and how this most emotional of politicians remained so calm under the stress remains a mystery. He did not lose his temper. His voice did not rise as the blows rained on him. Perhaps he was still in a kind of trance, unable to understand what was going on and where events were leading. What we saw that day was the inexorable beginning of the end of the Soviet Union, as power slipped from its president to the president of Russia. In turn, this meant that Gorbachev's own time in power was up.

Gorbachev appeared not to realize this. In Foros he had told us with pride that the coup plotters did not understand that the country had changed over the six years of perestroika. Their · attempt to turn back the clock and reverse the changes was bound to fail. Now Gorbachev himself behaved like a man out of touch. He did not seem to understand how much the balance of power had changed in the three days of the coup. The Communist party's Politburo had destroyed the last few shreds of its authority. Russia's leadership had taken supreme power into its hands. Gorbachev thought the defeat of the coup was symbolized by the return of the ousted president to his seat in the Kremlin. But it was another president in another place who had defeated the coup.

Gorbachev's first mistake was not to go to the White House immediately on returning to Moscow. Had he gone to the balcony with Yeltsin and publicly thanked the Russian president and the crowds below, he might have reaped some sense of triumph and created a bond with the few who openly resisted the coup. He failed to appear there either on his immediate return or the next day. It was left to Yeltsin to savour the victory as a quarter of a million people gathered outside the White House on the Thursday afternoon beneath a blazing blue sky after three days of drizzle. 'You braved the danger, cold and rain to defend Russia and democracy,' he told them. The pre-Soviet red, white and blue flag of Russia was raised over the building as the crowd cheered. Gorbachev, meanwhile, spent Thursday in the Kremlin. It is true there was pressing business. He had to appoint new men to run the army, the ministry of the interior, and the KGB. He sacked his foreign minister, Alexander Bessmertnykh, for not having denounced the coup. Gorbachev wanted to speak on the phone to a string of world leaders. But he should also have thought of his constituency at home. Once again the contrast was drawn: Yeltsin the politician of the Russian masses; Gorbachev the man of closed-door meetings, happier in recent years to press the flesh of crowds in foreign capitals than meet his own people.

Ironically, like the coup leaders whose only public appearance on their first day in power was an evening press conference at which they performed disastrously, Gorbachev left the Kremlin on Thursday only for a press conference. It was almost equally disastrous. The answer which most people remembered, as vividly as Yanayev's shaking hands the Monday before, was Gorbachev's comment that the Communist party could still be reformed. The remark flew in the face of reality, and made Gorbachev look as though he was somehow defending its leadership. The next afternoon, as Gorbachev stood at the rostrum of the Russian parliament, looking like a defendant in the dock, Yeltsin indicated that the Communist party was over. 'Read the minutes of the last meeting of the Soviet government,' Yeltsin ordered him. 'Read them out aloud.' Gorbachev obeyed. The minutes showed that the government, all but one of whose members was a party member, had accepted the coup. Then in Gorbachev's presence Yeltsin triumphantly signed a decree suspending the activity of the Russian Communist party and ordering the confiscation of Soviet Communist party property on Russian territory. Gorbachev looked appalled, as he tried to plead above the deputies' deafening applause, 'Be democratic, be democratic'.

The next day he saw Alexander Yakovlev at the funeral of the three young men killed when tanks tried to break through a barricade across an underpass under Moscow's ring road. He asked Yakovlev to come to the Kremlin afterwards. Shakhnazarov, Vadim Medvedev, a former ideology chief, and Chernyayev were with Gorbachev. They suggested Gorbachev call a plenary meeting of the central commitee or even a special party congress. 'I was the only one who wasn't a party member,' Yakovlev told me with a smile later.[8] The guru of perestroika appeared to relish the moment when he had helped to finish the party off. 'I said we were discussing a phenomenon which no longer existed. The party had sentenced itself to death. Finished. During the coup we didn't hear any announcement from it. Later it said it did not support the putsch. But it didn't object to it either.' For three days, Yakovlev argued, the party kept quiet. What party in any developed democratic country would have done nothing if its general secretary was arrested by rebel forces, he asked? Like other observers in Moscow, Yakovlev was aware that Kryuchkov, Yazov and other hard-liners had for months been trying to resist a new Union treaty but he had not expected the coup. I went to see him three days before it, and asked him about the rumours. 'From my experience I don't think there can be a military coup. I don't think they can take power, or do anything with it,' he predicted.[9] Later that day, Yakovlev was telephoned by his wife who had just heard on the radio that the central control commission, the party's disciplinary watchdog, was demanding his expulsion. He resigned in anger, denouncing what he called the influential Stalinist grouping which had formed inside the party's leadership.

After listening to Yakovlev that Saturday afternoon Gorbachev took the momentous decision. He would resign as general secretary, recommend the central committee to meet to suspend itself, and leave it up to the party's millions of ordinary members to decide whether to try to start again. As he ended a lifetime in the party Gorbachev could not bring himself to make the announcement. It was left to a news reader on television. In a special broadcast at 9.30 p.m. on Saturday evening, 24 August, prime-time programmes were interrupted for the bulletin. 'After all the dramas of the preceding days – the tanks in the streets, the barricades, the liberated president, the euphoria, the funeral, the triumph of Boris Yeltsin – could a man in a grey suit on a television programme reading a piece of text on a desk in front of him really change the world?' I wrote in the *Guardian* next day. 'He could, and he did. "The central committee of the Communist party of the Soviet Union should take the difficult but honest decision to disband itself. Republican Communist parties and local party organizations will decide their future by themselves." In another country it would be like pronouncing the end of the monarchy or the voluntary winding up of a religion, an abdication of something with which people had grown old, for good or ill, for all their lives . . . For several million party members it must have been as though the announcer were handing them a gun and asking them to do the decent thing.'

Although he had resigned as Yakovlev recommended, Gorbachev left it to ordinary party members to decide what to do. He later said this showed he did not think the party was a political corpse. His position was that he could no longer work with men who had betrayed him. 'The structures had discredited themselves and did not deserve my support. They had also discredited themselves in front of the people . . . This does not mean that all Communists had given up their socialist convictions.' [10]

Gorbachev's point was important, since he was accused by hundreds of Communists, including such former colleagues as Ligachev and Ryzhkov, of betraying the party when he resigned. It was an extraordinary continuation of old-fashioned thinking, as though the leader is all-powerful and does not have the right to resign, while the rank and file must wait for new instructions. Ligachev, Ryzhkov and all the others who complained of Gorbachev's 'treachery' could have tried to rally the party after August, had they wished. It was only some months later when they saw Yeltsin's popularity beginning to slip that most of them made any move to do so.

One reason for the party's immobility, even though it was still a legal entity, appeared to be fear. Knowing that Russia was not a democratic country, Communists were worried about a witch-hunt by revenge-seekers once they were seen to be on the run. The morning after Gorbachev's resignation I went round to the Oktyabrskaya hotel. With its vast, marble-lined entrance hall and tropical creepers hanging down from the balconies, it was one of the most luxurious hotels in Moscow. It belonged to the central committee, and that Sunday it was the only piece of party property in Moscow which had not been sealed. An elderly driver in a black Volga parked by the entrance at first refused to admit he was a party member. A grandfather and war veteran, he remembered driving Andropov, the high point of thirty years behind the wheel. When I expressed surprise that a person without a party card could have had such a job, he confessed he had kept quiet because 'it's difficult to be a party member now. I'm worried about persecution, a return to 1937'. While he seemed to represent the kind of members who would quietly fade away, inside the hotel I found the other type, the officials who would try to make money out of their old positions. A young security guard was relaxed about the party's collapse. 'During the coup it dug its grave,' he commented without regrets. Yuri Ivanov, the duty manager, was equally calm. Two years ago, he pointed out, the hotel had started opening its doors to non-party foreign visitors and charging them hard currency. He was sure this trend would accelerate. He was right. The hotel remained under Russian government control and soon changed its name to 'Presidentskaya'.

Although the party had been declining for months, the almost total desertion of its membership after the coup was astonishing. In Eastern Europe and the former East Germany Communist parties re-formed themselves into socialist ones, the CPSU fizzled out with barely a sound. This was all the more remarkable in that the Eastern European Communist parties could legitimately be accused of long-term collaboration with a foreign power. For decades they had been creatures of the Soviet Union. Although they had sometimes tried to resist Soviet pressure, and in two cases, in Hungary in 1956 and in Czechoslovakia in 1968, the Russians used troops to bend the local Communist party to their will, the parties refused to die. They always re-emerged as Moscow's ally. In spite of this tainted past, they survived again in the post-Communist world, albeit drastically reformed. In most cases the old leadership resigned or was voted out, but thousands of rank-and-file members stayed loyal to their beliefs and ideals and refounded the party under a new name. In Lithuania the old pro-independence Communist party, under its existing leader Algirdas Brazauskas, changed its name and programme, and was re-elected to power in November 1992.

In Russia it was different. The first few efforts to revive Communist parties made little headway. Nina Andreyeva, the Leningrad chemistry lecturer who had caused a storm with her notorious letter in 1988, formed an All-Union Communist party of Bolsheviks. In

November the Russian Communist Workers' party was founded with a programme of Stalinist nationalism. Some former members of the Marxist Platform set up the Russian Party of Communists. Roy Medvedev, a leading historian and member of the last central committee, founded the Socialist Party of Working People. It did not claim to be the heir to the CPSU's property, but unlike the other new Communist groupings it accepted the last party programme, 'Towards Humane, Democratic Socialism'.

The first meeting of this 'left-wing party of socialist orientation' was a sad affair. 'Seventy-three years of Communist rule, in spite of all the distortions, have not destroyed the idea of socialism in Russia,' Medvedev told a dozen friends. He was crouched on a sofa with three people in a room of the Hotel Rossiya. One person was sitting on a table which supported a television set. Another squatted on a bedside table. Anatoly Denisov, a member of the Supreme Soviet – leaning against a refrigerator – criticized Gorbachev for not summoning the central committee before resigning. In these pathetic surroundings the group discussed the text of its manifesto. 'There is a chance of creating a strong party of like-minded people, united round good ideas, generous goals, and comradeship,' it declared optimistically. But it accepted that the old party could no longer be revived. 'However bitter it is, we must recognize that the CPSU in its former guise has exhausted its usefulness and lost public confidence. It bears great responsibility before the millions of ordinary people whose hopes it betrayed and who have had to carry the heavy burden of conflict, lawlessness, and poverty.'

In Eastern Europe the former Communists had one advantage over their Russian equivalents. General elections were held soon after Communism fell. This helped to give the ex-Communist parties a chance to focus themselves and campaign for support. In Russia there were no early elections. But this is not the whole explanation for the Communists' initial retreat from politics. Fear of a witch-hunt was a factor, though this also applied to Communists in Eastern Europe. Yeltsin banned both the Russian and Soviet Communist parties in November 1992 but this did not make it illegal for Communists to found new parties. The main reason for apathy seemed to be that the party had long ago become a structure of government and a career ladder for individuals. It had no independent existence as a force for change or a reservoir of new ideas. There was a wider element. In Russia, the former Communists were not alone in being unwilling and unable to put together a new organization and gain substantial support. Public alienation from active politics for over seventy years and the weak tradition of party life in Russia before 1917 guaranteed that party politics of any ideological stripe would find it hard to grow.

A year after Yeltsin banned the party, the Constitutional court ruled that his decrees were only valid in part. Local branches were entitled to resume their activity and elect new structures and a new leadership. By then Russia had lived through a year of painful economic 'shock therapy'. Many Communists were angry with Yeltsin's role in destroying the Soviet Union. The whole party had had time to recover from its shock. The fact that earlier fears of a witch-hunt had not been borne out was also a source of encouragement. In early 1993 party members began 're-registering' and electing delegates to the 'Second Extraordinary Congress of the Russian Communist Party'.

It was held in a former trade union rest-home in pleasant woods on the northern outskirts of Moscow. Organizers said three applications for halls in the city had been rejected. The party claimed to have 450,000 members, making it the largest in Russia, though this was only 3 per cent of its former peak. The sensation was that seven of the twelve men arrested for their role in the August coup attended. Most had only just been released from more than a year's imprisonment pending trial. Delegates gave them a standing ovation. It was as though no one wanted to believe that anything had changed. The past eighteen months were a nightmare, which the morning sunshine, as it glinted on the crystals of fresh snow outside the rest-home, was driving away.

Although the revived Russian Communist Party had to operate in new multi-party conditions, its stance was more conservative than that of the defunct CPSU, at least of its Gorbachevian wing. While the Socialist Party of Working People could be described as social-democratic and in line with the last programme statement adopted by the CPSU in 1990, the Communist Party of the Russian Federation, as it was renamed, was backward-looking. The major change was its talk of a strategic alliance with nationalist forces. Its new leader was Gennady Zyuganov, a forty-nine-year-old former teacher and party propagandist from Oryol who became a Central Committee official in the last years of perestroika. He later joined the National Salvation Front (see Chapter Thirteen).

The party took advantage of growing public disenchantment with Yeltsin's fast-paced economic reforms, and won 12 per cent of the vote in the December 1993 elections. By then a number of its members had helped to form the Agrarian Party, which won almost 8 per cent, largely from peasants unhappy with the moves to break up the collective farms and with the increase in prices which discouraged investment in agriculture. Taken together, this gave the Communists and their allies a fifth of the national vote.

While the revived Communists fiercely attacked Yeltsin, they were even more scathing about Gorbachev. He was seen as a revisionist who had betrayed Communism and set in motion the forces which had destroyed the Soviet Union. While the extent of Communist support in the 1993 vote surprised those observers who had always described the system as one of terror which no one would willingly uphold, it was a reminder of how much the old Stalinist machine had already changed in the Brezhnev years. It had softened politically, and was able to produce economic stability and modest growth. A large number of Russians felt comfortable with it and had no fear of Communists.

The vote also showed once again why Gorbachev had failed to reform the party. The conservatives who obstructed him and later plotted his downfall were not just a group of officials cut off from public opinion. They had substantial backing for their cause.

3

End of Empire

7

The Imperial Rings

In Europe we were hangers-on and slaves,
whereas to Asia we shall go as masters.

FYODOR DOSTOYEVSKY, 1881[1]

We don't have the strength for Empire; and we don't need it.
Let it fall from our shoulders. It only weakens us, exhausts us,
and hastens our destruction.

ALEXANDER SOLZHENITSYN, SEPTEMBER 1990[2]

After the fall of Communism, there was much talk of nationalism as a new danger in Russia. Humiliated by the loss of empire, shattered by the drop in living standards that went along with the transition to the market economy and set loose from the false ideology of Marxism-Leninism, Russians would turn to nationalism for moral and psychological support, it was predicted. The argument had little evidence behind it, but Western analysts seemed to be reverting to old Russophobic instincts now that the Soviet Union no longer existed. There always had to be bad news out of Russia. If it was not aggressive Communism, then it would be aggressive Russian nationalism. As a headline in a British newspaper put it, 'The bear snarls as nationalism stirs'.[3]

In fact, Russians abandoned their empire with remarkable ease. The speed and smoothness with which they gave up control over vast territories which had been linked to them for decades was in marked contrast to the agony and turmoil which accompanied other recent withdrawals from empire. There was no Rhodesian-style unilateral declaration of independence by Russian settlers in Estonia when it became clear that Moscow was giving up, as had happened when the British government had announced the surrender of its last African colony a generation earlier. No Russians in Latvia turned to terrorism or set up their own army like the French pieds-noirs in Algeria.

As the empire Stalin built in Eastern Europe collapsed in 1989, not a single Russian shot was fired. The 'buffer zone' which was meant to protect Russia's Western approaches was conceded with barely a murmur. Only in the Baltics was there any shooting, but it did not last long and was quickly repudiated by the political leadership in Moscow. The use of Soviet troops in Tbilisi in April 1989 and Baku in January 1990 was aimed at protecting the local Communist party at its request rather than at preserving a Russian imperial position in Georgia and Azerbaijan. At that time the latter had hardly begun to be called into question. Even in Moldova, where the bloodiest confrontations between Russians and non-Russians took place, the issue was not a case of resistance to de-colonization, as the Moldovan claim to Transdniestria, the area in dispute, was historically unfounded. The area was only joined to the then Moldavia by Stalin after the war, in order to compensate for other regions he awarded to Ukraine.

One reason for this non-violent decolonization, particularly in Eastern Europe, was its speed. Events happened so fast that there was little time for hardliners in Moscow to put pressure on Gorbachev or demand that he resist. Decolonization was also helped by Russian political passivity. The absence of a civil society which made it hard for democratic reforms to put down roots helped in the case of the retreat from empire. Whatever they thought about it, few Russians were going to protest, or take political action to stop it. The priority for Russian families was their own economic security and the daily struggle to make ends meet. Perestroika inside Russia, and the doubts over whether it would bring the material improvements which Gorbachev promised, were more important than foreign policy.

Another key factor was the restraint shown by the independence movements in Eastern Europe. They were careful not to provoke the Russian garrisons or to take any action against individual Russians which might have produced cries for retaliation. But the overriding reason for the bloodless Soviet withdrawal was Gorbachev's decision to permit democratization and not to intervene to stop the process. It took four years of perestroika for Eastern Europeans to realize that this was his policy for their region. After so many brutal Kremlin clamp-downs under previous Soviet leaders, it was hard to believe that Gorbachev was different. When the message was finally understood after his various visits to the region and particularly his United Nations speech in December 1988, the house of Stalinist cards in Eastern Europe collapsed in a matter of weeks.

Russians had three empires. The oldest was the 'inner one', the fourteen non-Russian republics which together with Russia formed the Soviet Union. It included almost exactly the same territory as the Tsarist empire. Only Finland and parts of Poland had been lost. Like classic empires, it was acquired over a period of more than a century through setting up trading posts, followed by military conquest and civilian settlement. But there was an important difference. Unlike the empires of the Western European powers, which were almost entirely overseas, and officially described as the metropolis and the colonies, the Russian empire was a land ring of foreign territory joined to and running round core areas inhabited by Russians. In the discussions leading to the establishment of the Soviet Union in 1922, the Bolsheviks repeatedly talked of Russia as the centre and the other republics as the periphery.

The two 'outer' rings, Eastern Europe and the Third World, were of much more recent origin. The Third World empire meant little to Russians. It was a loosely-knit group of outposts which mainly provided Moscow with military facilities in its drive to achieve global strategic parity with the USA. It consisted of other socialist countries, like Cuba or Vietnam, or those which Soviet planners described as 'states of socialist orientation', such as Angola, South Yemen and Ethiopia. When Gorbachev's new policy of 'solving regional conflicts by political means' took wing, the ties with these states were quickly abandoned with minimal public discussion, let alone resistance in Russia. On the contrary, the wave of anti-Communism in the mainstream press, particularly after the August coup, gave enthusiastic support to the breaking of these ties, and regimes such as Fidel Castro's which survived the sudden cuts in Russian aid were regularly vilified. The arms supplies and financial support which were organized by the Communist party for various Third World guerrilla forces and liberation movements were listed as criminal in Boris Yeltsin's indictment of the party before the constitutional court in 1992.

Russian attitudes to non-European peoples are as infected with racism as those of other colonial powers. They may be worse in that few Russians had the opportunity to meet or become friendly with non-Europeans. Unlike most metropolitan capitals, Moscow never felt like the heart of an empire, a cross-roads of different races and skin colours. Because of the restrictive system of residence permits the vast majority of its population were Slavs. The few Georgians and Azerbaijanis who became prominent in the private markets under perestroika were quickly dubbed the 'blacks'. Vietnamese workers in hostels and communal flats in provincial Russian towns were regularly picked on by the police. By the end of perestroika African students in Moscow were living in fear, and many did not dare to go out at night except in groups.

The bloodiest and most expensive Soviet involvement in the Third World was the decade-long intervention in the Afghan civil war. Around 15,000 Soviet soldiers died in the struggle. When Gorbachev announced that he wanted to withdraw Soviet troops, the decision was almost universally welcomed in Russia. For hundreds of thousands of working-class and peasant families this was Gorbachev's greatest achievement. The fear that their sons would die in a distant war was removed as he brought the boys home. There was no nostalgia in Russia to match the mood among some older people in Britain when the troops withdrew from 'East of Suez'. There were no conservative complaints of an 'Afghan syndrome', allegedly sapping the country's will to stand up for its foreign interests, like the 'Vietnam syndrome' which Henry Kissinger and Ronald Reagan deplored in the USA in the late 1970s and 1980s as an irritating restraint on Washington's ability to intervene in the Third World.

In Russia it was rather the reverse. The painful experience of Afghanistan was accepted by virtually every politician and the public as a warning against interventionism. This made it easier for Russians to retreat from the Caucasus and Central Asia, and even to accept the collapse of the Soviet Union. Fighting between the two southern republics of Armenia and Azerbaijan over Nagorno-Karabakh was seen as a repetition of the Afghan civil war, a futile struggle between wild mountain peoples, in which Russian troops had better not take part. 'Let them kill each other without us' was the usual street reaction. Russians reacted approvingly when Yeltsin said he would withdraw the troops from beyond the Caucasus in 1992. Ethnic troubles in Central Asia produced the same popular response. When troops were used in the Northern Caucasus, Abkhazia and Tajikistan, it was mainly to protect fleeing Russian civilians and evacuate refugees rather than to seek to change the political map. Although these were undeniably 'colonial' operations, they were part of a general strategic withdrawal. They were not intended to preserve an empire which most Russians recognized was finished.

Eastern Europe was a different case from Afghanistan and the Third World. This 'outer ring' of empire was more closely connected to the Soviet Union. It straddled the historic route from which two invasions of Russia had come this century, and it was hardly surprising that Stalin and his successors would want to keep it under close control after the victory over Nazi Germany in the Second World War. Khrushchev set up the Warsaw Pact to give an international flavour to the arrangement. The pact was an alliance in name only since Russian forces dominated it and Russian generals took all the strategic decisions. Most Russians accepted this arrangement without question. With its huge Soviet death toll, the war left a deep scar in virtually every Russian family. Its impact was kept alive by countless ceremonies at war memorials in every town and population centre. Twelve- and thirteen-year-olds in Pioneer uniforms took turns to stand stiffly at attention, guarding the eternal flames. Young couples laid wreaths on their wedding day. The Cold War was also a deeply ingrained concept. Official state propaganda that the Soviet Union faced a military threat from NATO, a re-armed West Germany and the West in general was widely believed.

Yet even this Eastern European empire was felt and seen differently in Russia from the way the populations of Western powers viewed their colonies. For one thing Russian civilians did not settle in Eastern Europe, except for a handful married to local people. The Soviet presence in East Germany, Hungary, Czechoslovakia and Poland consisted of an embassy, military garrisons, the KGB, and a few state-owned trading concerns. The military garrisons were isolated from the local population and Soviet troops were under strict orders not to fraternize, except under controlled conditions, the so-called 'Druzhba' or 'Friendship' occasions when delegations met local groups and visited schools or factories. Otherwise, troops were confined to barracks and military exercises. In Czechoslovakia before the invasion of 1968 and in Bulgaria and Romania throughout the post-war period there were no Soviet troops.

Second, Eastern Europe was largely out of bounds for Russian tourists. Occasional groups travelled there, again under tightly supervised conditions. Eastern Europe, although in theory part of the Soviet 'camp', was considered alien territory. The traveller, crossing by train from the Soviet Union to Poland, would find barbed wire and watch-towers on the Soviet side of the frontier. It was as though Poland was already part of 'the West', a threatening culture from which Russians must defend themselves. This marked the third peculiarity of Russia's Eastern European empire. The centre did not feel it had a civilizing mission towards the colonies or was in some way their cultural mentor. It is true that Stalin and his successors laid down certain 'socialist' principles which the states of Eastern Europe had to follow as they built Communism. But everyone was aware that this was ideological orthodoxy in the service of Russian state security. Any sign that the Eastern Europeans wanted to develop their own model, like the Prague spring of 1968, was firmly squashed, not because it might end up with a different form of socialism but because the Kremlin saw it as the first step towards leaving the Soviet camp. Even if they had never travelled to the area, Russians instinctively knew that Eastern Europe had a long cultural history and was economically more developed than the Soviet Union. Since its people lived better, there was little scope for Russians to 'civilize' them.

Germany was slightly different. In spite of its high level of development, Germany had produced Fascism, and Russians were anxious that it should not happen again. The Russian occupation of East Germany, and the creation of the German Democratic Republic, were meant to install and foster institutions which would root out Fascism once and for all. Russians were taught that the people of the GDR were 'good Germans', the heirs of the pre-war anti-Fascist German Communist party, who were anchored in peace-loving socialist democracy thanks to Soviet advice and control. In East Berlin, on the fortieth anniversary of the GDR, even as he was privately urging Erich Honecker to reform before it was too late, Gorbachev publicly put the traditional sentiment in clear terms: 'In their reminiscences our many war veterans note that when they entered German territory Soviet servicemen regarded the Germans not only as a defeated enemy but also as a great people which had been driven to disaster by criminal authorities and found themselves in need of help to stand up again.'

When the local Communist parties lost power in Eastern Europe in 1989 and moves towards unifying Germany began, some of the older generation's doubts and fears revived. By then the geo-political situation had changed. Visits by Gorbachev to West Germany, the warmth of relations with the USA and the climate of accelerating nuclear disarmament, as well as the passage of time since 1945, encouraged Russians to believe that the Germans had repudiated their Nazi past. The notion of a Soviet retreat from Eastern Europe and the GDR was not seen in a tragic light. There were important constituencies in the Soviet army's high command and some senior Communist party figures who were angered by the process, but they had little support among ordinary Russians. Talking to Russians in those heady days of 1989 and 1990, I rarely found concern over the end of the Eastern European empire. In as much as Russia was believed to have subsidized its allies by selling them cheap oil and gas and giving them expensive arms most people welcomed what they thought would be the saving of money involved in the change.

The collapse of the Soviet Union was altogether more traumatic. Although many Russians felt the other republics had also been a drain on their economy, their attitudes were shaped by deeper and more complex feelings. The Soviet Union had existed for almost seventy years and was the continuation of the Tsarist empire. Even if the Baltic states had only been reincorporated in 1940, Russians knew that they had been Tsarist before that. Russians travelled regularly throughout the Soviet Union with no sense of crossing borders, or needing to learn other languages. They assumed everyone would or should speak Russian. In the Slavic republics, Belarus and Ukraine, many Russians were barely conscious that there was a local culture. They took holidays on Ukraine's Black Sea coast without ever thinking it was outside Russia. Official state propaganda that Soviet rule was benign, and that a unique multinational state had been created, seemed to most Russians to coincide with reality. Whatever they thought about the disparity between word and deed when it came to the economic achievements of state socialism, on the national front the picture looked correct. While local languages and customs survived in the republics and autonomous regions, virtually everyone could speak Russian. The dream of an eventual merging of the other nationalities into a new whole, which, it went without saying, would be dominated by Russia, seemed plausible.

For most of the twenty-five million Russians, or one out of every six Russians who lived outside the borders of the Russian Federation according to the 1989 census, the collapse of the Soviet Union was a special disaster. Tens of thousands of Russians had settled in Central Asia by the late 1930s, as teachers, doctors and political administrators. Others came during and after the Second World War during the wave of industrialization, as workers, engineers and managers. By 1989 they almost outnumbered the native populations in Kazakhstan and the capital cities of Kirgizia and Uzbekistan. Russians had also emigrated to the Baltics in vast numbers. Because of their strategic location, the three Baltic republics were riddled with rocket bases, garrisons and other military facilities, and many Russian officers chose to stay there when they retired. Much of the industry of Latvia and Estonia was built and staffed by Russian workers. None of these categories had special economic privileges which would make their standard of living higher than that of the local population. When they began to be spat at or attacked in the nationalist press as 'occupiers' and 'parasites' they found it hard to understand. Nevertheless, once the Baltic independence movements emerged and grew in strength, many Russian settlers decided to throw in their lot with them rather than contemplate having to return to the chaos of Russia.

In Central Asia the settlers' life-style was often poorer than that of the indigenous populations. One of the surprises of travelling there in the dying days of the Soviet empire was to see how difficult life was for Russians. Unlike Europeans in Africa, the Indian sub-continent and South-East Asia, the Russians in Central Asia did not enjoy large homes and palatial clubs staffed by servants. I remember Boris Khatuntsev, a journalist on the main Russian-language paper in Fergana, a town in the valley of the same name which links three republics, Uzbekistan, Tajikistan and Kyrgyzstan. The valley is one of the most fertile in the region, rich in vines and fruit. To reach his flat we walked past the walls of spacious Uzbek compounds where children played in the grass and goats grazed. Married sons built their own rooms in the extended family's compound, which became a hive of mutual support. By contrast, Khatuntsev, like most other Russians in the town, lived in a tall block of flats with the same chipped concrete staircase and creaking lift which one found anywhere in central Russia. He and his wife had two cramped rooms for themselves and their daughter.

Fergana town was laid out on a grid by its nineteenth-century Russian conqueror General Skobelev, with tall poplars shading its dusty streets. In 1989 a group of local Uzbeks massacred around forty Meskhetian Turks, descendants of a small minority deported to the area by Stalin. The motive for the ethnic killing, and what triggered it off, was still unclear several months later when we were in Fergana, but the episode had poisoned ethnic relations. Khatuntsev wore a permanently anxious look, although he clearly liked the town where he had lived for more than twenty years after moving from Voronezh in central Russia. He told us that 20,000 of Fergana's 130,000 Russians had already left, and most of the rest were planning to follow. 'The Turks have gone. The Tatars have gone, and all the Jews. I have nowhere to go. If I go back to Voronczh, who will give me a flat?', he asked desperately. Khatuntsev and his wife, Natasha, came to the area because she was a champion Soviet cyclist. 'We preferred the climate and the good roads,' she explained as we sat on the sofa in their small living-room, crouching over the supper table. 'I have cycled for Uzbekistan fourteen times, but now when I go to the bazaar, they say, "Go back to Russia". When they don't give me my change, and I ask for it, they just repeat, "Go back to Russia",' she added with understandable bitterness.

Two years later, after the USSR had collapsed, we stopped in Namangan, another town in the Fergana valley. A middle-aged woman in a green raincoat was standing at a bus-stop, the only Russian in a crowd of sixty people. She was the fifth generation of her family to live in the town. She told us proudly that one of her ancestors had been the commissar of foreign affairs of Turkestan and knew five Central Asian languages. His statue stood in the republic's capital, Tashkent. 'I understand almost everything in Uzbek, but I can't speak much,' she admitted. By then local feelings of nationalism were growing and the scope for inter-ethnic contact had begun to narrow. 'We've separated from the Uzbeks now. There's a mutual distancing going on.' Her grown-up son was in Moscow, her daughter was planning to leave, but she and her husband would stay. 'I suppose we'll be isolated. But my mother is old. She wept when we said we were thinking of leaving, so we'll stay,' she said wistfully. 'We've already decided to become Uzbek citizens. But we wanted the children to go, for our peace of mind.' An overcrowded bus drew up at the stop and she squeezed in with her shopping bags. It was a fleeting conversation, but her sad, dignified face seemed to express the end of a Russian era which would never be restored.

The Russian imperial paradox was that Russians did not feel the Soviet Union was an empire. This made it even harder for them to understand the views of non-Russians than it was for other imperial nations. The first outbreak of nationalism in any of the Soviet republics during the Gorbachev era occurred in Kazakhstan in 1986 when the Politburo in Moscow appointed a Russian to be the first secretary of the local Communist party. Hundreds of Kazakh students marched through the capital, Alma Ata, with placards saying, 'Are we worse than Russians?' Nikolai Ryzhkov, the Soviet prime minister, later admitted, 'It never came into anyone's head that the nomination of a Russian could provoke an explosion of national pride.'[4]

Russians rarely had any sense that they were living in a multi-racial or multi-cultural community, in which Russians were just another national group with no greater claims than anyone else. Their numerical strength combined with political dominance to produce an understandable feeling that there were Russians and others, and the 'others' were supposed to learn Russian and accept Russian leadership. 'Each of us Russians has a genetically determined perception of our country in all its scale, vastness and diversity of language, culture and people. We are all like this, and we feel fine in this country,' said Gorbachev in September 1990. Thanks to that pronoun 'our', what was intended as praise for Soviet internationalism sounded more like complacency and pride in a Russian empire.

In contrast to the Western European nation-states, Russians had created their empire at the same time as their state, and not as a subsequent development. Russians did not go overseas, as the English, French, Dutch, Spanish and Portuguese had done, to capture territories inhabited by different people as a conscious extension of the economy of the national state. The Muscovite principality was busy uniting other Russian cities, like Novgorod and Vladimir, into its orbit at roughly the same time as it was expanding outwards across the adjacent land-mass against non-Russian peoples. The two processes, forming a Russian state and acquiring a non-Russian empire, went hand in hand. This was not always a policy of unprovoked aggression, but often, as with Ivan the Terrible's capture of Kazan on the river Volga, in order to win back from the Tatars lands which had been Russian before. In the north-east the expansion was designed to drive out and create buffers against Polish and Swedish invaders. Along the Black Sea the outsider was the Turk. Only in the case of Central Asia and the settlement of the Pacific Coast in the second half of the nineteenth century was Russian expansion prompted by the imperialist urges typical of Western Europe, the desire for trade routes, raw materials, and control over territory so as to deny them to others.

In Central Asia, unlike Eastern Europe, Russians felt they had a civilizing mission, first to bring universal literacy and then industrial development. It was the classic colonial outlook which ignored local cultures and customs and did not recognize their antiquity. In Transcaucasia, where Georgia and Armenia had ancient civilizations and as high a level of literacy as Russia, the Tsars and their colonizing emissaries felt they were creating a belt of Christendom against the Islamic masses to the south, and in particular against the influence of Ottoman Turkey.

After the fall of Tsarism, the Bolsheviks held on to the empire they had inherited. Compared to their Russian predecessors, they felt they had an extra justification as missionaries of enlightenment. They had won the civil war against the White counter-revolution, and one reason – historically true – was that their policies towards non-Russians were more intelligent. The civil war was in fact two wars: one between the Reds and the Whites; the other a war of the non-Russians against both. Several of these non-Russian peoples managed to get away or were taken over by other foreign rulers. Finland and Poland won full independence on their own. Bessarabia joined Romania, and five Byelorussian-Ukrainian provinces were conquered by Poland. The Tsarist empire's three Baltic possessions, Estonia, Latvia and Lithuania, became independent with the help of German and Allied forces. But the impressive Bolshevik achievement was that more than 80 per cent of the Tsar's former subjects became citizens of the Soviet federation, and half of these people were non-Russians. Evan Mawdsley in *The Russian Civil War* comments accurately: 'The multi-national Russian empire, the famous "prison of people" did not break up, a remarkable development in an age of nationalism.'[5]

One factor was that the Russians outnumbered each individual national minority, with the exception of the Ukrainians, by about fifteen to one. It was hard for most of them to achieve independence by force of arms. But the Bolsheviks' social revolution had some attraction for the minorities. Whereas the Whites proclaimed a goal of 'Russia, One and Indivisible' and branded the other nationalities as separatists, the Bolsheviks rejected Russian chauvinism. They offered various forms of autonomy and self-government, however flawed these might eventually turn out to be.

When the civil war was over and they set up the Soviet Union in 1922, the Bolsheviks argued fiercely over the role of the republics. The arguments which Gorbachev and his colleagues were to use during the debate on writing a new treaty for the Soviet Union were remarkably similar. *Izvestiya TsK KPSS*, the journal which the central committee started during the wave of glasnost, published twenty-two previously unknown documents in 1989 on the way the party organized the formal unification of Byelorussia, Ukraine, Armenia, Azerbaijan and Georgia with the Russian Soviet Federation of Socialist Republics, the RSFSR.[6] Publication of the documents was intended to show that Lenin wanted a federation of sovereign states rather than the unitary state which Stalin created, since Gorbachev wanted to prove the Leninist credentials of his own project for a looser union.

In August 1922 the Politburo ordered the drafting of a resolution on relations between the RSFSR and the 'independent' republics. As general secretary of the party and people's commissar on national affairs, Stalin produced a draft which recommended that the governments and economic organs of the republics would be formally subordinate to directives from the RSFSR. Foreign affairs, military issues, railways, post and communications would be the exclusive responsibility of the RSFSR. Only education, health, agriculture and justice would be under republican control.

In a letter to Lenin, Stalin justified his recommendations by saying Moscow had to choose either to let the republics have genuine independence and settle matters of common interest by talks between equals, or to unify them into a single economic whole. The latter option would include 'genuine internal autonomy' of the republics in the sense of language and culture. Lenin opposed Stalin's plan and persuaded the central committee to propose that the non-Russian republics form a federative union with the RSFSR rather than becoming part of the RSFSR. The central committee resolution also gave the republics the right to secede. Lenin argued that the whole internationalist movement in Asia and elsewhere would be undermined if Russians appeared to be overriding non-Russians' interests.

Lenin's looser plan for the republics was meant to be only a temporary, tactical concession, since his other writings make it clear he favoured a gradual switch to a unitary state. He hoped the non-Russians would soon see its advantages. Although Stalin was forced to adopt Lenin's position on the federation, he acted on his own with the smaller nationalities. Some were given language rights. Others, such as the Kurds, were suppressed. The boundaries between republics often left peoples of the same group divided by administrative boundaries. In the Caucasus scores of different ethnic groups with separate languages ended up in a crazy quilt of adjacent autonomies. Later, Central Asia was carved into five republics which did not properly correspond to the ethnic distribution. Samarkand and Bukhara, two mainly Tajik cities, were deliberately put into Uzbekistan, to try to weaken the Tajik republic. The drawing of borders was not always done maliciously, as there is no such thing as a perfect map, since people rarely live in compact ethnic units. Whatever the original motives, many of the border issues were to explode into conflict under perestroika.

After Lenin's death, Stalin's gradual creation of a totalitarian political system and a centrally planned economy inevitably altered the nature of the Soviet federation. While a union of separate republics remained in form, Stalin changed its substance. Almost everything came under central control, a position which remained until well into Gorbachev's time. The economy was treated as a single whole and central ministries in Moscow decided to build factories on green-field sites without any chance for republics to object. On the principle that industrialization was progressive in itself, republics were given industries which they did not want or need because it fitted in with Moscow's plans. Central Asia was seen as a vital supplier of minerals and raw materials. Natural gas fields and mines of uranium and precious metals were opened without any control by local politicians or economic managers. At the same time vast areas of Central Asia were made over to cotton production, with serious effects on people's health from the excessive use of toxic chemicals and without proper consideration of the effect on local agriculture or the water supply. The catastrophic drying-up of the Aral Sea is only one of the consequences of the error of thinking of water as a free resource. Between 1960 and 1990 the population of Central Asia increased by 140 per cent, enormously raising the demand for food and water. Yet cotton production rose in the same period by 100 per cent. It was delivered to the rest of the Soviet Union at low prices as a 'patriotic duty', and Central Asia did not even have many textile factories of its own.

One element of the initial 1922 idea of a looser federation generally remained in place under Stalin. The Kremlin decided to rule the Union via a network of local Communist élites from the various republican nationalities. It was not like the French in Algeria, or the British in India and the settler colonies such as Rhodesia and the Cape, with their large civil service recruited and brought out from the metropolis. Although Russian was the official language, the concession of formal independence within the Union as well as local language rights in schools and the media meant that non-Russian cultures survived. At times the authorities in Moscow tried to Russify the republics through changes in educational and language policy, but there were also periods when central policy shifted back towards encouraging local culture. In every republic far more books were published in Russian than in the local languages. Stalin manipulated the alphabets to try to cut people off from their past. In Central Asia Arabic script was first replaced by Latin and then a decade later by Cyrillic. In all the republics Sovietization was often little more than a camouflage for Russification. None of these campaigns destroyed local languages and cultures completely, although it was taken for granted that non-Russians who wanted to progress up the Communist ladder of power – and there was no other – would have to learn Russian and be assimilated into Russian culture.

By the end of the 1980s the Soviet Union, itself the continuation of the Tsarist empire, was the longest-surviving European empire. But Russians did not perceive it as that. They felt the Soviet Union was genuinely an international family. Because it was one continuous land-mass with no customs posts or border controls, it felt like a single harmonious country. Russians saw no sign of the resentment and tension which non-Russians felt towards them.

When this empire began to unravel, far faster than any other

European empire had done, the process was a trauma. The British, French and Portuguese saw their empires come to an end over a period of roughly thirty years. In France and Portugal the process caused a major upheaval in the political system. In Britain the psychological wounds took a long time to heal. Russians went through a similar ordeal in thirty months. Fortunately, the empire collapsed from the outside in. The first of the imperial rings to break was the outer one in the Third World, symbolized by the retreat from Afghanistan. This part was widely welcomed by Russians. Eastern Europe went next. Here the mood was general indifference, in a few quarters mild concern. When the Soviet Union itself started to crumble, Russians were already prepared psychologically. There was shock, anger and worry over the economic consequences, as the impact of broken trade links led to a general slump in production in Russia as well as in the former Soviet republics. But the damage was containable politically. The main reason was simple. The freedom which encouraged Eastern Europe and the Soviet republics to break from Moscow's embrace was the same freedom which Russians were also enjoying, thanks to Gorbachev's perestroika.

Farewell, Afghanistan

Slowly, very slowly, after the war, you begin to think, to imagine, to remember what happened – the ruined villages, the expressions on people's faces.

YOUNG VETERAN OF THE AFGHAN WAR, MOSCOW,
FEBRUARY 1989

One of the strangest sights on the first day of the August coup was an advancing column of tanks beside the Manezh exhibition hall in the centre of Moscow. The hall was holding an exhibition on the

Afghan war, and the front of the building was covered in large camouflage nets. From a distance it looked for a moment as though the tanks were blasting through the netting and emerging from the hall itself, a surreal re-enactment of the long Soviet intervention in Afghanistan. It was only a fleeting image, but it served to link the horror and futility of sending tanks into the Soviet capital with the horror and futility of the Afghan war.

Inside the Manezh, the exhibition offered an equally powerful combination of images. It had been put together by an *ad hoc* committee which included representatives of the defence ministry, the foreign ministry and the KGB, alongside grass-roots veterans' groups and the Committee of Soldiers' Mothers, a tough body of lobbyists who had became one of the sharpest thorns in the Soviet army's side. Sensibly, they did not try to agree on a common interpretation of the war. We would still be waiting for the exhibition if they had. Instead, they decided to share a common space and let each point of view speak for itself. The one issue on which there seemed to be general consent was that Leonid Brezhnev was vain and senile when he launched the intervention in 1979. The first exhibit was a video clip of the old boy having yet another Hero of the Soviet Union medal pinned to his chest by a doddering fellow-member of the Politburo. The award must have irritated the professionals in the high command as much as it did the conscripts and their families.

The army section of the Manezh exhibition was a display of rockets and weaponry, plus a straightforward summary of dates and battles, and the casualty list of some 15,000 Soviet dead. It suggested the army had performed a difficult task with honour. The foreign ministry exhibited a series of large cards with expanded quotations from secret cables sent to Moscow by Soviet diplomats in Kabul, recounting conversations with Hafizullah Amin, the former president of Afghanistan, and their replies. This part of the exhibition was designed to show that far from being a hasty affair the invasion was a response to repeated requests from Amin. The cables demonstrated how often the Afghan leader had asked the Soviet Union to send special forces and police disguised as advisers if necessary, to protect his regime, and how often Moscow had refused – until December 1979. The KGB display was especially revealing. It explained how a crack unit, the same Alpha team which reconnoitred Boris Yeltsin's White House during the 1991 coup, assaulted Amin's palace at Darulaman and killed him. The central flaw in Moscow's futile effort to legitimize its intervention – the fact that the man who did the inviting was liquidated by his guests – was being made plain to Russians for the first time.

Pride of place in the unofficial exhibits was given to the Committee of Soldiers' Mothers for a sad collection of mementoes of their children: letters from the front, hat badges, photographs in cheap, gilt frames. There was an impressive gallery of drawings and pictures by Russian artists. Most of them were official war artists, sent to Afghanistan on delegations, to portray the heroism of the men under fire. Invariably their pictures gave a deeper and gloomier view than they were meant to show. A canvas by Gennady Zhivotov was called 'Boys playing at War'. It showed Brezhnev and Babrak Karmal, who became Afghanistan's leader after the invasion, signing a Treaty of Friendship. Their sharp outlines, flanked by an array of advisers, filled the lower third of the frame. Above them, cut off at the knees and hovering in a ghostly half-light against the khaki mountains of the typical Afghan landscape, were four young Russians in uniform. Two were wounded, two seemed physically unscarred, but all four stared out of the canvas with the same dull pain.

Every war is the private soldier's war, but the nine-year adventure in Afghanistan hit the infantry more than most others. Conscripts were sent to a battleground of which they knew nothing and with no convincing explanation of what they were fighting for. Vague talk of performing their 'internationalist duty' did not prepare them. Many spent months on guard duty at mountain outposts with no relief or break. Others were bundled into helicopters for hair-raising search-and-destroy missions. If they were wounded, little was done for them when they returned to the Soviet Union. Unlike the veterans of the Second World War, disabled 'Afghantsy' had to fight an ungrateful bureaucracy to get wheelchairs and ground-floor flats. If they died and their bodies were recovered, coffins were sent back to their families but no explanation was given as to how or where their sons had died. Their tombstones – at least until well into the Gorbachev period – were not allowed to mention they had fallen in Afghanistan. Anything which might have revealed the war's casualty toll, or have become a focus of public protest, was forbidden.

Shortly before the Soviet withdrawal was completed in February 1989, I invited four young veterans to come round and watch a Yorkshire Television documentary on the Afghantsy. I had first met Igor a few months earlier at a strange reception offered by a group of disabled American veterans of the Vietnam war. They had come to Moscow out of what they described as a sense of kinship and solidarity with another generation of victims of super-power intervention in the Third World. I met Igor and his friends several times more after the Americans had left. They came from the industrial suburb of Lyubertsy, a shapeless collection of high-rise flats and waste ground about twenty miles east of the city centre. They had formed a club with forty members and were collecting money to erect a monument to their dead friends, since the state was clearly not going to build one. The video impressed them. It was more detailed and sensitive than anything shown on Soviet TV, they said. They quickly started reminiscing, as they often did. 'They never trained us properly,' Igor complained. 'All they told us was that Afghans were different and had a different climate. They gave us a pocket dictionary and a bit of paper telling us what not to do. That was it. "Don't fraternize. Don't look at women. Don't go into cemeteries. Don't go into mosques".'

The veterans found that most Russians still did not want to think about the war, or why it happened. It was the same with most Afghantsy. Only a minority bothered. Leonid, who stayed in the army after Afghanistan and became an officer, said that most soldiers felt they were doing their duty: 'Your motherland sent you. Many people stay thinking like that. Actually, you still feel that but over and above it you wonder what the point was.' Their first glimmerings of the war's political context came when they realized how little contact they had with Afghans, the people they were supposed to be helping. They talked to only a few adults, usually uniformed police troops. The rest were the small Afghan boys who hung round the barracks, offering cheap drugs. 'You felt the aim was to get us hooked,' Yuri commented. He remembered being in Herat in February 1985 when Soviet troops captured a group of forty-eight mojahedin. Later they got hold of a copy of *Izvestiya* which said the Afghan army had captured them. Another time they found a cache of rebel weapons. Army photographers posed Afghan troops in front of them.

Gorbachev's great achievement was to end the pretence of a non-war, to start honouring the conscripts for what they had done and to bring the troops home. The decision to withdraw preceded his change of line on Eastern Europe. In July 1985 the central committee, according to a secret document released in November 1992, instructed newspapers and television to step up their coverage of the war, authorizing them to show 'individual cases' of Soviet casualties, 'no more than one a month'.[7] It had always been stated Soviet policy that the troops would leave as soon as a stop was put to 'interference' from outside by mojahedin trained and armed by Pakistan, Iran, China and the USA. The Soviet Union had been negotiating on this basis for more than four years through a United Nations mediator. In October 1985 the Politburo decided to 'speed up the withdrawal', the implication being that the troops would all leave. But Gorbachev was not making the withdrawal unconditional. He hoped for international guarantees and the survival of a friendly regime in Kabul. The new policy had three prongs: to give more impetus to the United Nations' negotiations over Afghanistan; to try to find a more broadly based government in Kabul; and a final push to try to seal the border with Pakistan so as to prevent the mojahedin from coming in and out. Gorbachev hinted at the new policy in his speech to the twenty-seventh party congress in February 1986, a year after coming to power. He referred to the Afghan war as a 'bleeding wound'. His phrase was new, and although he did not announce a timetable for a pull-out, it was clear that he was recognizing the war could never be won.

In Afghanistan, however, unlike Gorbachev's tactics in Eastern Europe, there was to be no policy of letting existing leaders stay in power. Sensing the new mood in Moscow, Karmal launched a ten-point policy of 'national reconciliation'. It gave concessions to private businessmen, allowed for the establishment of a multi-party system, and widened the revolutionary council. But Gorbachev felt it was not enough, since it offered nothing to Afghans outside the country, particularly to the mojahedin. To achieve a peace settlement they would have to be encouraged to join negotiations or return. Gorbachev decided that there would have to be a change of leadership in Kabul if a negotiated settlement was to be reached which could allow the Russians to leave with dignity. Speculation, apparently promoted by Soviet officials, that Karmal was ill mounted in the small diplomatic community in Kabul. On a visit to Kabul in March I saw him for an hour and a half in what turned out to be his last interview with a foreign correspondent. Smoking one Western cigarette after another, he claimed that his health was fine and that the policy of national reconciliation was serious. A few days later he was summoned to Moscow for what was described as a private visit. In a government villa on the Lenin Hills, Gorbachev gave him the news that the Russians were going to pull out. 'His expression changed. He looked distraught,' recalled Nikolai Ryzhkov, who was sitting beside Gorbachev.[8] 'Now?', asked Karmal. 'Not immediately,' Gorbachev told him, 'but we're going to do it. We're not going to sit in Afghanistan for ever.'

Gorbachev wanted more political changes to prepare the ground for the withdrawal. Karmal opposed them. The Russians kept him in Moscow for a month, an enforced delay which prevented him attending the anniversary celebrations for the April 1978 revolution which had brought the Communists to power in Kabul. His absence was a clear political signal that he was out of favour, especially when an article in *Pravda* attacked him on the same day for being too slow in introducing reforms. Even under Andropov, the Russians had been saying privately that Karmal would have to go as part of a diplomatic agreement to secure a new government in Kabul which would not threaten Soviet interests. Russian diplomats told this to Diego Cordovez, the United Nations' negotiator, as early as 1983.[9] Moscow's main fear was always that the USA would use Afghanistan as a base against the Soviet Union, after it was forced out of Iran when the Shah fell to the Khomeini revolution. The Russians were less interested in the internal set-up in Afghanistan than in its geo-strategic position.

Gorbachev changed the policy by insisting that Karmal go even before a settlement was in sight. The central committee of the People's Democratic party of Afghanistan met and bundled Karmal out of office as general secretary in May 1986. He was replaced by Mohammed Najibullah, a tough, bull-like figure who had trained as a doctor but became head of the secret police. Najibullah came from one of the main tribes along the Pakistan border, and the Russians hoped this could help him create a buffer zone which would prevent mojahedin infiltration. Karmal still had some political support in the party and he was allowed to stay on as Afghan president.

Soviet troops, beefed up by crack special forces, made their last effort to seal the border. Like similar efforts to clear the Panjshir valley, one of the main approaches to the Kabul valley from the north-east, the move was only a temporary success. As soon as the troops withdrew, the mojahedin returned with the support of what was left of the local population. Thousands had fled to Pakistan. By November 1986 the political overtures which Moscow wanted to be made to the mojahedin and the other exiles had failed to bear fruit, partly because Karmal, as president, was still able to block them. When the Soviet Politburo met in Moscow on 13 November, Gorbachev told them, 'We must finish this process in the swiftest possible time'.[10] Anatoly Dobrynin, the central committee secretary for international relations, took the bluntest line. 'Karmal must be got rid of. But we must remember that, as far as national reconciliation is concerned, not a single member of the Afghan Politburo supports Najibullah,' he asserted.

Vladimir Kryuchkov, then the deputy KGB chief, was sent to Afghanistan to tell Babrak Karmal that he had to make way for another man. It was a classic operation which Karmal later recounted to a Soviet reporter from the newspaper *Trud*. The reporter was able to talk to him on several occasions during his virtual arrest in a villa near Moscow for four years. He published his story after Karmal returned to Afghanistan in 1991.[11] 'A senior figure came to see me to recommend that I go to the Soviet Union to rest and get well,' Karmal told him. 'When you want to go back, we will bring you back here. Then this senior figure added, "Now, comrade Karmal, you should be very careful. Your enemies may kill you." "No," I replied. "Only my friends can kill me now." ' Karmal was replaced as president by Najibullah, who now had a freer hand. He promptly offered a six-month ceasefire, and then suggested meeting mojahedin representatives on neutral ground – an offer which for the first time accepted them as equals. Later in 1987 he promised them seats in the cabinet and suggested the exiled king could return to Afghanistan.

Gorbachev and Shevardnadze became increasingly impatient. They repeatedly shortened the timetable for the withdrawal of Soviet troops from the original offer of four years. They had hoped to arrange an end to the civil war at the same time as Soviet troops withdrew, but the mojahedin and their principal backers, the Pakistani army high command and the USA, were against this. The new Afghan leader's offers to the mojahedin were turned down out of hand, since the mojahedin expected to win a prompt military victory once the Russians left. When accords were finally signed in Geneva in 1988 they provided for a Russian withdrawal over a period of only nine months. Very little else was agreed. There was no ceasefire, no end to outside arms supplies and no plan for continuing negotiations. The United Nations' mediator was merely asked to try to promote 'an intra-Afghan dialogue'.

On the day the last Soviet units were preparing to cross the River Oxus, Afghanistan's northern border, to Uzbekistan and home, I flew from Moscow to Kabul. The Afghan capital had been

abandoned by Soviet troops some days earlier, and Russian friends
questioned my sanity. It would be my fourth visit to the country
since the Soviet invasion, and I felt sure the Najibullah regime
would hold out for a long time after the Soviet withdrawal. It
seemed cowardly not to put my faith to the test. The mojahedin
were hopelessly divided, spent much of the time fighting each other
and had failed to capture and hold any major Afghan city during
the war so far. They had the support of much of the rural
population but this was not enough to mount a full-scale offensive.
To capture the capital would require a degree of co-ordination that
they had never shown. The best field commander, Ahmed Shah
Massoud, who operated in the north-east, could interrupt the
highway from the Soviet border to Kabul but was not in a strong
enough position to capture the capital. The population of Kabul,
which had suffered from indiscriminate rocket attacks by the
mojahedin, seemed in no hurry to embrace them. There was no
sign of any political activity in the mojahedin's favour, no protest
strikes or demonstrations. The educated élite did not endorse
Najibullah with any enthusiasm but they were more afraid of the
kind of society which the Islamic fundamentalists, who dominated
the mojahedin forces, wanted to build. A crucial final factor was
that the Soviet Union intended to go on supplying the country
with food, fuel and arms supplies. For all these reasons Najibullah
survived for over three more years. His fall came when the political environment changed. Yeltsin's government, in the shadow of
the collapsing Soviet Union, opened talks with the mojahedin
towards the end of 1991 and agreed to stop supplying fuel to the
Afghan army. The Afghan leader had already made a serious
mistake. He helped the process of disintegration by upsetting the
tribal balance in the north of the country, when he appointed a
Pashtun general in place of a Tajik in the city of Mazar-i-Sharif.
The move, coupled with the news of the new Russian attitude,
caused dissension and some panic at the top of the regime. When
General Rashid Dostam defected and joined forces with Massoud's
wing of the mojahedin, leaving the north undefended, the die was

cast. On the point of arrest by rebels from his own side, Najibullah
fled to the United Nations' compound in Kabul. Senior minsters
of the regime, now thoroughly demoralized, started talks with the
mojahedin and let them enter the capital without a shot being fired.

The myth of Najibullah's imminent collapse in 1988 was partly
fed by exaggerated accounts of the mojahedin's military prowess.
There was a popular notion that the arrival of the American Stinger
shoulder-fired missile had won the war and made the Russians give
up. The doughty mojahedin were shooting down too many Soviet
helicopters and making search-and-destroy missions too costly, it
was claimed. But it was March 1986 when Gorbachev took his
decision to change the leadership in Afghanistan and start the
political concessions which would lead to an early withdrawal,
whereas the Stingers did not start to come into use until the end of
that year. At the time Gorbachev made up his mind, the evidence
was that Soviet forces had stabilized the military situation in the
country, perhaps even marginally widening their areas of control
round the three main cities, Kabul, Mazar-i-Sharif and Jalalabad.
On my visit in March and April 1986 I was taken under escort to
places farther from the three cities than had been allowed before.
But control of the cities and the ability to run supply convoys on
the roads between them were not enough to win the war. Two-
thirds of the country's population was beyond the government's
reach, in refugee camps in Pakistan and Iran or in villages in
mojahedin hands.

The Russians did not lose the war. They realized after six years
that they could not win it, though in the case of an intervention
aimed at pacifying a country, this amounts to failure. The remarkable thing was that the Soviet high command accepted this
without objection. Even in the early years of the intervention,
before Gorbachev came to power, there were no signs that the
military were demanding massive reinforcements, unlike their
counterparts in the USA during the Vietnam war. The original
invasion force of 100,000 men was raised by only 15 per cent
over the period of the war. This appears to confirm later disclosures

that the generals never wanted the war in the first place. After Soviet troops withdrew, no generals complained that the politicians had lost the war by not giving the army the tools to do the job. There was no talk of 'nuking' the mojahedin or bombing their bases in Pakistan. During the November 1986 Politburo meeting Marshal Sergei Akhromeyev, chief of the general staff, delicately blamed the politicians. 'There is not a single piece of land that the Soviet soldier has not conquered. Despite this, a large chunk of territory is in the hands of the rebels. We control Kabul and the provincial centres but we have been unable to establish authority over the territory we seize. We have lost the struggle for the Afghan people,' he told the civilians.

In September 1988 after the first stage of the pull-out was completed, Najibullah appealed to Moscow to leave some troops behind to guard the highway from the north to Kabul. Ironically, the man he dealt with was General Valentin Varennikov. Varennikov later worked closely with the August putschists and was also involved in the Soviet army operations at the Vilnius television tower in January 1991. But while he was ready to use the army, even against Gorbachev's wishes, to preserve the Soviet 'inner empire' Varennikov saw Afghanistan as of little importance. According to secret cables he sent to Moscow, 'In our view, our troops must not stay in Afghanistan under any circumstances. Such a step would bring us nothing but harm. The Soviet Union would suffer an unpredictable blow on the international scene and at home'.[12]

In justifying their pull-out, the Russians used the argument that the regime of Hafizullah Amin, the leader the KGB later admitted to killing, had mistakenly pursued excessively radical policies and tried to force socialism down the throats of a conservative, Islamic people. Since then policies had been moderated and Islamicized to make them more acceptable to Afghans, but this meant the original revolution of April 1978 which Moscow was trying to defend no longer existed. The line was put most graphically by Alexander Prokhanov, writing in *Literaturnaya Gazeta*. 'Since those December days when the USSR's troops went into Afghanistan, the Kabul government's political course has changed many times. State meetings are preceded by a mullah saying prayers. The flag is no longer red and has a green Islamic stripe. The party has stopped talking about building a socialist society. It has renounced the monopoly of power, and proclaimed pluralism.' Prokhanov's conclusion from these changes was that, 'All this makes it possible to say that the original aims which the People's Democratic party of Afghanistan proclaimed have not been achieved . . . That being so, the presence of Soviet troops in the country loses its meaning. Departure is inevitable and logical.' [13]

The fact that it was Prokhanov who made this case was interesting. In the last months of the USSR Prokhanov was one of its most fervent defenders. He edited a nationalistic newspaper, *Den'* (Day), which was one of the strongest critics of Yeltsin. He also bemoaned the collapse of the Soviet empire in Eastern Europe because he feared that as a result of unification Germany would come to dominate the whole of Europe. Yet, like General Varennikov, this imperial hawk was willing to give up Afghanistan. His view-point well illustrated the difference between Russian attitudes to the various imperial rings. Even those who worried about the Soviet Union and Eastern Europe accepted that Afghanistan was not a prize worth keeping.

Eastern Europe

Each country can act independently. In the past
Moscow conducted the orchestra and everyone else listened.
This is no longer the case.

YEGOR LIGACHEV, BUDAPEST, APRIL 1987 [14]

The day after the Soviet invasion of Czechoslovakia in 1968 Alexander Yakovlev was sent to Prague to oversee Soviet journalists who were to cover the event and to help to set up a tame new Czechoslovak press. At the time he was deputy head of the propaganda department of the CPSU central committee, and this was a vital assignment. Officially the despatch of troops was described as friendly assistance, but Yakovlev was shocked by what he found. 'I saw gallows with effigies of Soviet soldiers hanging there. I saw graffiti, saying "Vanyka, go home to your Manyka". People were shouting "Fascists, Fascists". I wondered why we had come.'[15]

It was almost impossible for Yakovlev to leave the Soviet embassy. The building was crowded with the team sent from Moscow, plus resident diplomats who did not dare to go into the street. Yakovlev was particularly struck by the fact that several pro-Soviet members of the Czechoslovak party leadership were also sheltering in the Soviet embassy. Yakovlev applied to return to Moscow and five days later left. Whatever his private views, he suppressed them well enough to be given an award for his work in the post-invasion period. He continued as deputy head of propaganda for several more years. Neither then nor throughout the period of perestroika did Yakovlev make any public mention of his impressions of Prague, and he only felt free enough to divulge them after he had retired. Yakovlev summed up the experience as 'an important school for me. You cannot imagine how useful it was for me. . . . It had the greatest sobering effect.' Yakovlev was not the only senior figure with Czechoslovak experience who came to work for Gorbachev. Georgy Shakhnazarov had been in Prague. Ivan Frolov, who got to know many of the Czech reformers when he lived there in the early 1960s, resigned from a senior job in the central committee after the invasion. He made no public protest but went off to edit the journal *Voprosy Filosofii*, in disgust, as he now says, with the Soviet intervention.

Gorbachev himself visited Prague a year after the invasion with a delegation of members of the Supreme Soviet but at that stage he appears not to have decided it was wrong. When I asked him how he felt about the intervention on that visit, he reacted evasively, saying it was 'painful'.[16] He had never previously discussed his views on the subject in public. Since his first answer was ambiguous, and he could have meant a 'painful necessity', I pressed him a second time. 'They doled us out with very little information about what was really going on,' he replied. He only joined the central committee in 1971 and it was not until he came to Moscow in 1978 to be the secretary in charge of agriculture that his 'possibility of getting information was broader, though still limited'. He learnt then about what he called 'the alternative view of those events' and 'got access to closed material and books by foreign authors which were available to high-up people who were on the right distribution list'.

By 1979 when he became a member of the Politburo, he revealed, 'I already understood that there were signs of disease in the whole system which we called socialist and in the Eastern European alliance system.' Suppose as a member of the Politburo he had asked to see the archives on 1968 and the Czech events, would that have aroused suspicion? 'Absolutely, absolutely,' Gorbachev laughed. 'It was out of the question.'

In supreme power six years later, Gorbachev decided that Moscow must withdraw any threat of pressure on Eastern Europe. This was a view which was widely shared in the Politburo, including by people such as Yegor Ligachev who later came to lead the resistance to radical reform (see the remarks he made on a three-day visit to Hungary in 1987, quoted on page 174). Of course, few expected that the Eastern European Communist parties would lose power, just as they did not expect the CPSU to lose it in the Soviet Union. The feeling was that those countries like Poland and Hungary which were making political reforms should be encouraged while the conservative ones like East Germany, Bulgaria and Romania should be gently advised that they would do better to seek more popular support. Gorbachev wanted closer links with Eastern Europe, not looser ones. It was no accident that in one of his earliest pronouncements as general secretary he described the maintenance of close ties with Eastern Europe as his 'first commandment'.[17]

Just as perestroika was aimed at making the Soviet Union more efficient politically and economically, Gorbachev's initial hope was that Comecon, the Eastern European economic block, would become more effective. The Russians were annoyed at the way they subsidized the area with cheap oil and gas and in return imported consumer goods which were often too shoddy for the Eastern Europeans to sell in the West but were considered good enough for the Soviet market. They wanted more Eastern European capital investment to develop resources in the Soviet Union and more collaboration on high technology projects. In December 1985 Comecon adopted a fifteen-year programme on scientific and technical progress.

Gorbachev assumed that the Communist parties of Eastern Europe could be reformed in a similar way to the reforms he hoped to achieve in the CPSU. But a few of his colleagues were already thinking the unthinkable. Asked later whether he was surprised that the parties had to leave the political stage, Yakovlev said, 'Not at all. I expected it'. He had enough friends and acquaintances in Eastern Europe to know it was 'absurd to keep the system'. He had come to the view that Comecon, the Soviet-dominated Council of Mutual Economic Assistance, could not work on non-market principles and that the Warsaw Pact was merely a fig-leaf for Soviet power. 'If a war broke out, it would not be the Warsaw Pact that fought, but the Soviet Union. The Pact had no relevance to real life. It was something for the military,' he said.[18]

Ivan Frolov recalled that in 1987 Yakovlev suggested to him in a private conversation that what should happen in Eastern Europe was 'Finlandization'. By this he meant a kind of non-Communist social-democracy and a foreign policy of neutrality but good relations with the Soviet Union. 'I laughed, and didn't answer. We wouldn't have wanted that then,' Frolov told me.[19] A firm opponent of any use of force in Eastern Europe, Frolov said that the trouble with the Soviet position had always been an absence of any real political and economic leverage in the region. Outsiders exaggerated the Soviet Union's influence. A combination of their own errors and wrong policies, plus constant Western propaganda, had lost the Eastern European Communist parties most of their support before their leaders realized it. Gorbachev's delicate efforts to encourage change were meant to rectify this, but they were doomed.

No signs of the new political thinking on Eastern Europe emerged publicly in the early years of perestroika. At the twenty-seventh party Congress a year after he came to power, Gorbachev spoke only briefly and in general terms about the region. The Congresses, held once every five years, are occasions for laying out the broad lines of policy, but on this subject there was little sign of any change from the Brezhnev era, when the Soviet Union had continually put pressure on its Eastern European allies.

The first possible hint of a new policy emerged that summer, although it was so obscure that few people paid any attention. At the end of a conference in Stockholm on confidence-building measures in Europe, held under the auspices of the Conference on Security and Co-operation in Europe (CSCE) the Soviet Union in September put its signature to a document which included the following passage: 'The signatories will abide by their commitment to refrain from the threat or use of force in their relations with any state, regardless of that state's political, social, economic or cultural system and irrespective of whether or not they maintain with that state relations of alliance.' It was a small paragraph in a long text adopted by every European state plus the United States and Canada, and Moscow may have thought it was a purely formal commitment.

As Gorbachev started to travel in Eastern Europe the following year, what had been slowly crystallizing in Moscow took more definite shape. A new policy of non-interference began to be launched publicly. On a visit to Prague in April 1987 Gorbachev said, 'No party has a monopoly on the truth'. His remark was not a criticism of the conservative Czechoslovak leader, Gustav Husak, but rather a disclaimer, implying that Moscow was not going to force its allies to adopt their own perestroika. As such, it disap-

pointed many Czechs, who turned out in large crowds to greet
Gorbachev in the hope that he would help to restore the ideals of
the 1968 reform movement. The Soviet Union's perestroika looked
similar to what Alexander Dubček had been trying to do before the
Soviet-led invasion crushed it. Nevertheless, the non-intervention
policy was a major breakthrough, even though it logically followed
that Moscow could not start intervening to remove hardliners. This
would be as bad as the old habit of intervening to block progressive
reforms. Using nothing but the force of argument to persuade the
conservatives to reform was unlikely to work. Kurt Hager, the East
German ideology chief, dismissed Soviet perestroika as irrelevant.
'When your neighbour puts up new wallpaper, it doesn't mean you
have to too,' he said. In Moscow this was seen as a sign of 'how far
we had already lost control,' Ivan Frolov remarked of Hager's
comment later.

Gorbachev and Yakovlev hoped that when the message of military
non-intervention sank in, hardline leaders like Gustav Husak in
Czechoslovakia, Erich Honecker in East Germany, and Todor
Zhivkov in Bulgaria would realize they were on their own, no
longer able to rely on Moscow to bail them out of crises. The lesson
was that they had better make reforms while they could. The so-
called Brezhnev doctrine, under which Moscow had long claimed
that its allies' sovereignty was limited and could be overridden by
the Kremlin, was buried.

The first test of the new policy came in Poland in June 1989,
when elections were held and every Communist party candidate
was defeated. The Soviet Union had held its own contested elections
three months earlier, a move which made possible the experiment
in Poland. The Polish results were far more dramatic, and opened
the way for the first coalition government with non-Communists
since the war. (Poland's electoral law, which provided for contests
in only some of the seats, still left the Communists in a reasonable
bargaining position.) Yet, as in Sherlock Holmes's story of the dog
which did not bark, Moscow uttered no sounds of disapproval. It
was an astonishing reaction, in marked contrast to the way the

Chinese Communist party had just sent in the army to smash the protests in Tienanmen Square. 'One day we may look back on the first week of June 1989,' I wrote at the time, 'as a turning point in European history. What did not happen in Warsaw last Monday was as dramatic as what did happen in Beijing the day before.'[20]

The Polish Communists' defeat was a more clear-cut, decisive and fundamental challenge to that country's establishment than the demonstrations in Beijing were for the Chinese leadership. It was nationwide and reflected the mood of every class and interest-group. Yet no tanks moved into the streets and no troops emerged from the barracks. The Polish leader, General Wojciech Jaruzelski, was the same man who had brought in martial law with Soviet backing to try to break the Solidarity movement eight years earlier. Now he was offering a coalition government. The lesson of the years in between had not been lost on Jaruzelski or on Gorbachev and his associates in Moscow. Martial law failed and the Communists were obliged to release Solidarity's leaders from detention. Over the next few years the movement was allowed to regroup, revive and resume its activities. In Hungary, meanwhile, in the same week as the Polish elections, the Communist government was renouncing its monopoly of control over the army and offering the increasingly powerful opposition a share. Imre Nagy, the leader of the 1956 uprising who had been executed by the Russians, was reburied amid full national honours. There was no objection from Moscow.

Gorbachev publicly proclaimed his historic 'Hands Off Eastern Europe' policy to the Council of Europe in Strasbourg a month later. Arguing the case for a 'common European home' he said: 'The social and political order in some countries changed in the past, and it can change in the future too, but this is entirely a matter for each people to decide. Any interference in the internal affairs, or any attempt to limit the sovereignty of another state – friend, ally or any other – would be inadmissible.' In Poland a month later the smaller, traditionally pro-Communist parties in parliament broke ranks and joined Solidarity. The change of forces led to the appointment of a non-Communist prime minister, the respected Catholic intellectual and Solidarity activist, Tadeusz Mazowiecki. Again, Moscow's reaction was relaxed. *Izvestiya*, the newspaper which usually gave the government's line, described the development as 'natural'.[21] A few weeks later Gorbachev gave Mazowiecki a warm reception in the Kremlin.

Whereas divisions had arisen in the Politburo over Soviet domestic policy, the leadership was agreed that Moscow had to accept the changes in Poland. An analysis prepared for the Politburo and released when the central committee's archives were opened after the August coup showed remarkable agreement between such different people as Yakovlev, Shevardnadze, Yazov and Kryuchkov. Drawn up by a team representing their various departments, it said the Soviet Union should be 'ready to develop co-operation with the new Polish government, the Polish parties and the forces represented in parliament' and should start treating Poland as a genuine ally.[22] 'We must give up the practice of merely informing our allies ... we must carefully consider our partners' opinions,' it said. The document recommended that the Soviet Union should set up diplomatic relations with the Vatican, so as to improve its contacts with Polish Catholics and improve its image in Poland. There was no hint of any use of the Soviet Union's economic power to destabilize Poland – 'our interest is in the Solidarity leadership and government overcoming the economic crisis, and normalizing the political structure in Poland' – though it did say that the two countries should move to hard currency trading. It said that there were a number of factors which would help to maintain 'friendly and good-neighbourly relations' between Poland and the Soviet Union, even if their governments were no longer ideologically close. These were the geo-political situation in Europe, traditional links between Slavic peoples, the Poles' 'German syndrome', and the Polish economy's dependence on Soviet trade.

The joint analysis accepted that the new Polish government might eventually raise the issue of leaving the Warsaw Pact, but its thrust was to pre-empt any rise in anti-Sovietism in Poland by ensuring that Moscow behaved as correctly as possible. 'It is essential to find approaches in our contacts with the new Polish government which would not arouse suspicions of any lack of trust on our side, and would not lead to reducing the level of co-operation of our two states.'

Gorbachev's policy of non-interference applied to his relations with the Chinese communists also. It was adhered to with extra-ordinary diplomatic delicacy. In Beijing in 1989 he had been at great pains not to alienate his hosts by criticizing their hardline position while at the same time expressing discreet sympathy with the student demonstrators. He persuaded the Soviet press not to mention that the protesters had disrupted the visit, or to go into detail about their demands. Asked at his Beijing press conference how he would react if similar protests took place in Red Square, he looked tense for a moment. The Soviet and Chinese sides had agreed to abandon any common model of socialism but 'you are trying to push me towards telling the Chinese what to do,' he answered his questioner. Then, in effect, he told them. 'If a similar problem arose in the Soviet Union, we would discuss it, and try to solve it within the political process in the spirit of glasnost and democracy which we have adopted.'[23] The Tienanmen massacre took place several days after he left China, but he remained equally diplomatic. He took issue with the official Chinese portrayal of the students, when he told a press conference on a visit to Bonn that he did not have information to judge whether they were 'counter-revolutionaries'. Then he added, 'All of us are terribly concerned at what is happening in China. All of us want the process of reform and change in that country not to fail.'

Gorbachev was equally diplomatic with the Czechoslovak Com-munists. In response to the changes in the Soviet Union, the Czechoslovak party dropped Gustav Husak in December 1987 but in his place chose Milos Jakes, a man who was only marginally less hardline. Jakes visited Moscow in April 1989 and was given the same delicate message as the Chinese. Perestroika and democratization were helping to draw people into politics in the Soviet Union and to form a society based on consent rather than coercion. It was something which political leaders anywhere should think about. At the end of his talks with Gorbachev Jakes announced a number of changes, including plans for contested elections and an offer for non-Communists to become ministers. But the litmus test for any Czech leader was the invasion of 1968, and Jakes's line was unbudging. He justified it by saying that civil war had been prevented. 'We're not going to change the conclusions we made at that time,' he declared at his press conference in Moscow. In Hungary the Communist party leadership had recently revised its line on the Soviet use of troops and tanks to put down a popular uprising in 1956. The Czechs were not willing to go that far and Gorbachev was willing to honour that. True to his own non-interventionist line, he would not comment on the invasion unless the Czechs did so first.

Nevertheless, *Izvestiya* was allowed to give a gentle push. On the eve of the twenty-first anniversary of the invasion it published three long interviews with participants. One was with Kirill Mazurov, a Politburo member at the time, who revealed that he was sent to Prague disguised as a general in order to mastermind the operation. He told his wife he was going to Central Asia. General Ivan Pavlovsky, the Warsaw Pact's top military commander in 1968, described the Soviet forces in his *Izvestiya* interview as 'uninvited guests'. Nevertheless, both men still claimed the intervention was correct since it was the height of the Cold War and the Kremlin rightly feared the West was trying to exploit instability in Eastern Europe. A young paratrooper gave a different view. He told *Izvestiya* his unit was advised that West German forces were about to invade Czechoslovakia. When he arrived the reality hit him. Everything was peaceful and calm, and angry Czechs kept asking why the Russian troops had come. He was ashamed, but did not say then what he felt now: 'Forgive us, Prague.'[24]

Some three months after the *Izvestiya* pieces, a wave of student protests and industrial strikes brought down the Communist

government in Czechoslovakia. The new government, a coalition
of liberal Communists and non-Communists, promptly issued a
statement condemning the 1968 invasion. Within a matter of
days Gorbachev invited the Warsaw Pact leadership to Moscow
where they issued a statement deploring it too. Like the young
paratrooper in the interview, they were apologizing twenty-one
years late.

The trigger for the Czech protests was the toppling of East
Germany's Erich Honecker. In this Gorbachev played no small
part, thanks to his policy of non-intervention. But East Germany
was always the most sensitive link in the Eastern European chain,
and there were some hesitations by Gorbachev when the party's
control finally began to split. He had made several fruitless efforts
to suggest the East Germans should change, first on a visit to East
Berlin in May 1987, and then when Honecker visited his Black Sea
dacha. Yakovlev was sent to Berlin with a similar message in early
1989. The East German crisis began to boil up seriously when
Hungary opened its borders to Austria in September 1989 and
hundreds of East Germans who had travelled to Hungary under
visa-free rules crossed to Austria. It was like a small breach in the
Berlin Wall. Although the journey via Hungary to Austria was
long, East Germans had an open door for the first time. At
the same time other East Germans started climbing into the
grounds of the West German embassy in Prague to seek asylum.
The East German government protested to Hungary and tried
to enlist Moscow's support. Gennady Gerasimov, the Soviet
foreign ministry spokesman, described Hungary's opening of the
border as 'a very unusual and unexpected step'. The official
Soviet news agency TASS accused West Germany of violating
international law by giving the East German asylum-seekers
documents for travel to the West.

The statements were cleared with the Politburo and appeared to
indicate some anxiety in Gorbachev's mind. Yet they fell a long
way short of full support for Honecker's position. The foreign
ministry statement on Hungary's action was low-key and Tass

made no criticism of Chancellor Kohl and the West German government. Gorbachev was not willing to jeopardize the new détente with West Germany, with its promise of massive financial aid, which he had forged on his triumphant visit to Bonn in June. When he travelled to East Berlin three weeks later, his mind appeared to have been made up. Honecker must be reminded that Moscow would not intervene to save him. October 1989 was the fortieth birthday of the German Democratic Republic, and Honecker was determined to turn it into a jamboree. The Communist leaders of all the Eastern European countries, including Romania's Nicolae Ceausescu, attended. Ceausescu was particularly alarmed by the changes in Hungary and Poland and suggested to Gorbachev that the Warsaw Pact consider using troops. The Soviet leader firmly ruled it out, Georgy Shakhnazarov, Gorbachev's aide who sat in on the meetings said later.[25] In his private talks with Honecker, Gorbachev spoke of the Soviet Union's perestroika. 'He did not utter a harsh word or tell him he was a conservative. He just said, "Everything in the world is changing. None of us can go on acting as we used to",' Shakhnazarov recalled. The East German leader lectured Gorbachev on the changes which the GDR had already made. Arguing that East Germany had had its own perestroika several years earlier, he cited a long list of economic achievements, from the country's industrial advances to its comprehensive welfare benefits. The trouble was that most East Germans compared their society with West Germany, not with the rest of Eastern Europe, and they wanted political liberalization. As had happened with Gorbachev's other visits to Communist countries, enthusiastic crowds turned out in Berlin to cheer him, hoping he would help them to press for reform. It was the great irony of his trips out of Moscow. In the Soviet Union he wanted supportive crowds but no longer got them. In the West they fêted him like a star, and he relished it. In the Communist world the crowds begged for his influence but he had to be the diplomat and turn them gently away.

As the crisis in East Germany sharpened over the next few

weeks, Alexander Yakovlev was sent to Berlin to reinforce the warning. 'They just couldn't believe that we'd let things take their course. I had to keep telling them we wouldn't interfere,' he said later.[26] Strict instructions were given to Soviet troops not to leave their barracks. With Moscow pledged to non-intervention, the East German party lost control. Honecker was replaced by his crown prince, Egon Krenz, who gave orders for the Berlin Wall to be opened in a desperate effort to stop the street protests and win the party popular support. But the party split and the old leadership was swept away.

The collapse of old-style Communist rule in East Germany was one thing, but no one had expected that it would lead so quickly to unification. After the Berlin Wall was breached, Gorbachev initially hoped there would be a confederation of the two German states with a long transition period before unification. He strongly backed the confederative plan proposed by Hans Modrow, the East German prime minister. When that proved impossible after the pro-unity East German Christian Democrats won the first post-Communist elections, Gorbachev still hoped to keep the united country out of NATO. He made various proposals, including a neutral Germany, and a Germany in both NATO and the Warsaw Pact simultaneously. The French were in no hurry for German unification either. Britain's Conservative government was also not keen, but as a loyal supporter of NATO and an American military presence in Europe it was concerned that a dilution of NATO or any hint of a neutral Germany could harm the alliance. The British and Americans had their eyes on the unravelling of the Warsaw Pact, and thought that an agreement on a two-alliance Germany would artificially prolong the Pact's life.

Everything depended on Kohl. As West German Chancellor, he was the lead-player, and once he made it clear he wanted the earliest possible unification on his terms, his French and British allies fell in line. Whatever they felt privately about a strong new Germany, they could not voice their doubts about unity in public. It would have looked 'un-European', as though they still did not trust the Germans more than forty years after the war. Anchoring a united Germany in NATO would at least continue to keep it in check. Besides, in the euphoric mood of conservative triumphalism over the fall of Communism, absorbing East Germany into NATO was the most dramatic way of signalling victory in the Cold War. Stalin's occupation of Eastern Europe, and the creation of the Warsaw Pact and Comecon, were all based on the proposition that part of Germany was and would always remain in the socialist camp. Now it had become 'one of us'. There could be no finer symbolism than this.

United Germany's adhesion to NATO suggested to many influential Russians that the Soviet Union had not only lost the Cold War, but the Second World War as well. It was one thing for the Soviet Union to give up its empire in Eastern Europe. Most army officers were willing and able to come to terms with this. For NATO to annex part of that empire, as they saw it, was a more difficult concept to swallow. A number of senior officers, and not only those involved in the August coup, felt that NATO was merely strengthening its position at the Soviet Union's expense. Rather than matching the diminution of the 'threat' with an equivalent contraction of NATO, the Western alliance was enlarging its field of operations. The cutbacks in NATO's nuclear and conventional arsenal and troop strengths in Europe did not lessen this perception. It helped to keep alive a mood of suspicion and resentment, which further undermined Gorbachev's authority.

'This is why we took so long to agree to united Germany's membership of NATO,' Eduard Shevardnadze explained. 'Look at our country, at the position we were in at the beginning of 1990. Look at the way our people felt and the tightness of the string which the opponents of perestroika had drawn. It could break at any moment.'[27] Throughout the second half of 1990 and in early 1991 Western leaders debated how to help Gorbachev in his struggle with the conservatives. The talk was mainly of economic aid. They could have helped him more by changing their own security policies. But this would have meant a complete re-ordering of priorities, since Western leaders wanted to weaken and disarm the Soviet Union. They wanted to keep Gorbachev in power not for his own sake but because they felt that under him they had more chance of achieving a controlled dismantling of the Soviet empire.

Disappointment with the West's unwillingness to match the momentous changes in Eastern Europe continued in sections of the Russian élite, particularly among military leaders. It was not by chance that in early 1992 Yeltsin proposed to NATO that Russia become a member. He was worried that NATO still saw itself as an anti-Russian alliance. If Russia joined, this would force it to reassess its goals.

Yeltsin's proposal was promptly rejected, but NATO leaders later accepted that a role for Russia had to be found. They offered it a place in the 'Partnership for Peace', a system for giving non-NATO members joint training and exercises with NATO. By this time, in the spring of 1994, Yeltsin was the one to play coy. He insisted on a parallel declaration emphasizing Russia's special status.

It was a far cry from the early phase of his presidency when his primary aim was to remain on the best possible terms with the West. In Washington in 1992 he achieved what he later told friends was his greatest triumph, apart from the heady days resisting the August coup. He won thirteen standing ovations from the US Congress for a rousing anti-Communist speech in which he pledged that Russia had become a new country without imperial ambitions.

Although Yeltsin, prompted by the military leadership and many parliamentary deputies, subsequently moved to a more assertive foreign policy, this did not include calls for reviving Russian control over Eastern Europe, nor for re-establishing the Soviet Union against the will of the various republics. With the exception of Vladimir Zhirinovsky, all leading Russian politicians accepted that the empire was dead.

8

The Soviet Disunion

*We do not have autonomous republics, but rather
provinces subject to the centre. The union of
republics within the USSR ought to be based on the
principle of attraction, like a friendship or love
affair.*

YURI AFANASYEV, HISTORIAN, SEPTEMBER 1988[1]

The Baltics Break Loose

It was the first time I had ever been asked to join a conspiracy to
overthrow an elected government. Along with one other reporter I
was half-way up the stands in a football stadium in Riga, the capital
of Latvia, on 15 January 1991. Around a microphone two rows
below us a small group of men in fur hats and army uniforms
gathered in the cold. On the field some 15,000 expectant demonstrators paraded their demands on posters, while stamping up and
down to try to keep warm.

Almost all the slogans were in Russian. Their anger was directed
partly at Gorbachev, but even more at Boris Yeltsin, then
chairman of the Russian parliament. 'Yeltsin – political prostitute'
proclaimed a placard, carried by an elderly woman obviously
furious at the way the Russian leader was flirting with Baltic
nationalists. A large red banner held up by two men screamed, 'We

ETERNAL RUSSIA

want presidential rule'. A heavy-set man came to the microphone and introduced himself in Russian as chairman of the republic's strike committee. 'The Latvian government has ignored workers' wishes,' he declared. 'We intend to start an indefinite political strike. We want the Committee of Public Salvation to take power into its hands. I call on everyone to listen to the Committee's demands. We promise to guarantee order.'

Next at the microphone was Lieut-Colonel Alexander Avdeyev, who said he represented the 'Co-ordinating Centre for Officers of the Baltic Military District', a group which included men from the army, police and KGB. Five of the centre's members were in the Committee of Public Salvation, he told the crowd. 'The army should stick to military matters and the politicians to politics,' he said, correctly enough. Then he added ominously, 'But sometimes politicians don't do what they should'.

A Soviet army helicopter flew low round the stadium, as hundreds of people waved in greeting. With its industrial muscle and military support apparently both in place, it was time for the conspiracy's political arm to swing into action. Word of the existence of a Committee for Public Salvation had been going round Riga for some days and Alfred Rubiks, a member of the Politburo of the Soviet Communist party – and therefore nominally a member of Gorbachev's team – had been strongly rumoured to be one of its co-chairmen.

Now Rubiks came out of the closet. 'Let me give you my opinion of Yeltsin,' he said to expectant cheers as he took the microphone. 'He has gone behind the backs of the people to sign treaties with Estonia, Lithuania and Latvia. Who gave him that right? Let him introduce order to Russia first. Let him feed and clothe his own people.' Someone in the crowd shouted Judas, and the cry became a chant for a few minutes.

Besides being in the Soviet Politburo, Rubiks was head of the pro-Moscow wing of the Latvian Communist party which had split from the majority faction a few months earlier over the issue of maintaining the Soviet Union against Baltic independence. Warming

190

to his theme, Rubiks said the Latvian Communist party supported the strike committee's demand for the Latvian government's resignation. If it refused, the Committee of Public Salvation would take power itself. 'We don't want dictatorship, but what we have now in Latvia is the worst example of nationalism. We need presidential rule so as to avoid bloodshed.' When Rubiks had finished, Oyars Potreki, another member of the pro-Moscow Latvian Communist party's leadership, read out a resolution for the crowd to adopt. 'This meeting demands that the All-Latvian Committee of Public Salvation takes on itself the responsibility for Latvia's fate. It proclaims the transfer into its hands of all state power in Latvia for a period of stabilization, and announces the dismissal of the Popular Front parliament and government. It entrusts the chairman of the Salvation Committee to produce a list of names for Latvia's new Council of Ministers.' Potreki then asked the crowd to signify by a show of hands whether they supported the seizure of power. Mine and that of my companion remained firmly at our sides. Our neighbours had seen us taking notes and presumably realized we were reporters, but it was an uncomfortable moment.

A football ground seemed an odd place from which to proclaim a *coup d'état*. Unlike the attempt by shadowy forces in neighbouring Lithuania to seize the television tower by means of tanks two days earlier, or the putschists in Moscow in August who acted first and then announced themselves, the conspirators in Latvia were making open declarations before taking any measures. For most of January 1991 the international media spotlight was on Lithuania. Its flamboyant leader Vytautas Landsbergis, and the English-speaking staff of returned American and Canadian émigrés who ran his parliamentary press service, made it a natural focus. But for us reporters that day in Riga, the open announcement of the transfer of power to a Salvation Committee in Latvia – the first such move in the Soviet Union – posed a difficult conundrum.

Was it a sign of despair, an act of defiance by Russians in Latvia designed mainly to boost morale? That seemed a possible explanation. After all, the crowd spilling out into the street after the meeting had not been asked to march to parliament or government headquarters. Some calmly waited for trams or drifted home on foot. But there was a more sinister alternative. Did the conspirators feel confident of quickly gaining support, since non-Latvians formed nearly half the population of 2,600,000 in the republic? And had they received approval from high-up forces in Moscow, in the KGB or the Kremlin itself?

I felt the coup announcement was a move of genuine menace, the intensification of a serious campaign to roll back the Popular Front and halt the drive to restore Latvia's independence. It was not just that the Russian population of Latvia was twice as big as that of Lithuania. A large proportion of them were army officers, some still serving and an estimated 100,000 in retirement. Latvia was the headquarters of the Soviet Union's Baltic military district and had the biggest Soviet troop contingent of the three republics. Boris Pugo, the newly appointed hardline Soviet minister of the interior, was a Latvian and a former first secretary of the Latvian Communist party. Many of Latvia's biggest enterprises were heavily staffed by Russians, and a strike would have had a devastating effect. Viktor Alksnis, the 'Black Colonel' and a leading figure in the pro-empire 'Soyuz' group of deputies in the Soviet parliament, was Latvian.

In the Kremlin Gorbachev and his advisers were also focusing on Latvia rather than Lithuania. 'We all thought something big was about to happen, but in Latvia not Lithuania,' Vitaly Ignatienko, his press spokesman, explained later.[2] At the end of December there had been a series of explosions, fifteen separate incidents in a single week, outside branches of the pro-Moscow Latvian Communist party and various army buildings. 'Judging from appearances, it isn't coincidence. Someone is professionally preparing a disaster,' Ignatienko quoted Gorbachev as saying. The president was convinced it was a well-planned provocation since the explosions caused attention but carefully avoided injuring anyone. As a result of the tension Marshal Yazov, the defence minister, and Boris Pugo, the interior minister, signed an order allowing for joint patrols by the army and police. These detachments were on the streets of Riga. It was all the work of nationalists, Pugo assured Gorbachev.

The two men also used their forces in other contexts, either to seize and allegedly safeguard Communist party buildings which were in dispute because of the split into pro-Moscow and pro-independence wings, or to round up draft dodgers and deserters. This further added to the tension. Early one morning in January a group of paramilitary police, the OMON (an acronym for 'special assignment police'), who were nominally under Boris Pugo's control, had stormed the headquarters of Riga's main publishing house. Kazimiers Dunders, its director, was arrested by the OMON as he left home. After twelve hours he was released but was forbidden to go to the publishing house. To avoid further trouble he took refuge in the Council of Ministers' building, where he was given an office and a small room to sleep, which he proudly showed me. 'The order to seize the publishing house came from the central committee of the Latvian Communist party. I assume from Rubiks, with the approval of Moscow,' he said.

Dunders had been a party member since 1957. Even when it split into pro-independence and pro-Moscow wings in 1990, Dunders remained with Rubiks's pro-Moscow group. Three months before the OMON'S seizure of the publishing house, Rubiks had summoned Dunders to his office. 'He put on a tape-recorder, and started to interrogate me. Why had I betrayed the party? Why had I stolen party property? I replied that the Latvian government, elected by the people, had taken over the publishing house and was operating it legally. "We live here," I reminded him, but he said the government was only the Popular Front, as though he did not recognize its authority,' Dunders recalled. After the meeting, he went home and wrote a letter resigning from the party. 'I saw it as a reactionary force, resting on the officer corps,' he explained.

The social headquarters of that corps was the officers' club, an imposing building in Riga's city centre. In a small reception room there Lieut-General Oleg Zinchenko, the head of the political department of the army in the Baltic military district (the senior political commissar) was at pains to project himself as no hawk. 'Many officers support Colonel Alksnis's call for the imposition of presidential rule,' he said, 'but I don't agree. We have a struggle here over law. The Latvian parliament adopts laws which go against the Soviet constitution, and against international conventions on human rights. Circumstances can only be changed by a referendum on whether the republic should be in the USSR or not. We won't do anything,' he assured me. 'The military doesn't decide whether to have a referendum. We're not Mozambique or Nicaragua where ten colonels can get together and mount a coup.'

The correctness of his views on the constitution did not stop the general from spilling out a series of complaints against the Popular Front government and its majority in parliament. Officers and soldiers were constantly being insulted in the street. The army had been forbidden to build new quarters for its troops, on the grounds that there were environmental problems. No new state flats were being given to officers, and when current army tenants left, their flats were repossessed by the government. 'As a result more than 10,000 army people have no flats and have to live in barracks with shared facilities, or in expensive privately rented rooms,' he said. Two years earlier, there were fewer than 5,000 in this position, but the withdrawal of Soviet divisions from Eastern Europe to the Baltics was making things worse.

General Zinchenko was upset over the new law providing for Latvian young men to do alternative service instead of accepting conscription into the Soviet army, 'which means that only around 37 per cent of our call-up quota has been fulfilled'. He was incensed at the Latvian parliament's resolution in November to cut off water and gas to army barracks (a move which the government later rescinded). He claimed that ration coupons for food and compensation payments for price increases were not given to army families. Putting his complaints into a wider context, he said he was unhappy that the Soviet retreat from Eastern Europe was happening so quickly, and that now the Soviet position in the

Baltics was under threat. 'It is our exit to the sea, as well as the area through which so many invasions from the West have come. We went into Eastern Europe as a victorious army in 1945. Why don't our former wartime allies also pull out, and form a demilitarised zone?', he asked.

General Zinchenko's irritation seemed to mirror the views of the officer corps, even if they differed over how to respond. For the army leadership in Moscow the immediate issue was the failure of the conscription drive. On 7 January, on instructions from Moscow, Colonel-General Fyodor Kuzmin, the commander of the Baltic military district, had telephoned the prime ministers of the three Baltic republics to advise them of the imminent arrival of extra Soviet troops to round up deserters and draft dodgers. If the local authorities helped in the process, then the troops might not be needed.

General Kuzmin was an unusually tall man with a ramrod figure accentuated by his long grey Soviet army greatcoat. The day before the public proclamation of the Salvation Committee he had appeared at a round-table meeting of all political groups which Anatolys Gorbunovs, the chairman of the Latvian parliament, had managed to call together in Riga's town hall. On the Russian side the meeting became another sounding-board for a string of complaints. Anatoly Alekseyev, the chairman of Interfront (short for International Front), said the state-owned Latvian television and radio did not reflect the Russian point of view. Interfront had been set up over two years earlier, in deliberate opposition to the Popular Front. Its name was meant to suggest that it represented the views of all the minorities in Latvia, though in practice it was dominated by Russians. When the grim-looking General Kuzmin took the microphone, he confirmed one's worst suspicions. Far from trying to take a statesmanlike or neutral view, the general spoke like a combination of a Communist party loyalist and a trade union representative of the Soviet army. He demanded that the Latvian parliament rescind all legislation which contradicted the Soviet constitution. He said the army's living conditions were miserable and warned that its patience was not limitless. He called for the Latvian police to be disarmed. 'Communists are fed up with being insulted. You must realize there is such a party, and it has many members, including among the army,' he concluded.

The Russians at the round table, like those in the football stadium the following day, were clearly the hawks. There was an alternative view. Russians who had been born or lived a long time in Latvia tended to support independence, particularly if they had higher education or were in one of the professions which did not directly depend on Moscow. I went to see Vladlen Dozortsev, a Russian member of the Latvian parliament, and the editor of the journal *Daugava*. He had been living in the republic since 1951. 'I joined the Popular Front on the first day,' he announced proudly, as we sat in the anteroom of the parliament chamber. He pointed out the extraordinary Soviet stained-glass windows in the mock-Gothic hall, which showed happy people showering bouquets of flowers on the Soviet troops which entered the republic in 1940.

The Popular Front had won two-thirds of the votes in the 1990 elections, which showed that many Russians had supported it. Dozortsev conceded that the Popular Front had since then lost some of that support. 'Only between 45 and 50 per cent of non-Latvians back the PF now, compared to two-thirds a year ago,' he said. One reason was disappointment with the government's decision to raise prices. Another was that people expected too much too soon. Some had been upset by the government's discussion of a new citizenship law which might limit the rights of recent settlers. Dozortsev said the Moscow authorities had sent in between 12,000 and 18,000 Russian peasants every year after the war to work in factories which were under Moscow ministries' control.

If the mood among Russians was divided, the same could not be said of the Latvian community. With the exception of a few highly Russified Latvians like Rubiks and Alksnis, who had lifelong connections with the Communist party apparatus or the Soviet officer corps, the vast majority were in favour of the Popular Front and its drive for independence. The notion of a 'love affair' between

Moscow and the Baltic republics was out of the question, as Yuri
Afanasyev well knew when he made the comment quoted at the
head of this chapter. The shotgun marriage of 1940 was over, and
most Latvians wanted a divorce. A key motive was anger at the way
the demographic situation in Latvia had changed as a result of
Soviet rule, now that glasnost was allowing the facts to emerge. In
1935 Latvians comprised 77 per cent of the republic's population.
By 1989 they were only 52 per cent. It was not just the massive
Russian immigration but also the deportations of Latvians to
Siberia. In 1949 when forced collectivization of agriculture began,
thousands of private farmers and their families were herded off to
camps. Estimates vary from 43,000 to 144,000. The latter figure
would be one out of every ten Latvians.[3]

The Soviet attack on the television tower in Vilnius produced a
massive outburst of defiance in Lithuania, but even more so in
Latvia, where people expected a similar onslaught. In Vilnius the
next day crowds rallied round the parliament building, erecting
concrete barricades to protect it against possible attack. In Riga the
entire old city was blocked off by heavy lorries and mounds of
stones and concrete blocks set up as barricades. The Council of
Ministers' building in the modern part of the city was also ringed
with bulldozers, cranes and dump-trucks. Crowds kept vigil for
several nights at bonfires in the streets, singing national songs and
dancing in the snow. The Protestant cathedral which had been used
as a concert hall in Soviet times was turned into a huge first-aid
centre and canteen for the thousands of unarmed volunteers. The
precautions could not protect every building, and that night OMON
troops, the Black Berets, attacked a suburban police station as well
as the police academy and seized weapons. Five days later, when
some of the tension had abated, they also struck the Latvian
interior ministry in a separate part of the modern city, near the
river which runs through Riga's central park. Black Berets stormed
the building, killing four people, but then left again after a few
hours. The OMON's spasmodic performance suggested they had
no overall plan. Like the original founding of the Committee of

Public Salvation, which had looked threatening at the time, subsequent events belied it. The strike by Russian workers which its leaders promised fizzled out. The Committee was never heard from again.

In Lithuania a similar 'National Salvation Committee' was a more pathetic affair. It refused to name its members. At a press conference in the Soviet officers' club a few days after the storming of the television tower, Juozas Jarmalavicius, the ideological secretary of the small pro-Moscow Communist party, claimed to be in charge of 'links to the National Salvation Committee'. On the platform with him was a representative of the Soviet ministry of defence, Major-General Yuri Nauman. Jarmalavicius, who denied being a member of the Committee, told reporters that he used to receive its material by courier but had been invited to a flat in Vilnius the night before to meet the chairman and members of the Committee. 'I know these people. They are well-known in the republic. They are workers, peasants, leaders of the creative intelligentsia from Vilnius and other cities. Most are Lithuanians, but there are Russians, Poles and other nationalities.' Even more directly than the similar Committee in Latvia, the one in Lithuania said it wanted to create a situation of 'dual power' with the power of the 'bourgeois-nationalist Supreme Soviet' balanced against its own. This would trigger Soviet intervention since dual power could lead to civilian bloodshed unless the Soviet president stepped in and imposed presidential rule, according to a statement given to us at the press conference.

General Nauman said the National Salvation Committee had appealed to the military commander of Vilnius, Major-General Vladimir Uskhopchik, to take the television and radio centres under control 'in order to stop provocative actions'. The General said the Committee had to remain anonymous because the Lithuanian parliament had threatened to kill its members. 'I am sure you will understand why we do not give their names now,' he concluded. A 'diary of recent events' distributed to us by the information centre of the Communist party said the Committee had imposed a curfew on 13 January, a few hours after the attack on the television tower. Journalists pressed Jarmalivicius and the General to explain how an unnamed private body could take such decisions. The real reason for the Committee's anonymity appeared to be that, even more than in Latvia, it was unsure of popular support. Only 20 per cent of the republic's population was non-Lithuanian.

The main riddle in the Latvian and Lithuanian events was whether they had been planned with Gorbachev's approval. Gorbachev had been moving towards a tougher stance towards the Baltics for several months. He had also taken a number of legal and constitutional steps which could be used to justify a crackdown. His assumption of the executive presidency in March 1990 gave him the power to declare a state of emergency or impose presidential rule in any part of the Soviet Union. The following month he accepted Nikolai Ryzhkov's advice to impose an economic blockade on Lithuania in an effort to make the republic's parliament revoke its declaration of independence. In December 1990 he issued a decree demanding that republican governments enforce conscription laws. It was this decree that Marshal Yazov, the defence minister, relied on in announcing on 7 January that extra troops were being sent to the Baltics, allegedly to round up deserters. Towards the end of 1990 Gorbachev sacked Vadim Bakatin, his liberal interior minister, and replaced him by the hardline Boris Pugo. This was a further sign of the mounting pressure from pro-empire forces which led to Eduard Shevardnadze's bombshell resignation as foreign minister in December 1990. He coupled it with warnings that the country was threatened by an imminent dictatorship. Yet the day after the Vilnius events, Gorbachev said, 'I only learned about it in the morning. The report came as a surprise to us all.'[4]

Many Russian liberals refused to believe Gorbachev's version. They saw him as a puppet or even a willing ally of the conservatives. They warned that the next step by the hardliners would be an attempt at a coup in Moscow. The morning after the Vilnius shooting several deputies from 'Democratic Russia' and other supporters of the movement held a protest march through Red Square, claiming the Lithuanian and Latvian events could be the start of a general clampdown. When Pugo and Yazov both later became members of the August conspiracy, those arguments gained strength. The Baltic crackdown was a 'rehearsal' for the August coup, it was argued. But the chain of events is not sufficient to prove that. One could equally argue that the failure of the Russian-speaking audience both in Russia and in the Baltic republics to respond positively and support the military drama should have warned the August plotters not to proceed in Moscow.

The more likely explanation is that the hardliners were not yet certain what to do in Moscow but were testing the ground and the possible reaction. They clearly hoped to do something to reverse the Baltic republics' independence. Whether or not it was a 'rehearsal', what happened in the Baltics was real enough. Yazov and Pugo were probably lying when they denied giving orders for the crackdown in January. They had certainly set in motion a chain of events and a political climate in which local commanders and Communist party leaders could expect to receive retroactive support from Moscow or at least be able to act with impunity.

For this there were good precedents. In April 1989 Soviet troops had viciously broken up a peaceful demonstration in Tbilisi, the Georgian capital, using sapper's spades and a powerful disabling gas. Twenty civilians were killed. Some liberals tried to prove that Yegor Ligachev had taken the decision, on the grounds that in Gorbachev's absence on an official visit to London he had called a meeting of Politburo members at which the recommendation was made to bring troops into the city to guard public buildings. But the decision was upheld by Gorbachev on his return, and no evidence was produced that the Politburo ordered these troops to disperse the crowd. This appears to have been a decison by the Georgian Communist party leader. Although he later resigned because of the local outcry, the significant point was that the Politburo did not insist he be removed nor did it denounce the use of force.

Nine months later the Politburo itself openly used force to protect the Azerbaijani Communist party from a series of mass demonstrations by the republic's Popular Front who were on the verge of seizing power. Tanks and heavy artillery were used to smash through street barricades and arrest hundreds of Popular Front supporters. More than 130 people died. There was little protest from liberals in Moscow and none from Western governments. A pogrom against Baku's Armenian community, which left scores dead and prompted thousands to flee the republic two days before the tank assault, denied the Azerbaijani Popular Front much outside support. Although the Front blamed government provocateurs and the KGB for the anti-Armenian outrages, the truth of these charges was impossible to ascertain.

The Latvian and Lithuanian events the following year appeared therefore to fit a pattern in which the centre would either step in to endorse a *fait accompli* or else turn a blind eye to whatever was done on the ground. Gorbachev's disclaimer of any prior knowledge of the attack on the TV tower may well have been genuine. His error was not to have done anything immediately afterwards to condemn the events in the strongest possible terms and punish those who perpetrated them. Anatoly Lukyanov's view was that Gorbachev did not know the details of particular operations in advance, but had approved a general policy of tough action. Speaking two years later, shortly after his release from prison before the coup trial, when his attitude to Gorbachev was severely critical, he nevertheless exonerated him on this issue. 'Don't blame everything on the centre,' he said.[5] 'The OMON and military in Riga and Vilnius were put in a position where they could act on their own, but base themselves on the local Communist parties.' Gorbachev's spokesman, Vitaly Ignatienko, said that Yazov and Pugo 'pulled the wool over Gorbachev's eyes'.[6]

Ignatienko and three of Gorbachev's senior advisers, Alexander Yakovlev, Vadim Bakatin and Yevgeni Primakov, who were members of his presidential council, discussed the crisis and decided to urge Gorbachev to fly to Vilnius. There he should address the

Lithuanian parliament, acknowledge the republic's independence, and pay his respects to the dead. Gorbachev agreed with the plan and said he would go next day. But next morning he told them he had been warned by his security people that his safety could not be guaranteed. (His security chief later joined the August plotters in their bid to preserve the Soviet Union.) Gorbachev's failure to take strong measures was a major blunder, which lost him much of his last remaining credit with the reformers and suggested to the hard-liners that their pressure on him was working. No one was punished for the affair. Neither Yazov nor Pugo were sacked. Gorbachev did not even remove Alfred Rubiks from the Politburo.

The ineffective crackdown in the Baltics was almost a caricature compared to earlier patterns of Soviet intervention in Hungary and Czechoslovakia. There were, in outline, the same ingredients; allegedly angry loyalist populations, strike threats by aroused workers, news media that were said to have been captured by one-sided bourgeois forces, and invitations from local Communist parties for Moscow to intervene. There was even, as in 1956, a good choice of timing. Just as the West was meant to be distracted from Hungary by the crisis over Suez, in the 1991 case it was busy with the Gulf war.

But in every other way the crisis showed how much things had changed. At a banal level there was the fact that we reporters could camp all night in the Lithuanian parliament building or rent rooms from sympathetic Vilnius residents with a ring-side view of the square just in case of an attack. A year earlier, during the economic blockade, Moscow-based Western journalists were officially barred from Lithuania, and we all obeyed. More important, in 1991 the Kremlin was obliged to deny its involvement, whether or not it was true. The international climate, the end of the Cold War, and the image – as well as the reality – of perestroika made it impossible for Gorbachev to accept responsibility for the bloody crackdown.

The collapse of Communist rule in Eastern Europe was also a crucial factor. The three Baltic republics had been the last to enter the Soviet Union, when their independence was removed by means of Stalin's 1939 pact with Hitler. What they were asking for was not secession from the USSR but the restoration of independence, very much on the same lines as the new post-Communist governments of Eastern Europe had been doing over the previous year. While the rest of Eastern Europe had never been formally annexed, the Baltic Popular Fronts saw this as only a trivial difference. One of the tragedies of Gorbachev's reaction to the Baltic events was that neither he nor his colleagues initially recognized this. Their response to the Baltic events differed markedly from the way they behaved towards the end of Communist rule in Poland.

In Chapter 7 I reported on the secret Politburo analysis of the Polish events, which accepted them as inevitable and recommended that Moscow work as calmly as possible with the new government in Warsaw. A month earlier an analysis for the Politburo on Poland's small neighbour Lithuania by the ideological department of the central committee came out with an astonishingly tough set of recommendations. It called for the restoration of censorship in the republic, for the prosecutor-general to bring charges against 'extremists, nationalists, and anti-Soviet elements', and for Soviet government ministries to examine the legality of the financial operations of Sajudis, as the republic's Popular Front was known.[7] Although the Politburo did not accept these extreme recommendations, the policy it adopted was significantly harsher towards Lithuania than Poland.

By any simple measurement of territory this was strange. The 'loss' of Poland would mean much more for the security of the Soviet state than the 'loss' of Lithuania, or even of all three Baltic republics together. Poland was larger and strategically placed on the Western approaches to Russia. But territory was not the issue. To the Soviet leadership the Baltics were part of the sacred 'inner empire'. Even though they had only been incorporated into the USSR in 1940, their brief period of independence since 1918 was seen as an aberration. Gorbachev and his colleagues could not accept that the three republics had been annexed by force in 1940 against the will of the majority. In Moscow they were seen as an inalienable part of the Soviet Union's political, economic, and military space.

In the turmoil of perestroika the issue of a new dispensation with the republics had come late on to the agenda. Reform of the party, changing the electoral structure, permitting glasnost and modernizing the economy were all being implemented before the idea of a new nationalities policy emerged. As Russians, Gorbachev and his Politburo colleagues failed to appreciate the strength of other people's nationalism. When anti-Armenian violence broke out in Azerbaijan in early 1988, followed by heavy pressure on the few Azerbaijani communities in Armenia to pack up and leave the republic, the Politburo again saw the events as a provocation either by a small group of ambitious nationalists or else by reactionary Communist 'mafias' bent on sabotaging the pro-perestroika local leaderships.

In the Baltics nationalism took an even more dangerous form, as far as the future of the Soviet Union was concerned. The memory of pre-Soviet times was more vivid, as was the feeling that Sovietization had held the area's development back and changed the ethnic balance. Once more the Politburo did not read the signals properly. Anatoly Lukyanov, who as chairman of the Supreme Soviet became the most prominent parliamentary obstacle to a looser form of union, disclosed that the party leadership saw things in class rather than national terms. 'The Politburo well understood that in the Baltics we were not having to deal with nationalist movements for self-determination but with a concealed movement for the restoration of capitalism,' he told me in 1993. 'The Popular Fronts wanted to restore capitalism. Later they didn't even hide it.'[8]

In fact, the movements in the Baltic republics raised a mixture of political and economic demands. They first surfaced in 1988 when a group of Estonian economists, all Communist party members, came up with a plan for republican financial autonomy, modelled on the ideas for enterprise self-accounting which Gorbachev and his colleagues had already approved. This was not just a tactical ploy by the Estonians. In every republic there was antipathy to the

THE SOVIET DISUNION

way the centre had dominated the planned economy in the past. Decentralization was a natural part of relaxing the command-administrative system and allowing republics to decide the costs of imports from and exports to other parts of the USSR. That the impetus for Baltic independence came from local Communists, joined later by nationalists who had fought against the party under Stalinism, underlined the broad base of the movement. It also made it virtually unstoppable.

The exact moment when the collapse of the Soviet Union as a federation became irreversible will be debated for years. Some suggest it was when Moscow imposed its embargo on Lithuania in April 1990. Others say it was the Russian parliament's declaration of sovereignty in July 1990. Still others say it was the failed coup of August 1991. I put the occasion down as the meeting of the Lithuanian Communist party's central committee on 25 June 1989, more than two years earlier. The event went unnoticed on the day. By chance I was the only foreign correspondent in Vilnius, though the party meeting was not my reason for being there. I had gone to cover the Popular Front of Byelorussia which was holding its founding congress in a trade union hall in the Lithuanian capital. The red and white banner of the last independent pre-Soviet Byelorussian state flew over the building, as hundreds of nationalist delegates met 'in exile'.

Byelorussia had the reputation of having the most conservative party leadership in the Soviet Union. It had done everything in its power to block the formation of informal political groups, from using water-cannons to break up meetings to sacking activists from their jobs. In other republics Popular Fronts already existed but when the Byelorussians applied for a hall to hold their first conference, the party authorities in Minsk refused. Yefrem Sokolov, the first secretary of the Byelorussian Communist party, denounced the movement as 'extremist' and called on branches to deal severely with party members who supported the Front. Denied a hall, the Front approached its Lithuanian neighbours, the Lithuanian Popular Front, known as Sajudis, for permission to meet in Vilnius.

205

Sajudis agreed. More important, the Lithuanian Communist party which was then still in power, did not object.

This was a dramatic sign that the Soviet Communist party was already beginning to break up along republican lines. Gone was the solidarity with the Byelorussian Communists which Sokolov had hoped for. It was a fascinating decision, though not in itself a watershed. The Communist parties of Armenia and Azerbaijan had been trading charges and counter-charges over the issue of Nagorno-Karabakh for more than a year already. The Lithuanian party's snub to the Byelorussians was in the same category.

The sensation came a few hours later when the Lithuanian party's central committee met behind closed doors to hear a report by Algirdas Brazauskas, the Lithuanian party leader. The meeting took place on the same day as the Byelorussian Popular Front's founding congress. Brazauskas's speech was a dramatic challenge to Moscow. 'A Lithuania without sovereignty is a Lithuania without a future,' Brazauskas declared, as he announced his recommendation that the Lithuanian party break ranks with the Soviet Communist party. No republican party had ever dared raise such a demand. Word of its contents began to leak out that night in Vilnius. Those were the days when Moscow offices of foreign news agencies still waited two or three days for the republican press to arrive in the capital by mail. The agencies and newspapers did not yet have correspondents or local reporters in the Baltics, and there were no fax machines. By buying a copy of Lithuania's Russian-language party paper at a Vilnius news-stand I had a two-day advantage. Brazauskas announced that a special congress would be held later in the year to formalize the decision to split from Moscow. Algimantas Cekuolis, a senior member of the party, graphically explained the central committee's complaints to me: 'We have no programme, statutes or autonomy. We are like a regional branch, which receives orders, is subject to inspections and has to have its leadership changes and promotions approved from the centre.'

Brazauskas himself was a product of this centralized system, and had spent most of his life as an economist in the Lithuanian state planning commission. Gorbachev engineered his selection as party secretary in 1988 to replace a conservative, but the new leader quickly showed his dissatisfaction with the old style of relations. His threat of a split from the Soviet Communist Party infuriated Gorbachev, who put enormous pressure on the Lithuanian Communists to back down. He called a central committee meeting of the Soviet party in January 1990 and persuaded the Lithuanians to delay their congress so that Brazauskas could come to Moscow to attend it.

Brazauskas told the central committee that Lithuania would remain in the Soviet Union, even though his party wanted to be independent of the CPSU. But speaker after speaker denounced the Lithuanians and attacked Brazauskas personally. Nursultan Nazarbayev, the Kazakh party leader, described the Lithuanians as traitors. Yegor Ligachev said they had succumbed to the separatists. Gorbachev sounded apocalyptic: 'Today in this Kremlin hall the fate of the world is being decided. Where do we go after this plenum? A great deal depends on that – the fate of the country, the fate of socialism, the fate of the world.'[9]

In a last throw, Gorbachev travelled to Lithuania to urge the Lithuanian Communists to stay within the fold. For three days the Soviet leader travelled round the republic, meeting groups of workers, talking to crowds in the streets, and finally holding a stormy televised session with the republic's leading Communists. Neither he nor any of his predecessors had spent so much time in one non-Russian republic before. The subliminal message was that Gorbachev was visiting a foreign country and that Lithuania was already independent. His persuasion failed, and a few weeks later 82 per cent of the delegates at the Lithuanian party congress confirmed their intention to break away from the Soviet party. The rest formed the pro-Moscow faction which became the backbone of the 'National Salvation Committee' a year later.

The Lithuanian Communists' move was partly an attempt to compete with the nationalists in the first free elections which were due in February. But the move was more than that. Few Russians, including Communist party officials like Gorbachev and Ligachev, knew how much the LCP had suffered under Moscow's rule. When a Lithuanian worker asked Gorbachev during his visit to the republic whether he knew how many Lithuanians were sent to Siberia in the 1940s and died there, Gorbachev snapped, 'I don't want to talk to this man any more. If people in Lithuania have attitudes and slogans like this, they can expect hard times'.[10]

I was given a hint of the Lithuanian party's feelings by Vladimir Berezov, a genial figure who was second secretary of the party. It was a month after the announcement that the LCP was going to break from the Soviet Communists. The party's headquarters in Vilnius were no longer a fortress, and visitors could walk upstairs and along corridors without an escort. Berezov was a Russian born in Lithuania, who had married a Lithuanian and spoke better Lithuanian than Russian. His forefathers had moved to the republic decades before. He pointed out that Lithuanian Communists were repressed by Stalin almost as severely as other groups. After Soviet troops entered Lithuania in 1940, six of the eight veteran members of the republic's original revolutionary government of 1919 were executed. Scores of other Communists were purged on the grounds of being nationalists and within eight months of Lithuania's incorporation into the USSR 70 per cent of its members consisted of people sent from Moscow. The party was turned into nothing more than a junior branch of the Soviet party.

Gorbachev's attempt to bully the Lithuanian Communists backfired. It increased public support in the Baltics for leaving the Soviet Union. As the Popular Fronts expanded their demands for independence, their mood encouraged centrifugal tendencies in other republics. This forced Gorbachev to change his mind and announce his willingness to consider a new Union. He proposed a kind of USSR *à la carte*, in which each republic could decide what degree of voluntary association to have: either a federal status, a looser confederal status or associate membership. He mentioned the analogy of the Tsarist empire, where different areas such as Finland or the Emirate of Bukhara had had special status.

Gorbachev was too late. The three Baltic republics held parliamentary elections in the spring of 1990, just as Russia did. This was the planned follow-up to the first Soviet elections for a Congress of People's Deputies in 1989. In the Baltics the Popular Fronts won the elections, transforming themselves into legitimate governments which Gorbachev could not denounce as unrepresentative. At the end of March the Lithuanian parliament proclaimed the republic's independence. Gorbachev's use of an economic blockade to try to make them abandon their independence was a disastrous move, which undermined his protestations of good faith. It failed partly because the 'centre' had already lost control over the economy. Many Russian and Byelorussian state enterprises surreptitiously supplied Lithuania in defiance of the blockade. When Gorbachev pushed through the Soviet parliament a law allowing republics to hold a referendum on leaving the Union but only after a five-year period of transition, the Baltic republics scoffed at it. It was easier for them to declare independence unilaterally.

The Soviet leadership's use of force in Lithuania and Latvia in January 1991 differed from the interventions in Hungary and Czechoslovakia a generation earlier not only by its inefficiency and half-heartedness. It prompted open protest in Russia. The Russian establishment split, with large sections of the intelligentsia and many parliamentary deputies refusing to go along with the crackdown. Boris Yeltsin played the key role, as he was to do again during the coup in Moscow. On the eve of the attack on the television tower in Vilnius he signed a politicial and economic treaty in Moscow between Estonia and the Russian Federation. The text recognized Estonia as 'an independent, sovereign state' and as Arnold Ruutel, the chairman of Estonia's parliament put it at a press conference that evening, 'the timing is significant'. Tension between the Kremlin and the Baltic republics had been rising for days, and Yeltsin was trying to give a Russian signal which was different from the Kremlin's. Immediately after the attack he flew to Tallinn to meet the leaders of Latvia and Estonia, and suggested that the United Nations intervene. He called on Russian forces to disobey orders for a crackdown and said Russia should think of creating its own army. This was a precursor of his succesful attempt during the August coup to split the armed forces and create a new loyalty to Russia rather than to the Soviet Union.

Yeltsin's move had a strong effect on Russian public opinion in the Baltics. Gorbachev expected the Russian communities in the Baltics to play a role by supporting Moscow against the Popular Fronts. The vast majority did not, even though dissatisfaction with the Fronts had been growing. The use of force increased local Russian support for Baltic independence, especially when it became clear that Moscow had lost. Over the next two months the Baltic republics held referendums. In Latvia and Estonia substantial percentages of Russians voted for independence. In Latvia there was a turn-out of 88 per cent, of whom 73.1 per cent voted for independence, which means that around 65 per cent of the entire electorate said 'Yes'. Although there was no breakdown of the results by ethnic origin, the figures suggest that between a third and a half of the Russians were in favour of independence. In Estonia on a turn-out of 82.8 per cent, 77.8 per cent voted for independence, which produces a roughly comparable estimate of Russian support.

Some Russians may have acted from a survival instinct. Realizing that Moscow had lost its grip on the area, they wanted to show their credentials as loyal citizens of the Baltic republics. With economic troubles mounting in Russia, others felt there was more chance of progress in an independent republic than in the mess their original homeland was in. Whatever fears they might have about being second-class citizens they preferred to side with the independence cause. The phenomenon was different from that of the vast majority of English and French settlers in their former colonies. It was one more sign of the relative weakness of Russian nationalism.

If the Russian population of Latvia turned out to be remarkably tolerant of the independence movement, either supporting it or giving grudging acquiescence rather than the defiant resistance which the Salvation Committees hoped for, this was even more the case in Estonia. Estonia also had a large Russian population, some 470,000 people. In many ways its structure was similar to that of the Russians in Latvia – a large number of post-war industrial workers, and a belt of better-educated Russians living in Tallinn, many of them second- and third-generation residents. The difference was that there were fewer military men, and that the relative share of Russians in the Estonian population was lower. But what made the issue more sensitive for Estonians was the speed and scope of the change since the war. Whereas a quarter of Latvia's prewar population was non-Latvian, Estonia was an almost entirely mono-ethnic country. By 1989 the Estonian share was down to 61 per cent. This dramatic shift eventually led to the Popular Front's being outflanked on the right by an ultra-nationalist movement, called the Congress of Estonia.

Its strong growth was to some extent unexpected because the pro-Moscow Russian patriots in Estonia, unlike their counterparts in Latvia, played a low-profile role. Estonia was the only one of the three republics not to have a Committee of National Salvation. It was the only one where Soviet troops did not use force, perhaps because they sensed they would have little support from the Russian population, and because the pro-Moscow Estonian Communist party was weaker and less vocal than its Latvian and Lithuanian counterparts.

After independence the three Baltic republics almost seemed to change character. In Lithuania, where the government had been the most provocatively anti-Moscow, Vytautas Landsbergis became the first Baltic leader to sign an agreement with Moscow on the withdrawal of Soviet troops. He and the parliamentary majority which he led did not weaken the progressive citizenship law passed in 1989 which was based on the 'zero option'. Anyone living in the republic for at least two years could become a citizen. Yet even these acts of moderation were not enough to save him from criticism by his old rival, the centre-left Algirdas Brazauskas, who had fought strongly for the republic's independence as leader of the Lithuanian Communist party. After 1991 he transformed it into a Social-Democratic party and defeated Landsbergis in the parliamentary elections in 1992, partly on economic issues but also on the need for better relations with Russia. Perhaps because the non-Lithuanian population was relatively small, at about 20 per cent, the issue of nationalism faded once the republic gained independence. In February 1993, Brazauskas was elected president of Lithuania, in a political comeback as remarkable as Yeltsin's two years earlier.

In Latvia and Estonia the position was different. Nationalism became stronger after independence, as the governments felt they had a freer hand to deal harshly with the Russian population once the Soviet Union collapsed. Having removed the 'partocrats' of the Soviet period, the republics came under the control of 'ethnocrats'. The Estonian parliament, led by the Popular Front, adopted a citizenship law which gave automatic rights to people who had been Estonians in 1940 at the moment of the Soviet incorporation, and to their descendants. Others would have to wait two years from the day of independence before applying, and even then they would have to pass a language test. This effectively meant that Russians could not vote in the first post-independence elections in September 1992, which produced a further swing to the right.

On a visit to the largely Russian town of Narva in north-eastern Estonia in November that year I found considerable bitterness. Because the town was almost 95 per cent Russian, even those who tried to learn Estonian found no chance to use or practise it. They were voteless. In Tallinn, the Estonian capital, Russians had less excuse for not learning Estonian, which was one reason why feelings against them were high. But some liberal Estonian intellectuals nevertheless argued that it was bad politics to punish present-day Russians. The education system was gradually being switched to give more emphasis to Estonian so that the younger generation would learn Estonian. Why not leave the adults alone, especially as so many voted for independence?

The good thing about Estonia's 'ethnocracy' was that it was non-violent. Russians in the republic appreciated this and reacted calmy. They recognized that it was not Central Asia, the Caucasus or even Moldova. In spite of the discrimination, very few Russians emigrated from Estonia or the other Baltic states after independence.

Ukraine Departs

Ukrainians had to pay a high price for being occupied by the Mongols, the Poles and the Lithuanians. But only the Russians invaded our souls.

LEVKO LUKYANENKO, FORMER POLITICAL PRISONER AND
LATER A CANDIDATE FOR THE PRESIDENCY,
SEPTEMBER 1989

Lieut-Colonel Vladimir Chernyshev sat rigidly in his chair, explaining with some reluctance why he refused to swear an oath of allegiance to Ukraine. His commanding officer, the deputy head of the former Soviet interior ministry's academy in Kharkov and the main source of his embarrassment, watched attentively. 'I wanted the Commonwealth of Independent States to have a united army. When I joined the Soviet army in 1978 and took my first oath, I felt I was an internationalist. I suppose I'm not ready to serve just one state.'

Colonel Chernyshev, in his mid-thirties, was a Russian, as was his commanding officer. It was January 1992, barely a month since the CIS came into being, and neither man had expected, even six months earlier, that they would be faced with pledging allegiance to a state in which they were an ethnic minority. Russians have always considered Ukraine to be an inalienable part of their world, particularly such cities as Kharkov in the Eastern part of the republic where over half the population is Russian. Suddenly, with the collapse of the Soviet Union, Ukraine took over the academy and announced it would be part of the new state's national guard. The senior man swallowed his doubts, and one Saturday afternoon in early January led his fellow-officers and cadets out along the Moscow road to the tall grey memorial to the thousands of soldiers who fell near Kharkov in the Second World War.

They died defending the Soviet Union. Now in a glade of pine and birch trees he and his men would line up and take their oath to Ukraine. He acknowleged it had been difficult but justified it on the grounds that there was no contradiction with the oath to the Soviet Union he took when he joined up in 1966 in the Soviet Far East. 'That also committed me to defend the people of Ukraine among others. With the new oath I'm merely specifying my position,' he argued stiffly as we sat in a bare reception room in the academy.

Behind the dilemmas of the loyalty oath some hard economic thinking had taken place. Earlier in his career Colonel Chernyshev had served in the most varied places of the Soviet Union, first the Caucasus and later above the Arctic circle. He had been delighted when he was posted to the milder climate of Ukraine two years earlier. Now he would have to look for a new job, but what made it easier was that his mother-in-law had a flat in Moscow where he and his wife would move. Only two other officers declined to swear their loyalty to Ukraine, he disclosed. 'Many of my colleagues had no choice. I'm not surprised so few refused'.

The commanding officer strongly disagreed with Chernyshev's view that more officers would leave Ukraine if they could. He pointed to the result in the recent referendum on Ukraine's independence. Voters were asked whether they supported the declaration of independence which the Ukrainian parliament passed after the failure of the August coup. Seventy-eight per cent of the academy's men voted yes. Since almost exactly half were non-Ukrainian, that meant that a majority of the non-Ukrainians had voted for it, and, he stressed, the ballot was secret. Officers and cadets were not trying to curry favour with the new authorities.

Support for independence was repeated in the referendum in all the areas of compact Russian settlement in Ukraine. In the mining town of Donetsk the pro-independence majority was 83.9 per cent; in Odessa 85.3 per cent; in Kharkov as a whole 86.3 per cent. For Russians in Russia the result was a double shock. It was surprising enough that Ukrainians wanted to leave the Soviet Union. That most Russians in Ukraine agreed with them was almost incomprehensible to people in Moscow, particularly to the Soviet leadership in the Kremlin. Yet to reporters who visited the republic regularly in the three or four years before the formal break, the development was not unexpected.

The rise of Ukrainian statehood in 1991 was one of the success stories in the demise of the Soviet Union. Both the old Communist establishment and the new Ukrainian nationalists were able to prevent the independence movement from splitting along ethnic lines. While Boris Yeltsin and Leonid Kravchuk, the first president of the new Ukraine, argued for months over the future of the Black Sea fleet and the status of the Crimea, relations between ordinary Ukrainians and Russians in Ukraine remained calm. Any analogy with Yugoslavia was rejected by almost every Russian or Ukrainian one talked to. There was no major religious difference to burst open like the one which turned the Orthodox Serbs against the Muslims in Bosnia, or even like the clash between Catholic Croats and Orthodox Serbs. The Croatian Ustasha Fascists and the Serbian Chetniks had slaughtered each other in their thousands during the Second World War, and the memory remained vivid enough in Yugoslavia to re-emerge in the 1990s. By contrast, Russia and Ukraine had unified in 1654 and not been to war since.

This did not mean that Ukrainians were reconciled to Russian rule. Rising Ukrainian nationalism was a major factor in the post-revolutionary civil war from 1917 to 1920, which was fought in large part on Ukrainian soil. Although this was not a war between Ukrainians and Russians as such, Ukrainian nationalists took advantage of the civil war to break from Russia and proclaim a short-lived independent state in 1918. When the Ukrainian Bolsheviks regained the upper hand, they reintegrated the state into

Russia, reluctantly accepting Lenin's insistence that there could be no self-determination for Ukraine. This was a change of view. In 1914 Lenin had described Ukraine as Russia's first colony: 'It has become for Russia what Ireland was for England, exploited to the extreme, receiving nothing in return.'[11]

The Ukrainian Bolsheviks had minimal support from the peasantry, even before the collectivization campaign and the famine of the early 1930s. But Ukrainian hostility to Bolshevik rule was not an ethnic issue. In the first days of the Second World War some Ukrainians greeted the invading Nazis as liberators, but the movement was not widespread. While eye-witness accounts suggest that most people were glad to see the Soviet authorities retreat, they watched the invading Germans with caution. Their restraint was justified since the Nazis soon turned on Ukrainian nationalism more viciously than the Bolsheviks had done.

In spite of Ukraine's bloody history in the first half of this century, Ukrainian-Russian relations continued on a surprisingly high level of harmony. The two peoples were not in a state of perpetual suspicion and enmity as Poles and Russians were. Ukrainians and Russians had been ethnically one when the first Eastern Slav state began to be formed in the tenth century – Kievan Rus, that is, Russia based in Kiev. Its Prince, Vladimir of Kiev, was the first of the Eastern Slavs to accept Orthodoxy and was baptized in AD 988. Later, when the Princes of Muscovy created a new power centre in Moscow and became the main force among the Eastern Slavs, ethnic and linguistic differences developed. Several centuries later, when Moscow became the main colonizing force, Ukrainians were given a label which they were to find insulting. To the west were the 'White Russians', the Byelorussians, between Smolensk and the Polish border. The Russians of Muscovy who had now spread their influence south to the Caucasus and east as far as the Pacific Ocean were the 'Great Russians'. Ukraine was called 'Little Russia', or Malorus. Although the phrase was geographical in origin, it could not help being felt by Ukrainian nationalists as demeaning.

Russians started to settle in Ukraine from the eighteenth century, particularly in the regions to the east of the River Dnieper, known as the Left Bank, as well as in the Crimea and along the Black Sea coast. In the western regions Russian garrison towns were set up to defend against the Poles. Migration continued up to and throughout the Soviet period. Under Catherine the Great it was a widescale and deliberate policy. Russians moved to Ukrainian towns and Ukrainian peasants were forbidden from settling in them. All Ukrainian provinces were governed from St Petersburg, just like any provinces in Russia. Outside the towns the gentry of the Left Bank quickly allowed themselves to be Russified in order to join the Russian system. Thousands changed their names. The result was that there was even less entrepreneurship in Ukraine in the nineteenth century than there was in Russia itself. Development of the southern steppe area was almost entirely financed by Western European capital. Ninety-three per cent of Ukrainians in 1897 were classified as peasants. From 1804 until the 1917 Revolution the Ukrainian language was banned from schools as a subject and a medium for instruction.[12]

This almost total suppression of Ukrainian culture eased somewhat under the Bolsheviks. They permitted a controlled Ukrainianization of the party and administrative élite. The establishment of a Ukrainian Soviet Socialist Republic and a Communist party of the Ukraine were partial concessions to national feeling. But Ukraine was to suffer the catastrophe of collectivization, the artificial famine of 1932 and 1933 and the purges. Stalin's ruthless policies of requisitioning grain, with troops and police being sent into villages to seize whatever they could find, left three million people dead.

After the Second World War Ukraine's agriculture revived, thanks to its generally rich soil. Its better local food supplies, as well as its climate, attracted hundreds of Russian settlers. By 1989 when the last census was taken 21.9 per cent, or roughly one in every five inhabitants of Ukraine, was Russian. In many of the cities of the east they were a majority. Other areas were heavily Russified.

Ukrainian parents spoke Russian at home, and had to send their children to Russian schools because there were no others. In Donetsk there were no Ukrainian-language schools, and even in Kiev only a quarter of the children went to them. This long process of Russification and the high degree of intermarriage between Russians and Ukrainians over centuries played a major role in blurring distinctions and keeping ethnic relations even-tempered. In a 1991 poll in Donetsk one-third of the population described themselves as Russian, one-third as Ukrainian. The rest did not know what they were and fell back on the vague definition 'Slav'.

General Konstantin Morozov, the first defence minister of independent Ukraine, was branded a traitor by some officers in Moscow. He had a Russian father and Ukrainian mother. Asked at a press conference how he felt about serving Ukraine rather than Russia, he replied with a laugh, 'Very comfortable'. Vladimir Grinev, the jovial bushy-haired deputy chairman of the Ukrainian parliament, reflected the confusion of identity which many feel. 'My mother is a Ukrainian, and I grew up without a father,' he told me. 'But I consider myself a Russian, since I went to a Russian-language school and was raised on Russian literature and culture.' He had once asked his mother why she registered him as a Russian so that the entry for his nationality on his internal Soviet passport said 'Russian'. 'She threw up her hands and said she did not know.' Grinev played an important role in winning Russian-speakers in eastern Ukraine to the idea of Ukrainian independence.

In a set of small rooms off Kiev's main street shortly before the independence referendum I met the leaders of the Rus Society, a group which claimed to defend Russian speakers' interests and wanted to maintain the Soviet Union. One room was a gallery with pictures on Christian religious themes and landscapes. Plying me with cognac, they ran through their complaints. I thought they sounded mild. 'We have no problems yet on language and education,' said Yuri Kudryavtsev, 'but on several occasions vandals have daubed statues and monuments which are sacred to Russians.' Vladimir Lozovoy, a large man with a flowing black beard, was a

member of an Orthodox religious order. Though his father was
Ukrainian and his mother Polish, he described himself as Russian.
'I feel part of the great Russian tribe. I respect Russian culture and
am worried by this rise of Ukrainian provincialism. I can get
Ukrainian books in Moscow as well as Russian ones, but here
nowadays you can only find Ukrainian books.' In spite of their
complaints, none of the five men was planning to emigrate if
Ukraine split from Russia. They did not expect many other Russian
speakers would.

Another reason for the relative placidity of Ukraine's move
towards independence was the way the republic's Communist party
embraced the nationalist cause. It meant that a broad political
alliance for independence was formed several months before the
USSR collapsed. In Moscow Gorbachev saw this as cynical
treachery, and Leonid Kravchuk, who had once headed the Ukrainian Communist party's department of ideology, was second only to
Boris Yeltsin as the man the Soviet president found it hard to
tolerate. In their determination to block the Union treaty and save
the USSR, the coup plotters felt similarly about Kravchuk. Ukraine
was the only republic which received a visit from one of the
conspirators. General Valentin Varennikov, the commander of land
forces who took a tough line with Gorbachev at his Foros dacha on
the first day of the coup, flew to Kiev the next day. The hatchet
man of the otherwise incompetent team, Varennikov promised
Kravchuk not to impose a state of emergency or bring troops into
the streets provided the Ukrainian leader did not publicly oppose
the coup. Trying to stop Ukraine's drift out of the Union was one
of the plotters' main objectives. They failed, and Kravchuk
continued on his course to independence with redoubled vigour
after the coup crumbled.

Some of Kravchuk's opponents in Ukraine's anti-Communist
camp saw this as cynicism, a device to keep the old nomenklatura
and himself in power. Kravchuk is an ambitious man, and he
realized that to oppose nationalism would be political suicide. He
had seen how Yeltsin played the Russian nationalist card against

Gorbachev, and understood that he could also use Ukrainian opposition to 'the centre' to win popular support. Nevertheless, his switch to a nationalist position helped Ukraine as a whole, since it prevented the republic being split on the issue. Kravchuk also prevented the party from splitting into pro- and anti-independence camps largely on ethnic lines, as happened with the Communist parties in Latvia and Lithuania. This might have led to bloodshed, as it did in the Baltics.

The nationalist movement in Ukraine emerged into the open relatively long after the beginning of perestroika, and more than a year later than similar movements in the Baltic republics and Armenia. It started as a protest over the environment before taking on an open political form. The slowness of Ukraine's protest was surprising in that Ukrainians had a more serious ecological cause for concern than any other republic. The explosion of a nuclear reactor at Chernobyl in April 1986 less than 100 miles from Kiev was a national trauma, yet it was only gradually that a political reaction developed. It took two years before an ecological movement, Zelenyi Svit (Green World), was created. Its aim was to press for a faster clean-up of the area and to get accurate information on the disaster's medical effects. Green World joined forces with intellectuals who were raising the issue of Ukrainian history and language. A Ukrainian Memorial society was founded in the autumn of 1988 to demand compensation for Stalin's victims and to start uncovering the scores of secret mass graves. They broke the taboo on the famine of 1932 and 1933 which Stalin deliberately promoted during his collectivization drive. Until then, party officials refused even to acknowledge there was a famine, let alone that it was man-made. In February 1989 Dmytro Pavlychko, a distinguished poet, started a Language Society named after Ukraine's great nineteenth-century writer, Taras Shevchenko. It campaigned to have Ukrainian declared the republic's state language and revived in schools and universities. The three groups combined to discuss the formation of a Ukrainian Popular Front, which they called the Popular Movement of Ukraine for Perestroika, or Rukh (Movement) for short.

A key factor in the slow emergence of these non-party groups was the fierce opposition of Vladimir Shcherbitsky, the first secretary of the Ukrainian Communist party who had ruled the republic since 1972. The change came with the nationwide elections to the Congress of People's Deputies in March 1989. Communist officials in Kiev suffered a huge defeat, even surpassing the humiliation which voters inflicted on party leaders in Leningrad. Of the fifteen officials who stood in Kiev only one was elected. The losers included Valentin Zgursky, Kiev's mayor, as well as Konstantin Masik, the first secretary of the city party committee.

Emboldened by their triumph Rukh's supporters called a protest meeting on the third anniversary of the Chernobyl disaster. For the first time the party authorities did not dare to ban it. On the contrary they tried to take it over, as I discovered when I joined some 50,000 people streaming into Kiev's Dynamo stadium. Spelt out in lights on the electronic scoreboard were four words: 'Chernobyl: memory and vigilance'. The defeated mayor and party secretary were standing by the microphones. One of their officials conducted the meeting and chose whom to call to speak. There was a heavy police presence, watching the stands to make sure no one strayed on to the pitch. But what officials wanted to confine to a memorial event insisted on becoming a meeting about the present and future. 'Chernobyl hasn't taught us anything,' Volodymyr Yavorivsky, a popular writer and at that time still a Communist party member, told the crowd. 'An undemocratic society cannot be allowed to use high-risk technologies. The only way to make things safe is to have more democracy.' Behind in the stands a group enthusiastically waved a banner saying 'Chernobyl – leadership irresponsibility, contempt for the popular masses, absence of glasnost, a warning to future generations'.

Before the anniversary, the party press had come out with several articles and interviews claiming everything was under control, and that adequate radiation checks were being done on the ground, water, locally-grown food and people so that there was no cause for alarm. After the cover-up in the first days and weeks after the explosion, many Ukrainians had lost faith in any assurances the party gave. 'The ministry of health gives out too little information,' claimed Alla Yarushynska as she sat on the terraces watching the rally. A campaigning journalist from Zhitomir, sixty miles from Chernobyl, where new radiation hot spots had just been discovered, she beat a party official in the March elections. One of the biggest rounds of applause went to a speaker who angrily declared he had seen ministry documents urging officials not to publish the full facts about radiation doses. Speakers who claimed that there was no cause for concern were booed and whistled by the crowd, who shook their banners rhythmically.

One group managed to get on to the pitch, led by a man carrying a child's coffin draped in black. The police did not dare to stop them. They marched up close to where the mayor was standing. He was in office at the time of the Chernobyl explosion and did nothing to warn parents not to let their children play outside as radioactive clouds went by. He even ordered the May day parade with its traditional accompaniment of flag-waving youngsters to go ahead through Kiev. The coffin-carrying marchers walked past the mayor, unfurling a banner which said 'Stop the May Day parade this year as a sign of respect for the dead'. 'If he has a conscience, Mr Zgursky should resign,' demanded Les Tanyuk, a Rukh supporter, through the microphones. The mayor bit his lip and said nothing.

Gaining confidence and widespread support, Rukh was able to hold a founding conference in Kiev the following summer. Shcherbitsky was still in power (Gorbachev persuaded him to retire a few days later) but the Ukrainian leader gave his consent to the occasion. Rukh made compromises. It agreed not to hold a rally or march to the city centre and not to parade in the street with the blue and yellow flag of the short-lived independent republic of 1918, which Rukh wanted to restore in place of the flag of Soviet Ukraine.

Shcherbitsky was not the only hardliner in the Ukrainian party leadership. Yuri Yelchenko, its ideological secretary, strongly criticized Rukh, a few days after its conference, at the central committee meeting in Moscow on nationality policy. He even suggested that rules be worked out for disbanding nationalist organizations. But Leonid Kravchuk, then head of the ideological department and a relatively junior figure, seemed to be taking a more forward-looking position. He attended Rukh's conference, sitting modestly near the back of the hall. He told me when we sat down for an interview in the corridor that he found many of the nationalist speeches contained 'very strong but just points'. The Communist party had gradually come round to accepting Rukh's right to exist, he admitted, though 'the logic of the political battle is implacable. There cannot be two centres of power here. They are our opponents, but we must defeat them through argument.' The main thing he feared was bloodshed, he said. 'I hope there won't be confrontation between us.'

Kravchuk's measured comments suggested he was well aware of the strength of the nationalist case. He pointed out that he favoured making Ukrainian the republic's official language. Perhaps he was already learning how to steal Rukh's political clothes. At the time, however, no one had any inkling that he would emerge as the country's president. Two other appearances impressed me more. Levko Lukyanenko, a gaunt man with a grey beard, was introduced as a political prisoner who had spent a total of twenty-six years in custody, among other things for advocating a referendum on Ukraine's secession from the Soviet Union. There was much talk at the time that Nelson Mandela might soon be released from his South African prison after the same number of years. I had never met a man who had lost a quarter of a century and I wondered why the world had not heard of Lukyanenko, or how he could look so composed. (Two years later he ran against Kravchuk in the presidential election and was soundly beaten.)

The other star of the Rukh conference was Adam Michnik, the editor of the newspaper of the independent Polish trade union movement, Solidarity. A shambling figure in light blue jeans, he prophetically described the two neighbours, Ukraine and Poland, as 'post-Communist nations' but urged the Ukrainians not to antagonize Gorbachev, since the keys to democracy in the Soviet Union were in Moscow.

In those early days much of Rukh's focus was on Western Ukraine, the areas which Stalin seized from Poland under the Molotov-Ribbentrop pact. The region was different from the rest of the republic, and had been under Austrian or Polish influence for centuries. Its religion was Uniate, or Greek Catholic, a blend of Orthodoxy which accepted the Pope as the church's head. Stalin suppressed the Uniates and closed most of their churches, giving the rest to the Orthodox. In 1989 Uniate congregations which had for years held services secretly in the forests started to seize the churches back. The following spring Vyacheslav Chornovil, another former political prisoner, won the elections to become head of the regional council in Lvov, Western Ukraine's capital. The region was one of the first to dismantle a Lenin statue. It was the first region in Ukraine where human rights activists exhumed mass graves in which the NKVD, the forerunner of the KGB, had buried its victims. Naturally, Western Ukraine was the first part of Ukraine to raise the demand for independence from the Soviet Union.

At first the demand seemed absurd. Rukh leaders in Kiev were not thinking of secession themselves. They thought Western Ukraine was a special case. The Rukh conference in September 1989 adopted a milder demand. It called for the political and economic sovereignty of Ukraine and a new Union treaty. Though more moderate than the Western Ukrainians' position, the call for sovereignty was radical compared to the recent past. As Ukrainians rediscovered their history, a new national consciousness developed throughout the country. The crisis of the Soviet economy also gave a powerful push. Traditional party economic managers began to be convinced that decentralization and breaking from Moscow would help them to prosper more rapidly.

After Shcherbitsky's resignation, the Communist party moved quickly to adopt Rukh's policies. After their poor showing in the

Soviet elections of March 1989, the more far-sighted Ukrainian party leaders saw that to prevent a similar defeat in the republican elections of March 1990 they would have to support sovereignty 'within a renewed Soviet federation', as their electoral manifesto put it. Thanks partly to this change of line, the Communists won some three-quarters of the seats and the so-called 'Democratic Block', centred on Rukh, took a quarter.

Rukh called its parliamentary block the People's Council. Its nationalist tide continued to flow, and in July parliament adopted a Declaration on Sovereignty which went further than that passed by the Russian parliament. It also passed a law on Ukraine's economic independence.

A two-week-long student strike outside parliament in October 1990 forced the next change of pace. By then Kravchuk had become chairman of parliament after Vladimir Ivashko moved to Moscow to be the CPSU's deputy general secretary. The students demanded that conscripts into the Soviet army should only serve in Ukraine, and that the new Union treaty be rejected. The Communist majority in parliament was already beginning to split into 'sovereignty Communists' and 'imperial Communists'. The former sympathized with the nationalists and parliament accepted most of the students' demands. Conscripts would only serve outside Ukraine if they wanted to, and no Union treaty would be signed before there was a new Ukrainian constitution.

The following spring Gorbachev tried to dragoon the republican leaders into signing the Union treaty by calling a nationwide Soviet referendum. The question to be asked was unclear and designed to elicit a positive answer. While the nationalists denounced the referendum as illegal, Kravchuk cleverly proposed adding a second question – 'Do you agree that Ukraine should be part of a Union of Soviet sovereign states on the principles of the declaration on the state sovereignty of Ukraine?' The electorate voted 70.2 per cent in favour of Gorbachev's question, but 80.2 per cent for Kravchuk's.

On 27 June parliament in Kiev was due to discuss the draft Union treaty and decide whether to sign it. Demonstrations outside the parliament helped to sway some deputies. Kravchuk himself was already looking ahead to the presidential elections due on 1 December and did not want to be accused of stampeding parliament into the treaty. When parliament decided to postpone its decision until September so as to give more time after the summer break for deputies to study it, Gorbachev had to give up his hopes of early success in holding the Union together. The blow came on the eve of his visit to London to meet the Group of Seven leading industrial countries where he had wanted to show them that his country was stable enough to receive Western loans. In spite of the Ukrainian disappointment Gorbachev managed to persuade Yeltsin and the Kazakh president, Nursultan Nazarbayev, to agree to the signing ceremony for 20 August. But what had been too tight a treaty for the Ukrainians seemed too loose and decentralizing for the coup plotters. Their putsch unravelled the treaty. After it, there was almost no chance that Ukraine would ever sign.

Although they began as political opponents, as Kravchuk had observed at Rukh's founding congress in 1989, Kravchuk and Rukh had converged on two important issues. They had broadened the independence struggle to cover economics as well as politics, but narrowed it to focus on statehood instead of nationalism. The dominant ideology for both of them was state-building rather than ethnicity, and citizenship rather than language. Bohdan Krawchenko, the Canadian historian of Ukraine's independence movement, who became an adviser to the government in 1991, remarked that Kravchuk and Rukh 'always referred to the people of Ukraine rather than the Ukrainian people'.[13] The phrase recurred in the oath of the new National Guard, which the majority of Russian officers at that interior ministry academy in Kharkov solemnly accepted – 'I swear always to be loyal to the people of Ukraine ... I take my oath to defend the Ukrainian state'. As Krawchenko commented, 'the distinction is crucial'.

9

Russia *v.* the USSR
Yeltsin *v.* Gorbachev

You don't have to be a president to be a politician.

GORBACHEV, 18 DECEMBER 1991

The Final Days

A light snow coated the cobble-stones of Red Square and a wind was blowing fiercely through the Spassky Gate, the Kremlin's pedestrian entrance for official visitors. Grigory Revenko, President Gorbachev's chief of staff, was walking in as we came out. It was a fortuitous encounter and neither I nor Michael Dobbs of the *Washington Post* who was with me knew Revenko well. Was the president doomed? I asked him, chancing my luck. Two days before Richard Nixon's resignation or two hours before Margaret Thatcher's, a senior official on either of their teams would have sent a foreign reporter packing with a crisp 'No comment' or some other evasion.

Revenko, like most Gorbachev loyalists, was a convert to glasnost. 'The president has no power now,' he replied with no hesitation and a wan smile. 'Gorbachev's fate is decided. He has no physical opportunity to work or carry out his duties. He will keep his position only as long as it takes the new structures to replace the old ones.' In the lobby of the Soviet parliament we had just heard

Georgy Shakhnazarov, another close Gorbachev adviser, being equally candid about his boss. 'He's holding up very well. He's a courageous, convinced man. But in life you always have to be ready to move from one stage to another. Everything has a beginning and an end.'

A week earlier it had become inevitable that Gorbachev would have to go, since the USSR of which he was president was itself coming to an end. At an extraordinary meeting in an old Brezhnev hunting lodge in the Byelovezhsky Forest near the Polish border at Brest on 8 December 1991 Boris Yeltsin and the leaders of the other two Slav republics, Ukraine and Belarus, came to an agreement to replace the Soviet Union with a Commonwealth of Independent States. For Gorbachev the news was not entirely unexpected but he was shocked by the way it was done. Yeltsin first told the US president, George Bush, by phone and only then asked Stanislav Shushkevich, the Belarus leader, to ring Gorbachev and give him the fateful news.

Although the drive for increased sovereignty in the main Soviet republics had been accelerating fast since the collapse of the August coup, Gorbachev was still hoping he could hold together a loose confederation with a place for himself in the centre at the head of various inter-republican committees or councils. It was not to be. The second Peace of Brest (at the first one in 1918 Lenin had been forced to give up huge slices of the Russian empire) did away with any notion of a union, a confederation, or a centre.

The agreement by the Slav troika faced the leaders of the other Soviet republics with a *fait accompli*. Nursultan Nazarbayev, the president of Kazakhstan, was particularly angry, first at not being consulted, and second by the notion that the Slavs were taking decisions behind the backs of Central Asia and the southern republics. As the fourth nuclear-weapons republic in the USSR, he should have been invited by the others, he felt. He called the Byelovezhsky agreement 'a throwback to the Middle Ages'. But Nazarbayev was a realist, and after his initial anger saw he had no choice but to go along with it. Gorbachev tried to fight the move at first, calling it 'illegal and dangerous'. He issued a strong public statement which was read out on the evening television news, saying three men could not take such key decisions on their own. He urged the summoning of a special session of the Soviet Congress of People's Deputies. The idea was doomed when the various republican leaders met to discuss the Brest agreement and decided there was no way to resist. Once he saw that there was no chance of enough deputies coming to Moscow to form a quorum for the Congress, Gorbachev also realized there was no way out.

In the Russian parliament at the end of the August coup, he had been subjected to a merciless hounding by Yeltsin and his triumphant supporters. Now the humiliation was to last a fortnight, as the reins of power were prised from his hands. There was no precedent to follow, no formal handing over, no ceremonial departure, since a country had never come to an end like this before. One by one, the remaining bastions fell to Boris Yeltsin by decree. The Russian leader signed an order liquidating the Soviet foreign ministry. He took over the KGB and the Soviet interior ministry, ordering their staff to merge into a new Russian security organization. Finally the Kremlin fortress with its famous high brick walls and ancient watch-towers itself fell to the enemy. 'All buildings, including the Kremlin, as well as the property, assets and foreign currency belonging to the Soviet presidency ... are transferred to the management of the Russian administration,' said one of Yeltsin's many decrees.

It was hardly surprising that Gorbachev's temper sometimes broke. At a long meeting with Russian reporters on 12 December he accused Yeltsin of plotting behind his back and mounting in effect a second coup.[1] Gorbachev said he had the first inkling of it during a talk with Yeltsin on 5 December. The subject was the Ukrainian referendum on 1 December with its massive vote for independence. To Gorbachev's question as to how he saw a future Union Yeltsin was evasive. He could not imagine a Union without the Ukraine, he kept repeating. Was he sorry about that, or privately pleased? Gorbachev could not be sure. The two men emerged from the meeting looking grim. 'It was very difficult, very difficult,' Yeltsin told waiting reporters.

Gorbachev argued that the Ukrainian vote did not mean that the USSR's second largest republic wanted to break away. The referendum was not a mandate for secession, unlike the one in Armenia six months earlier where the question had been unambiguous: 'Do you want Armenia to be outside the Union?' Gorbachev urged Yeltsin to sign the draft treaty for the new Union of Sovereign States (USS) which they had tentatively agreed on two weeks earlier. 'My job is to force you to be the first to sign,' Gorbachev said he told Yeltsin. That would convince the other republics to sign, leaving Ukraine isolated. Yeltsin refused. He told Gorbachev he was flying to Minsk on 7 December to meet the Belarus leader and would suggest that Leonid Kravchuk, the Ukrainian president, came too. 'If we can't convince Ukraine, we'll have to think of something else,' Yeltsin told Gorbachev.

It was unclear what that 'something else' was, but Gorbachev told reporters he felt a constitutional coup was in the offing. He sensed there was a 'secret plan'. 'The issue was not Ukraine. The Ukrainian factor was exploited by the Russian leadership. Their position was obvious for a long time. They just played the Ukrainian card,' Gorbachev snapped. He told reporters he had in his possession a paper written by Gennady Burbulis, Yeltsin's right-hand man, who had recently been appointed Russia's first deputy prime minister. Its gist was that Gorbachev was trying to re-create the old Union centre under the guise of a confederation and this must be resisted. 'Russia has already lost half of what it gained after the August putsch. Cunning Gorbachev is weaving a net to restore peace. This is not good for Russia. The process must be stopped,' the paper said, according to Gorbachev.

Although the paper was marked 'Strictly Confidential', Burbulis's views had been well-known for some time. A former lecturer in Marxism-Leninism at a government institute in Sverdlovsk, Burbulis was the forty-six-year-old leader of a young guard of politicians and economists whom he had brought to Yeltsin's side after the coup. His father was Lithuanian but had lived most of his life in Russia. A long-time member of the communist party, Burbulis founded a pro-democracy political club, called 'Discussion Tribune', in Sverdlovsk in 1988 and was elected to the Congress of People's Deputies the next year. As a member of the Interregional Group of Deputies, a loose faction of democrats which became known as the official opposition in the Soviet parliament, Burbulis caught the eye of the future Russian leader. They were both from the same town. By 1991 Burbulis was a firm anti-Communist. He and Yegor Gaidar, the leading economist in the group which Burbulis assembled, urged Yeltsin to ban the Communist party, which he did on 6 November, and to break with the Soviet Union. They advised Yeltsin that any new economic union would help the other republics feed off Russia rather than help Russia. They also urged him to offer the United States dramatic nuclear arms cuts so that all nuclear weapons could be removed from the territories of Ukraine, Belarus and Kazakhstan. Russia would remain the only nuclear state in the former USSR.

The Inter-regional Group of Deputies had first raised the idea of a 'Commonwealth' instead of the USSR two years earlier, though they called it a commonwealth of sovereign, rather than independent, states. Under the original draft there would have been a central body with a co-ordinating role. By the autumn of 1991 Burbulis had dispensed with that, seeing it as vital to remove Gorbachev, who in his eyes was still the linchpin of the old Communist-dominated apparatus. On 7 December the Burbulis plan went into high gear. In Minsk Yeltsin addressed the Belarus parliament, saying there were four or five ideas for the future shape of the country, one of them a 'commonwealth of independent states'. Kravchuk, meanwhile, was thinking along similar lines. At a press conference in Kiev, before leaving for Minsk, he also used the word 'commonwealth' and said he had a proposal to make to the other two leaders in this regard. From Minsk, now in the company of Shushkevich, the Belarus leader, Yeltsin and Kravchuk travelled to the hunting lodge at Byelovezhsky Forest near Brest. The talks lasted twenty-four hours, with drafting groups working all night.

At a press conference in Moscow later, Burbulis and another of the Russian young guard, Sergei Shakhrai, were at pains to reject the notion that the Russians took the initiative. 'Everyone chipped in. There was an extrordinary sense of collective work,' Burbulis said. An abrasive confrontational personality, Burbulis liked medical metaphors. At a dinner with the Foreign Correspondents' Association in October 1992 he referred to the opposition in the Russian parliament as people 'pathologically unwilling to accept our economic programme', and described Gorbachev as a man 'whose sickness is that he was brought up in a system where your personal future and your job were totally linked'. After the meeting near Brest, Burbulis denied that they had killed off the Soviet Union. The three leaders had declared that they were forming a commonwealth because the Union was already dead. 'Our declaration was a medical diagnosis,' Burbulis said drily.

Yeltsin had already done much to take away the centre's power before he went to Brest. Russia had stopped paying federal taxes, a move which other republics followed, leaving the Soviet treasury without a budget. On 30 November Yeltsin promised to guarantee all Union officials' salaries. On 5 December, the day of his tense encounter with Gorbachev over the Ukrainian referendum, he signed a decree promising to pay all army officers' salaries from 1 January, regardless of which republic they were based in. He also gave them a 90 per cent increase in pay. This was the muscle behind Yeltsin's constitutional moves against the Union, and it left Gorbachev virtually powerless.

Two days after the Brest summit, Gorbachev made his last move to try to forestall the process. He asked the defence minister, Marshal Yevgeni Shaposhnikov, to summon to Moscow the entire corpus of senior army commanders from the USSR's various military districts. Gorbachev's address was a flop, a disastrous mixture of calls for reform and misplaced morale-building. He said the army should stick to its professional business and not get involved in politics, and urged the men in uniform not to panic over the disarray in the Union. One participant described the president's performance as 'pathetic', and when Yeltsin addressed the same group the next morning, he sensibly stuck to bread and butter issues, reminding them of his promise to raise salaries. It was clear that Yeltsin, not Gorbachev, held the purse-strings and the army's loyalty.

Gorbachev's final days were spent in adjusting to what had become an unstoppable transition. Hopes that there might at least be some form of dignified ceremony to mark the hand-over of power and the end of the Union, had to be abandoned. All that Gorbachev could do was prepare his resignation speech and send diplomatic notes to the world leaders he had known, thanking them for their support. Six days before his farewell broadcast I arranged an interview in the prestigious yellow stucco building in the Kremlin where every leader since the October Revolution had worked. Near Lenin's office and private apartment, which were still kept as a museum for special visitors, Gorbachev was preparing to hand over to Yeltsin. The red-carpeted corridors looked the same as always. Huge burgundy-coloured filing cabinets stood in an alcove near the lift, giving the impression that furniture removal was under way. In fact, the cabinets had been there for months. There was no whirr of shredding-machines, no plastic bags of papers being secreted down the stairs. 'It's not as though the enemy is at the gate. We don't feel under siege,' Alexander Likhotal, one of Gorbachev's spokesmen, told me. He used to be a senior official in the central committee's international department, and well remembered the time, four months earlier, when an angry crowd stood beneath his window, demanding that the building be sealed. 'That was not a pleasant experience, and yet I felt it had a certain historical justice. It was part of an inevitable process. In their last months the people running the party were doing nothing but obstructing reform,' he said. 'Now it's rather the reverse. I feel physically secure, but sad that perestroika's efforts to find a constitutional way of making changes seem to have taken so little root. Society and the press have not yet got to the point where they object to the way the decision to end the Union was done behind people's backs.'

On 25 December Gorbachev was to make his broadcast and sign his resignation decree. There was a brief flutter as Andrei Grachev, his press secretary, and Yegor Yakovlev, promoted from being editor of *Moscow News* to head the central television service, discussed whether the signature should come before the speech or vice-versa. Yakovlev wanted the signature last, so that viewers would see it. Gorbachev said he would do it immediately, before the broadcast began. He took a pen and signed the paper. The cameras were turned on, and looking solemn but composed, the abdicating president summed up his seven years of reforms. He described perestroika's greatest domestic achievement as the fact that 'society has received its freedom and been liberated politically and spiritually', though he pointed out that society still had a 'low level of political culture'. Internationally, the Cold War was over. The country had given up foreign interference and the use of troops abroad. At the end of his ten-minute address, Gorbachev expressed alarm at the collapse of the Union, and that people had 'lost their citizenship in a great country'.

After the speech Yeltsin was supposed to meet Gorbachev in the Kremlin for a brief ceremony in which the nuclear codes would be passed over. But the Russian leader was angry at the tone of Gorbachev's speech and refused to come, suggesting that they meet on 'neutral ground' instead. His action seemed to underline Gorbachev's point about the country's low political culture. The departing president was forced to give Marshal Shaposhnikov the codes and ask him to pass them on. When the Red Flag was lowered over the Kremlin that night for the last time, it disappeared with as little formality as Gorbachev's own slipping away. 'Not one of the presidents of the sovereign states, the former Soviet republics, considered it possible to come to Moscow during those days, or even to phone me, although long years of close and comradely relations had linked most of us.' Gorbachev wrote bitterly two months later.[2]

The Russian Idea

Gorbachev had been destroyed by two of the things he had created, or at least allowed to come into being. One was republican nationalism. The other was Yeltsin's burning rivalry. In the 'Russian idea' the two merged. By conviction and instinct Yeltsin was no more of a Russian nationalist than Gorbachev and it was only shortly before the Brest meeting that he decided to destroy what was left of the Union. What Yeltsin did was to use the national idea to undermine and unseat his enemy. His was what one might call 'instrumental nationalism' – nationalism as a means to an end – as opposed to the deeply-felt nationalism of the Russian ideologues who are discussed in Chapter 13. This is not to say that Yeltsin was purely motivated by ambition, rivalry and his love of being popular. Under perestroika he gradually developed a gut instinct in favour of a more open form of politics to replace the Soviet Union's Communist system, and his conversion to the principle of market economics was certainly genuine. But these changes of heart came late and were initially prompted by other, more limited, motives.

Yeltsin had come to Moscow in June 1985 when he was appointed central committee secretary in charge of construction. This had always been his special field and the move was logical. He had spent most of his career in his native Sverdlovsk, acquiring a reputation as a hard-driving and energetic party official. Yeltsin is not a man who reads much or who likes to get information from briefing-papers and memoranda. His style has always been to go out and listen to meetings of organized groups, or address complaints in person. In Sverdlovsk he answered letters and took phone calls from ordinary people on television. For a local party secretary this was unusual but in no way politically dangerous, and not in itself a sign of a commitment to building democratic institutions.

Yeltsin was not an industrial administrator or economic manager. A party secretary was more concerned with matters of infrastructure, trying to get more money from the centre for local road-building, housing and schools. In Moscow, Yeltsin met a tough administrative challenge. A few months after being posted there, he was appointed first secretary of the capital city's party organization. He initially refused the job, perhaps sensing it would be beyond him. Moscow had been run for years by the corrupt Viktor Grishin and its administration had become a hotbed of bribe-takers and inefficiency. Yeltsin set about sacking officials in large numbers, a move he carried out with bluntness and some courage, but it was not enough. The system itself was rotten, as Gorbachev and other members of the new Politburo also sensed. (Yeltsin had been promoted to the Politburo in February 1986.)

Yeltsin began to lose heart. In trying to sack party officials he was meeting resistance from Yegor Ligachev, who was in charge of the central committee secretariat. He was also getting tired of what he considered Gorbachev's self-satisfied monologues at Politburo meetings. In September 1987 he wrote to Gorbachev saying he wished to resign. It was an unprecedented move for a Politburo member to make, at least since the 1920s. Many had resigned 'on grounds of ill-health' but everyone knew that this was a euphemism for being sacked. To go voluntarily was unheard of in recent years. Why did Yeltsin do it? It seems there was no reason or strategy. It was another sign of impulsiveness, as well as the culmination of months of exhaustion, overwork, and ill-health. He was sent to hospital with severe chest pains soon afterwards. Gavriil Popov, a liberal future mayor of Moscow, accused Yeltsin of panicking and said his style of trying to run Moscow was 'theatre'. Yeltsin was an authoritarian 'vanguardist' who confused the art of governing with giving orders and dismissing people. Lev Sukhanov, who became one of Yeltsin's closest aides a few months later, said it was not a weak decision. 'A weak man would have carried on. He wanted to show he could not work in that environment.'[3]

In his autobiography, Yeltsin describes his motive as frustration. 'I needed the help of the whole Politburo . . . the capital city is such a complex, conglomerate entity where virtually every strand of the country's political, economic and social fabric criss-cross and intertwine . . . but far from getting their help, I had noticed there was an active unwillingness in the Politburo to help the city in tackling the problems that had built up'.[4] If frustration was the impulse, then Yeltsin was probably expressing a combination of feelings which many Politburo members must have shared, a sense that change was urgent and vital, desperation about how to achieve it, plus fear that if the process went too far too fast, they might all be out of work. If it was so hard to change one city, how much more difficult was it to change a nationwide system?

The strange element in what Yeltsin later admitted was not a very coherent resignation speech to the central committee in October 1987 was that he did not call for a speeding up of perestroika, or an abandonment of the old system, as one might have expected from a radical. He called for a slowing-down. 'It seems to me we must perhaps take a more cautious approach to announcing a realistic timetable for perestroika in the coming two years,' he told the central committee. Nikolai Ryzhkov, as a former director of Uralmash, the huge engineering firm in Yeltsin's home-town of Sverdlovsk, knew him better than most members of the Politburo. He put Yeltsin's departure down to two factors. After almost two years in the Moscow job, Yeltsin realized people would soon start asking why so little had changed. It was therefore better to get out before the blame was put on him. The second factor was a vague sense that 'the wind was beginning to change, euphoria over perestroika was evaporating and he could somehow exploit it'.[5]

Yeltsin's resignation speech contained criticism of Gorbachev and Ligachev, a strong dose of self-criticism and an attack on perestroika's failure to improve ordinary people's standard of living. Gorbachev was furious with the speech, both for the content and for its timing on the eve of the seventieth anniversary of the October Revolution, when he wanted to convey an impression of party unity. Yeltsin was forced to leave his hospital bed in November and attend a humiliating meeting of the Moscow party committee where one official after another attacked him. He said in his autobiography that the doctors had drugged him so much that he could not defend himself.

According to Yeltsin, Gorbachev expected him to retire altogether.[6] But Yeltsin was still only fifty-six and asked for another job. Gorbachev created a special one for him, back in his old field, construction. He was made first deputy chairman of Gosstroi, the State Committee for Construction, a job with ministerial rank. A man who liked to denounce privileges in public found it hard to give them up himself. Sukhanov explained how difficult it was for Yeltsin to lose the perks of office. Switching from the Zil limousine allowed to Politburo members to the smaller Volga of a minister was a small shift which still left Yeltsin far better off than most Russians. Yeltsin did not like it. 'It was as though there were two people inside Yeltsin. One was the senior party official, used to power and privilege and lost when it was taken away. The second Yeltsin was a rebel, rejecting or rather beginning to reject the games connected with the system. These two Yeltsins fought against each other, and I won't be wrong if I say the struggle was fierce, and victory by no means sudden.'[7]

This inner struggle was understandable enough. Yeltsin had risen from the most humble beginnings to the apex of Kremlin power. He was born to a peasant family in February 1931 in the village of Butko in the Sverdlovsk region of the Urals. His mother was illiterate. They lived in a small house and owned one cow, but when this died in 1935 Yeltsin's father moved to Perm to work as a labourer on a building site. They found a room in a communal hut but were too poor to buy much furniture and the whole family, now including three children, slept on the floor. They lived in these conditions for ten years, an experience which marked Yeltsin for life. Schooling was rough and ready but Yeltsin did well. He loved volleyball, in spite of losing two fingers on his left hand while playing with a hand-grenade he had stolen as a boy. After graduating from the Urals polytechnic, he worked for fourteen years as a construction engineer. He was then asked to work with the Communist party's city committee in Sverdlovsk. His energy and extrovert personality impressed his superiors and within a relatively short time he was summoned to Moscow and asked by Brezhnev to take over the job of first secretary of the entire party apparatus in Sverdlovsk. Gorbachev was in charge of the rural region of Stavropol at the time, and the two men, one the head of an industrial area, the other head of an agricultural one, often telephoned each other to organize barter swaps of metal and timber for poultry and meat.

After his dramatic downfall, Yeltsin's main goal during the first few months in his new job was to recover from the blow of his sacking, his illness, his loss of status and the damage to his self-confidence which went with it. As usual, his chosen path was to get out and meet people. He was still a member of the Moscow city council and he began to visit constituents from the suburb of Ramenki which he represented. Then came the nineteenth party conference (see Chapter 5) which Yeltsin wanted to use to achieve his rehabilitation. He hoped the party delegates would restore him to favour. If that failed, then at least his speech, with the criticisms of Gorbachev and the party apparatus which he planned to make, would be published and he would be able to present himself to the public as a martyr. In Moscow, a small cult had already developed around him as a grass-roots democrat struggling against the party apparatus.

It is not clear when Yeltsin himself decided that a personal comeback was not enough and that he could challenge Gorbachev for the top job. It appears to have been after his massive election victory in March 1989 when he won 89.6 per cent of the vote. The first session of the newly elected Congress of People's Deputies would choose its chairman. He would automatically become the Soviet head of state. Yeltsin's supporters were told by an aide to Anatoly Lukyanov, Gorbachev's close colleague, that every job in the new Supreme Soviet had already been earmarked and there was nothing for Yeltsin. This annoyed the deputies from Sverdlovsk, Yeltsin's associates, and they resolved to find someone to nominate him. Burbulis was going to do it, but the deputies decided it would be better to find someone from another region. 'The aim was to put down a marker,' Sukhanov recalled.[8] But when his name was put forward, Yeltsin publicly withdrew his candidacy for the post of chairman. He realized that Gorbachev would easily win.

During the election Yeltsin had felt the power of public opinion and begun to see it as a real weapon for bringing the Communist party under control. Gorbachev had promoted the idea of contested elections and a genuine parliament as a way of bringing fresh blood into the system and removing the Communist party from duplicating the work of government. He had not meant to replace the party altogether. Yeltsin wanted to go further. In his speech to the Congress of People's Deputies he called for laws to limit the party's power and free the press from its control. He also backed Baltic demands for greater sovereignty. This was not yet a move to weaken the Soviet Union, or a sign that Yeltsin was already thinking of Russian sovereignty. It was rather that Yeltsin wanted to form a coalition of reform in the Soviet parliament and the Baltic deputies could form a solid part of it.

In parliament, Yeltsin came into close contact with the Russian liberal intelligentsia for the first time in his life. When they formed the Inter-regional Group of Deputies, Yeltsin was an obvious person to invite on to its leadership board. It was strange to see him on the platform in the hall of the Film-makers' Union at the group's inaugural meeting next to Andrei Sakharov, Gavriil Popov (who had recently criticized his authoritarian style) and Yuri Afanasyev, the radical historian. The bear-like figure and former party apparatchik seemed out of place. Everything about him was different: his size, his image of brute strength, his background, his blunt style of speaking. Although Gorbachev was no intellectual either (and the Moscow intelligentsia often ridiculed his bad grammar and pronunciation of Russian, which some said was less educated than Yeltsin's), his body language, facial expressions, and a certain softness which seemed to surround him allowed him to fit easily into an intellectual environment. Yeltsin, by contrast, was an unguided missile. That was how his new allies saw him, and an early plan for him to head the Inter-regional Group was modified so that it would have five co-chairmen rather than him alone.

Nevertheless, Yeltsin was a crucial figure to have on board. Pavel Voschanov recalled the way the radicals felt. Voshchanov had worked at the State Committee for Construction in charge of its economics institute and got to know Yeltsin when he moved there after his resignation from the Politburo. He later became Yeltsin's press secretary. 'I remember my first impression. He produced such internal energy that I came to understand that he was a battering-ram and could destroy that system.'[9]

Voshchanov realized that Yeltsin 'was no great thinker or intellectual, but as an apparatchik he knew how to take advantage of the system's internal contradictions'. Some of Yeltsin's enemies, like Anatoly Lukyanov, consider that Yeltsin was not an independent figure in the early days. He was used by the opposition movement. 'They needed someone to carry the flag. I had long conversations with Sakharov at the time, and he was always very critical of Yeltsin. The opposition people were clever. They saw this seed was being thrown on fertile ground. He was a man of ambition and with a sense of populism. He needed the moral and financial support which they could give him.'[10]

Voshchanov, who worked closely with Yeltsin for three years from soon after his humiliating departure from his high party position, says Yeltsin's feeling of insult was still deep and fresh three months later. Yeltsin often spoke about it. It was not a desire for revenge against Gorbachev at that stage, more a sense of competition. He wanted to create a counter-balance. 'When Yeltsin felt support from the public after his dismissal, he realized his power. Since then their relationship shaped as a balance. Which of them would lead the population? Which of them would control public opinion? Yeltsin was the mirror-image of Gorbachev,' Voshchanov said. At times this desire to be on a level with Gorbachev became absurd. On his first visit to the United States in September 1989, as an MP and not yet Russia's leader, Yeltsin almost cancelled a visit to the White House because he had not been promised a meeting with President Bush.

It was on his first American visit that Yeltsin seems to have decided to try to become Russia's leader. The first session of the Congress of People's Deputies had disappointed the radicals. In spite of the unprecedentedly open debates, the majority of deputies supported the Gorbachev line of gradual reform. With the prospect of elections to a Russian parliament the following spring, the radicals were shifting their attention to this body. In the old system it had been even more of a rubber stamp than the Soviet parliament, and completely subordinate to the Politburo. But in the new conditions of free elections, especially if there were no reserved seats for one-third of the deputies as there were in the Congress of People's Deputies, it could be a powerful body. That was the idea which excited the radicals, including Yeltsin. It was a time when new thinking had taken wing beyond all expectations. The Communist party apparatus was on the defensive. Gorbachev's economic reforms were running into the ground. The notion of a complete end to the Communist system and a shift to market economics was gaining strength.

Sukhanov, who was with Yeltsin on the American trip, described the deep impression made on Yeltsin by a visit to a supermarket in Texas. Yeltsin knew that the choice of food in Western shops was far wider than anything in Russia, but seeing it for himself nevertheless stunned him. On the plane from Texas he did not want to speak to anyone for some time. 'I think it's likely that the last prop of Yeltsin's Bolshevik consciousness finally broke after Houston. His decision to leave the party and join the fight for supreme power in Russia may have ripened at that moment of mental confusion,' wrote Sukhavov.[11]

With his triumph in the March elections and his subsequent performance at the Congress of People's Deputies, Yeltsin was articulating the anti-apparatus, anti-élite mood which had been building up for decades but which no one of rank had ever expressed before. Yeltsin became a national safety-valve. His contacts with severe critics of the party, such as Sakharov, Afanasyev and Popov, strengthened both his mental commitment to the anti-Communist cause and gave him the comforting feeling of having allies and being part of a movement. In early 1990, Sukhanov, Burbulis and his other close associates urged him to run for election to the Russian parliament and then to become its chairman.

Yeltsin's interest in the Russian parliament was not motivated by Russian nationalism in any genuine sense. Nor indeed was this true of the other 'instrumental nationalists', the Communist conservatives who started to agitate in September 1989 for a separate Russian Communist party within the framework of the Soviet party (see Chapter 6). From different positions each was using the 'Russian idea' against Gorbachev. The combined assault from both flanks made the concept of Russia respectable again. The old notion of 'much-suffering' (mnogostradal'naya) Russia – one of the long-held notions of Russian nationalists – re-emerged and became the vogue. People produced a string of complaints. Russia had no Academy of Sciences. Russian villages were dying. Russia did not have its own police force. Russian culture, its songs, its history, its folklore, had all been suppressed in the name of the creation of a new Soviet state. While every other Soviet republic was allowed its dance-groups, its ethnic costumes on television, its national days, only Russia was without all this.

Neither the Communist conservatives nor the pro-Yeltsin radicals, fortunately, turned this new-found nationalism against other ethnic groups. For the Communists this was impossible, given the long tradition of Soviet 'internationalism' and their desire to preserve the USSR. They could not very well argue that the other republics were exploiting Russia and at the same time insist these republics must not leave the Union. While the conservatives' 'instrumental nationalism' was used against Gorbachev, that of the radicals was directed against the whole Communist system. They saw other nationalities not as ethnic enemies but as political allies in the struggle. From this was born the notion that Russia had itself been colonised – by the 'centre'. The whole country had been exploited by a small layer of party functionaries to benefit themselves and build up a huge and useless military machine.

Now it was time to liberate Russia. De-Communization became decolonization.

Yeltsin's decision to turn his attention to the Russian parliament and virtually stop attending the Soviet one fitted naturally into this new climate of thinking. In March 1990 he ran in Sverdlovsk and was elected as easily as he had been in Moscow the previous year. The difficulty was to be elected by the Russian Congress of People's Deputies to be its chairman. This time Yeltsin worked hard for the post, and his supporters were assiduous in lobbying deputies. Gorbachev helped him enormously, first by calling a central committee meeting which tried to discipline party members into voting against him, and second by making a poor impromptu speech at the Russian Congress. It was a direct attack on Yeltsin, accusing him of not being a socialist, of calling for the disintegration of the USSR, and of following a policy which would lead to anarchy. He was also helped by the feeble showing of Gorbachev's favoured candidate, Alexander Vlasov, who admitted that the old Russian government had been little more than a post office for complaints sent to the Union ministries. Vlasov pulled out before the first round of voting and left his place to a hardliner, Ivan Polozkov, who frightened the centrists as well as the radicals.

Although Yeltsin was using the Russian idea to compete with Gorbachev, he still appeared to believe in the Soviet Union. To have come out for a break-up of the USSR, or even for the independence of the Baltic states in May 1990 would have put paid to his chances of being elected chairman of the Russian parliament. He therefore argued that as Russia's leader he would be the best man to work with other republican leaders to transform the Soviet Union. Appealing for support in his bid for the chairmanship, he told the Congress he favoured a new Union treaty, but was vague on whether it should be a federation or a confederation. 'I have never advocated Russia's secession,' he said. 'I am in favour of the Union's sovereignty, equal rights of all republics, the autonomy of the republics so that the republics are strong and with this strength reinforce our strong Union.'

The rest of his programme was radical. He called for a law on land, to give private peasants greater rights. He wanted an end to nuclear testing on Russian territory. He proposed legislation to bring the various security organs under a single minister responsible to parliament. The KGB should no longer be at the service of a single political party. He advocated a gradual move to a professional army, and the provision in the meantime of alternative service for conscripts with conscientious or religious objections. He suggested the formation of a Council of Economic Advisers to work out a transition to a market economy. He called for a law on Russian sovereignty, a new Russian constitution and direct elections to a new executive presidency for Russia. He talked of shifting prices to international levels and a convertible rouble. After failing to win on the first ballot, Yeltsin modified his position to win over deputies from the army, promising them that he favoured keeping the Soviet army and not allowing it to break up into republican armies. On the third and fourth ballots Vlasov came back in and Polozkov withdrew. Yeltsin won 535 votes, just four more than needed.

Within two weeks Yeltsin had fulfilled his promise and brought to the Congress a declaration of Russian sovereignty, which was passed by an overwhelming 98 per cent of the deputies. Yet even with this declaration Yeltsin showed no sign of wanting to undermine the Soviet Union. The handful of deputies who voted against it were unhappy with an amendment brought in so as to win conservative support. This said that while the constitution and laws of the Russian Federation were supreme on Russian territory, any disagreement with Soviet law should be resolved in line with the Union treaty. The critics pointed out that the Union treaty gave primacy to Soviet law, so that the two clauses contradicted each other, meaning that the 'declaration is not a legal document but an empty political statement', in the words of Oleg Rumyantsev, who later became executive secretary of Russia's constitutional commission. But even as a purely political statement the declaration had enormous force. The very next day Gorbachev's spokesman, Arkady Maslennikov, announced that the president favoured a completely new Union treaty to replace the one of 1922. It would guarantee republics 'real economic and political sovereignty'.

By then Yeltsin was the darling of the radicals and all those who wanted to destroy the Communist system. He was also the champion of the ordinary Russian, commanding huge popular respect. But he had little power. For all the republican declarations of sovereignty, the country was still governed by the Union authorities, as became clear when the Russian parliament tried to start its own market reform programme, the 'Five Hundred Days', and found it rejected by Ryzhkov's Union government. In October Yeltsin told the Russian Supreme Soviet: 'Here we just sit and adopt resolutions and do not know whether they will be carried out, because all the real power is in their hands. They have the apparatus – the administrative, state and party apparatus, the army, KGB and other structures. We have none of that.'

Yeltsin tried to resolve the paradox of influence without power by urging Gorbachev to form a coalition government in the centre. The aim would be to push through a reform of the economy on market lines against the resistance of Ryzhkov's government and to work out a new relationship between the centre and the republics. It was an inherently incompatible package. Gorbachev was being asked both to share power and to reduce the role of the centre. When the pro-empire conservatives in the army and the Union parliament began to put pressure on Gorbachev to preserve the Union, Yeltsin's offers were rejected.

Yeltsin increased his demands. He wanted to gain control of the KGB and the army and undermine their support for maintaining the centre. At the end of 1990 Yeltsin demanded for the first time that Russia have the right of veto over Soviet nuclear weapons, the right to nominate the Soviet defence minister and to control KGB communications on its territory. In early 1991 he stopped suggesting a coalition government and went to the opposite extreme. In a prime-time television broadcast in February 1991 he called on Gorbachev to resign.

Yeltsin was still arguing for maintaining the Union, though now on confederal lines. But he was also putting his words into action by withholding part of Russia's tax contribution from the Soviet budget. Ironically, it was President Nazarbayev of Kazakhstan, later to be so angry over the Brest agreement, who first raised the notion of a Union without Gorbachev. After one of the many meetings at Gorbachev's country residence of Novo-Ogaryevo, Nazarbayev suggested a novel formula. Until then the talks were known as Nine plus One, because Gorbachev and nine republics were taking part. The three Baltic states had severed all links with the process. Armenia, Georgia and Moldova were waiting to see how they would turn out. In order to try to bring all the republics back in, Nazarbayev proposed they switch the focus to economic co-operation and hold talks in Alma Ata, the Kazakh capital. The formula would be Fifteen plus Zero, since Gorbachev would not be invited. The other republics did not accept the idea at the time, but the stone which Nazarbayev had thrown later prompted an avalanche. The taboo subject, a confederation without a centre, was in the public domain.

Yeltsin was still busy strengthening his personal position. Mindful of his narrow victory when the Russian Congress of People's Deputies chose its chairman, Yeltsin wanted the security of a popular mandate. Again by a small margin, he persuaded the Russian Congress to change the constitution and authorize nationwide elections for an executive presidency with a five-year term. In June 1991, Yeltsin was overwhelmingly elected president with 57 per cent of the votes. His nearest rival, former Soviet prime minister Nikolai Ryzhkov, who was also trying for a comeback after being sacked by Gorbachev, won 16.85 per cent, less than a third as many votes. Vladimir Zhirinovsky, an unknown populist, came third with 7 per cent. But Yeltsin was not bent on destroying the Union. To the chagrin of the radicals in the Russian parliament, he agreed to sign the new Union treaty in August, and would have done so if the coup had not intervened and changed the whole face of the country's politics.

Throughout the summer of 1991, before and after the coup,

Gorbachev argued that the national referendum in March had shown that the public wanted to preserve the Union. Just over 61 per cent of the electorate voted yes. But the question had been slanted, and Gorbachev himself changed his line in April, accepting the notion of a confederation which was a far looser option than the voters had been offered in the referendum. It was the coup which doomed the Union, coupled with Ukraine's position. Kravchuk was determined not to be outflanked by the nationalists. But Yeltsin accelerated the process by some ham-fisted comments after the coup. He suggested that Russia would have to review the borders of any republics which did not collaborate with it. Kazakhstan and Ukraine saw this as a threat to seize their territory. It stiffened Ukrainian determination to break with Russia.

Whether Gorbachev and Yeltsin could have held the Union together if they had been able to collaborate is purely hypothetical. The two men were at each other's throats, and if the choice was between saving Gorbachev and the Union or destroying them both, Yeltsin was bound to pick the latter. The Union was not quite dead, as Burbulis implied, when the leaders of Russia, Ukraine and Belarus met in the Byelovezhsky Forest. But to cure it required efforts which none of them was willing to take.

According to Andrei Grachev, Gorbachev's chief spokesman, the Soviet president was hoping that the public would protest their agreement and demand that the union be preserved. 'He invited society to give him a push, to demand some action from him and provide a mandate,' he recalled.[12] But Russia did not yet have a civil society, willing or able to put pressure on their parliaments. Most people were too concerned with the daily problems of economic survival to take action on behalf of the Union. It was not an issue about which they cared deeply, and they were used to decisions being taken above their heads. In Grachev's words, 'After losing faith in Gorbachev's project and in him personally, society which had taken him at his word so often was speechless. For the umpteenth time the people kept silent.'[13]

4

Towards New Institutions

10

Parliament, Soviet-style

Opposing the Congress of People's Deputies to the party,
or the Supreme Soviet to the central committee is
demagogy.

VADIM MEDVEDEV, CPSU IDEOLOGY CHIEF, JUNE 1989[1]

Many of the members of the Soviet Union's first genuinely elected Congress of People's Deputies recognized that it was anything but a parliament. Only one party was represented. There was no official opposition. Above all, discipline was totally absent. Even the very loose agenda was rarely observed. 'It's Hyde Park,' said one deputy after its first session in June 1989, 'a string of unrelated speeches, neither responding to nor even referring to what anyone else has said.' 'It's a trade union meeting,' complained Sergei Stankevich, one of the youngest and most radical Muscovites to become a deputy.[2]

Whatever definition was best, here at last was a rough-and-ready democratic institution of a kind which Russia had not seen for roughly seventy years. If Russia was to make the long march towards a functioning civil society in which conflicts would no longer be swept under the carpet or dealt with by repression, the Congress of People's Deputies might be the beginning. Some saw August 1991 and the defeat of the coup as the door which would unlock democracy. Others chose a later date, the banning of the Communist party in November 1991 and the demise of the Soviet

Union a month after that. But the real breakthrough towards new institutions was surely earlier than that. Although the establishment of the Congress of People's Deputies had been decreed from on high by the Communist party without any popular input, the elections for places in it had produced an explosion of grass-roots political activity. Now that the Congress was opening its proceedings, the country at last had a forum in which issues could be aired, conflicts debated and, with luck, solutions agreed.

For those of us who sat in the gallery, wandered the lobbies or watched compulsively on television, it was marvellous theatre. Held in the glass-fronted Kremlin Palace of Congresses, which doubles as a concert hall and a stage for opera and ballet, it seemed to infect deputies with the drama of its setting. The costumes were infinitely more varied than those of any Western parliament. Deputies ranged from the peacock poet Yevgeni Yevtushenko in a cream-coloured, pinstriped suit to Metropolitan Alexi, later to become the Patriarch, in a tall white headdress and black robes. Army officers of every rank wore their uniforms and in the warm spring weather dozens of deputies were in shirtsleeves and without ties.

It seemed light years from the rigidly formal final session of the old Supreme Soviet when a brave woman deputy from Latvia, the head of the republic's Union of Artists, had asked to take the floor to propose an amendment to Politburo-sponsored changes in the constitution. The vote was about to be taken and everything was supposed to be wrapped up. The other 1499 deputies, the press gallery and the diplomatic corps had watched in awe as she walked the lonely thirty yards to the rostrum. Her courage in breaking ranks had been extraordinary. In the new Congress such independent spirits were represented by the hundreds. From the opening minutes the mood was clear. Before it could even choose a presidium, Vilen Tolpezhnikov, a doctor at a Latvian hospital, strode to the podium and asked for a minute's silence for the twenty people killed in Tbilisi when troops had dispersed a street meeting the previous month. The Politburo rose tentatively. This was not in the script and Politburo members looked to each other for guidance, unsure if it was official. But it was impossible not to respond to the speaker's call, so they and everyone else stood stiffly to attention.

The next shock came ten minutes later after the Congress's presiding committee had been selected and the official agenda was read out. The plan was to move rapidly to electing the country's head of state, the chairman of the presidium of the Supreme Soviet. 'Any proposals?' Gorbachev asked from his seat on the platform. Andrei Sakharov's hand shot up, and Gorbachev invited him to the rostrum. To make the first speech at the new parliament in front of a live television audience was a triumphal rehabilitation for the once dissident and exiled physicist. After years of being an 'unperson', ignored in the official media and confined to a small flat in the closed city of Gorky, Sakharov was in the limelight. He was not overawed by the honour. Stooped over the rostrum, he went straight to the business he had in mind.

Sakharov had three suggestions. First, he wanted the Congress to have the final say on all legislation. His remarks were an implicit attack on the notion of an inner and an outer chamber. The new procedure held that the 2,250-person Congress would choose a full-time Supreme Soviet. The Congress would meet only twice a year, while the real work of parliament would be done by the roughly 450-person Supreme Soviet. Like Sakharov, many deputies were wondering what the point of being elected was if they were to hand everything over to one-fifth of their members. Sakharov's second point was that the Congress should have a wide-ranging debate on the country's problems before electing the head of state. Thirdly, he proposed, there ought to be more than one candidate for the presidency, and each one should lay out his manifesto. He supported Gorbachev for the post, but not to provide the Congress with a choice would be 'shameful'.

Gorbachev responded with little enthusiasm, but had to let the debate proceed when several deputies supported the idea of alternative candidacies. Since his own candidacy was under discussion, he gave up the chair to Anatoly Lukyanov. Alexander Obolensky, an engineer from Murmansk in the Arctic circle, who proudly declared he was not a member of the Communist party, put himself forward in an eloquent twenty-minute speech, which included a call for a constitutional amendment to remove the party's leading role. Although Gorbachev was only opposed by one unknown candidate, Lukyanov was nervous. Before having a vote on the candidacies, he asked Congress to decide whether to include Obolensky's name on the ballot. The vote went 689 in favour to 1,415 against. The motion was defeated, and Gorbachev could relax. His name was on the ballot, unopposed.

The vote showed that the reformers were in a minority of roughly one-third of the Congress. Although that meant they would not be able to get their way, such calculations did not matter greatly in that first session. Its key achievement was to raise glasnost to unprecedented heights. Deputies of all tendencies started to flex their muscles, as they saw they had the right, as elected representatives, to information. What was the size of the budget deficit? How much had the Afghan war cost the country? How much was the Soviet Union's foreign debt?

The Congress was covered live on radio and television, and the country almost came to a stop. People stayed at home, watched in their offices and factories, or listened to transistors. The newspapers gave several columns to readers' letters. There were outspoken comments from people, complete with the names and towns they came from. 'I think M. S. Gorbachev puts pressure on speakers in the way he chairs the sessions,' wrote a soldier, A. Petrov from Moscow, in the newspaper *Trud*. 'How could Mikhail Sergeyevich [Gorbachev] allow himself to say, as he called for a vote, "The overwhelming majority of deputies usually support my proposals"?' asked V. Petrenko from Fedosia. Petrenko's point was that Gorbachev always put his hand up quickly when votes were taken, almost as a signal for delegates to take their cue from him. Electronic voting was installed a few weeks later. This saved the tellers' time, but also stopped such open manipulation.

The Congress symbolized the party's shrinking role by reducing

Politburo members to the level of other deputies. Instead of sitting on the platform, as they did in the old Supreme Soviet, they sat in a block at the side of the hall. Even this irritated some deputies, who felt they should be dispersed among the ordinary seats. Politburo members responded to the challenge by shedding their aloofness. In the old days foreign correspondents and most Soviet ones, with the exception of television reporters, *Pravda*, and *Izvestiya*, were penned into an upstairs gallery above the chamber. We only had access to the deputies' area in small groups for ten minutes at a time, shepherded by an official. Written applications for interviews had to be made in advance. In the new Congress we could mingle with the mighty at will. We had full access to the lobbies and the restaurant at any time. One evening I was in the main foyer in a group surrounding Ligachev as he extolled the state farms of East Germany and Czechoslovakia. As I pushed on to another scrum round Boris Yeltsin, a colleague tugged my elbow. 'Look, over there, Alexander Yakovlev.' Sweet was the dilemma of choosing which top Soviet figure to ignore.

Although the Congress differed greatly from the old Supreme Soviet, the key question was whether Russia would get an efficient legislature for the first time in its history. The last Tsar, Nicholas II, had allowed a parliament, known as the Duma, to be formed in 1905, but it never sat for long periods. It was not elected by universal franchise. Its powers were strictly limited. It was constantly shut down and reorganized, while the Tsar ruled in the interim by decree. Now, after three quarters of a century, Russians had a new chance. The Congress of People's Deputies had several obvious flaws. One-third of the membership had been elected on a restricted basis and there was no multi-party system. But could it develop into a democratic chamber, with clearly-defined responsibilities and genuine powers, and able to pass laws which society would obey?

The first obstacle was the continuing existence of the Politburo, the embodiment of the 'leading role' of the Communist party which was still enshrined in the constitution. When he had persuaded the nineteenth party conference to accept the principle of contested elections and a full-time parliament the previous year, Gorbachev had not intended to dismantle the Politburo. He had wanted to create a rival source of power which he could use, if necessary, to weaken the influence of the Communist party's conservatives. Creating an elected chamber was not designed as an anti-Communist move. It was an anti-conservative, pro-perestroika move.

Gorbachev failed to foresee that parliament would start to develop a life of its own. After an initial period of enthusiasm when the Congress first opened, he gradually became less keen to encourage it. He paid lip-service to the notion of parliament, but began to look for ways of reducing its powers. In any country the legislature is both a source of opposition as well as a partner in government. Gorbachev seemed to focus mainly on the former aspect. The Supreme Soviet provided him with a platform on which he could have built a broad coalition for reform, but Gorbachev was unwilling to use it. When parliament opposed him, or rejected his plans, he became touchy and irritated instead of seeing it as part of the normal give and take.

Gorbachev's suspicions of parliament only increased the deputies' striving for independence. Even without this mutual tension, the Congress of Peoples' Deputies was bound to develop a separate identity which would pit it against the government. Unlike Western European parliaments from whose ranks the government of the day is formed, the Congress had no way of bringing down the executive. Its position was closer to that of the United States Congress, where the constitution provides for a separation of powers between legislature and executive. In 1989 the Soviet Union did not yet have a presidential system, but it had an executive party. Its powerful Politburo was not accountable to the legislature.

When the first session of the Congress of People's Deputies adjourned and its inner chamber, the new full-time Supreme Soviet, started to define its powers, it was not surprising that the foreign model which deputies found most relevant was that of the United States Congress. Gorbachev was not willing to give the

Supreme Soviet the right to nominate the prime minister and appoint the government. That would remain the prerogative of the Politburo. But, like the US Congress, the Supreme Soviet wanted to have the right to reject ministerial appointees. Like the US Congress, it also set up permanent commissions which could summon ministers to explain their policies. It also hoped to be given statutory oversight over the security organs, such as the KGB.

The first flexing of the new Supreme Soviet's powers came when it started to exercise the new right it had been given to confirm ministers. Nikolai Ryzhkov, the prime minister, survived the process with relatively little difficulty but nine of his appointees to the council of ministers were turned down. They included a former deputy minister in charge of water resources, now proposed as minister, whom deputies accused of ruining Central Asia, and Vladimir Kalashnikov, the obkom secretary in Volgograd. Kalashnikov would later be sacked by his party colleagues for high-handed actions (see Chapter 6). What annoyed deputies was that he had lost in the elections to Congress in March, but was then proposed as a minister.

One of the hardest confirmation hearings was suffered by Marshal Dmitri Yazov, reappointed by Ryzhkov to be minister of defence. It was only two years since Gorbachev had first appointed Yazov, allegedly as a reformist general who would be willing to restructure the military on new lines. But when he faced the deputies in the new Supreme Soviet he came under sustained fire. Some took exception to his age – sixty-six. More tellingly, several deputies, including some in uniform, accused him of representing the conservative old guard and not being willing to contemplate a phasing-out of conscription and the move to an all-volunteer army. To see junior serving officers unembarrassedly interrogate a Marshal of the Soviet Union was one of the more astonishing experiences of the new parliament. Yazov was held responsible for all the abuses of military life which the press was uncovering, from poor safety conditions on board nuclear submarines to the widespread bullying of conscripts.

With the exception of the ecology movement, no aspect of the slowly emerging civil society was more impressive than the organized activities of soldiers' mothers on their sons' behalf. Given the determination of Soviet women, and the fact that the issue they were protesting about was senseless death, soldiers' mothers easily became militant. The first such organized group, Hope (Nadezhda), aimed to get more information on young men missing in Afghanistan or held as prisoners by the mojahedin. When the Congress opened, a separate group of 300 women presented a petition demanding that their sons be released from the army so as to continue their studies. The Committee of Soldiers' Mothers, which was formed soon afterwards, widened the demands to a general attack on conditions for conscripts, in particular 'non-combat deaths'. Hundreds of young men were dying in the army as a result of bullying, accidents and suicide. Unofficial estimates suggested that since 1985 some 15,000 soldiers had died in the Soviet Union, as many as fell in the Afghan war. In 1990 and 1991, as ethnic conflicts erupted in several republics and interior ministry conscripts were sent to maintain the peace, the Committee of Soldiers' Mothers had a new cause for their demonstrations outside parliament.

Gorbachev initially imagined that friction between the parliament and the Politburo would be overcome by the fact that the vast majority of deputies were Communists. This was a forlorn hope. New institutions create new loyalties, and deputies soon saw the value of their new parliamentary power. More important, Communist party discipline had already broken down and the crucial division was not between Communists and non-Communists but between reformers and conservatives. One of the key points was the future of the party itself. Communist and non-Communist reformers agreed that its powers had to be reduced.

When a number of the reformers decided to set up the Inter-regional Group of Deputies (IRG), the first 'horizontal' alliance not under Communist party control, it was promptly dubbed 'the opposition'. They adopted a manifesto saying they were creating the group because Congress was not being given the chance to hear alternatives. In the absence of a multi-party system, they hoped to be allowed to address the Congress with a policy statement instead of the few minutes individual speakers were allowed. If the prime minister outlined his economic policy, then the IRG should be able to make a considered response as leaders of alternative factions did in other countries. The group intended to co-ordinate the reformers into a single voting block. A key aim was the abolition of Article Six of the constitution, which sanctioned the Communist party's monopoly on power.

The group's founding conference at the end of July was attended by 393 Congress deputies. By September when it adopted its full programme, the group committed itself to the introduction of a market economy. It called for private ownership of the means of production to be legalized, and for state intervention in the economy to be reduced. All forms of property, from state-owned to private and co-operative should be guaranteed equality under the law. On Union issues, it called for a new constitution which would guarantee the sovereignty of the republics. They would decide which powers to delegate to the centre rather than the other way round. About 90 per cent of the IRG were members of the Communist party. Three-quarters were Russian.

Gorbachev was hostile to the Inter-regional Group from the start. He told the Supreme Soviet he thought it would make it 'more difficult' to take decisions.[3] The group was denied access to the Congress's printing equipment and, thanks to friends, published its first statement in *Sovietsky Fizik* (Soviet Physicist), the little-read journal of Moscow's Kurchatov Institute of Atomic Physics. A conservative faction set up the 'Soyuz' (Union) group a few months later in February 1990. They wanted to preserve the Soviet Union and resist the pressure for republican independence. Soyuz was more militant than the IRG, and as the threat of the USSR's disintegration grew, they repeatedly called for Gorbachev's resignation. Neither of the groups were stable coalitions, let alone embryonic political parties. They met irregularly, had no internal discipline and developed splits among themselves.

The parliament's first six months were its most successful. Apart from establishing itself as a chamber of glasnost with certain rights over the government and some opposition functions, it helped Gorbachev by laying the foundation for the 'law-based state' he was advocating. The Supreme Soviet became a kind of factory of laws. It adopted a law on agricultural leasing, and on the presumption of innocence in criminal trials. It repealed the old laws banning 'anti-Soviet propaganda' and 'slandering the Soviet system' which had been used to imprison dissidents. It granted the Baltic republics economic autonomy and adopted a law on the freedom of the press. Some of its most important actions were in the economic field, where it became a real source of pressure on the government, forcing it to take more account of the hardships of everyday life. The Congress had one important power. It approved the budget. In an economy with controlled prices and no understanding of inflation, deputies eagerly approved extra spending, increasing pensions, raising child benefits and giving groups of workers higher wages. Deputies helped the government resolve the 1989 miners' strike. Representatives of miners' districts travelled to the pits and acted as intermediaries in negotiations with the government. Workers still trusted the Supreme Soviet, though they said they had lost faith in the party, government and trade unions.

In spite of its initial period of success, the parliament turned out to be doomed. Gorbachev's creation of an executive presidency in March 1990 weakened it enormously. Just when parliament appeared to be winning sufficient legitimacy to start challenging the Politburo, Gorbachev changed the rules of the game again and set up a new source of power. The final blow was the collapse of the Soviet Union. As the country's only prominent 'all-Union' body, the Soviet parliament became a sounding board for the tensions which grew between the centre and the republics. But deputies from the more militant republics increasingly lost faith in it, or deliberately tried to destroy it as a symbol of the Soviet Union. The Lithuanians walked out first, followed later by the other deputies of the Baltic republics. Finally, after the August coup, the

Russian liberals boycotted its sessions, leaving it without a quorum.

Ironically, the first threat to their power, the establishment of an executive presidency, was supported by a majority of the legislators even though they were cutting the ground from under their own feet. They included many members of the Inter-regional Group. They were motivated partly by a desire to reduce the power of the Communist party's apparatus, and partly by admiration for the American system with its strong executive president. At the back of many of their minds lurked the old Russian hankering for a 'strong hand'. Few Russian deputies acknowleged that every Western European democracy, with the exception of France, had a parliamentary rather than a presidential system, and that this might also be worth studying. If they did, they tended to dismiss it by saying the Soviet Union had no time to develop multi-party politics.

Gorbachev, paradoxically, opposed the idea of a presidency at the beginning. As late as October 1989 he was telling the Supreme Soviet that it would concentrate too much power in the hands of a single person and would undermine parliament.[4] His plan was to use parliament and elected soviets throughout the system to eliminate the duplication created by the party's interference. He changed his mind for four reasons. First, he was encountering growing resistance to perestroika from the Politburo and the central committee but the Supreme Soviet had shown it could not be a full replacement. Something else had to be found. Second, the Supreme Soviet was showing disturbing signs of opposing his own policies and trying to take the lead in reforming the country. This was not to Gorbachev's liking. Third, as ethnic tensions started to explode in more and more areas, Gorbachev began to feel that he needed a quick and authoritative instrument to handle them. Finally, there was Gorbachev's pride and love of power. As chairman of the Supreme Soviet, Gorbachev was bound to consult the other forty-one members of the presidium of the Supreme Soviet. In effect, the Soviet Union still had a collective head of state. If he became president, Gorbachev would stand alone and be relieved of the burden of regular attendance in parliament. He would be an executive and a legislator combined, able to issue decrees which had the force of law.

The notion of a presidency split the Inter-regional Group. Yuri Afanasyev, the outspoken historian who was rector of the State Historical Archives Institute, said that the deputies should not approve the presidency until they had adopted a new constitution. There had to be guarantees against the emergence of a new dictatorship. The country's problem was not that there was a lack of executive power, but a lack of trust in the leadership. People had lost their faith, he argued. In order to restore this, the president must be chosen by direct, popular elections. Sergei Stankevich, whose academic work had been a study of the United States Congress, said that a strong president had to be balanced by a strong parliament. 'If the law is adopted in its present form, the president can do almost anything. We can still feel the great totalitarian tradition in this country, and this is a good reason for us not to rush things'.[5]

The presidency issue was first raised at the Supreme Soviet in February 1990, where it obtained a heavy majority, 347 in favour and twenty-four against. Forty-three abstained. The Inter-regional Group divided in three directions. After decades of authoritarian government in Russia, it might have been thought that what the country needed was to build up and develop a parliamentary tradition. Even if it took some time, this would be the better path to follow than setting up a new executive system. In its first months of life the Congress and the Supreme Soviet had shown the advantages of open debate and dialogue on matters of state. The election campaign had given thousands of people the chance to join in political life. Now parliament was narrowing the system down again. It was a strange abdication of its powers.

The closest vote in the Congress turned out not to be over the creation of the presidency, which passed easily after the Supreme Soviet's endorsement. It centred on whether the president would be allowed to remain as general secretary of the Communist party. Gorbachev, after all, had continually argued for an end to the duplication of state and party functions. Now he was being asked to put his money where his mouth was. The radical democrats favoured the idea of non-duplication. As president, Gorbachev would be more inclined to cut the party's remaining power if he was no longer its general secretary. The conservatives in the party also supported the change, though for different reasons. They wanted him to vacate the party's top post so that they could elect one of their number to replace him. They sensed that the party still had considerable moral authority over the security apparatus, the army and the KGB, as well as in the vast regions of Russia where its bureaucracy remained intact. If they had their man as general secretary, he might be able to turn Gorbachev into a purely figurehead president, isolated in the Moscow Kremlin.

Gorbachev wanted to keep the two posts, mainly as an insurance policy. He was afraid that if a conservative took control of the party this could block all hope of reform. Once again, the IRG split. Sobchak voted to give Gorbachev the right to hold two posts, but the majority went against. The constitutional amendment was as follows: 'The person elected to the post of president of the USSR shall not hold any other political or government post.' In favour of the motion were 1,303 deputies; against were 607. But the yes vote fell some way short of 1,497, the required two-thirds needed to change the constitution. Gorbachev had won.

With its powers reduced, parliament ceased to play a decisive role. Legislators complained that it was little more than a talking-shop, yet they were the ones who decided that this should be its fate. There were still some important debates for it to hold. The main one was over the transition to a market economy, which most Soviet economists were saying was inevitable. The politicians agreed in theory, but found it hard to decide on the first steps. Ideological reservations were not the main problem. Deputies wanted to minimize the pain of change. In the spring of 1990, when Ryzhkov came forward with a plan for a gradual transition to a regulated market economy, starting with the removal of subsidies on bread prices, deputies strongly objected and the prime minister was forced to back down. Later parliament was the scene of fierce battles over Gorbachev's initial readiness to back a faster transition, the 'Five Hundred Days'. They supported a compromise plan, 'The Basic Principles', which was a switch back to Ryzhkov's more cautious approach.

The arguments over market reform and the mounting crisis in the economy produced a mood close to panic in the Supreme Soviet. Having already handed much of their power to the president in March, they proceeded to give him the rest a few months later. In September by a vote of 305 to 36 the Supreme Soviet authorized Gorbachev, until 31 March 1992, to issue decrees on any economic matter, from price increases and property rights to the budget, salaries and the financial system. The aim was 'to accelerate the formation of an all-Union market'. Although the Supreme Soviet would have the right to override these new economic decrees, it seemed unlikely they would want to.

A minority of deputies, including Boris Yeltsin, were not happy with the Supreme Soviet's abdication. They took issue with a comment by Gorbachev that he might have to introduce presidential rule in some areas and suspend the activities of the local soviets. They feared he might even dissolve the parliament of the Russian Federation, of which Yeltsin had recently become chairman. Gorbachev ignored protests, arguing that the situation was desperate. 'There are all the signs of an emergency ... The situation is fraught with danger, and action is vital ... The trouble today is that the system of executive power is not functioning.'[6] Gorbachev did not state why, if executive power was already not working, it would make any sense to add new powers. In reality, the crisis of authority was not caused by restraints on the president's power. It was caused by a breakdown of the old system and the lack of public consensus on a new one. The republics were increasingly unwilling to take their orders from Moscow. As for the market economy, people were still not ready to take the risks involved. Private businessmen were afraid of confiscation. Peasants would not accept free land until they were sure their crops would not be seized or taxed away. Foreign investors were uncertain of the long-term political climate.

Having willingly abandoned its last leverage on the situation, parliament degenerated into the caricature which its critics were already accusing it of being. It still served a function as a sounding board for grievances but it took no serious action. The main issue in its last year of life was the break-up of the Soviet Union. By then the Inter-regional Group had virtually disappeared. The Baltic members of the Supreme Soviet no longer played a part in Moscow, while the Russian reformers started to take more interest in the Russian parliament, as indeed did many of the Russian conservatives.

When Gorbachev started discussing a new Union treaty with republican leaders in April 1991, the Soviet parliament was effectively pushed aside. Even Anatoly Lukyanov, the chairman of the Supreme Soviet, complained that key decisions on the future of the Union and of the Supreme Soviet were being taken behind its back. The criticism was legitimate but Gorbachev correctly saw that no decisions on a new Union would stick unless they were negotiated with the leaders of the various republics. The USSR Supreme Soviet had lost its political and moral authority. It was already a lame duck. Under the Union treaty, the Congress of People's Deputies would be abolished and new elections would be held for a new parliament with different powers.

The Supreme Soviet's final fling came in June 1991 when prime minister Valentin Pavlov ended a report on the country's economic situation with an appeal for a drastic expansion of the cabinet's powers. It should be able to issue decrees without getting the president's agreement. He claimed Gorbachev was too busy to attend to every detail. In effect, the government wanted to set itself up as a rival to the president. Pavlov's plea was endorsed by the KGB chief Vladimir Kryuchkov, the defence minister Dmitri Yazov, and the interior minister Boris Pugo. With the hindsight of the August coup, Pavlov's move can be seen as a kind of trial balloon. It was an effort to undercut Gorbachev and find a constitutional way for someone else to issue the state of emergency and restore central control over the economy which the president was reluctant to do. Even at the time, many analysts saw it in that light, although Lukyanov tried to put them off the scent. 'There is no governing centre in the country today . . . The cabinet is making this plea . . . We need decisions and instead people are speculating "What if the cabinet usurps power?" This is ridiculous,' he told deputies in closed session, according to one of those who heard him.[7] Deputies from the Soyuz group welcomed Pavlov's speech. Yevgeni Kogan, a Russian-speaker from Estonia, told the chamber: 'Let's strip the president of his powers. He's not using them anyway. Let's give them to someone who will.'

Gorbachev was slow to react, and it was not until 21 June, four days after Pavlov's request for more power, that he attended the Supreme Soviet himself. He attacked by name Viktor Alksnis and Yuri Blokhin, two of the most vocal Soyuz deputies, but spared Pavlov, claiming there was no crisis, and that Pavlov had not thought his ideas through properly. Putting all his remaining authority on the line, Gorbachev proposed a resolution that Pavlov's request be passed to the president for further study, a polite way of killing it. The Supreme Soviet duly obliged and voted for it. But the most significant aspect of the debate was that only 307 of its 542 members attended the session. A severe constitutional crisis was under way. The issue of who ruled the country, the president or the prime minister, was out in the open. The conservatives were mounting a mini-putsch, and yet almost half of parliament's members did not bother to turn up.

A legislature which had been hailed with such excitement as the most democratic forum in modern Russian history was fizzling out into impotence barely two years later.

11

Lure of the Strong Hand

*Talking about Russia one always imagines that one is talking
about a country like the others; in reality this is not so
at all. Russia is a whole, separate world, submissive to the
will, caprice and fantasy of a single man. Whether his name
be Peter or Ivan, no matter. In all instances the common
element is the embodiment of arbitrariness.*

PETER CHAADAYEV, 1854[1]

The defeat of the August 1991 coup was not only a personal
triumph for Boris Yeltsin. It was a victory for the Russian parliament, whose headquarters, the White House, had been the focal
point of resistance to the plotters. In the euphoria of success, many
deputies felt there was a real chance for rapid change in Russia at
last. The Soviet government which had blocked the Russian parliament's plans for radical reform was discredited and in disarray.
The Communist party had been suspended. The prospects seemed
bright for a fast transition to a market economy without the
hesitation which Gorbachev had shown. All that was needed was
the slap of firm government from Boris Yeltsin in Moscow, and a
clear system for carrying out his decisions and ensuring that there
was no more foot-dragging in the provinces. No one was surprised
when the Russian Congress of People's Deputies, at its first session
after the coup, voted by a large majority to give Yeltsin special
powers to rule by decree. He could issue any legislation he liked

and he could also appoint his own administrators in every region and large city with the authority to overrule the elected local councils.

The caveat in this extraordinary transfer of power was that it would last for only a year. The Congress of People's Deputies remained the highest organ of state, according to Article 104 of the constitution, and after twelve months it would decide whether to renew the arrangement. Congress would keep its right to authorize the budget and other government spending, though the government itself would be subordinate to the president.

As Yeltsin's economic reforms started to bite in 1992 and living standards for most Russians collapsed, the mood changed. A growing number of deputies felt it had been a mistake to hand so much power to the Russian president, as the Soviet parliament had done with Gorbachev before them. Parliament should not have abdicated its newly-won rights, especially as the price which the government was asking Russians to pay for its economic 'shock therapy' seemed so high. A cry went up to modify the reforms, but for this to be done the Congress of People's Deputies needed to reassert its primacy. Fierce battles developed between the president and parliament throughout 1992 and 1993 over who was to be the sovereign power in Russia.

The conflict was natural in a country which had an authoritarian tradition and no experience of an independent legislature. Yeltsin and the deputies could not even agree who should decide the issue. Should the Congress of People's Deputies draw up a new constitution for Russia, or should there be a specially elected constituent assembly to do the job?

Ironically, it was the anti-Communist camp which began the struggle against the Russian parliament. In this they were building on a line of argument first raised during the Soviet period when Igor Klyamkin and Andranik Migranyan, two staff members of the Moscow think-tank, the Institute of the Economics of the World Socialist System, gave a provocative interview to *Literaturnaya Gazeta*. It was August 1989, less than six months after the Soviet parliament had started work. The two liberal academics criticized parliament and argued that the Soviet Union needed an 'iron hand' to secure a peaceful transition from totalitarianism to democracy.[2] Citing a number of the reforms decreed by the Tsars in the nineteenth century, they advocated a 'benevolent dictatorship'. They recommended that the dictator be Gorbachev. In their view he should break with the Communist party bureaucracy and set up a Committee of National Salvation to rule by decree. It was a strange foretaste of things to come, harking forward to similarly-named committees which were to emerge in Latvia and Lithuania and Moscow itself.

The Soviet Union had to be reformed, the two academics recommended, by means of the speediest possible introduction of a market economy. A dictatorship was necessary for two reasons. There was no other way to smash the power of the Communist party apparatus, and the switch to the market would require unpopular austerity measures which would be resisted if people had full political rights. On no account, therefore, should perestroika's political reforms outstrip the economic reforms. Without using the phrase, they were proposing a kind of Chinese variant, with the crucial difference that they were anti-Communists.

Their article produced a storm of mostly hostile replies. Political perestroika was in its heyday. The new Congress of People's Deputies had just finished its first session, and the issue of transforming the economy had not yet moved to centre stage. Flushed with the exciting changes, the liberals attacked Klyamkin and Migranyan with vigour. Yet, as time went on, it seemed the two men's views were not so much wrong as premature. Although the word 'dictatorship' was avoided, the Russian debate over the transition from Communist central planning to a market economy two years later became increasingly dominated by the notions of strong executive power which Klyamkin and Migranyan had raised in 1989.

Several factors in Russia's intellectual and political tradition made this almost inevitable, and certainly no cause for surprise. The first was a kind of historic impatience. The immobility of

Russian society over long periods and the absence of any process of reform often steered the argument among politicians, especially political intellectuals, towards ideas of revolution and destruction. There was no other way, it seemed, to break out of stagnation except by means of a sharp and convulsive change. Half a century before the Bolsheviks, the Russian 'nihilists' argued that the only way to advance the wheel of history was to smash what was left of the old order. 'Such nihilism,' wrote Richard Pipes, the historian, 'was motivated not by a total absence of values, as conservative critics were to charge, but by the belief that the present already belonged to the past, and destruction, therefore, was creative.'[3]

In Western Europe the mainstream view among politicians has long favoured evolution, while 'revolution' is frowned on. This is not the case in Russia. Gorbachev used the labels 'stagnation' for the Brezhnev period and 'revolution' for perestroika, even though in practice what he was proposing was only 'evolution' and 'reform'. The great European upheavals of the last two centuries, the French Revolution of 1789, and the Russian Revolution of October 1917, had one key aspect in common. They dispossessed or destroyed a whole class of citizens. In Russia three classes were destroyed: the large private entrepreneurs plus the urban craftsmen and traders disappeared in 1918, while Stalin liquidated the peasantry a decade later. While the Bolshevik seizure of power made no major change in Russians' political psychology since its authoritarianism was based on long Russian traditions, it led to profound alterations in the systems of land and property ownership. In this sense it was a genuine revolution.

Gorbachev's evolutionary 'revolution', by contrast, had achieved neither of these things by 1989, four years after it started. The advocates of a market economy began to feel that only a real revolution would make the necessary changes. The new class of property-owners, the Communist party nomenklatura, which had controlled state assets since the early 1920s in the name of the working class, but in practice for their own benefit, had to be dispossessed. Its system of political power, and the institutions which sustained it, must be destroyed root and branch. Gorbachev's attempt to ease the Communist party to the side-lines and force its members to compete for power by means of elections was too slow, while the notion of a gradual, social-democratic switch to a 'regulated' market economy which prime minister Nikolai Ryzhkov proposed was thought to be a smokescreen for keeping the old planning system intact. To destroy it required radical surgery or 'shock therapy'. This approach coincided with the thinking of many Western advisers and governments. They were not going to live in Russia and had little interest in a gradual transition. Their advice also tended to encourage the concept of the 'strong hand' to take decisive measures.

One of the first to brand this line of thinking 'neo-Bolshevik' was Gorbachev. In a speech in Byelorussia in early 1991 he used the term to denigrate the radical democrats. It was a strange adjective to emerge from the lips of the general secretary of the Communist party, since if neo-Bolshevism was bad, that must mean that its parent, Bolshevism, was equally bad. By implication, Gorbachev was attacking Lenin. Until that point Gorbachev had never gone so far. He began perestroika by criticizing Stalin and Brezhnev and calling for a return to 'true Leninism'.

Criticizing 'neo-Bolshevism' was a new and fascinating step. Was it a cry of frustration and anger with the radical anti-Communists, and a way of tarring them with a brush which he knew they would resent? Or was it the product of a profound change of mind by Gorbachev? 'I was for a process which was revolutionary in its essence but evolutionary in its tempo. They have broken from the evolutionary path,' he told me.[4] Lenin himself had realized that there was a time for making changes slowly, he claimed. 'After the Revolution of February 1917 the Bolsheviks didn't use its potential or try to unite the whole spectrum of democratic forces. Instead, they moved towards a split, particularly with the Left Social-Revolutionaries. They should have worked with them and the Mensheviks. Lenin realized this at the end of his life,' he said.

In Russia revolutionary impatience has always tended to go with a primitive view of society and politics. The scheme is straightforward. There is an élite and there is the 'narod' (the people). Conservative politics are about maintaining order on behalf of the narod. Progressive politics mean leading the narod into a better future, like Moses taking the chosen people to the promised land. In both cases politics are viewed as a top-down process. Whether it is reform or revolution, it is always 'from above'. The vital ingredient is strong leadership, though this need not come from a single individual. It can come from a dedicated group of like-minded rulers.

In the nineteenth century the politically conscious sectors of the intelligentsia adopted this simplified approach, and it has been a constant of Russian politics ever since. Most ordinary Russians accepted it. They put their faith in the Tsar or Stalin to provide order and justice. People who had grievances would rarely band together with others to seek redress. They would go, as an individual, to petition the supreme ruler. Even Stalin's mass purges and executions, which left hardly any Russian families unaffected, did not eliminate this attitude. Some believed the dictator did not know what was going on, which only increased the need for the aggrieved individual to break through the wall of advisers and explain to the supreme ruler what was really happening.

Perestroika lifted Russians' fear but it could not change attitudes quickly. How often did one hear the phrase, 'We believed in Gorbachev, but now he has disappointed us', or 'We believe in Yeltsin. He will save the economy'? The word in Russian – 'verit' – has some of the overtones of 'trust', a concept frequently used in the West, where incumbents like to play the 'trust' card, asking voters whether they have confidence in the challenger's promises to run the country better. In the West this kind of trust is conservative. The issue is how to keep an existing system functioning efficiently. In Russia 'verit' is more than a matter of trust. It denotes a wish for change and has the quality of faith, the submissive belief in a saviour with all the religious overtones which go with that.

The October Revolution and the Bolsheviks' subsequent establishment of a monopoly of power exploited these long-established Russian attitudes. Support for the Revolution began with strong elements of faith. Later, the Bolsheviks built a typically Russian dictatorship by fusing the old Tsarist administrative system with their élitist concept of government. After his death they turned Lenin into a combination of icon and oracle. Stalin was made the unchallengeable dictator, and the Communist party was projected as a nationwide, enlightened élite, with branches in every corner of society and dedicated to leading the narod to a bright future. Even apparently sophisticated politicians still used the notion of 'faith' decades after Stalin's death. Ryzhkov's memoirs were called *Perestroika: a story of betrayals*, and Ligachev, in his book, repeatedly accused Gorbachev of treachery. The books contain little suggestion that the authors might also have made mistakes. It was as though everything depended on a single leader, and these two men bore no responsibility for what the Politburo did wrong or failed to do.

Although he ran as an anti-Communist, Yeltsin's triumphant election as Russian president in June 1991 owed much to this background. None of the five other candidates came anywhere near him. Yeltsin was the only man able to combine all the necessary qualities. He appealed to people's faith, to the desire for a strong leader and to the impatient wish to destroy the old system, while also exuding the sense that, although he was a product of the élite, he understood the narod since he was an authentic Russian 'muzhik' (little man) himself.

The simplistic concept of élite and people, combined with the tradition of strong leadership, left Russians unprepared for compromise and dialogue. One serious consequence was that it made it hard for strong political parties to develop. The lifting of the Communist party's monopoly in March 1990 led to the appearance of a host of new parties. By the summer of 1992 twenty-five had been officially registered in Russia, as well as fifteen political 'movements'. The Russian news agency Itar-Tass, counting unofficial parties and movements as well as those which had been registered, produced a total of 141. From one point of view this was an encouraging sign of a burgeoning civil society. After the years of enforced silence people were eagerly expressing political ideas. But if one looked at the new parties' programmes, they were marked by massive overlapping.

Why was it not possible for politicians to consolidate their forces rather than each starting a new party? Why was there this phenomenon of 'one leader, one party'? Once again the answer lies in history. The Russian intelligentsia has always believed in the power of word over deed, in the force of ideas to change established structures. All that is needed is to find the right formula. In the nineteenth century Russian universities were strong on philosophy, a tradition which the Bolsheviks expanded enormously in quantity, though not in quality, by establishing countless institutes of Marxism-Leninism and compulsory university courses in a narrow version of Marxist theory. When Russia's multi-party system took wing, everyone had his own manifesto or programme, as though all one had to do to change the world was to write out a solution on a piece of paper or publish it on a computer print-out.

Aversion to Stalinism's 'mass politics' with its compulsory attendance at rallies and May Day parades produced a counter-reaction. The notion of politics as a joint endeavour was rejected, making it hard to develop a more sympathetic form of collective politics or the art of seeking the broadest possible number of allies through compromise. Hostility to the Bolsheviks' perversion of ideology produced the misguided feeling that ideology was always a denial of common sense, and that politics required technical solutions in which values no longer needed to be considered. Most Russians took it for granted that socialism or any variant of it, including social-democracy, had failed. This also limited the scope for debate.

Out of this grew the 'personality politics' of Russia's first post-Communist period, which fed back into the old lure of a 'strong hand'. Moreover, the long years of dictatorial one-party rule had discredited the idea of parties as such. In most people's eyes, a party was not a forum for discussion or a vehicle for winning allies in the competition for power. It was at best a tight, disciplinarian structure; at worst an intellectual prison. Millions of people had been forced to join the party for the sake of their careers. The freedoms brought by perestroika included the freedom not to have anything to do with a party any more.

The first Russian parties after 1989 were best described as 'proto-parties'. They were embryos which might develop but, more likely, would soon be aborted as parties split and re-formed in the kaleidoscope of personality clashes among strong (and invariably male) leaders. Of the twenty-five officially registered parties, the largest at the moment of registration was the Democratic Party of Russia. It claimed a mere 28,608 members. The next largest was the Party of the Russian Christian Democratic Movement with 6,027 members.

In the first phase of multi-party politics, between 1989 and 1991, the lack of effective parties was not a major obstacle to democratization. The totalitarian system was imploding of its own accord, as a result of the decline of living standards, the onset of glasnost which undercut people's fear of a repressive security police and the centrifugal tendencies in the republics. Nearly all the proto-parties agreed that the Communist party had to be reformed out of existence, either by removing its role in government or by encouraging it to split and become a parliamentary party like any other.

The main anti-Communist opposition force was not a party but a broad-based movement known as Democratic Russia. It was set up to try to co-ordinate the strategies of the liberals before the March 1990 elections to the Russian parliament and to local councils. Profiting from the experience of the first polls to the Soviet Congress of People's Deputies a year earlier, Democratic Russia concentrated its campaigning on a number of key seats. The system had been simplified since 1989 and it was easier to nominate candidates and have them officially registered, if groups of citizens signed petitions in their favour. Democratic Russia won sizeable majorities in Moscow and Leningrad and took about 40 per cent of the seats in the Russian parliament. This turned out to be vital in engineering Yeltsin's election as chairman of the Russian parliament in May 1990 against Gorbachev's opposition.

But there were already signs that the movement would not last long. After becoming parliamentary chairman, Yeltsin announced that he was resigning from Democratic Russia. His argument was very Russian. Yeltsin claimed that as Russia's leader he should not be allied to any particular movement or party, but should represent all the people. His decision may have been made with an eye on the forthcoming twenty-eighth Congress of the Communist party, where he was planning to make an ostentatious gesture and resign from the party, using the same argument. In either case, it was a weak line, since in every democratic country the chief executive represents a party. By breaking his links with Democratic Russia Yeltsin seemed to be signalling that he did not want to accept the disciplines or responsibility of membership of a movement, or to be accountable to the Democratic Russia faction in parliament. It looked like a move towards executive independence and, at worst, autocracy.

Yeltsin could legitimately say that Democratic Russia was not yet a party. It was still only a movement. But there were Russians who argued it would be better if Yeltsin remained in it, precisely in order to help to turn it into a party. With his authority he could have done so. If he was genuine in wanting to establish a new democratic order in Russia, he had a duty to build a multi-party system to fill the vacuum left by the collapse of the Communists. Yeltsin chose otherwise. It was as though, writ large, he was behaving like the proto-parties' leaders. For an ambitious individual his party was a ladder to power, influence, publicity and a seat in parliament. Once elected, the leader discarded it.

In spite of considerable unhappiness inside Democratic Russia, most members accepted Yeltsin's decision. Its supporters played a major role in getting the Russian Congress of People's Deputies to vote for a constitutional amendment, setting up an executive presidency of Russia. They also campaigned eagerly for Yeltsin during the election. Although Yeltsin welcomed their help, he continued to project himself as an independent candidate. The concept of political parties was still so closely tied to the Communist experience that it was better not to be associated with any party at all. To many Russians parties were seen as nothing more than social parasites. 'Now we'll have to feed them too,' replied one middle-aged woman when I stopped passers-by for quick comments on the day the constitution was changed to allow other parties to compete with the Communists.

Yeltsin's aloofness from Democratic Russia was one factor in its decline. The other was that it had no real programme except opposition to the CPSU. Democratic Russia split over its attitude to the future of the Soviet Union. Before the August coup a pro-Russia wing, led by Yuri Afanasyev and Yelena Bonner, Sakharov's widow, appealed to Yeltsin not to sign the Union treaty. Later, as Yeltsin resisted any form of strong centre for the USSR, the leaders of three proto-parties walked out of Democratic Russia in protest. They were Nikolai Travkin of the Democratic Party of Russia, Viktor Aksyuchits of the Christian Democratic Party and Mikhail Astafyev of the Constitutional Democratic Party. Travkin was later to form a centre block in the Russian parliament with vice-president Alexander Rutskoi's People's Party of Free Russia. The others would start working with the Russian Communists and nationalists. What was left of Democratic Russia became just one of many small factions in the Russian parliament.

By the spring of 1992, with the Soviet Union dead, the Russian Congress of People's Deputies had become the focus for intense struggle between deputies and the president. They gained particular vehemence when the Congress of People's Deputies met for its ten-day sessions twice a year, since the Congress had the power to change the constitution. The underlying conflict was over economic reform, but it played itself out as a struggle over who was in charge of the economy. Liberals claimed the main reason for the Congress's hostility to Yeltsin was that it was under the influence of Communist conservatives, seeking revenge for the collapse of the USSR and the banning of the Communist party. The Congress had been elected in 1990 under rules which, they claimed, favoured Communist party officials. The argument was hard to sustain. It is true that the two-chamber system, with a 1,040-seat Congress of People's Deputies, and an inner Supreme Soviet of 248, chosen from among the Congress deputies, was modelled on the Soviet parliamentary system set up in 1989. But there were important differences. First, there were no reserved seats for representatives of 'public bodies', a device which increased the number of establishment Communists in 1989. Second, the nomination system had been simplified so that it was easier for independents and anti-establishment citizens' groups to get themselves or their candidates on the ballot. By 1990 too, the mood of protest against official Communist representatives had risen considerably from the year before.

The clinching point was the way support for Yeltsin declined over time. In May 1990 Yeltsin was chosen by 535 deputies to lead the Russian parliament. By April 1992 his support among the same body of deputies was more tenuous. Analysis of every deputy's voting behaviour showed that the centre of gravity had shifted from plus seven in favour of Yeltsin and his reforms to minus eleven against them.[5] At the watershed Congress in December 1992 which effectively forced Yegor Gaidar, the acting prime minister, out of office the swing against Yeltsin was stronger, reaching a figure of minus twenty. Some deputies were unhappy with Yeltsin's role in destroying the Soviet Union and wanted to punish him. There was also a hard core of Communists who could not forgive him for banning the party. But added together these people were a minority. Had Yeltsin been a more skilful leader, he should have been able to increase his support as memories of the climactic year, 1991, receded into the past.

In the absence of strong parties, the deputies were divided into a series of factions. To be registered officially as a faction, there had to be at least fifty deputies. The factions were loose, and deputies often switched from one to another, so that factions sometimes continued even when they had fewer than fifty members. There was no inner-factional discipline or instructions to vote in a particular way. Roughly one fifth of the deputies chose not to join any faction. The factions allowed for an easier distribution of seats on parliamentary committees and a method of choosing delegations for discussions with interest groups or for foreign trips. Faction leaders provided their members with briefing papers and organized meetings with experts. In turn the factions combined into blocks, although these were even looser. Their main aim was to give some indication of the general balance of forces, as well as providing a forum for policy discussion. Blocks tended to meet roughly once a month.

At the March 1993 Congress fourteen factions were registered. These had aligned themselves into three blocks. The largest was Russian Unity, claiming 301 members, which brought together the Communists and patriotic forces. They described themselves as the opposition. The block included the following factions: Communists of Russia (67 members) which stated in its declaration that 'the historic and cultural traditions and national characteristics of the peoples of Russia over many centuries have determined the predominance of collective forms of ownership', and that 'we do not reject the Communist idea that "the free development of each is the condition for the free development of all" but in present conditions our realistic goal must be socialism'; Russia (53 members), formed by deputies who had opposed the collapse of the USSR and wanted a stronger line against 'separatists' in the Russian Federation itself; Fatherland (51 members), a group which consisted largely of army officers and other 'patriots', but was very similar in its views to the 'Russia' faction; and the Agrarian Union (130 members), a grouping of deputies from country districts. The Agrarian Union was the largest faction in the Congress, simply because it united people as a broad interest group. While the bulk of its members came from the collective and state farms or from food-processing plants, it was also willing to defend private peasants. It argued that the terms of trade between town and country discriminated against farmers of all kinds, and it wanted to change this in the interests of all farmers.

There were two centrist blocks. One, called Creative Forces, was made up of three factions: Industrial Union (52 members), which represented the conservative wing of the managers of state enterprises, who favoured privatization via the transfer of assets to workers' collectives rather than via public auctions, as well as a 'republic with strong presidential power'; Workers' Union—Reform without Shocks (53 members); and Change—New Politics (53 members), which proclaimed the need for 'parliamentary professionalism, political pragmatism, firm principles, consistent democracy, a balance of power and a civilized market'. This last group was perhaps the most 'parliamentary' of all the factions. One of its main aims was to build up the role of parliament, though even this faction wanted to retain the presidency as a strong executive.

The other centrist block, Democratic Centre, contained three factions: Sovereignty and Equality (50 members), which consisted of deputies from the republics and autonomous regions of Russia and argued for the rights of ethnic minorities, including self-determination; Free Russia (55 members), which used to be called 'Communists for Democracy' and was linked to vice-president Rutskoi; and Left-Centre (62 members). Describing itself variously as 'liberal-democratic' or 'right-wing social democratic', it said the economic reforms started by Yeltsin had been launched in a disorganized way and should be adjusted. Privatization should concentrate on medium and small businesses, leaving state industries alone for the time being.

The Congress's other four factions did not form a block though they allowed individual deputies to join a grouping known as Coalition for Reform. Two factions, Democratic Russia (48 members), and Radical Democrats (50 members) were strong supporters of Yeltsin's reforms, and were almost indistinguishable from each other. Ironically, though, Radical Democrats espoused the slogan 'The free development of each is the condition for the free development of all', which was also part of the programme of 'Communists of Russia'. Consensus for the Sake of Progress (54 members) was formed in the autumn of 1992 with the aim of trying to find harmony between president and parliament while preserving the economic reforms. The youngest faction was Motherland (57 members) which saw its main goal as preserving Russia from disintegration on the pattern of the Soviet Union. Its members claimed that parliament and the president had put off the issues of a new dispensation for the republics for so long that centrifugal tendencies had grown alarmingly. They spoke out for a new federalism, and a 'centrism which would exclude left and right radicalism'. They borrowed the slogan, invented by Tsar Nicholas II's prime minister, Pyotr Stolypin – 'A great Russia without great convulsions'.

Several conclusions flow from this brief survey of the factions. First, the differences between many of them were minimal. Second, without exception they all favoured a republic with a balance of power between a president and parliament. None favoured a parliamentary system on the Western European model. Third, the ideological spectrum of Western politics did not yet apply. The fact that the faction 'Left-Centre' gave itself that name when its views would be more likely to put it in a centrist or even right of centre slot in Western Europe showed that Russian labelling was still different. 'Left' was used loosely for 'reformist' and 'right' for 'conservative' regardless of a faction's economic views. The Western equation of 'Left' for supporters of an interventionist state and 'right' for free marketeers was irrelevant.

The fourth and perhaps most important conclusion from the rainbow of Russian factions was that the description of the Congress as Communist-dominated was wide of the mark. The deputies' growing opposition to Yeltsin and his government throughout 1992 and into 1993 had causes which had little to do with the Communists in parliament. There were two large centre blocks with whom Yeltsin should have tried to work. If he had been successful at this, he would have had close to the two-thirds majority needed to make amendments to the constitution. At the least, he could have commanded a clear, simple majority. Yeltsin's government survived in April 1992 partly because economic reforms had only started, deputies saw little alternative to the way they were being conducted and the West put strong pressure on Congress. In an extraordinary piece of arm-twisting which might have caused an explosion of resistance in a more established parliament, Western governments said a 24 billion dollar loan package would be in jeopardy unless Yegor Gaidar, the then first deputy prime minister, remained in power.

One result of the system of factions rather than political parties was that it gave great power to Ruslan Khasbulatov, the chairman of parliament. In a developed party system, parliament's agenda is set by the ruling party or coalition of parties; in the British case, by the Leader of the House, in the USA by the Senate and House Majority Leaders. The Speaker is an impartial umpire who ensures that MPs observe the established rules of procedure. When parliament consists of factions, or even blocks, none of which has a majority, the situation is different. As practice developed, Khasbulatov acquired considerable skill in controlling the agenda both of parliamentary sessions, and of particular debates. He was ruthless in choosing which deputies to allow to speak.

By nationality a Chechen, Khasbulatov had entered politics early in life. He was a secretary of the Young Communist League at Moscow university for two years. Until his election to the Russian parliament in 1990, he worked for ten years as a professor of economics at the Plekhanov Institute of Economic Management in Moscow. Initially a strong ally of Yeltsin, he was appointed as Yeltsin's first deputy chairman of parliament. When Yeltsin was elected executive president, Khasbulatov at first found it hard to muster a majority of deputies to support him in his bid to succeed Yeltsin in the top parliamentary job. The August coup was the turning point. Khasbulatov played a prominent role in defending the White House, and at the next Congress was easily elected as its Speaker.

Abrasive, sly and arrogant, Khasbulatov played a formidable role in 1992 and 1993 in fighting to maintain and strengthen parliament's power. While no faction wanted Russia to be without an executive president, dispute centred on the degree of his powers. Mikhail

Poltoranin, one of Yeltsin's close friends who headed the Federal Information Centre, claimed that parliament wanted to turn the president into a figure-head like the 'Queen of England', as he put it. Initially there was little basis for the charge. If there were signs of absolutism, they were greater in Yeltsin's camp. Parliament's main interest was in watering down Yeltsin's 'shock therapy', which could best be done, most deputies felt, by removing Gaidar from power and bringing in men who were closer to the industrial managers. In practice, the government's reform programme had already been modified in the summer of 1992, so that the gap between the two sides was small. But Yeltsin felt parliament's demands were an invasion of his prerogatives.

The constitution inherited by Russia after the fall of the Soviet Union was indeed ambiguous. In line with Gorbachev's effort in 1988 to reduce the Communist party's role by returning 'All Power to the Soviets' under cover of Lenin's famous dictum, the Congress of People's Deputies was described in Article 104 as the supreme organ of state power. When the executive presidency was later created, a constitutional amendment described the country as having a separation of legislative, executive and judicial power. But Article 104 was not annulled, though Congress never made use of it.

The concept of a separation of powers was a major breakthrough for Russia. It struck at the heart of the monarchist and authoritarian tradition of centuries. Under Tsarism there had never been such a separation. The Duma which Nicholas II created at the beginning of the century was only consultative. In their struggle for power, and in their analysis of history, the Bolsheviks always took as a key breakthrough the concept of 'dual power' (dvoyevlast'e) which was achieved after February 1917. Dual power was not meant to be a permanent state of affairs, let alone a constitutionally recognized distribution of power. It was a temporary stage when one side was gaining ground and the other was losing. The issue was which side would be defeated, so that it in its turn could establish absolute power, either a revived Tsarism, or a bourgeois republic in the case of Russia in 1917, or the dictatorship of the proletariat.

Yeltsin and his radical supporters could not seem to free themselves from this way of thinking. Russia must either have a strong president or a strong parliament. It could not have both. Yeltsin's criticism of the Russian parliament exaggerated its power. In fact the Congress of People's Deputies and its inner full-time subsidiary, the Supreme Soviet, had no more power than their French and American equivalents in those two countries' presidential systems. In France, parliament had the right to approve the government's programme and could at any time pass a vote of no confidence in the prime minister. The Soviet parliament could not do this. It had given up its power to approve the president's choice of prime minister when it handed him emergency powers for a year at the end of 1991. Where the Congress was stronger than the French parliament was that the president had no right to dissolve it.

In this it was closer to the United States Congress. Unlike the US Senate, however, and the previous Soviet parliament, the Russian parliament had no power to reject ministerial appointments. Its main power was over the public purse. It approved the budget and could make changes or order its own spending programmes. Yeltsin wanted to remove this. Control over the Central Bank was also contested. In practice, although it was nominally under parliamentary control, the Bank operated independently like the United States Federal Reserve Board or the German Bundesbank.

Even during the period when the parliament had awarded him emergency powers, Yeltsin built up new executive authorities subordinate to himself alone. Some deputies suspected that if parliament won more control over the government, Yeltsin's aim was to relocate the real centre of power elsewhere. This trend had begun as soon as he was elected president in 1991. He created a State Council which was meant to become the main executive body while the government, at that time led by Ivan Silayev, would be confined to running the economy. Shortly before the April 1992 Congress Yeltsin created a five-man Security Council with supreme power to run the country, a move which some liberals described as an echo of the Communist party Politburo.

Throughout the summer of 1992 Yeltsin kept up his pressure on parliament with various threats to dissolve it. He had no authority to do so and could only have succeeded with the help of the army. In September he made a truce with Khasbulatov by agreeing to drop his threat in return for the speaker's agreement to his request not to hold elections for the heads of regional administrations. They had been appointed a year earlier under his emergency powers, but it seemed likely that if elections were held many of them might be replaced by critics of the reforms. As the December Congress approached, Yeltsin stepped up the pressure on parliament again. On a state visit to London he told British MPs that he might have to take firm measures and in a subsequent interview in a Russian paper he hinted at the imposition of direct presidential rule. He allowed his staff to accuse deputies of planning a 'creeping coup' aimed at stripping him of his power.

The occasion was an extraordinary dinner for foreign correspondents held in the government's offices on Pushkin Street. About twenty of us were invited by Mikhail Poltoranin, the deputy prime minister in charge of information, and Gennady Burbulis, who was then a state secretary, and still Yeltsin's main political adviser. Andrei Kozyrev, the foreign minister, and Anatoly Chubais, the deputy prime minister in charge of privatization, also attended. For three and a half hours the team of four embroidered a fantastic theme of revenge-seeking and conspiracy. We listened in amazement as Poltoranin accused Khasbulatov. 'A coup is being prepared under his wing,' he claimed. Poltoranin said the opposition was planning to topple the government at the forthcoming Congress and to introduce elections to the constitutional court so as to replace the present judges. 'This would then enable them to declare most of the president's decrees unconstitutional, get rid of the executive presidency itself and turn the president into an icon.'[6] Burbulis said that in some areas of Russia the police and prosecutors' departments had gone into 'invisible opposition'. This meant the government could not take action against local officials who violated the president's decrees on privatization and economic reforms. The ministers' unusual invitation to us seemed designed to elicit foreign support against the Congress, and prepare the ground for sympathetic coverage if Yeltsin chose to impose presidential rule to close the Congress.

Yeltsin reinforced his ministers' line by calling for the Congress to be postponed. By then the pressure on deputies had become counter-productive. Parliament voted a few days later to reject the president's call. It also passed a law giving Parliament the right to approve the prime minister and other ministers. Yeltsin still did not compromise. In spite of giving a conciliatory speech to the Civic Union, a powerful lobby group which represented the liberal wing of the industrial managers (see Chapter 12), Yeltsin continued to allow his tactics to be set by his three 'neo-Bolsheviks', Burbulis, Poltoranin and Gaidar. On the opening morning of the Congress Yeltsin launched the confrontation by offering to give up his emergency powers if deputies gave him the right to form the government. This was no deal since his powers had already run out. He was basically saying, 'Give me what I want, then I will not ask for it'. He compounded the blunder by circulating a draft resolution which would have turned parliament back into something like the rubber-stamp of the Brezhnev era. The draft upset even many of his supporters in parliament.

Yeltsin could still muster the support of slightly more than a third of the deputies. When Congress voted on constitutional amendments giving it the permanent right to approve the prime minister and other key ministers, the result fell just short of the necessary two-thirds majority. Nevertheless, Yeltsin made his wisest move of the two-week Congress. Recognizing that his victory had been narrow, he offered to let the Congress have the right to appoint the four security ministers (defence, foreign affairs, the police and the intelligence services). The implication was that he should have a free hand on the economy. Yeltsin's undoing was that Congress had no party system. Under the system of loose factions, it was impossible for faction leaders to insist that deputies accept the president's move as part of a deal. Yeltsin saw the point too late. When it became evident that Gaidar would still have trouble being approved as prime minister, Burbulis and Poltoranin urged Yeltsin to try to destroy the Congress.

Late that night they drafted a ringing 'Appeal to the People', attacking the Congress as 'impossible to work with' and calling for a referendum on 'Whom do you entrust with taking the country out of the economic and political crisis, this Congress, the Supreme Soviet or the President?' The appeal claimed the country was being 'pushed toward civil war'. Yeltsin was to read it out to the Congress the next morning.

Yeltsin was relying on Russians' inclination towards a 'strong hand'. He also exploited the fact that parliament's image was worse than his own. State-controlled television and radio had for months been feeding on the renewed popular apathy about politics to portray parliament as an unruly talking-shop, full of deputies who lived off the public purse. Mention of the danger of 'civil war' was intended to heighten fears of insecurity, which would also tend to make people rally round the president, as father-protector. Viktor Sheinis, a long-time Yeltsin supporter, heard about the president's plan to make his appeal a few minutes before he was due to deliver it. 'I thought it was a terrible mistake. Along with two other deputies, we tried to have a word with him, but he was already in his seat. He just waved us away,' he recalled.

The speech was a disaster, especially as Yeltsin misread his text. At the end, according to Arkady Murashev, another of Yeltsin's associates, he was to invite all the deputies who agreed with him to join him in the Kremlin's St George's Hall 'during the break'. Yeltsin forgot to use this phrase, and strode out of the Congress chamber. His plan was that at least a third of the deputies would follow. He hoped then to convince them to stay out of the chamber, depriving the Congress of a quorum and forcing it to close. But because he forgot to mention his meeting with the deputies would be 'during the break', many of his potential supporters did not understand the plan. They were still stunned by the speech and remained in their places. A furious Yeltsin found only about 150 deputies with him. This was the first sign that he had miscalculated. The second came when he left the Congress building and drove to the Moskvich car factory to repeat his attacks on the Congress at a staged meeting with workers. Their response was only lukewarm.

Yeltsin's clumsiness united Congress. It passed a resolution charging him with exceeding his authority. Vice-president Rutskoi criticized Yeltsin, saying he would not back him. 'For me the highest order is the constitution, the law, the Congress, and the people,' he told cheering deputies. They summoned the three security ministers to address the Congress to reassure them that no coup was planned. 'We shall not let the army be pulled into solving political battles,' promised General Pavel Grachev, the defence minister, whose defection to Yeltsin's side during the August coup had played an important role. It was a humiliation for Yeltsin. His discomfiture was compounded when Valery Zorkin, the chairman of the constitutional court, appeared as an umpire in the squabble, calling for talks between Yeltsin and Khasbulatov.

A furious Yeltsin signed a decree sacking Burbulis. Typically, in his tough style, he did not even phone his friend to explain his action. (Several days later, he gave him another job.) For the last three days of the session Yeltsin was on the defensive. He was forced to allow Congress to have its say in the nomination of the prime minister after all. He would select five candidates and deputies would then vote on each of them, as if in a beauty contest. The result was that Yeltsin's favoured candidate, Yegor Gaidar, came third out of the five, and Yeltsin had to drop him. There were two consolations. Congress passed a resolution renewing his special powers for another four months, and they accepted that a referendum would be held in April on the basic principles of a new constitution.

While the two-week session was a defeat for Yeltsin, it was a step towards the establishment of democracy in Russia. Unlike the Soviet Congress of People's Deputies which handed its power to Gorbachev, the Russian Congress had stood its ground against the president. It was the first hint of a real separation of constitutional power.

There was, of course, much to criticize in the Congress's behaviour. It was volatile and unpredictable. A few deputies hogged the limelight and the microphones. Others rambled and spoke off the point. It was rare for a deputy to deal with a preceding speaker's argument. But it was a mirror of Russian public opinion. Most deputies, like most Russians, were confused and uncertain, frightened that their country was slowly becoming ungovernable, aware that something was going seriously wrong with the economy, ready to accept that there was no theoretical or practical alternative to the market, but hoping and believing that there must be a way to make the transition more sensitive and gradual.

Some deputies, like Andrei Golovin, the co-ordinator of the faction Change—New Politics, argued that having factions meant the Congress was more democratic than the Westminster system. Without party discipline, deputies were free to vote according to their own beliefs rather than taking instructions from party whips. Others felt the factions were a necessary transition stage towards a party system. Elections were the focus round which factions would coalesce into parties, and Russia had had no parliamentary elections since 1990.

Several Russian political analysts argued that parties could only develop on the basis of well-defined interest groups in Russian society. The Soviet system had left Russian society atomized and without social classes. Until Russia developed private property so that people had something to defend, there would be no basis for a party system. Alexander Yakovlev, once the guru of perestroika, took this view. He became a supporter of Russia's Republican party, which he saw as the embryo of a party of private entrepreneurs.

Whoever would turn out to be right, the Congress had shown that it could play a key role in forming a civil society. Pressure groups, citizens' lobbies and social movements need a forum of competing political forces, to which they can direct their arguments and complaints, and from which they can hope for redress. An autocrat, or even a popularly elected president, cannot fulfil that function to the same extent, since his or her position does not encourage discussion and debate. But there were also negative signs. A poll conducted by the Moscow-based Institute for Social Research in early 1993 found a high degree of 'party-phobia' among Russians. Only 10 per cent described themselves as supporters of a particular party.[7] A poll taken by an American research organization found a rise in the number of Russians favouring authoritarian rule. The Washington-based Times-Mirror Centre for the People and the Press polled people in November 1991 and November 1992. In 1991 it found that 39 per cent of respondents wanted authoritarian rule. A year later the figure had risen to 51 per cent.[8]

In March 1993 Yeltsin announced a plan to impose 'special rule'. The move was condemned by Khasbulatov, Valery Zorkin, the chairman of the constitutional court, and Vice-President Rutskoi. Yeltsin backed down and narrowly survived an impeachment vote in Congress. Next month he felt the tide had turned when he won a nationwide referendum on his economic reforms. Although the result went against him in many parts of Russia, Yeltsin treated it as a landslide win. Confident that the public would support him against parliament, Yeltsin dissolved the Congress and the Supreme Soviet in September 1993. His stated aims were to rule by decree for three months so as to push through more of his economic reforms and hold elections for the lower house of a new two-chamber assembly. The irony was that the Congress had voted for such an assembly eighteen months earlier at a time when the conflict with the president had not degenerated to the level of political warfare. What was unresolved then and was still in dispute in September 1993 were the powers of the new assembly. Would the government be accountable to parliament or the president? In the context of Russian history, Yeltsin's wishes were clear.

12

Big Shock, Little Therapy

*Russia in one respect represents an exception to all
the countries of the world . . . the people have been
brought up, systematically over two generations,
without a sense of property and legality.*

SERGEI WITTE, THE TSAR'S PRIME MINISTER, 1905

*For the economist – if
economics is a science with its own laws – all
countries from the point of view of stabilization are identical.*

PYOTR AVEN, MEMBER OF THE GAIDAR TEAM, 1992[1]

Looming above the political conflict, which raged throughout the
first part of Yeltsin's term in office, over 'Who should run Russia –
the president or parliament?', there was an even more deeply felt
argument over the economy. Had the Russian economy been in good
shape, the constitutional clash over the distribution of power in the new
republic would have been incomparably calmer. But Yeltsin inherited
a situation which was already bleak by the time of the August 1991
coup. Output was falling for the first time for many years. Economic
ties between the fifteen Soviet republics had been disrupted by the
uncertainty caused by each one's demands for sovereignty, by
disagreements over currency and payments and by ethnic conflict. Trade with Eastern Europe, the former area of the

Council for Mutual Economic Assistance (Comecon), had slumped sharply after being put on a hard-currency basis in place of the inter-governmental clearing system of the past. As a result, the chronic shortages of food and other basic commodities in every Russian city had become even worse. Many city governments as well as enterprises with large work-forces were increasingly reverting to barter to try to find food suppliers with whom to swap industrial goods.

It was in this grim context that Yeltsin decided to entrust the country's economy to a team of completely new men, unconnected to the traditional power-houses of the Soviet regime, the State Planning Commission (Gosplan) and the military-industrial complex. Led by Yegor Gaidar, they were mostly academics in their mid-thirties with a theoretical grounding in macro-economics but no administrative or managerial experience. They were united by a burning desire to break the old system and bring in a market economy so quickly and drastically that the changes they made would be irreversible.

Within a few months of their taking charge, vice-president Alexander Rutskoi described them as 'young boys in pink pants, red shirts and yellow boots'.[2] The first part of his phrase, up to the bit about the pink pants, was subsequently quoted on numerous occasions in the Russian and Western media, usually in a favourable context, designed to suggest that they were brilliant young whizz-kids. But by referring to red shirts (the reference to yellow boots is obscure) Rutskoi was trying to compare them to the Bolsheviks. His charge was that they were a 'wrecking team'. Far from trying to reform the ailing economy, they were following in an old Russian nihilist tradition – first destroy, and then think what to do next. Gaidar did not deny that destruction was his first goal. When he took power in early November 1991 he said he was forming a 'kamikaze government'. It was a suicide mission which would not last long, but would with luck sink its target beyond the reach of any salvage operation.

Gaidar had been planning his attack on the state-controlled

economy for several years. Born in 1956 to an old Bolshevik family (his grandfather commanded a Red Army regiment and later became a famous children's writer under Stalin) Gaidar was a research analyst at the economic faculty of Moscow State University from 1981 to 1987. He had contacts with the most progressive think-tanks which had been allowed to flower when Gorbachev came to power. One was the Central Economic Mathematical Institute, led by Nikolai Petrakov, which became the home to the Club for Democratic Perestroika (see Chapter 1). The other, with which Gaidar had closer ties, was the Institute of the Economics of Forecasting and Scientific-Technical Progress, led by Stanislav Shatalin. Both men became advisers to Gorbachev. Two of Gaidar's ministers, Alexander Shokhin and Andrei Nechayev, passed through the Shatalin Institute.

Gaidar had his first brief brush with power in 1983 as a junior member of a state commission for economic reform set up under Yuri Andropov after Brezhnev's death. Through the commission he got to know a group of young economists from Leningrad, including Anatoly Chubais, later the influential minister in charge of privatization, and Sergei Glazyev, later minister of foreign economic relations. Under Gorbachev, when the informal political movements started to emerge, young economists also began to meet for weekend seminars and conferences. Gaidar and his friends were among the most talked-about and active. In 1987 he was appointed a columnist for the reformist party weekly, *Kommunist*, and later the economics editor for *Pravda*.

By then Gaidar was coming into contact with Western economists, particularly of the monetarist school. He visited the Hoover Institute at Stanford University in California, and attended a conference in Paris in May 1991 organized by Pyotr Aven, another future minister, at which the idea of trying to attach themselves to Yeltsin was first seriously aired. Those were exciting times, intellectually and emotionally, with something of American politics about them – young and ambitious specialists searching the horizon for a candidate who might be a winner, and to whom they could offer their talents and enthusiasm.

They made their move on the first morning of the August coup. A few hours after Yeltsin had climbed on to a tank outside the White House to issue his famous call for resistance, Gaidar and several of his friends assembled in the Institute of Economic Policy which he had founded under the auspices of Abel Aganbegyan, another of the leading perestroika economists. Gaidar decided to resign from the Communist party, and go over to the White House. For the next several days he met repeatedly with Gennady Burbulis, Yeltsin's chief political adviser. The two men came from different intellectual fields but were remarkably similar in character and politics. They were young, clever, academic, arrogant, confrontational and infused with impatience to destroy the old system.

When the coup collapsed, it was obvious that power had shifted dramatically from the centre to the republics. The issue in the Yeltsin camp was how much further to push it. Although the Union treaty which had been due to be signed on 20 August was clearly dead, Gorbachev was trying to maintain some form of political confederation and a single economic space. Burbulis and Gaidar were suspicious of both ideas. Burbulis invited the Gaidar team to retire to a dacha in the Russian government's compound at Arkhangelskoye to produce a programme for an independent Russian economy. They were also asked to write the economic part of the speech which Yeltsin would make to open the Russian Congress of People's Deputies at the end of October.

A fierce battle was going on inside the Yeltsin entourage. When Yevgeni Saburov, a deputy prime minister, flew to Alma Ata in early October to sign an economic treaty with the other republics, he was repudiated by the rest of the government for allegedly giving away too much of Russia's sovereignty. Although Yeltsin signed the document after further changes, it had been watered down to being a mere statement of intent rather than a set of co-operative obligations. The Burbulis-Gaidar line was growing in influence. Two weeks later Gaidar commented: 'Russia must have its own monetary and fiscal policy and its own bank. We must move to treating all other republics as sovereign states.' On macro-economic policy Gaidar's main argument was that subsidies should be removed and all prices, except those for energy, should be freed across the board. 'To make a switch to market prices in one motion is a severe, forced but necessary measure,' Yeltsin told Congress in the speech which Gaidar had written for him. The Gaidar calcula-tion was – again in Yeltsin's words – 'everyone will find life harder for approximately six months, then prices will fall and goods will begin to fill the market. By the autumn of 1992 the economy will have stabilised.'[3] Gaidar was appointed deputy prime minister in charge of economic policy a few days later.

His reforms were aimed at destroying the old system, not of course for its own sake. The idea was to create a fully-functioning market economy on its ruins. To claim that Gaidar had no positive goals would be absurd. But a strategy of 'shock therapy' with a high risk of killing the patient was deliberately chosen, so that if the reforms failed there would at least be no chance of the old central-ized state-owned economy continuing. In this sense his critics were right when they charged him with introducing a political rather than an economic programme, or at least trying to achieve a political goal through economic means.

Price de-control was intended to shake up the economy and force those enterprises which could not compete without subsidies to shut down or become more efficient. The soaring government budget deficit would be cut. Money would start to fulfil its proper function. Instead of queues chasing scarce goods at artificially low prices, goods would in future be rationed by price. There would be enough in the shops and people would decide what they could afford to buy. Gaidar accepted that the economy was heavily monopolized, but he argued that even monopolies would have to lower their prices again if they raised them too high and demand fell. As Pyotr Aven put it in the extraordinarily unrealistic interview from which the quotation at the beginning of this chapter was taken, 'Inflation is a phenomenon of monetary-credit policy. If there is no money, there can be no growth in prices'.

Asked why he was starting his reforms with price de-control, Gaidar said it was because prices were the only thing which the government still controlled. All the other levers had already ceased to operate. His remark was the essence of neo-liberal economics. The main aim was to get the government out of the business of running the economy and leave it to the market. Gaidar admitted he would like to be able to limit the money supply but that was in the hands of the Central Bank which was officially under the control of parliament, though open to persuasion from the government. The Gaidar reforms were often described as 'monetarist'. As a kind of shorthand for 'neo-liberal' or 'non-Keynesian', this was an acceptable label, though in strict terms they were not monetarist, since the new government accepted it could not fully control the Central Bank's credit policy or its printing and issuing of money.

The second element of the Gaidar strategy was rapid privatization. State-owned enterprises would be required to turn themselves into joint stock companies within a year. This was called commercialization. No longer would they be tied to the state in terms of supplies of inputs and the disposal of their product, with central ministries arranging how they obtained their raw materials or components and telling them to whom to deliver their finished items. They would have to prepare their own financial plans. The only input the state would provide would be credit. But even here a system of commercial banks would be set up with competitive interest rates and lending policies. Once commercialization was achieved, shares would be sold to the public, so as to reduce the power of the old directors as well as giving ordinary Russians a direct stake in the new market economy.

Gaidar's third key principle was that there should be a single exchange rate for the rouble. Any Russian firm or individual should be freely able to buy and sell roubles for hard currency at designated banks. This too was designed to 'make money mean something', as well as forcing Russian companies to face competition from foreign goods and services. Foreign investors would be encouraged to put their money into Russia, secure in the knowledge that the rouble was freely convertible.

Gaidar's insistence on shock therapy, and his determination to act quickly, arose from the experience of the previous two years. Under Gorbachev the Soviet government had attempted at least six different reform programmes. In 1989 Leonid Abalkin had produced the first serious proposal to introduce a market economy, but the best known was the 'Five Hundred Days' programme drawn up in September 1990 by Stanislav Shatalin, the director of the Institute through which many of Gaidar's friends had passed, and Grigory Yavlinsky, another ambitious young economist. It provided for a substantial devolution of economic power to the republics and a packet of legislation aimed at creating the basis of a market economy. There were laws on banking, stock exchanges, industrial privatization, private farming and foreign trade. The Shatalin plan aroused fierce resistance from the directors of state enterprises and from the central ministries in Moscow. They had the sympathetic ear of Nikolai Ryzhkov, the Soviet prime minister, as well as of many deputies in the Supreme Soviet. As a result the Supreme Soviet rejected the plan.

Gorbachev asked Aganbegyan to produce a synthesis, which would merge some of Shatalin's points with those of Ryzhkov. Known as the 'Guidelines for the Stabilization of the National Economy and the Transition to a Market Economy', the compromise tilted towards the Ryzhkov version. The significant aspects of the Guidelines were its pace and the sequence of events it proposed. First, there should be a gradual establishment of the legal framework for a market economy combined with the destatization of property and the 'cleaning-out' of the country's finances. This could take two to five years. Only after this was done should prices be decontrolled across the board. There were undoubted problems with this approach. As long as central ministries continued, small businesses found it difficult to get licences and credit. The destatization of property, envisaged in the Guidelines, concentrated on leasing arrangements and co-operatives, which by mid-1990 employed only 4 per cent of the workforce, or the piecemeal selling of state property such as equipment and vehicles. It did not envisage selling many state enterprises as such.

Nevertheless, the Guidelines were in tune with Russian conditions, in accepting that it would take time to restructure a heavily monopolized economy in a country with no understanding of private property and market disciplines. The Guidelines proposed a large reduction in the budget deficit by means of cuts in defence spending and a gradual reduction in the state's wage fund. Companies would increasingly have to pay for wage increases out of their own earnings. Above all, the Guidelines assumed that the government would control the transition to the market economy. It would be a regulated transition to a regulated market, rather than an attempt to switch the economy over to market forces in one go.

The Gaidar strategy was very different. Some critics claimed he had taken it from the International Monetary Fund. This was not strictly true. Although it adopted many general IMF prescriptions, such as free prices and currency convertibility, it was not worked out directly with the IMF. The neo-liberal ideas of economists such as Hayek and Friedman formed its intellectual basis, as well as the political advice of a new generation of Western economists such as Jeffrey Sachs, who had been involved in the Eastern European economies since the fall of Communism, in particular Poland's shock therapy. But the overriding factor which encouraged Gaidar to climb into the kamikaze pilot's seat was the intense atmosphere of political, propagandistic and intellectual pressure from Western governments and much of the Western media, who were anxious to see the Communist system destroyed root and branch. Although the party was virtually defunct after the August coup, a myth was created that the old nomenklatura was planning revenge and could make a come-back unless the market economy was speedily introduced. Hence the premium on 'irreversibility', as though there was some discernible safe limit which could be reached, and everyone could then breathe freely.

This climate of Western advice was inspired by one of the deeply felt tenets of the ideology of anti-Communism, namely that Communists never give up power voluntarily, let alone peacefully. In fact, the collapse of Communist power in Eastern Europe had just produced a graphic refutation of that thesis. Communist governments not only retreated bloodlessly, with the exception of Romania, and to a small extent Albania, but many of their officials admitted they were exhausted and dispirited, and only too glad to go. Where there was truth in the Gaidar/Western line was that some individuals from the old Communist system would try to maintain their power and position in spite of the change in the political and economic environment. But this was a normal human process of adaptation, a matter of instinct and survival rather than of ideology. Gaidar only had to look in the mirror as well as all around him. Most of the Yeltsin team, starting with the boss, were former Communists. The political underpinning of shock therapy was flawed since the Communist system was discredited and incapable of comeback by the autumn of 1991, before Gaidar launched his attack. The real issue was how to find an evolutionary transition to the market economy which would be practical in Russian terms.

Gaidar's second strategic mistake was not to recognize the specific features of the Russian economy. He was excessively influenced by the claimed success of Poland's post-Communist economic experiment. Michael Ellman, professor of economics at Amsterdam University, has pointed out there were six respects in which Poland differed from Russia.[4] First, there was no control on wage increases in the state sector in Russia. This point was accepted by Gaidar, when he told parliament in December 1991 that this 'is impossible in our conditions'. Without a strong trade union movement, which is one of the key elements of a civil society, Russia could not expect the kind of voluntary wage restraint which Poland's Solidarity movement was able to adopt at least for a time.

Second, the state sector in Russia was much larger than in Poland, so that more of the economy was run along administrative lines and therefore minimally responsive to market stimuli. When prices were decontrolled, firms raised them to virtually any level they thought fit, and did not lower them when demand fell. In any case, the most responsive sector of any economy is the consumer goods sector but in the Russian economy this was one of the least developed areas, producing a relatively small share of total output. In Russia the bulk of the economy was raw material processing, heavy industry and chemicals. State firms assumed that they would run up debts to each other, and the government or Central Bank would soon bail them out, as it had always done in the past. This, they thought, made more sense than lowering their prices and cutting revenue.

Third, Poland's shock therapy was introduced to an economy where 40 per cent of employment was in the private sector, predominantly in agriculture but also in construction (27 per cent) and industry (15 per cent). This was not the case in Russia. Fourth, Russia's depression was also more severe than Poland's when the changes occurred, so that the margin of political tolerance in Russia was lower. In 1991 national income fell 19 per cent, largely because of breakdowns in supply. The new policy could not afford a very heavy further drop if pressures for reflation were not to mount. In fact, in the first six months alone of the Gaidar programme in 1992, national income fell another 20 per cent. This was bound to lead to political pressure to reverse course.

Fifth, Poland had a credit policy which provided for a rate of interest above that of inflation, so that enterprises had to use their loans productively. This was not the case in Russia where the Central Bank was unwilling to stop loans or call in debts because this would have increased the depression and led to closures and massive unemployment. The final difference between Russia and Poland concerned exchange rate policy. Poland managed to achieve a fixed exchange rate at the same time as it started its shock therapy. Russia was not able to do this. However, instead of postponing the move altogether until stabilization of the economy had been achieved, Gaidar brought in a single exchange rate six months after starting his programme, when inflation was already galloping as a result of the price decontrol. It was a disastrous step, which led to a massive demand for dollars, a further collapse of the rouble and a haemorrhage of the newly acquired hard currency to accounts abroad. With the economy in such chaos as a result of the price increases and the production slump Russians with access to funds scrambled for a safe haven. Their mood amply matched the behaviour of foreign investors who were equally reluctant to put money into such an unstable economy. Figures for capital flight are always impossible to ascertain since most of it is concealed, but estimates at the beginning of 1993 put it at between $2.5 billions (10 per cent of annual export earnings), according to Sergei Glazyev, the then minister of foreign economic relations, and $10 billions, according to Western monetary officials.[5]

Within days of the lifting of controls on prices, the first errors in Gaidar's predictions became visible, in line with warnings which many critics had given in advance. Controls were removed from 90 per cent of goods on 2 January 1992, and raised to new ceilings on the remaining goods, including bread, vodka, public transport and energy. The following day prices rose by 250 per cent. But this was not a one-time jump as Gaidar and his team hoped. It led to a vicious cycle of price rises throughout the economy. Companies cut output but continued to raise their own prices to compensate for the higher cost of their inputs. Most of the economy was based on the so-called non-cash rouble, with transactions being written into firm's accounts, and not being transferable into cash. In response to the price leaps, firms covered their increased costs by writing up debts to each other. At the beginning of 1992 inter-enterprise debt was 39 billion roubles. By the middle of June it had reached a colossal 3.2 trillion roubles. Gaidar should have predicted this but his neo-liberal economic ideology did not take account of the realities of the Russian economy. It was one more tragic Russian example of theory taking precedence over practice.

Managers were behaving rationally by piling up debt, since interest rates were below the soaring level of inflation and they were convinced that political pressure would oblige the government to write off the debts instead of risking the bankruptcy of the entire economy. Soviet industry used to be organized into 7,664 product groups, and the extraordinary degree of monopolization – a pre-Revolutionary Russian phenomenon which was exacerbated by Soviet planners – was illustrated by the fact that 77 per cent of these items were made by a single firm. While inter-enterprise dealings were cleared in non-cash roubles, cash was needed to pay wages and pensions. The speed of inflation, and the politically inevitable mark-up of wages and pensions to prevent the population falling too far behind, were so rapid that the economy was soon faced with a massive shortage of cash simply to pay people. Millions of people were told to wait for one or two months before getting paid, or were sent away from their factories on temporary unpaid leave.

The government's projections for cutting the budget deficit were also made to look foolish. In a memorandum to the IMF in March 1992,[6] Gaidar said the deficit would be equivalent to 0.9 per cent of Gross National Product in the first quarter. In reality, according to Philip Hanson, professor of Soviet economics at Birmingham University, the deficit in the first quarter was running at between 8 to 10 per cent of GNP.[7] Hanson blamed the government for the high deficit, arguing first that it had underestimated the predictable difficulty of collecting its new taxes, such as value added tax, and also because output fell so much as a result of price decontrol.

By April 1992 political pressure on the government for a change in course was intense. At the Congress of People's Deputies Gaidar had to accept that the Central Bank was going to loosen credit policy and write off the inter-enterprise debt. As a consequence the government rewrote its forecast on the budget deficit. Towards the end of the second quarter Gaidar recognized what he should have seen in the autumn of 1991. His message to parliament, introducing the draft budget in June, said that 'under the existing conditions of the real existing structure of the Russian economy and the acuteness of the social problems, it will be impossible this year to stabilize the economy by means of the classic forms of monetary regulation of a market economy'.[8] The government accepted that the deficit would rise to at least 15 per cent of GNP. It abandoned its plans for a credit squeeze so tight that it would, according to its own estimates, have put five million people out of work in the second half of the year.

Even without the 'second shock' which mass unemployment would have produced, by mid-year almost a million Russians had lost their jobs, the majority of them women. This was partly a result of dismissals of office workers, and partly because of the reduction of creche and kindergarten places, as factories tried to cut non-production costs. Inflation had wiped out millions of people's savings in a matter of a few weeks. Small businesses and the few private farmers found it hard to invest. Because of the absence of hire-purchase or instalment buying in the economy, people used to save the full amount in order to buy large items, such as television sets or cars. Millions found themselves unable to buy as the price shot up before they were ready to produce the cash. Those who had already accumulated 80 or 90 per cent of the old purchase price were predictably furious. In the first half of 1992 retail sales were only 58 per cent of what they had been a year earlier.

Consumption of food also dropped sharply, as people changed their diet to try to make ends meet. According to official estimates, about half the population was living below the poverty line by mid-1992. Government spending on public services such as transport, education and health declined, with a consequent drop in standards. Low pay for teachers, doctors and scientists forced trained people to drop their professions and try to find a niche in the emerging commercial structures, which were often not based on new production but on buying and selling state assets, or on imports.

By the autumn of 1992 Gaidar's reforms were being criticized by virtually every independent economist in Russia, including Shatalin and Yavlinsky, the authors of the first market programme. Yavlinsky had spoken out already in April. 'Liberalizing prices without privatizing the economy and breaking the monopolies in the state sector was a major mistake,' he told me in the office of his think-tank, Epicentre, high up in the old Comecon building opposite the White

House.[9] 'There have to be two stages: first instititutional changes, even constitutional changes, in order to develop private property, and only then macro-economic policies. You have to combine the two. Without the first part, everything else is just playing tricks.'

Shatalin's attack was timed for the eve of the December session of the Congress of People's Deputies. 'If economic policy is not changed,' he wrote in a long and withering analysis, 'the collapse in output will continue and Russia may lose half its industrial production. This is only comparable to the combined results of the First World War, the Revolution, and the civil war.'[10] He argued that some 80 per cent of the population had suffered a halving of their real incomes.

Perhaps the most important theme of Shatalin's article was that there were two broad approaches in world experience to creating and running a market economy, the liberal model and the socially-orientated model. The choice was not between economic efficiency and social justice, but between two models which could guarantee a reasonable level of both but by using different techniques. In the socially-orientated model the government played a greater role in economic management, taxing incomes and stimulating job creation, and in providing funds for education, health and culture.

In a developed market society Shatalin's discussion would have been considered a statement of the obvious. In the Russian context it was like a thunder-clap. The Gaidar team, its supporters in parliament, and almost the entire pro-government press had succeeded in framing the discussion on market economics into a simple issue of 'for or against the market'. The level of economic literacy in Russia was so low that it was almost impossible to put across the notion that a person could be for the market but favour getting there by different means from those chosen by the government. The idea of a strong government role in running the economy was denounced as 'socialist', and therefore a hold-over from the previous system. Being critical of Gaidar meant that you were either a Communist or a supporter of the old nomenklatura.

Shatalin's record as a firm believer in the market gave him a credibility which few others enjoyed. His article had enormous influence, especially as he wrote that Russia was more suited to the socially-orientated approach 'because of its historic conditions, the level of social welfare achieved in the framework of the planned economy and in the mentality of its society'. 'The liberal approach means going against the will of the majority and destroying the social welfare guarantees and the material basis for paying for them which people have managed to reach at such great sacrifice,' he said. It was not surprising that Ruslan Khasbulatov, in an address to the Congress a few days later, used almost exactly the same argument about the existence of two pro-market approaches as Shatalin had done. His speech was more warmly applauded than Yeltsin's, and on the eve of the 1993 referendum Yeltsin started using the phrase 'socially-orientated market economy' himself.

Nevertheless, Gaidar's price decontrol had achieved one of its aims. He had broken the last elements of the state planning system. The kamikaze pilot had succeeded, or as Yavlinsky put it, 'the pill has been swallowed'.[11] When Viktor Chernomyrdin, Gaidar's successor as prime minister and an industrialist of the old school, in early 1993 tried to reintroduce price controls on some food items and other basic commodities, Yeltsin's new economic adviser, Boris Fyodorov, said it was impossible and unenforceable. He was right and Chernomyrdin soon backed down.

The economic and human cost of the Gaidar strategy was catastrophic. 'The Russian stabilization plan of January 1992 failed to stabilize the monetary economy and destabilized the real economy,' Michael Ellman concluded.[12] Although by mid-1992 Gaidar had conceded his failure to balance the budget and had therefore started to change his goals, he refused to admit his error explicitly, let alone resign.

At the Congress in December 1992 he claimed that the programme had been a success because people had not rioted or gone on strike. This was a dangerously lame defence. One reason was that the government sensibly gave generous wage increases to key groups in the workforce, such as the miners and the oil-workers. Another was that Russians have little practice in strikes. The organization and solidarity which they require depends on a strong civil society. The strikes of the final years of perestroika were exceptions to the rule, and they mainly affected a few industries and regions. The passivity of Russian workers who failed to heed Yeltsin's appeal for strikes during the August coup was more indicative of their general unwillingness to protest.

Mass unemployment might have changed the mood, and the government did not take the political risk of provoking unrest. By 1992 most of the unemployed were demoralized women workers. They were scattered round the country and not in a position to take collective action. The government was justifiably afraid that if large plants began to close, especially if they were the main employers in a single town, there could be trouble. Russian industry was heavily concentrated in a relatively few giant factories. Some 1,000 large companies, each employing on average 8,500 people, produced half the country's industrial output.

While Gaidar had succeeded in destroying the state's ability to control prices but had failed to stabilize the economy, what of his aims for privatizing industry and encouraging 'popular capitalism' so that citizens would become shareholders and small-scale entrepreneurs? For most of his year in office Gaidar worked closely with Anatoly Chubais on a scheme for selling companies to the public via auctions at which people could use free vouchers. The vouchers began to be distributed in September 1992. Each had a nominal value of 10,000 roubles and every person, children included, was entitled to one. The logic was that people had helped to build up state industry with sweat and blood during the long years of Soviet rule, and they were entitled to a return.

The same argument applied with more force to workers in particular plants. They felt they had contributed to creating 'their' factory, and when it came to privatization they wanted the major share rather than letting shares be scattered throughout society. They were also afraid they would lose control if shares ended up in the hands of one or two powerful outsiders. Battles developed in parliament over the point, and the government was obliged to modify its line, so as to allow the workforce of any company to have the option of taking a controlling share of 51 per cent. They would be given a block of shares free, and have the right to buy others at a privileged low rate. The remaining shares would be sold at auction. The scheme was backed by directors, who also wanted to retain control within the company and felt they could operate more easily with their 'worker-shareholders' than with outsiders. At some plants the government was obliged to retreat even further and accept that the workforce be allowed up to 80 per cent of the shares.

The government saw the issue as a struggle between the nomenklatura and the public. It argued that widely dispersed shareholding was more healthy, and would lead to a more efficient check on management. The counter-argument fitted more naturally into Russian tradition and won the day. Under changes made by Gorbachev in the early years of perestroika the workers in any plant, operating as a collective, were given the right to elect managers. It was aimed at encouraging economic democracy and giving people a greater incentive to modernize and improve industrial practices. In a burst of pride Gorbachev told a meeting in January 1988: 'Nowhere in the West do they elect directors and foremen. Nowhere in the West do work collectives endorse plans. This is what constitutes our socialist democracy.'[13] But the new law was resented by managers, who persuaded the then prime minister, Nikolai Ryzhkov, to repeal it three years later. Nevertheless the spirit of the original reform seemed to live on, and when privatization started, Russian workers were more interested in taking shares in their own companies than in buying them in other companies as a speculative investment.

The Bolshevik cake factory went on sale in Moscow in December 1992, the first share auction in the capital city. Senior officials of the committee on state property, the main government body in charge of privatization, were on hand as well as advisers from the European Bank who had subsidized the running of the auction and the hire of a hall in Moscow's main exhibition centre. When the doors opened at 9 a.m., a crowd poured in and formed up at tables for share application forms. It looked an impressive display of popular capitalism. But when we started to interview the buyers, it turned out that most were the factory's own workers. Special buses had been organized to take them to the auction site, and they had been given time off work. They did not want to lose control of the plant, they said. Anatoly Andreyev, a driver at the plant, was sitting with his wife at a table filling in a share application. 'I don't want to invest anywhere else. I'm not the sort of person to buy and sell shares in the street,' he explained. 'We don't want to go back to the old system,' he went on, as his wife nodded her head in agreement. 'But if Gaidar brings people to disaster, what's the good of that? His grandfather carried a sabre and made the October Revolution. Now he's doing the same thing.' Marina Vinakurova, a department head, who was standing with other women in a queue for applications, was more cheerful. She took the share issue light-heartedly. 'It's better to have shares in the factory where you work. A game is a game. We're learning,' she laughed.

What was true at the Bolshevik cake factory was reflected throughout the economy. Figures released by the committee on state property in January 1993 showed that workers in 64 per cent of the first 2,520 large firms which turned themselves into joint-stock companies had voted for the option which gave them a controlling interest.[14]

The switch from centrally owned state property to ownership by individuals was an important reform. It could mark a key step towards a civil society in which people took greater responsibility for their environment, in this case, the enterprises which provide the lifeblood for the economy. The interesting thing was that Russians' main motive in share-owning was conservative. It might well be that at a later stage a secondary market would develop, with people trading on stock exchanges in shares of companies with which they had no connection. In the first instance they were more interested in their own enterprises.

Shatalin was one of several economists who welcomed the shift towards worker shareholders. He argued that Russians were not ready to become shareholders on a mass scale. Faced with their one free voucher, people would either sell it or invest it. Not many would seek to become capitalists and buy other shares, mainly because so few had the money to spare, but also because they had no interest in acquiring shares. The voucher idea would lead to two possible results. One was that there would be 'a broad stratum of small or minimal rentiers getting miserable dividends on the shares they buy with their voucher'. The other, which Shatalin considered more likely, was that the vouchers would be bought up by a few rich speculators and asset-strippers 'with no interest in the more efficient use of destatized property'.[15] He argued for distributing shares to workers' collectives instead of using vouchers and auctions.

As for the so-called 'small privatization', the selling of shops and other businesses in the service sector, Shatalin pointed out that this was going very slowly. By the end of 1992, after a year of the scheme, only 7.7 per cent of the country's retail shops had been privatized and only 2.7 per cent of cafés and restaurants. In the field of personal services, like hairdressers and shoe repairs, it was 6.5 per cent.

The most conspicuous signs of flourishing private business were not in industry or the service sector. They were to be found on every main street in Moscow, St Petersburg and other Russian cities. Kiosks sprang up, selling a narrow range of mainly identical items – drinks, coffee, shirts, shoes and cosmetics. Nearly everything was imported. The sales people were mainly in their twenties. The kiosks clearly satisfied a need even though there was little competition between them. Kiosk owners reported that new 'mafias' had emerged to control them, demanding protection money to save the kiosks from being smashed up. Even the trellis tables in Moscow's pedestrian areas, where traders sold souvenirs and dolls for foreign tourists, were under threat from similar racketeers. The owners had to pay a share of their takings or risk the consequences. Many

Russians complained that the kiosks did nothing to raise production in the local economy. The goods on sale were foreign, and the profits made by the new entrepreneurs were spent on importing goods for their own consumption, from Japanese hi-fi systems and music centres to the Mercedes and BMW cars which started appearing on Moscow's streets. Any profits left over were stashed away in banks abroad rather than invested in Russia.

The optimists argued that although Russian capitalism was making a rough start a healthy climate of longer-term risk-taking and honest entrepreneurship would gradually evolve. The pessimists disputed this. Low-level speculation and dishonesty would only breed the same vices on a larger scale, they feared. Indeed, there was considerable evidence that this was already the case. Managers of the large state-owned monopolies were selling state assets on the black market and exporting Russia's precious raw materials abroad, often outside official channels, so as to avoid tax and keep the proceeds for themselves rather than for their companies. As even Anatoly Chubais, the privatization minister, once put it: 'Property in this country belongs to whoever is nearest to it.'[16]

Down on the Farm

Valentin Novikov was not in a good mood. He had driven us out to the fields where he and the other private farmers were supposed to be cutting hay. It was already 11 a.m. and at least two men had not turned up for work. 'A day lost is a day never made up,' muttered Novikov, a ruddy-faced man in his early forties, as he stared grimly round, hoping to catch a glimpse of recalcitrant friends. Since the men broke loose from the collective farm the previous year, they were free agents. They did not have to work if they felt like a long lie-in. This was one such occasion, the morning after an ancient country festival known as Elijah's Day, which villagers celebrated with generous helpings of vodka.

While the collective farm workers had Elijah's Day off as well as the next one, Novikov wanted the new entrepreneurs to show a greater sense of responsibility. Relaxing for one day off might be acceptable but they should avoid a second day of drinking and take advantage of the dry weather, he maintained. If it rained the next day, the hay would be sodden. 'I've harvested my hay. Now I have to run after the others. My nerves aren't good enough to go on helping them for nothing,' he grumbled.

As we drove back along the bumpy dirt-road to the village, we met a rusty bus coming the other way. Two of the missing farmers were in it. Alexei Osonov was barefoot and drunk. His wife, a kindergarten teacher, was sitting some ten feet from him. She was angry and refused to speak to him, having apparently exhausted herself getting him out of bed. 'I don't know if it's better to have left the collective farm. You have to work more,' Osonov complained, as we tried to interview him. Alexander Khrustalov was also the worse for wear, though marginally more articulate. 'The people who stayed on the collective farm look badly on us, but we won't go back. We'll work,' he said, not entirely convincingly. 'We're the strongest, but even we are collapsing.'

A third man on the bus, Ivan Kazakov, was able to explain the position better. He had never been a member of the collective farm, but came up from Turkmenistan eighteen months earlier when he heard that private farmers were getting land. His parents had settled in Central Asia and he was born there. He decided to get out as the independence movement started. 'In Turkmenistan I lived in town. People there get two days off a week, and I earned five times more, but I was attracted up here by the land. Sometimes I think it was a mistake.' Kazakov was given 136 acres of land but no equipment. He thought he could buy some, but found it was impossible to get a loan.

We were in a village called Shagot in Yaroslovskaya Oblast, some 200 miles north-east of Moscow. It was eight months after the start of the Gaidar reforms, and the prices of farm machinery had risen dramatically. A tractor which cost 3,500 roubles in 1991 cost

350,000 roubles a year later. Farmers like Osonov and Khrustalov who had been in the collective for many years had been granted some equipment as well as land when they set up on their own, though not as much machinery as they needed. They helped Kazakov out. 'We've created a voluntary private kolkhoz (collective farm),' he said. 'We have to help each other. There's no other way.'

I had first visited the area more than a year earlier, when the idea of private farming was in its first bloom. At that time Osonov and Khrustalov were optimistic. They were among the youngest and fittest members of the collective farm, a dairy-producer with the odd name of Blessed Shoots. Osonov was twenty-seven, and had been born at Blessed Shoots. Khrustalov, a little older, had spent ten years there, and was the farm's chief agronomist. We sat on a bench outside a wooden single-storey cottage, along with the farm chairman Mikhail Nogibin. Blessed Shoots had been created in the 1930s at the height of Stalin's collectivization drive. By 1991, thanks to the exodus of peasants to the town, it was a residential community more than a working farm. Children and old people made up 40 per cent of its population. Out of its 470 people only 287 were workers, and half of these had non-farming jobs as clerical staff, teachers, drivers, cleaners and cooks in the farm's canteen. A quarter of the workforce had left in the six years since perestroika, and nineteen of the farm's forty settlements had been abandoned. The clumps of cottages stood empty. It was a typical case of the denuded Russian farm community. Near Moscow and other big urban centres better-off city dwellers would buy up the derelict cottages for use as weekend homes, but Blessed Shoots was too far away from any large town to make this feasible.

When word came through that Boris Yeltsin had signed a decree making it possible for collective farm members to demand their share of land and equipment and start up on their own as private entrepreneurs, fifteen men announced their intention to do so. The prime mover was Valentin Novikov, the man we found in such a state of irritation a year later. A natural leader, he persuaded the others that they would do better outside the farm.

The chairman was not against the idea. 'If people want to work, good luck to them,' he told us. But other farm members were not so relaxed about the advent of the market economy, and the prospect of private enterprise. Led by the pensioners, they were concerned that if fifteen of the best farmers withdrew, the rest would suffer. According to Yeltsin's decree, they could not refuse to let them have their rightful share. What they were entitled to do was to decide what land to give them. The fifteen naturally wanted land as near as possible to their cottages. The farm collective, meeting as a democratic body, said no. The issue was argued and debated, and in the end the fifteen were given land about six miles from where they lived. 'It's not the farthest corner of the farm. There are more distant spots,' the chairman said. The men were awarded 110,000 roubles, five tractors, one car, a combine harvester and 100 cattle.

Although they were private farmers, in practice their independence was limited. For one thing, they could not sell their land to anyone else for ten years. After that, they would have to get permission from the local council. The aim of the decree was to prevent speculation in land, with collective farmers selling their share to rich businessmen who would not bother to farm it but keep it for residential development. This was a prospect which seemed unlikely for land as isolated as Blessed Shoots. The second restriction was that the new farmers were required to sell their milk to the collective farm. This was not necessarily a bad thing, since they had no milk lorries or refrigeration, and would have found it hard to drive to town to sell milk on their own. But it put them in a subordinate position, especially as they also had to buy their fuel from the collective farm, as well as renting equipment and buying spare parts. 'They're dependent on us at every step,' the chairman acknowledged. 'If we refused them help, they'd have to come to us on their knees.'

In spite of the difficulties, the farmers were ready for the challenge, they assured us. Eighteen months later, their mood was noticeably more pessimistic. Heavy drinking on Elijah's Day looked like an effort to escape. Among the collective farm members the atmosphere had soured further. We learnt that the chairman, Mikhail Nogibin, had been voted out of office by the assembly of members. A majority decided he had been too generous to the private farmers, by awarding them too much equipment. On our first visit in 1991 we already heard complaints that the government was raising prices on industrial goods more steeply than on farm produce, making it hard for farmers, whether collective or private, to invest in new machinery and modernize. By 1992 they had been hit by the Gaidar government's 'shock therapy' with the lifting of restrictions on the prices of all industrial goods and a big increase in fuel prices. Angry farmers complained that the way the switch to the market economy was handled undermined one of its stated purposes – to boost agricultural production and encourage private farming.

In the regional centre of Yaroslavl, Alexander Bartsov was head of the association of peasant farmers. But even he was against any wholesale break-up of the collective farms. 'If we transfer all funds to private farms in one go, there'll be a collapse of agriculture,' he said. 'There have to be people who want to farm,' he added, putting his finger on one of the major issues of the Russian countryside. The slaughter of thousands of peasants in the 1930s, plus the famine, coupled with the rapid shift of many of the survivors to industrial work, significantly reduced the number of people with farming skills. The miserable infrastructure of the countryside – dirt roads, poor schools, derelict shops, a shortage of hospitals, as well as any form of entertainment – widened the gap between town and country. When private farming was finally legalized again, two generations after collectivization, there were few people willing to take it up, particularly among those who had become city-dwellers.

Faced with the danger of a collapse in agriculture, the Gaidar government retreated from some of its anti-subsidy reforms within a month of starting its shock therapy. Retail prices for milk were fixed and the prices paid to farmers were raised by means of state subsidies. The aim was to encourage them to go on producing milk in spite of the high price of feed rather than kill their cattle and turn them into meat. Vladimir Bardakov, the chief engineer of Yaroslavl's main dairy, said in August 1992 that only 75 per cent of the 1991 volume was being delivered by the farms, because of a fall in output. There had also been a sharp drop in milk consumption, he pointed out. Much of the milk in Yaroslavl is sold from cisterns in the street. They are a kind of tanker pulled by a lorry which can park at strategic points near blocks of flats. People prefer to bring their own jugs and buckets because the milk is cheaper than when you buy it in cartons. 'Last year there were forty cisterns operating every day. Now we need only twelve,' Bardakov reported.

At the town's meat-processing factory 100 yards up the street, it was the same story. Supplies from the farms were down by a quarter, but so was consumption. The trend in Yaroslavl was repeated throughout Russia. Figures published by the United Nations Food and Agriculture Organization in September 1992 showed a nationwide drop of 34 per cent in milk consumption and a 16 per cent drop in meat-eating.[17] At the same time there was a sharp rise in the consumption of the traditional Russian staples, bread and potatoes. This reversion to a less wholesome diet was happening in a country where nutritional standards were already low in comparison with developed nations. Consumers faced shortages of fresh fruit and vegetables for several months of the year.

The high price of food, as a result of inflation, accelerated the demand for private allotments of land. This had already started under perestroika. Then people wanted a guaranteed supply of their own produce because of constant shortages and queues. Under Gaidar the main factor pushing people back to the land was the prices in the shops and at the peasants' markets. Local authorities allocated land free, and at weekends hundreds of city-dwellers worked on their patch of ground.

This was not a genuine expansion of private agriculture, since there was no marketable surplus. It was a throw-back to a more primitive form of economic survival. In his satirical novel about the future, entitled *2040*, which was written as a prediction for the

Soviet system rather than for the market economy, Vladimir Voinovich described a Moscow in which every balcony housed a live pig. Food production had collapsed and everyone did what they could to survive. By 1993 it had not reached that point but there was a massive increase in animal husbandry and vegetable gardening for home consumption. Many peasants who obtained their share of land from the collective farms took it out of market production, according to Vice-President Rutskoi, who was put in charge of agriculture. Of the 128,000 individual farmers registered by the end of the first half of 1992 only 3,000 were producing for sale rather than for themselves and their families, he reported.[18]

Miners and Unions

As you drive through the southern part of Siberia's Kuzbass, the heartland of Russia's coal industry, the main highway skirts small pit villages where horse-drawn carts still trundle along side roads. In the smaller settlements most people live in wooden cottages, with a coal-shed in every garden. In the bigger towns there are shoddy blocks of flats made of prefabricated concrete and a few older, stronger-looking buildings put up, they tell you, by German prisoners-of-war. Suddenly a huge lid of smoke comes into view, hanging over the horizon. This is the city of Novokuznetsk, where residents claim Yuri Gagarin could see the pollution from outer space when he became the first man to circle the earth.

In the great mining strike of 1989, the biggest in Soviet history, Novokuznetsk was the headquarters. Almost the entire Kuzbass came to a halt as thousands of men walked off the job and, with their hard hats and working clothes still on, sat down in the central squares of several Siberian towns. Beside the Lenin statues and from the balconies of Communist party headquarters, from which most officials had fled, the leaders of spontaneously elected strike committees formulated their demands to the government: better pay and pensions, improvements in the poor safety standards which allowed one miner on average to die every day of the year, and an end to corruption. The miners insisted they be paid from the moment that they entered the mine at the start of the shift and not from the time they reached the coal-face, sometimes a journey of an hour, half-crouching and half-crawling underground. They complained that managers were using materials and even workers from the mines to build themselves country cottages. These men were sneered at as 'podsnezhniki' or snowdrops, people who grow under the snow because they have the special protection of the management.

Although their demands were mainly economic and social, in the Soviet Union to go on strike was a political act, a statement of defiance which dwarfed any street demonstration yet seen during perestroika. For one thing it was the working class which was moving. For another the miners had the power to hold the country to ransom. In most mining towns the workers' committees had become the temporary centres of power. Local Communist party and government officials had disappeared, or were keeping discreetly quiet at home, and the strike committees took on responsibility for public order and providing citizens with news and information.

But the miners' leaders were not sure how Gorbachev and the Politburo would react. 'It was our first strike. We were aware of the dangers,' Mikhail Kislyuk, a mining economist and member of the Kuzbass strike committee, said. 'Troops had been used in Armenia and Georgia not long before, and people were killed.'[19] Yuri Gerold, another strike leader, was sardonic: 'Everyone here felt afraid, although we tried to hide it. Sometimes we even joked: "Here we are in Siberia. The camps aren't far away." '[20]

Gorbachev and prime minister Ryzhkov were shocked by the strike, but quickly understood there was no way to repress it. Worried that other industries would come out too, in particular the oil men and the railway workers, they decided to go to the other extreme. They conceded virtually all the miners' demands.

317

In the Donbass it was a similar story. When I saw Aleksei Bokarev, the head of the regional strike committee, a few days after their victory, he still could hardly believe their success. 'Throughout the strike we maintained iron discipline. Alcohol shops were closed. We could not afford provocations,' he recalled. Government ministers had rushed to Donetsk, anxious to get the men back to work as fast as possible. While the strikers waited outside, government ministers negotiated with Bokarev and his colleagues in the Communist party headquarters. But when they signed a 47-point protocol of agreement, the crowd was suspicious of being cheated and urged Bokarev to go to Moscow to get the prime minister's signature. Their faith in the authorities was close to rock bottom after years of neglect and broken promises.

The next twenty-four hours were the most extraordinary of Bokarev's life. There was the flight to Moscow, three hours with Nikolai Ryzhkov, the flight back, a welcome at Donetsk airport by a police escort and a motorcade with flashing lights which whisked him back to the thousands of anxious men, still sitting in front of the concrete portico of the party building. 'I struggled to the microphone, held up the agreement with the prime minister's signature, and said just two words: "Lads, hooray." The tension evaporated. There were tears. There was laughter. Our man, a delegate from the working-class, had come back from the Kremlin.'

When it was founded in the first wave of Russia's industrialization before 1917, Donetsk was called Yuzovka, after a Welsh mining engineer, John Hughes. In the 1930s they renamed it Stalino, a symbol of a triumphant process which was going to take the Soviet Union into the lead as the world's number one industrial power. At its heart was the 'shock worker' movement, whose champion, Alexei Stakhanov, exceeded all known output norms by cutting his way through 102 tons of coal in a single six-hour shift. 'He wasn't crazy. He was just a victim of the system. He thought he was building paradise,' Boris Grebenyuk, another of the new leaders told me. After a pause, he added: 'In a way, so did we.'

The trigger for the miners of both the Donbass and Siberia was the Congress of People's Deputies in May 1989. They experienced something novel – political arguments broadcast live and uncensored on television. Deputy after deputy criticized shortages, corruption and the dead hand of bureaucracy. Like many other citizens, Bokarev felt encouraged to act politically for the first time in his life. The second son of a peasant on a state farm near Ryazan in central Russia, he says his sense of injustice was first aroused in his last two years of school when he was drafted to work in the fields. 'We worked for twelve hours a day for three months without a day off,' he said. When he finished school, the state farm chairman refused to give him the internal passport which every citizen needs. He 'escaped' anyway, and became a miner. The Congress of People's Deputies inspired him to write out a list of demands which he read to his friends during a pithead safety drill in May.

The response was favourable but when he suggested calling a public meeting, the mine director called him in and told him the demands were unrealistic. The local trade union committee gave him the same message. Undeterred, Bokarev and his friends went ahead and held a meeting. They ended it by sending off two letters, one to the Congress of People's Deputies and the other, in traditional style, to the Communist party paper, *Pravda*. There the effort might have fizzled out, if it had not been for the miners in Siberia who went further and came out on strike. The spark of militancy flashed across to the Donbass, and the links which Bokarev had forged proved their worth. Within hours the Donbass regional strike committee was formed.

Over the next few months the strike committees became works committees while the official trade unions tried to find a new role. Fifteen months later in October 1990 miners from all over the Soviet Union converged on Donetsk to form a new Independent Union of Miners. By then, the euphoria of 1989 had evaporated, and the union had no clear line. Only some of the promised concessions had been implemented by the government. Miners were thrashing round for a firm approach to the new discussion of a market economy.

Just under a year after the collapse of the Soviet Union, I was in Novokuznetsk to try to find out what had happened to the miners' movement under the new structures of post-Communist power, and to see if the local pithead democracy had grown into something solid. The picture was confused and messy, a further illustration of the difficulty of creating a civil society in a short space of time. Several men who took leading positions in the workers' committees were dotted around the Kuzbass's key administrative structures, or had gone into private business. Mikhail Kislyuk had become the governor of the Kuzbass, appointed by president Yeltsin to head the Kemerovo region, as the area is officially known. Alexander Smirnov, a foreman in 1989, was Kislyuk's deputy, wielding power over the city of Novokuznetsk from the chair where the first secretary of the Communist party once held sway. Yuri Gerold, another leader of 1989, had started his own business to export coal.

At the pit level there had also been a change in power, though not what the miners had predicted when they had called for independence from the ministry in Moscow. In the past no one knew what an individual mine's accounts were, what its life expectancy was or how much profit it made. Miners wanted control over that information and the right to some of the profits. The result of the strike was unexpected. 'The mine directors have all the power now, much more than any Western mine-manager. They're complete owners of the mines,' said Vyacheslav Sharipov, the chairman of the Kuzbass branch of the Independent Union of Miners, as we sat round the table in Smirnov's grand office in the old Communist party building. With the mines' new sovereignty, and the collapse of the Soviet ministry of mines, local directors were taking key decisions on their own, even though some were elected by their workforce in the heyday of industrial democratization in the early Gorbachev period.

The practice of factory-wide elections was later abolished, and workers had little power of redress, except a new strike. But with many of their leaders now in different positions, with the realization that many mines were not solvent without major changes in work practices, and with minds diverted by the imminent prospect of privatization, there was no stomach or organization for a third strike wave.

Take the Abashevskaya mine at the bottom end of the Kuzbass. It makes its own contribution to Novokuznetsk's general dirt from a tall chimney-stack pumping out thick coils of black filth that float over the cottages and houses in the valley. The Independent Union of Miners has an office in the main building, but the three miners and a secretary sitting in the new premises were dispirited. With 33,000 roubles a month, miners earned more than twice the average Russian wage, but that meant little when you had miserable housing conditions and a local hospital which some refuse to use because standards of hygiene and equipment in it are so low. Seven hundred Abashevskaya miners had no flat of their own. They had to rent expensive rooms or live with their parents.

One result of the 1991 strike was that miners were told that part of the hard currency from coal exports would go to them. 'We have never seen any of it,' said Yuri Matveyev. In a few Kuzbass mines every worker had been given an account book where his hard currency allotment was recorded. He could order imported video recorders or refrigerators, or put part of it aside to buy a car. Not at Abashevskaya. 'In the last three months of 1991 our mine earned 860,000 dollars, and in January this year 250,000,' Yuri Matveyev commented. The director was in charge of it all and gave it to his friends, or to buy off people who protested.

The union branch was trying to recruit more members, but only claimed 700 out of the workforce of 3,400. Some 1,200 were in the old official union, which since the collapse of the USSR had also given itself the tag 'Independent' – the Independent Union of Coal-Workers. The official union had recovered from its low point during the 1989 strikes, partly thanks to the fact that it controlled sanatoriums and rest-homes and other social benefits. Ironically, with the onset of shock therapy, the old union had also become more 'independent' in criticizing the government.

Yeltsin's government had decreed that the mines, like other

industries, would have to be privatized, and that subsidies to loss-making pits would be reduced. They knew the union had set up a Fund for Social Guarantees which was trying to work out an overall plan for Russia's mines, and was pressing the government to provide money and organize retraining schemes for miners who would lose their jobs. 'In principle, we accept market conditions, but do not know what it will mean,' Matveyev said. The schemes being worked out in Moscow by the Fund for Social Guarantees had not been explained to them. In Moscow I went to see Igor Kozhukovsky, the Fund's head. 'I am not the one who's deciding to close a pit,' he told me, his air of confidence not entirely concealing some embarrassment. 'The market is doing that. All I'm doing is to prepare how the closures are implemented.'

Three years earlier, when the first wave of strikes brought the country's coal industry to a halt, he was working down the very Abashevskaya pit I had visited in Novokuznetsk. Now a senior official of the Independent Union of Miners, he was sitting in an office in Moscow a few doors away from those of the industry's management board. They were working on the final draft of a plan which envisaged the shutting of thirty-one of Russia's 238 coal mines. Another seventy-two 'have very little in view and will need massive investment to keep them open,' he said. Five of them were in the Kuzbass, though his pit was not among the threatened group. Kozhukovsky saw no irony in the fact that union and management were collaborating on the industry's future and considered it a step forward.

To draw up a balance sheet of the changes since 1989 would be difficult. There was a new union, organized from the grassroots, but it was weak, and short of both money and full-time, trained staff. The workers' committees still existed in most towns and some people had been given administrative power, but the local councils, elected in 1990, were suspicious of change. The workers' movement was split and confused over the value of a market economy and privatization. In another Kuzbass town, Belovo, which has a population of 180,000, and a third of the workforce in the mines, a survey made in May 1992 found 93 per cent on the 'edge of poverty', even though miners were earning about 30 per cent more than the average Russian wage.[21] The Russian government's shock therapy, with its jump in prices, had more impact on their lives than the strike gains three years earlier.

The strike wave of 1989 did produce a major psychological change. 'People understood who they are and what they stand for,' said Boris Lebedev, the Independent Miners' Union chairman in Belovo. 'People felt each other's strength, and felt they were free. It was the first time our generation had had this experience.' The strikes opened the door for the emergence of a civil society, but little more was done. Russian traditions of passivity and the lack of experience of self-organization lay heavily on people.

The distance still to cover became clear when I visited Olga Nevimbovskaya. She lost her husband in 1984 in a mine disaster in Belovo in which thirty-six men died. Eight years later she felt emboldened, and still angry enough, to form an Association of Families of Mine Victims to lobby for better compensation. There was no law requiring a lump sum or monthly payments. 'The mine gives whatever it feels like,' she said.

Russia's badly equipped mines and society's low culture of safety produce an accident rate far higher than in the West. In Belovo the Widows' Group had 599 members, including widows, orphans, and the parents of dead miners. In one block of flats there were twenty-seven families with members, partly because of the size of the 1984 disaster, but also thanks to Olga Nevimbovskaya's energy in creating a group at all. They were trying to provide counselling as well as material support.

The sad thing was that hers was the only such group in the Kuzbass. 'The press never used to report accidents. We still don't always hear, even when they happen in our own town,' she commented. How come there were no other such organizations in the region, or that the new union did not set some up? She shrugged: 'The bereaved are uncomfortable. They remind others of things they would rather ignore. In general, change here is very slow.'

13

Nationalism at a Low Level

*In this country it's shameful to be a patriot. It's an
in-bred difficulty which afflicts our educated classes.
Many of us became Marxists by accident, because there
was no other philosophy to adhere to. In all normal
countries the educated classes draw their strength
from patriotic pride.*

ALEXANDER TSIPKO, FORMER CENTRAL COMMITTEE
ADVISER, 1991[1]

It was called the National Salvation Front (NSF), and its aim, as
its founders made clear at their inaugural meeting one Saturday
morning in October 1992, was not to seize power or force the
president to impose direct rule, as similar 'Salvation Committees'
had tried to do in Latvia and Lithuania two years before. It wanted
to sound the alarm about what it saw as the destruction of Russia,
unite the widest possible spectrum of political forces in Russia's
defence and make Boris Yeltsin resign.

On a curtain behind the platform the organizers had suspended a
challenging line of verse from Pushkin: 'Arise, Russia, and be
strong.' Next to it, there was a picture of Minin and Pozharsky, two
seventeenth-century heroes, one a commoner, the other a prince,
who joined together in central Russia to raise an army which
marched on Moscow and liberated it from Polish invaders. But
none of the symbols which decorated the stage was more graphic

than the unusual juxtaposition of two flags, the red flag of the Soviet Union with its hammer and sickle and the black, gold and silver flag of the Tsarist empire with the double-headed eagle. On the face of it, the two flags represented polar opposites. The Bolsheviks and the Romanov dynasty had been mortal enemies.

President Yeltsin and his supporters preferred the red, white and blue flag of the provisional government under Alexander Kerensky which briefly ruled Russia after the Tsar's abdication in February 1917. It became the official Russian flag again in 1991. From their different standpoints the Tsarists and the Bolsheviks despised the Kerensky government as a weak bourgeois-nationalist creation, and it was not surprising that their political descendants spurned what was seen as its successor three generations later. The National Salvation Front had been formed by people who believed it was time to forget ancient antagonisms. The crucial issue for Russia was to form a 'left-right' coalition, a holy alliance of the reds and the whites who had fought against each other in the civil war. Though they had differed on so much in the past, the reds and whites of the Yeltsin era agreed in their claim that Russia's existence was in danger, with its economy at the mercy of foreign powers and its public life threatened by moral decay and political destruction from within.

The conference was opened by Academician Igor Shafarevich, a Christian mathematician who had been a dissident colleague of Sakharov and Solzhenitsyn in the 1970s but later adopted an openly anti-Semitic form of Slavophilia. Russia was suffering a similar fate to Germany's after the Second World War, he asserted. Its higher education was being smashed. Its economic power was being broken. In Germany's case the crime had been Nazism. Russia's crime was different but the punishment the victors were exacting was the same. Germany was gradually forgiven, he argued, because it became a docile political ally of the West. For Russia, he maintained, that price was unacceptable.

The NSF's organizing committee consisted of thirty men and six women (a higher proportion than in most Russian political groups). There were indeed reds and whites. Besides Shafarevich, the whites included Vasily Belov, one of the so-called village writers, and Mikhail Afstafyev, a member of the Russian parliament and founder of the Constitutional Democratic party. The reds numbered Viktor Alksnis, the notorious colonel who had been the mainstay of the Soyuz or pro-empire group in the Soviet parliament, General Albert Makashov, a former commander of the Volga-Urals military district, who had run against Yeltsin in the Russian presidential election in 1991 and later been sacked, and Sergei Baburin, leader of the 'Russia' faction in the Russian parliament, a vain man with a black goatee beard and a streak of grey in his carefully-combed black quiff.

The most interesting man on the platform was Alexander Prokhanov. A descendant of the Molokane, one of the many Orthodox sects which were heavily persecuted by the official church hierarchy in the pre-revolutionary period, Prokhanov had been a relatively unknown member of the village writers until he visited Afghanistan a few years after the invasion. When it became possible to publish something approaching to the truth about the war, he wrote two novels and several articles about the heroism and self-sacrifice of Soviet troops. Although he glorified the courage of the Soviet army, he made it clear the war was politically futile (see Chapter 7). His writings on Afghanistan propelled him to fame, and he became a senior member of the Russian Federation's Union of Writers and was awarded the Order of the Red Banner of Labour.

Prokhanov described himself as a statist (gosudarstvennik), not a nationalist. The Soviet experience and the Tsarist empire before it, with their strongly authoritarian centralism, had made many Russians anarchists at heart, a position which was in line, ironically, with Prokhanov's Molokane ancestors. Prokhanov had founded a weekly newspaper, *Den'*, which aimed, among other things, to change that. It called itself 'the newspaper of the spiritual opposition'. 'The state is not just a policeman and a tax collector. It is a religious and ethical value,' he told the NSF's founding meeting.

In the hall sat an estimated 3000 people. Hundreds more had tried to get in to the ticket-only assembly. They stood in the street listening to the proceedings through loudspeakers. Like other orators at the meeting, Prokhanov stressed that the Front would only work within the constitution. He believed it could eventually command a natural majority. 'The ideology of national salvation is the ideology of reconciliation,' he declared. 'We must end the civil war which is threatening Russia once again. The bones of the Reds and Whites must be laid again in a fraternal grave, and on its fresh mound we must pronounce the words of reconciliation. Social justice and national beauty bring patriots together.'

Prokhanov was more articulate and his language more colourful than that of most of the patriots who emerged from the ruins of the Communist system but his ideas reflected the dominant trend. He accepted the blurring of state and nation which was a special feature of Russian history. This did not mean that Russians did not feel pride in themselves as members of an ethnic group with a common language and significant cultural and intellectual achievements. But because the attempt to build a nation-state and an empire went hand-in-hand, the result was a relatively non-racist mentality. By 1850 fewer than half the Tsar's subjects were Russian. Language, religion and their political dominance clearly marked the Russians out from the other subjects of the empire but it was official policy not to glorify or encourage Russian nationalism. While overt nationalism might help to maintain the loyalty of the Russian peasant, it could have bad side-effects in destabilizing the borderlands, among Finns, Estonians, Latvians and even other Slavs, such as Ukrainians. It was accepted that the Russian empire was multi-national. This was as true under the Tsars as it was in the Soviet Union.

With the collapse of the Soviet Union Russians had to accept they had lost an empire. It was a blow economically as well as psychologically. The breaking of ties between the republics led to a huge drop in output. For Communist party activists and army officers who had maintained the equivalent of the front line in the Cold War, there was a strong sense of defeat. For the majority of people, there was a loss of confidence in the future. Would they become nationalists at last?

The first post-imperial years suggested that they would not. The essence of Yeltsin's 'instrumental nationalism', as I argued in Chapter 9 – his revival of Russia against the command-and-administrative centre – was anti-empire and anti-state rather than pro-Russian. He supported the independence of the Baltics and took advantage of the independence of Ukraine to destroy the Union and break the remains of the centralized Communist system, not primarily in order to revive the Russian nation. The 'gosudarstvenniki' such as Prokhanov had opposite priorities. 'I am an imperialist,' he said unashamedly, when I went to see him at the office of his newspaper shortly after the founding of the National Salvation Front. He found the end of the Soviet Union humiliating not because he had much sympathy for Communist ideology but because it meant the end of the Russian empire which the Union had inherited.

Prokhanov's charge against Yeltsin was that he had violated Russia's interests by undermining the Union. His second charge was that Yeltsin was betraying the country to foreigners by handing it over to Western market principles and allowing so many of its natural resources to be sold abroad. 'They are killing us off consistently and with impunity,' he maintained. 'At the hands of their paid agents the Americans are taking revenge on Russia for its recent greatness and refusal to submit. Our race, character and culture are being wiped out once and for all. They are stifling a temperament and a view of the world which were unique, and which, over ten centuries, had carved out a place in history through faith, understanding and love.'

Prokhanov's views contained strong echoes of the nineteenth-century Slavophile distrust of Western materialism as well as the isolationist anti-Western strain in Stalin's National Bolshevism. His belief in the priority of the imperial state coincided with the views of intellectuals like Nikolai Ustryalov and the Smena Vekh (Landmarks) movement in the 1920s. Originally opponents of the

Revolution, they later accepted it on the grounds that the Bolsheviks had the best chance of preserving and restoring the Tsarist empire. Sitting in his bare editorial offices opposite Moscow's main peasants' market, Prokhanov told me with some pride that Russians differed from Ukranians, let alone from other more distant Europeans, in their attitude to the state. At one extreme Russians had a special strain of anarchism. This was particularly the case among the Cossacks of the Don, the runaway serfs, who formed their own communities from the seventeenth century onwards, and in Siberia where serfdom never took hold, as well as among nonconformist Orthodox sects like that of his ancestors. At the other extreme Russians accepted a deep subordination to the state, a willingness to obey the Emperor and make sacrifices.

The concept of the martyr has always been strong in Russian folklore and the Russian consciousness, and the Orthodox church encouraged this trend. The first saints it officially recognized were Boris and Gleb, two young medieval princes who submitted without resistance when their elder brother had them killed. In an article, entitled 'Are you ready to stand up for Russia?', Prokhanov drew attention to the two horses on the standard icon of Boris and Gleb. Under the strict rules of stylized iconography, one was always coloured red, the other white. Reflecting the coincidence of this with his contemporary message, Prokhanov enthusiastically proclaimed: 'The two steeds walk side by side as a united people builds Great Russia again.'

Sacrifice, martyrdom and submission to the state – these are not the ingredients from which a functioning civil society is built. It is hardly surprising that Prokhanov did not believe in Western parliamentarianism. The Tsar's efforts at creating a Duma through reform from above were artificial, and ran up against Russian traditions at the base, he argued. 'They led to political chaos and civil chaos. After all, if there had been a civil society, there would not have been a Revolution. The fact that the Revolution succeeded shows there was only an imitation of one.'

The Tsar's mistake was to allow the creation of Western-style political parties, which were not able to develop because they were not suited to Russian traditions. All they could do was to weaken and destroy the strong centralized Russian state without putting anything constructive in its place. The monarchy, in his view, should have transformed itself gradually into a corporatist form of democracy, based on a modest amount of economic liberalization so that industry could keep up with technical progress. The post-Communist effort to import Western parliamentary practice was equally doomed, Prokhanov believed. Like other 'statists', Prokhanov promoted the notion of a special Russian quality, 'sobornost', as the basis of the social organization he wanted to see. The word is hard to translate, and perhaps the only appropriate English equivalent is 'fellowship'. Sobornost was meant to evoke the traditions of the peasant commune, as well as the values uniting a sacred community.

Yuri Senakosov is a leading specialist on nationality issues at Moscow University and, unlike Prokhanov, a political liberal. His analysis of Russian character is on many points remarkably similar, though less romantic in tone. 'Russians were pushed up north in the eleventh and twelfth centuries into the forest,' he told me one evening. 'This created a special type of personality, very different from the people of the steppe – closed in, passive, and respectful of the forest, which is mysterious, unknown and dangerous, yet also all-providing.' Over the next four centuries Russian life was dominated by the Tatars. 'At the beginning they destroyed churches, fortresses and settlements, but later they allowed Russia's princes to pay tribute and maintain their own customs. This has produced a strange extremism in the Russian character. Anarchy and nihilism go hand in hand with extreme obedience and submission.'

There were three main types of human mentality, Senakosov argued: the military mentality, marked by a strong sense of discipline, which was characteristic of Germans; the instinctual mentality, which warned you not to put your hand in fire or enter a radio-active zone; and the social mentality, which gave rise to political consciousness and the search for consensus and compromise. 'Russians have none of the three in any significant measure, so that you can get things like Chernobyl, enormous management irresponsibility and great individual heroism.' The tough natural environment and Russia's long history of surviving invasions created a sense of long-suffering combined with greatness. 'The Russian felt he must be a "veliki chelovyek", a great person, but we also developed the concept of Mother Russia, absorbing everyone to her breast and assimilating foreigners.'

One thing on which the National Salvation Front and the Yeltsinites agreed was that even without its Soviet empire Russia was a multi-national country, which must be recognized as such. Both talked of its inhabitants as 'Rossiyane', an old but recently revived noun meaning 'people who live in Russia' rather than 'Russkiye', ethnic Russians. In the same spirit the Bolsheviks created a series of autonomous republics and regions within the new Russian federal republic after 1917 in place of the governor-ships of the Tsarist administration. The Russian Federation had twenty-one republics and eleven autonomous regions. After perestroika the extreme nationalists like Vladimir Zhirinovsky, the head of the misleadingly named Liberal Democratic party, called for the replacement of these boundaries by the old Tsarist 'gubernii'. This was also the position of Solzhenitsyn, but not of the NSF or the Yeltsin administration.

But the NSF did believe that Moscow should take a strong line towards the republics. It accused Yeltsin of not doing enough to protect the Russian Federation from breaking-up as the USSR had done. Just as imported Western liberalism had led to the collapse of the Tsarist empire, the liberalism started by Gorbachev had caused the implosion of the Soviet Union, it claimed. According to Prokhanov, during Tsarist rule the state's firm hand had kept tight control of ethnic contradictions. Sometimes it had been done by force, sometimes by manipulation. But once it was relaxed, conflicts were bound to burst out, as had now happened again with perestroika.

Some analysts have claimed there is a serious danger of a 'red-brown alliance' in Russia, meaning a coalition of former Communists and Fascists. It was an argument used by many of Yeltsin's supporters, often with the explicit aim of frightening Western governments into providing economic aid. At the NSF meeting there were undeniable hints of Fascism. On each flank of the platform stood three guards in black uniforms. They wore high boots, leather straps across their chests, and black berets with a badge of the double-headed eagle. Others in brown camouflage uniforms and similar berets patrolled the lobby. They described themselves as members of the 'Russian National Legion'.

While this kind of group could form the basis of a rightwing paramilitary movement, there was little sign that any such development was gaining strength. The black shirts of the Pamyat movement had been in evidence at public rallies and meetings in Moscow and St Petersburg for at least four years before the collapse of the Communist system. They occasionally caused scandals, shouting down a meeting of the Writers' Union in early 1990, and storming through the offices of the popular newspaper, *Moskovsky Komsomolets*, in the autumn of 1992. Neither the impoverishment caused by 'shock therapy' nor Zhirinovsky's strong showing in the 1993 elections led to an increase in the numbers of organized black or brown shirts.

Movements like the National Salvation Front were better described as patriotic rather than nationalist. They were not so much against other nations or nationalities as in favour of the 'Russian idea'. They wanted to revive the 'third way', a special destiny marking Russians out from other Europeans. In its vulgar form this obviously could be the basis of racial prejudice and anti-Semitism. Russian history has had plenty of examples from the Tsarist 'Black Hundreds' with their anti-Jewish pogroms to the quotas against Jews in the Soviet period. Armenians, Georgians and other nationalities also had constant problems. But the perestroika reforms, the open proclamation of state respect for human rights, and the mass emigration of Soviet Jews, reduced the level of official anti-Semitism in the late 1980s and early 1990s. The NSF was not an avowedly anti-Semitic organization. Its antipathy to foreign influence was directed at Western liberalism and what its supporters saw as the over-hasty dismantling of the state economy. If a few 'patriots' argued that this was the fault of Jews, they were no more influential than those who claimed seventy years earlier that the importation of Communism into Russia was also the work of a Jewish conspiracy. By the early 1990s there was more hostility in Russian cities directed against Azerbaijanis, Armenians, Chechens and other 'blacks' from the Caucasus.

The overwhelmingly pro-Western tone of most Russian mass media made the NSF sound, by contrast, more extreme and reactionary than most of its members were. The Front was a loose coalition in which various points of view were represented. While some wanted a return to state economic planning, the majority opposed that. They accepted a variant of the market economy, which would in some ways be a restoration of the turn-of-the-century Russian economy, a form of state capitalism in which large and primarily state-supported corporations operating on market principles would, they hoped, revive Russian industry and create a national entrepreneurial class, protected from foreign competition. This, they said, was how Japan, South Korea and Indonesia had achieved high levels of growth in recent years, and Russia should emulate them. Russia's natural partners were other advanced economies in the Third World, the 'newly industrializing countries', rather than Western Europe or the USA. It was not surprising that the revived Communist party joined forces with the NSF since many of the leaders of this new entrepreneurial class would be the old Communist economic nomenklatura, who had transformed their state enterprises into joint stock companies, but still looked to the state for credit.

The key exponent of this 'national state-capitalism' within a socially-orientated market economy is Rutskoi, who was elected vice-president with Yeltsin in 1991 but was later sent to prison for six months. He calls himself 'an enlightened patriot'.

Like Yeltsin, Rutskoi is a former Communist, but unlike the president, he never accepted the strategy of a rapid switch to market principles. He preferred a gradual process with a high priority put on agriculture. Rutskoi's most important difference with Yeltsin was on the issue of nationalism. If Yeltsin's support for Russian sovereignty was 'instrumental' and consequently somehow bloodless, Rutskoi carries conviction when he talks of Russia's greatness. While Yeltsin had his moments of impulsiveness and high emotional intensity but could also disappear for days on end or withdraw behind a mask of impassiveness, Rutskoi always gives out an aura of energy and passion. In Russian politics this is an advantage.

Alexander Rutskoi was born into a military family in 1947 and graduated from the Yuri Gagarin air force academy in Moscow before commanding an air force assault regiment in Afghanistan from 1985 to 1986. He was twice shot down and spent several months in Pakistan as a prisoner of war. On return to Moscow he became deputy chairman of the city's branch of Otechestvo (the Society for the Rebirth of Russia), and in this capacity he was elected to the Russian parliament in March 1990 as one of the new generation of activists.

In those days Rutskoi was still a loyal member of the Communist party. What shook him was his experience as chairman of the parliament's committee on Afghan veterans' affairs and the social protection of servicemen and their families. Running up against the state bureaucracy for the first time on a sustained basis, as he tried to solve veterans' problems, and seeing its incompetence, harshness and lack of compassion even towards disabled war heroes, Rutskoi says he lost faith in the system. 'How can an oppressive power call itself Soviet?' he exclaimed indignantly in one interview.[2] He was also angered by the use of force in Lithuania in January 1991, and what he saw as the Communist party's sabotage of attempts to help peasants start private farms.

During the Russian Congress of People's Deputies, when Yeltsin was trying to push through his plan for an executive presidency, Rutskoi played a pivotal role. He led a group of 178 Communist party colleagues out of the official faction and formed a new one, called 'Communists for Democracy'. The mutiny tipped the balance of the Congress to Yeltsin's side. Yeltsin chose Rutskoi as his running mate for the presidential campaign six weeks later. Rutskoi turned his faction into a party, called Democratic Party of Communists of Russia, and was promptly expelled from the Soviet Communist party. After the August coup, in which he played a leading role as the main organizer of the White House's defences, Rutskoi renamed his group the People's Party of Free Russia.

From the start Rutskoi criticized the Gaidar reforms as too severe and subservient to the West. He formed an early distrust of Yeltsin's main adviser, Gennady Burbulis. In October 1991 he proposed himself as prime minister but was out-manoeuvred by Burbulis. An initial plan for him to head a Russian Security Council with control over the armed forces and the Russian KGB was also turned down by Burbulis.[3] After these setbacks Rutskoi virtually went into opposition to Yeltsin, at least as regards economic policy. He tended to support Yeltsin's desire for a strong presidency, but as the chairman of a political party, he also had an interest in protecting the rights of parliament. During the constitutional crisis of early 1993 he attacked Yeltsin, and when the president sacked him and dissolved parliament in September, Rutskoi joined the resistance at the White House. He was arrested after urging the crowd to seize the main TV station.

Rutskoi had made it clear during the 1991 campaign that he favoured a switch from central planning to the market economy. In June that year he organized the first congress of Russian businessmen. Later, as head of a state committee to supervize the conversion of defence industries to civilian production, he met scores of state enterprise directors, and was convinced by them that the process had to be done gradually. A month after the liberalization of prices, which he denounced as 'another experiment performed on the Russian people', Rutskoi joined the chorus of critics who argued that breaking up the monopolies should have preceded the freeing of prices. He said the transfer to the market should be administered by a strong centre which would gradually dismantle the monopolies and promote competition and labour discipline. While he supported foreign investment, he was suspicious of foreign loans administered by the International Monetary Fund, which were tied to Western monetarist prescriptions – 'free cheese in a mousetrap', as he phrased it once.

Rutskoi's views put him firmly in the camp of Russia's national entrepreneurs and state capitalists. His career gave him natural support among the military, but he strengthened this with repeated appeals for tough action to protect Russian minorities abroad, though without specifying exactly what he meant. His background as a chairman of the Society for the Revival of Russia naturally led him to the notion of 'Great Russia'. This did not mean a change in Russia's borders. It was meant to be a patriotic unifying idea which could encourage Russians to feel self-confident again. After his release from prison in 1994 he talked about the re-integration of the republics which had formed the Soviet Union, but exclusively on a voluntary basis.

In 1992 Rutskoi had drawn a distinction between 'enlightened patriotism' and 'primitive patriotism'. It struck a powerful chord, and his popularity ratings rose. His wild behaviour at the climax of the crisis in October 1993 lost him much support, but he remained a powerful figure on his release from prison even though his tone had shifted more towards the 'primitive' line. He described the Yeltsin administration as an 'anti-people police regime . . . serving the interests of the Western powers and international financial circles'. But Rutskoi's support for a more independent foreign policy in early 1992 had encouraged other positions of the new generation, who had impeccable democratic credentials. Two, in particular, could not be labelled conservatives, or ignorant of the West.

I first heard of Oleg Rumyantsev in 1987 when he was a young researcher at the Institute of the Economics of the World Socialist

System, and a founder of the Club for Democratic Perestroika. He played a key role at the first conference of political clubs that August (see Chapter 1). A specialist on Hungary, he travelled several times to Budapest as the democracy movement unfolded there, and as a founder of Russia's Social Democratic party attended conferences of the German Social Democrats and the Socialist International. Rumyantsev came from what he describes as an unpolitical family, though his parents had joined the Communist party for career reasons. They were not happy with the way he used his room in their flat, which I regularly visited, for printing leaflets on his computer and conducting his campaigns. Rumyantsev was never in the party nor an activist of the Komsomol, the Young Communist League. He decided to enter politics, he said, 'out of a wish for modernization, and when I saw that reforms in Hungary were going well. It also seemed a way to fulfil myself'. Four years later, disappointed with the West's policies towards Russia and by then a member of the Russian parliament, Rumyantsev joined the band of Rutskoi supporters, advocating a combination of democracy and patriotism but remaining independent of any faction.

Sergei Stankevich, another prominent young politician, also entered public life through the grass-roots clubs, in his case the Moscow Popular Front. Inspired by perestroika, he joined the Communist party under Gorbachev to try to increase the power of the reformers. He was elected to the Soviet parliament and the Moscow city council, where he became deputy mayor. After the coup he switched to Yeltsin's side and was appointed a State Counsellor. He travelled to Moldova with Rutskoi in April 1992 and became an adviser on ethnic issues. It was in this capacity that he too started to argue the cause of 'enlightened patriotism', warning the West that excessive insistence on an economic revolution could lead to a backlash.

If Rutskoi was the politician who first raised the banner of enlightened patriotism, the man who carried it most prominently on the economic front was Arkady Volsky. He, too, was primarily a politician rather than an economist, but he was not a member of the

Russian parliament and preferred to act as a lobbyist and power-broker on behalf of Russian industrialists. There were constant rumours that he wanted to become prime minister, but at least in the early years of the Yeltsin administration, when almost any government was bound to be unpopular, he chose to be a manipulator behind the scenes. Volsky worked for nine years at the huge Likhachev car factory in Moscow before joining the apparatus of the central committee. As a senior official in the influential department for machine building, which had general oversight over the factories of the military-industrial complex, he formed close contacts with the directors of state enterprises. At the end of the Soviet period he founded a kind of directors' lobby, called the Scientific and Industrial Union. When that died with the USSR, Volsky became head of a newly-formed Russian Union of Industrialists and Entrepreneurs.

The directors were divided over the market reforms. Those in the classic arms production sector felt most threatened by the end of the Cold War and were naturally the least willing to contemplate change. Conversion to civilian production would involve a major upheaval, and possibly the outright closure of their plants. Volsky was always on the more liberal wing, representing the plants with a better chance to adapt. While the traditionalists formed a parliamentary faction of sympathetic deputies, called the Industrial Union, headed by Yuri Gekht, Volksy put his group behind the 'Civic Union'. The Civic Union was a coalition which included Rutskoi's party, as well as the Democratic party of Russia, headed by Nikolai Travkin, and the Renewal party, headed by Alexander Vladislavlev, who was also Volsky's second in command at the Russian Union of Industrialists and Entrepreneurs. It was a powerful alliance which effectively took the lead against the Gaidar government at the Congress of People's Deputies in December 1992 where he was forced out of office. The Civic Union also opposed the Gaidar team on the issue of privatization, preferring a transfer of shares to the workers and management of enterprises rather than sales and auctions by means of vouchers.

While the Civic Union, representing the enlightened national capitalists, was generally successful in influencing government policy in Moscow, what was less clear was whether it would be able to help the government resist the break-up of the Russian Federation. By 1993 the centrifugal tendencies were still gaining strength and not only in the twenty-one republics which made up the Federation, in particular Tatarstan, Bashkortostan and Sakha (the former Yakutia). Several regions, including parts of Siberia, the Urals and the Far East, were also demanding greater economic rights. They felt Moscow had always imposed excessive control and the time had come to loosen the links. During the long debates in 1993 over a new Russian Constitution, Russia's regions insisted on equal status with the republics in relation to Moscow. Some of them had larger populations and more natural resources than the republics and they found it an anomaly that they should have fewer rights. Now they wanted the right to raise taxes and develop their own resources, as well as to be able to conclude deals with foreign investors or set up free economic zones. A number of regions in the Urals were considering amalgamating into a Urals republic, and there were similar tendencies among regions on the Pacific coast.

The trend was based on a long Russian tradition of regional patriotism, which was one of the factors that had always militated against the creation of a Russian nation. Under the Tsars there were major differences among Russians – Siberians, Cossacks and the Russians of the central regions, to name but three. The Tsars allowed a considerable amount of regional autonomy, leaving education, for example, under local control. The schism in the 1660s between the Orthodox hierarchy and those who became known as the Old Believers, as well as the other Christian sects, also played a role in differentiating Russians.

Stalin's imposition of totalitarian rule from the centre forced regionalism, as the sense of a separate cultural identity, to go underground. In its place a kind of clan feeling developed inside the Communist party. A party boss from a particular region, if promoted to run a ministry or central committee department in

Moscow, would appoint friends from the area as his deputies. This was also in part a reflection of the atomization of Soviet society under Stalin and the absence of other horizontal links. The only people to be trusted were from an official's own area. In the long years of the corrupt Brezhnev regime this clan feeling produced veritable 'mafias', the Uzbek 'mafia', the Krasnodar 'mafia' and the like. They were local party and economic élites who promoted each other's careers and had their collective hand in the state's till. Under Yeltsin some of these groups saw a way of preserving their power by raising the banner of local autonomy.

Some analysts argued that because Russians formed the majority of the population in at least nine of the republics, as well as in all the regions, there was little danger of secession from the Russian Federation. Certainly, the ethnic factor was a restraint. So was the lesson of the Soviet Union's collapse which had torn the economies of constituent republics asunder. People would think twice before converting their desire for economic autonomy into all-out political independence. But there was an alternative scenario for Russia, on the lines of what happened to the Spanish empire in Latin America when central control was loosened. The fact that the various provinces all spoke Spanish, had Spanish majorities, shared the same religion and had a number of powerful economic reasons for staying together was not enough to prevent them from breaking into separate states.

The contrast with North America is instructive. Civil society, as a separate area of political and economic activity outside the state structure, was more developed by the beginning of the nineteenth century in North America than in South America. There was a larger constituency of independent political forces able to see the advantages of merging a single economic space with a single political and administrative federation. Hence the foundation of the USA. But even in North America, the colonists split into Canada and the USA, and a century later the USA itself almost came apart through civil war. Russia was more similar to Latin America. Neither under the Tsars nor under Soviet rule was it able to develop a sense of national cohesion. With the iron hand of central control removed, the tendency for disintegration was very strong. Whether developments would go all the way, or stop at a loose form of federation, one conclusion was clear. The National Salvation Front's hopes for, and many Western government's fears of, a strong Russian national state would not be realized.

14

A Law-based State

Gogol called Russia a country of bad roads and fools.
Monarchy, partocracy, democracy – what's changed?
The roads are worse, and the fools more cruder.

NIKOLAI RYZHKOV, MAY 1992[1]

A side door opened in the modest room with its dull, whitewashed walls and in stepped thirteen judges, dressed in long black robes. The chairman of the court had huge, white, silken cuffs on his sleeves so as to give more authority to his hands as he read the verdict from a standing position. Everyone else in the court stood rigidly during the twenty-minute performance. It was the climax of the most controversial case in the Russian constitutional court's first year of life, its judgment on president Yeltsin's decision to ban the Communist party in November 1991.

Apart from the rule that the entire courtroom should stand during the judgment, a practice inherited from the Soviet Union, everything else was novel. The black robes, specially designed by Moscow's star couturier, Sasha Zaitsev, were a throwback to pre-Revolutionary traditions. The Bolsheviks had outlawed them as an echo of Western bourgeois courts, and decreed that judges wear ordinary clothes to show they were close to the people. The shape of the courtroom was different, with equal space for representatives of two sides, reflecting 'adversarial' proceedings which had always been foreign to Soviet courts. Above all, the existence of the court itself was new. With his stress on the need to make the Soviet Union a 'law-based' state, Gorbachev had brought in a constitutional supervision committee, but Yeltsin and the Russian parliament went one better as they formed the institutions for a new Russia. In July 1991 the Russian Congress of People's Deputies established a constitutional court, a new third arm of society with the right to sit in judgment on the behaviour of president and parliament.

The court could become one of the most significant institutions in Russia, and its judgment in the case of the Communist party was to be the test case. The petition had been brought by representatives of the party, but the court had decided to hear it in conjunction with a petition brought by the party's opponents, alleging that the party had repeatedly violated the constitution and had long been an illegal organization. During the several weeks of hearings, the court became a compulsory stopping-off point for the media as the Yeltsin side produced secret documents from the party's files, highlighting its aid to foreign parties and the tapping of its own senior members' telephones.

Another sensation was the judges' brush with ex-president Gorbachev, who repeatedly refused to appear as a witness. It was not that he felt he was above the law, since he had given evidence to the investigators in the case being prepared against the August coup plotters. But those hearings were private. Gorbachev argued that the case against the Communist party was a political show of dubious legality, where public hearings were being used for posturing by both sides. It was a bad decision which undermined Gorbachev's reputation as a reformer and weakened his stated commitment to a law-based state. All the other former Politburo members, who were summoned to appear, including Alexander Yakovlev, Yegor Ligachev and Nikolai Ryzhkov, did so without demur. They were not being asked to incriminate themselves or sit in a dock as though they were accused men under cross-examination in a criminal trial. The questioning was loose and easy to evade. Gorbachev's behaviour created a problem for the court. It could not turn a blind eye but it had minimal powers of enforcement, a maximum fine of 100 roubles. Three of the thirteen judges argued against summoning Gorbachev because they had no way to force him to appear, and they felt his refusal would lower the court's authority.[2] The state helped it out. When Gorbachev refused a second summons, the foreign ministry impounded his passport, preventing him from travelling to Italy on a long-planned lecture tour. Having slapped him on the wrist, the court later announced that it would no longer need Gorbachev's presence since enough evidence had been given by other witnesses.

While the episode showed that the court would not retreat in the face of an ex-president's defiance, how would it behave with a serving president? Encouragingly, it had given one ruling against Yeltsin within two months of starting work. It judged that his decision to merge Russia's security services and police (the old KGB and MVD) was unconstitutional because the president did not have the power to create new ministries or take major decisions on security without consulting parliament. Yeltsin accepted the judgment and withdrew his decision. The Communist petition against Yeltsin's ban was a far bigger issue. The president had put Sergei Shakhrai, his top legal adviser, in charge of defending Yeltsin's decisions. The ban had won him immense support from Western governments as a sign of Russia's fresh start and its new leader's anti-Communist credentials.

Valery Zorkin, the court chairman, was a slight figure with short grey hair and a rather mousey, timid face. His eyes tended to concentrate on the floor rather than on the person he was addressing. Seeing him scurry along the passage towards the robing room before each session, one felt Yeltsin only had to breathe out a little more heavily than usual and Zorkin would be sent flying. Now, dignified immeasurably by his white, silken cuffs, Zorkin delivered the complicated judgment. As he moved to the detail, the faces of the Communists in court changed from tension to relief. The Yeltsin side looked glum. The ruling was a surprise which neither the Communists nor Yeltsin's supporters had expected. On the first petition, the court declared that Yeltsin had acted unconstitutionally in banning the Communist party's local branches, and therefore the entire party as such. All he had a right to do was to ban the activities of its ruling bodies. On the second petition, claiming that the party had been illegal for most of its history – which some had hoped to turn into a kind of 'Nuremberg trial' of what they saw as a murderous and criminal organization – the court ruled that the case was beyond its competence. As for the question of Yeltsin's decrees expropriating the Communist party's property, the judges said he was only entitled to seize property which had been used for state or government purposes. The rest had to be given back. The ownership of disputed buildings which were used for both state and party goals was left to the arbitrage court to decide.

After the unexpectedly favourable judgment, the Communists could not contain their delight. They prepared a quick statement, welcoming the decision, and told a press conference they would immediately revive the party. As for the property issue, this was not so important. Valentin Kuptsov, a former central committee secretary, reminded us that the building where the constitutional court was sitting in a side road near to Red Square, was itself once used by the central committee. 'But the court need not worry. We shall lay no claims to it,' he smiled magnanimously. Andrei Makarov, one of the main lawyers for the Yeltsin side, testily told reporters in the passage outside the courtroom that the judges had buckled under strong pressure from conservatives.

Perhaps there should not have been such a shock. The court had already given several indications that it would be fair. When the Communist side complained that they had to conduct their defence on the basis of being a banned, property-less organization while the Yeltsin side had all the accoutrements and income of government at its disposal, the court offered to redress the balance. The Communists were given rooms in the court building, a room in the old Supreme Soviet annexe near the Kremlin, free use of telephones, two million roubles of expenses, and the right to summon government cars and drivers whenever they needed them. For us reporters it was like a flashback in time to see the black Volgas swish up to the front door with their Communist officials inside, or watch Yegor Ligachev stride through the corridors of the court building and attentively follow the proceedings, just as he used to do in parliament two years before. The dining-room downstairs was one of the best in Moscow. We queued there alongside these retired but surprisingly chipper luminaries of the Communist past. The prices, clearly still subsidised by the state, were in low amounts which were even measured in kopeks. Everywhere else in Russia inflation had already killed the kopek off.

The court disappointed the government team early on. On the face of it the government had a hard case to make in defending Yeltsin's ban on the party. When he issued it on 6 November 1991, the day before the anniversary of the October Revolution, the only law on political parties was a Soviet law which stated that the prosecutor's office or a court could ban a party. The presidency had no such right. To get round this, Yeltsin's lawyers argued that Russia's declaration of sovereignty in 1990 overrode all Soviet legislation, and that Soviet law only applied if it had been expressly adopted by the Russian parliament. The USSR Law on Public Associations had not been adopted by Russia and therefore did not apply. The only law which did apply, they maintained, was a 1932 decree issued by Stalin, and ratified by the Russian parliament in the same year, which permitted the liquidation of political parties by executive order without court proceedings.

It was strange to hear the new 'democrats' relying for justification on one of Stalin's decrees and its rubber-stamping by a cowed and phoney legislature. Their third argument was more convincing, and it was the one which the court, in part, accepted. Sergei Shakhrai claimed that the Communist party was not a normal political party but the ruling structure of the state. Its Politburo was the supreme executive, legislative and judicial power. As the popularly elected chief executive of the state, the president had the right to abolish another state structure. Andrei Makarov said the Communist party had waged a reign of terror against its own people and he would produce thirty-six volumes of evidence from 1917 onwards to prove it.

The weakness in the Shakhrai argument was that until March 1990 when Article Six of the Soviet constitution was repealed, the Communist party had had a legally sanctioned monopoly on power. For this reason the court decided, soon after the start of the proceedings, that it could only deal with the period after March 1990. This effectively weakened the effort to put the party's entire history on trial. It did not stop the Yeltsin side from making selective quotations from the pre-1990 archives, alleging, for example, that Gorbachev had concealed information about the Soviet massacre of Polish officers in the Katyn forest in 1940, or that the party had financed international terrorists. It was an unfortunate politicizing of the archives which angered many journalists and researchers who wanted access to all the evidence. Instead, they were told that the files on recent events were closed, except for documents which the government selectively released with the aim of putting Gorbachev and the Politburo in the worst possible light.

The court's judgment in the Communist party case was a sensible social and political compromise. It gave both sides some benefit, while defusing the mood of anti-Communist witch-hunting which some sections of the pro-government press had been fanning. It also exonerated and relieved thousands of mostly elderly Communist rank and file members who felt they had been condemned for the sins of their leaders. The judgment was a triumph for democracy in that it established the court as an independent entity and a vital pillar of the new order, separate from both the executive and the legislature.

The judgment also removed most of the doubts over the court's impartiality which had surrounded it from the beginning. The procedure for selecting judges was meant to guarantee the court's independence. The president nominated a list of twenty-three candidates from which the Russian parliament was to pick fifteen. They would then serve for life. Because of arguments about political balance parliament filled only thirteen slots, but this was considered enough for the court to start work. The judges chose one of their number to be the chairman. Some deputies were unhappy with the speed of the selection process. They had only five minutes to question each candidate. Other deputies complained there were not enough representatives of ethnic minorities, and only one woman.

What remained obscure at the end of the Communist party case was why the court had taken so long to decide to hear the Communists' petition against Yeltsin's ban. There were strong suspicions that Valery Zorkin, the chairman, was delaying it so as not to embarrass the president. The court was 'saved' in May when Oleg Rumyantsev, the executive secretary of the Russian Congress's constitutional commission, brought his petition questioning the party's constitutionality throughout its time in power. This second petition muddied the waters, and meant that when the case opened both sides were on the defensive. Rumyantsev had only just managed to get the Russian Congress of People's Deputies to pass an amendment to the constitution one month earlier allowing the court to rule on the constitutionality of parties. He did not explain his purpose at the time. Had the second petition been worked out with the government's lawyers? I asked Rumyantsev later. 'No,' he replied. 'It was my personal initiative, which I worked out after consultations with Zorkin. He headed a group of experts working with our constitutional commission and I knew him well.'

It was an astonishing disclosure, since in any system with a true separation of powers such a move by the country's top constitutional judge would be inadmissible. Moreover, the law establishing the court forbids judges from giving opinions on executive decisions before a case is brought. But, according to Rumyantsev, he only 'consulted' Zorkin. Zorkin decided that while Russia's new institutions were still feeling their way forward he should say what he thought. He justified his action by reference to the law's preamble which says the court's aim is to serve to strengthen Russia's constitutional order. His interventionist line upset several members of the court.

Zorkin upheld his case to great effect at the Congress of

People's Deputies in December 1992. While the battle raged between president and parliament over the powers of each branch of the state, Zorkin decided that the constitutional court had to step in as umpire. After Yeltsin's surprise 'Appeal to the People' with its call for a referendum on reducing parliament's powers (see Chapter 11), Zorkin was invited by deputies to give his view. He did not endorse the legality of the president's action and warned that the wording would have to be carefully chosen so as not to violate the separation of powers between president and parliament. Putting himself above both institutions, he ordered president and parliament to find a compromise, under his chairmanship if they wished. Otherwise, he warned, the court might have to consider the constitutionality of the actions of both side's leaders. It was a bold move. But it worked. Two days later, when passions had eased, Yeltsin, Khasbulatov and Zorkin met in the Kremlin to hammer out the compromise on which the Congress ended. Parliament would have a key role in selecting the prime minister, and a referendum would be held in April on the constitution.

The clash between parliament and president in September 1993 politicized the court completely. Yeltsin flouted the constitution by dissolving parliament. To try to prevent a legal challenge he even issued a decree to suspend the constitutional court. Zorkin quickly condemned the president but the move split the judges and prompted a minority to press for Zorkin's resignation. The court went into recess for more than a year. It was a sad chapter for an institution which had promised so much, but failed to create a precedent for Russian judges to stay clear of day-to-day political pressures.

With the constitutional court in uproar after only two years of operation, there was even less to admire in the state of criminal law or its application. The Soviet legal system, like the Tsarist system before it, was based on the primacy of the interests of the state over those of the individual. The law was used as an instrument, in some cases as a weapon, to defend the existing regime. Neither before nor after the October Revolution did Russia's rulers accept, let alone respect, the principle that there are basic human rights and freedoms which should be guaranteed by law and to whose protection the state must be bound.

A start towards changing this was made under Gorbachev and later by the Russian parliament. Several international conventions on human rights were ratified. However, these remained mainly declarative, and detailed legislation to back them up was either not passed or not implemented. The right to a passport, for example, was written into law, but action on implementing it was delayed for more than two years. The criteria for refusing a citizen a passport were left unclear.

Pre-Revolutionary Russian law, and Soviet law after it, were based on the Napoleonic code and the traditions of civil law, whereby judges are supposed to apply rules laid down in a legal code. Prosecutors and judges are servants of the state, and cases are conducted according to the 'inquisitorial' rather than the 'adversarial' system. In the former, both the judge and the prosecutor take a more active role. The pre-trial investigation is usually more important than the trial itself. Similar systems operate in many Western countries and there is no implicit reason why the defence side should not be properly safeguarded. Both the Soviet and Russian parliaments passed various amendments to the law which gave defence lawyers more rights than they had had before.

It would take more than a few good amendments to provide for a better system of justice. After years of subordination to the state, the best change would be a system under which judges and lawyers were made independent of the state. Retraining of lawyers and police was a vital need. Even these major reforms would be worth little, however, if the chief law enforcement officers were not themselves to show a greater respect for justice, and if the standards of public administration were not raised. The corruption in the public domain, which grew enormously under Brezhnev, appeared to become more widespread with perestroika and after the collapse of the Communist system. Sometimes it was worse than dishonesty. There was a fundamental unwillingness to accept that certain commodities, such as information, should not be for sale and that public officials have to renounce profit-making during their time in power. There was a basic misunderstanding of the market system, as though everything is for sale.

One of the most striking cases concerned Valentin Stepankov, Russia's prosecutor-general. As the man in charge of preparing the case against the August coup plotters, he had two potential ways of making money. One was by controlling access to the prison where they were held. An amazing number of journalists obtained interviews with the men in prison, a practice which would not be tolerated in most countries for the obvious reason that it could prejudice the conduct of the eventual trial. Worse than that, Stepankov used his privileged control of the pre-trial investigation to write a book on the case and sell excerpts from it to foreign publications. He was unabashed, claiming that he was merely charging for the 'creative work' involved in writing the book and in giving interviews on the case. He did not accept the concept of a conflict of interest, or the need to abstain from public comment so as to safeguard a fair trial. The American magazine *Newsweek* published parts of Stepankov's book for a fee under the title 'Kremlin Plot: the investigator's version'. It carried a coy introduction saying, 'Such disclosures in a US court case could be grounds for dismissal of the charges. In Russia rules are not so clear . . . Stepankov told *Newsweek* he wanted to counter the plotters' public version of events since "public opinion might influence the verdict". He may simply have been in the market for hard currency.'[3]

Reporters were often asked to pay for interviews or for access to government facilities. The Foreign Correspondents' Association compiled a 'White Book' of more than forty cases. The Associated Press was told in June 1992 that it would have to pay $800 for a visit to a strategic missile base near Moscow. The money was said to be for the base commander and for the fact that rockets would be taken off alert while the visit was under way. The Canadian Broadcasting Corporation was asked, and agreed, to pay $400 to film the spring 1992 call-up of recruits at a Russian army base. A

Belgian magazine requested an interview with the deputy head of the KGB in November 1991 and was told by letter the fee was $400. Even Yeltsin's bodyguards used their position to sell journalists access to the president. Pavel Voshchanov, his former press secretary, told Russian television in December 1992 that a semi-official press service called Alen acted as a go-between with the head of Yeltsin's security service. 'The head of the security service can give you close access to the head of state to make exclusive photos or hear things no other journalists will hear,' he said. 'I've never run into a situation where a small commercial enterprise would for money decide the question of contact between the head of the government and the mass media. To my mind we have again surprised the world,' he said.[4] Alen existed to sell professionals permission to film or photograph on Red Square, according to its director Alexander Kuznetsov. Japanese journalists from two competing television companies said Alen offered interviews with Yeltsin before his planned trip to Tokyo. They were told Alen was 'very close' to one of Yeltsin's aides. There was no evidence that Yeltsin knew of the promises.

While bribes in return for information were the area of corruption about which reporters heard most often, corruption was widespread in other fields. Bribes for licences, bribes for medical service, bribes for getting a state flat, bribes for permission to travel abroad, bribes for winning a university place and for taking a degree – all these were common in the Soviet period. Officials had arbitrary power and many used it to line their own pockets. With the arrival of the market economy, the scope for corruption widened immeasurably. In February 1993 Yeltsin told the All-Russia Conference on Measures to Combat Organized Crime and Corruption, meeting in Moscow: 'Bribes for export licences and quotas, preferential credits, special conditions for commercial structures and low-cost purchase of privatized state property have become a reality of our life. Around 40 per cent of businessmen and two-thirds of all the commercial structures are involved in corrupt transaction. Corruption within government departments is literally corroding the state structure from top to bottom'.[5] At the same conference vice-president Alexander Rutskoi said: 'More than half the criminal gangs investigated by federal security bodies in 1992 had corrupt connections with Russian administrative bodies.'[6] He went on to mention the unlawful remittance of hard currency abroad and the private export of Russia's oil, gas and other raw materials.

According to Rutskoi, crime had increased by 70 per cent over 1989. There was no area in which Russians and foreigners did not come across illegality. The police system was notoriously corrupt. Motorists were stopped on the road and asked to pay 'fines' under threat of having their passport impounded or being given a blood test with a used needle. A general rise in crime seemed to be the inevitable accompaniment of the market economy, with widening income differentials which brought desperation at the bottom of the social scale and glittering opportunities at the top. The collapse of state control over the main enterprises, their transfer into often dubious 'joint stock companies' in which directors were subject to minimal supervision, and the absence of clear laws on ownership led to massive theft of national assets.

Some argued that the extent of crime and corruption was a passing phenomenon, which would diminish as the reforms proceeded and a democratic system was established. People talked glibly of the period of the 'robber barons' and the Rockefellers in the nineteenth-century United States as the model which Russia would inevitably follow before gradually civilizing itself.

This was not the view of Yuri Boldyrev, the chief state inspector whom Yeltsin appointed in March 1992. The aim of the new post was to root out corruption, but it transpired that the job was meant to be more political than legal. When Boldyrev wanted to investigate friends of the president, he was told to lay off. When he tried to tighten up the law so that the massive programme for privatizing state property would be conducted openly, equitably, and with the minimum scope for back-handers, he was rebuffed. Finally, he was told his job was being 'reorganized' altogether. As a result his services would no longer be required.

His case was a classic example of the difficulty of creating and protecting the concept of a 'public interest' in today's Russia. In the urge to break from everything to do with the state – what Boldyrev called 'vulgar liberalism' – Yeltsin's 'democratic' team was refusing to take seriously the need for public control and accountability. 'In the old system we needed to protect citizens from the state,' said Boldyrev, when I visited him in his flat shortly after he became unemployed. 'Now we need controls to protect citizens from other citizens. If you just lift controls, you will be left with a new system in which criminals take over.'

One of the new generation of genuine Russian democrats, Boldyrev was a 28-year-old electrical engineer, who also had an economics degree, when he ran for the Soviet parliament in the first free elections in 1989. He was elected from Leningrad on an anti-Communist slate along with the passionate reformer, Anatoly Sobchak, who later became the city's mayor. The problem of corruption was one of Boldyrev's main interests, and he helped to draft the first Soviet law on the subject, shortly before the USSR collapsed.

A colleague of Leningrad's second most famous reformer, Anatoly Chubais, who became Russia's privatization minister, Boldyrev was a natural choice to head the newly formed State Inspectorate. But Boldyrev made it clear that he did not just want to investigate suspicious cases. He called for a system of privatization which, in his view, would minimize corruption.

In relieving itself of municipal and state property, the government had chosen a system of valuing buildings which only assessed the cost of the original bricks and mortars. Market value and inflation since the time of construction were left out of account. Property was meant to be sold competitively, but highly lucrative sites were virtually handed over to cronies of government officials at knock-down prices. Sometimes it was claimed that there was no time to organize an auction. At other times no public announcement was made that a building was available, so that no rival bidders emerged. Occasionally, it was said that some new 'fund' or public committee needed premises urgently. If there were auctions, the starting prices were artificially low, and the bidding was rigged so that all potential buyers were guaranteed something and did not compete with each other.

, 'We proposed a system of co-efficients,' Boldyrev explained. 'Depending on a building's age, appearance, and location, the original cost would be multiplied by a co-efficient. You can debate how radical or moderate a reform should be, but either way there must be protection against abuse. We were refused.' To deal with cases where government officials dispensed with auctions, and merely handed out property to friends or relatives, Boldyrev proposed that the illegal distribution of state property should be a criminal offence, punishable, if necessary, by a fine equivalent to the loss to public funds of a deal which was made at below-market prices. Again, he was refused. Officials could only be sacked, or suffer some other form of administrative sanction.

Boldyrev also suggested that citizens should have the right to bring civil suits, so that, for example, a group of entrepreneurs could complain that a factory or other property had been allocated without competition and seek redress. In the Soviet system this had always been a grey area. Party and government officials had enormous powers to distribute favours, licences and privileges. With the collapse of the Soviet system Boldyrev hoped that new laws would be brought in. Yeltsin's men, Yegor Gaidar, the prime minister, and Anataly Chubais, the privatization minister, were not interested, he said. 'One argument was speed. They wanted to move fast, and argued that when you cut wood, chips will fly. It's the Bolshevik notion that the end justifies the means. The other idea was that in the first stage of accumulating capital you create a new group of owners as fast as possible. Only then can you get private investment. I saw it as giving a right to criminal groups to get rich quick.'

Boldyrev pressed for an anti-monopoly committee, which would be independent. But it was put under Anatoly Chubais' state property administration. 'Even then, it was not given premises to work in. Then they set up a tax police to check on non-payers. I had to argue five times for them to get a building. A year ago, a currency control inspectorate was created. It was meant to deal with illegal exports of hard currency. They were given no room, no staff, no wage fund. The government simply sabotaged it. Decrees were issued, but not fulfilled,' he complained.

Boldyrev's first run-in with President Yeltsin himself came a few months after his appointment. Suspicions were mounting about the way property was being privatized in Moscow. Boldyrev started to prepare an investigation of Yuri Luzhkov, the mayor. Yeltsin called him in and told him to stop the investigation. 'Did he give a reason?' I asked Boldyrev. 'Yes.' he replied. 'He simply said, "We support Luzhkov".' Boldyrev stood his ground, saying he could not halt an inquiry on the basis of an oral instruction. The president then put it in writing. 'If somebody learned that the American president stopped an investigation without explanation, I don't know what would happen to that president. In Russia, society does not consider this unacceptable.'

Moscow's Olympic stadium was one of several odd deals. The mayor authorized 45 million roubles of the city's budget to be spent on new seats for the huge building, which was last modernized for the 1980 games. A few days later it was privatized at a cost of only 90 million roubles. The building was handed to its 'works collective', which, Boldyrev pointed out, meant mainly its managers. When a large factory is given to its works collective, there is at least a substantial workforce of several thousand people. What kind of workforce does a stadium have? At the time of the stadium scandal, a three-room flat in Moscow cost around 5 million roubles. Here was a whole stadium going for just eighteen times that amount. In the rush to get private enterprise going, the government allocated a large sum of money to a pro-Yeltsin group, called AKKOR, the Association of Private Farmers. AKKOR could hand out cheap credits, farm machinery and tax privileges. In a Western country some system of control and auditing would be mandatory. Not with AKKOR. 'The state transfers its authority and finances to individuals and leaves them alone. We said there should be a follow-up to check on the use of the money, and whether the incentives had paid off, and what advantage was taken of the concessions.' He found no interest in the idea. 'Yeltsin's words to me were "It is not necessary now",' he said.

Boldyrev's year in office was not just a chronicle of frustrations. Even if corrupt officials were never prosecuted, they could be sacked. In one year he had the top men in four of Russia's 89 regions and republics removed. These were the men who had been put in charge in 1991 after the Communist structures were banned. Three were pro-Yeltsin appointees. In Pskov the head of the regional administration was illegally exporting petrol, food and metal to nearby Estonia without paying customs duty. In Krasnodar, Vasily Dyakonov, another Yeltsin man put his brother-in-law in charge of some sort of 'fund' to which former Communist party buildings were allocated. In Lipetsk, the local boss received a new car cheap after helping the manager of the area's largest factory obtain credits from the Central Bank. In Voronezh the top man and his deputy were sacked for allocating cars ordered for ordinary citizens to their friends and relatives instead. The fact that three of the four dismissed officials were Yeltsin men did not persuade Boldyrev that the Russian government was even-handed. 'I insisted three times that Dyakonov be sacked. Only on the third occasion did they take action.'

In spite of his bitter experiences Boldyrev wanted to remain in politics, and was elected to the Russian parliament in the ticket led by the young economist Grigory Yavlinsky in December 1993. Boldyrev was one of that rare band of centrists in Russian public life, without a past as a Communist functionary, with firm reformist credentials, and with a clear wish to create independent institutions for a democratic society which would be more permanent than the liberal slogans of whatever team happened to be in power.

Another victim of the chaos and immorality in the administration was Alexei Kazannik, a law professor from Omsk. He first came to prominence in the heyday of perestroika when he resigned his seat in the Supreme Soviet to create a vacancy for Boris Yeltsin. It was an unusual gesture of generosity which had no reward, and Kazannik returned to obscurity in Siberia. Four years later, after Yeltsin sacked the dubious prosecutor-general, Valentin Stepankov, on the grounds that he was taking parliament's side in the battle with the president, Yeltsin's team remembered Kazannik. The upright professor was brought to Moscow and made prosecutor-general.

He did not last long. 'The reason for Russia's crisis is ineffective and immoral power at all levels,' he said shortly after he resigned from the job less than six months later.[7] Kazannik's break with the administration came after parliament voted for an amnesty for Rutskoi, Khasbulatov and the other men arrested after the storming of parliament in October 1993. The new constitution gave deputies the right to issue amnesties, and Kazannik said that although he did not like the deputies' decision, it was legal. Yeltsin quickly issued a decree ordering officials to ignore parliament's decree.

Kazannik phoned the president and begged him to withdraw the decree. 'He very angrily said *Nyet*,' Kazannik recalled later, 'and I said "Boris Nikolayevich, you're consciously violating the Constitution," and he again said *Nyet*. Then I said, "Accept my resignation, because I can't fulfil your order." And he said, "*Nyet*. Find a way out, but don't carry out the amnesty."'[8] The prosecutor-general gave instructions for the prisoners' release, and resigned.

Back in Siberia, he revealed that he had had previous problems with the administration. The investigation his office was making into the October crisis would probably have ended in charges against both the parliamentary rebels and Yeltsin's top officials for criminal abuse of power, but he had been warned not to proceed. On corruption, he said: 'I'm amazed at how this administration breaks people. Some it buys with apartments and cars, some fall into a situation in which they compromise themselves.'

After his few months as a Kremlin insider he concluded that the president and his team operated on the basis that 'The law is very loose, it can be bent any way it suits you.' It was an old Russian saying which predated Communism and easily survived its collapse.

15

The 'New Russia'

*Bring in enlightenment gradually, if possible avoiding
bloodshed.*

MIKHAIL SALTYKOV-SHCHEDRIN, SATIRIST, 1869[1]

It was a summer weekend, almost exactly two years after the
August putsch. Once again Russians heard a stunning announcement, no less unexpected than the 1991 declaration that an
emergency committee had taken power because Mikhail Gorbachev
was too ill to continue as president. This time the broadcast hit
every adult in the land, not just those who were politically engaged.
All banknotes printed before 1993 would be invalid from midnight
the next day. People would have two weeks to change up to 35,000
roubles for new money. Amounts above that would have to be
deposited in their savings banks for six months. With inflation
running at 750 per cent a year, and interest rates at about one sixth
of that, the move was nothing less than confiscation.

The images of that frantic weekend will stay fresh for a long time
in the minds of everyone, Russian or foreigner, who was in Russia
then. Disconsolate old people crowded savings banks to try to swap
the suddenly worthless money. 'I just got my pension yesterday,
and now it's been annulled,' shouted Vera Ivanova with tears in her
eyes. 'The authorities do exactly what they please. It's just crazy,'
said Marina Fyodotova, an assistant hotel manager. Many
privately-owned street kiosks closed rather than have to take the

359

doomed notes as soon as the government's decision was made known. State shops were told to carry on accepting the old money as usual, but not all did. The 1993 money had no note less than 100 roubles, so at a stroke shops lost their change. Long queues formed in breadshops as helpless cashiers urged people to buy three or four loaves to bring their total up to 100 roubles. If the amount was not exact, change was offered in sweets.

Rather than have to deposit their money and watch it erode with inflation, many better-off Muscovites rushed to unload it. The upmarket shops had never been so busy. Customers piled dozens of bottles of drinks into cardboard boxes or bought scores of shirts just to get rid of their money. The black-market traders quickly saw an opportunity for easy profits. They started buying the old money for new at half-price or less, confident that they would be able to change it eventually.

People who were away from home were in the biggest panic. In the chaos of Russia's transport system it had long been almost impossible to buy return tickets. You travelled somewhere, and then worried about your journey back. Since no one had credit cards, the abrupt 'money reform' left thousands of holiday-makers unable to pay for their train or plane tickets home. 'It's an anti-people move,' commented an irate Yuri Afanasyev, one of Russia's most distinguished reformers, as he chose a uniquely Russian epithet to describe the authorities' action. 'How can they do something which so diminishes people's basic dignity?' His question was well-aimed since everyone, regardless of their age, status, or income, was made to feel equally angry, foolish and helpless that weekend. The answer, regrettably, was that the move fitted in with a long line of Russian government actions over the centuries, in which the public's feelings and interests were completely ignored. As Sergei Shakhrai put it at a press conference a few days later, 'The decision was reasonable. They just forgot that people live here.' The authorities were able to get away with it for another classically Russian reason. In most other countries, including Western Europe and the United States, the shock decision might well have provoked violent demonstrations and the smashing of bank windows. In Russia crowds complained and shouted, but complied.

While the decision was shocking enough, the way it was taken was no less worrying. The Central Bank and the government had been planning it as one of two options for some months. It was directed against the other republics in the Commonwealth of Independent States which still used roubles. The Russian government accused them of dumping roubles on the Russian market, thus contributing to inflation, and had tried in vain to get them to agree on a common monetary policy. The sudden withdrawal of old money was designed to force the republics into submission. Those governments which accepted a common policy would be allowed to change their notes, a bank official explained. The rest would lose them. The bank, said the official, wanted to withdraw the notes as an agreed measure, but in the end chose the 'tough' option of doing it unannounced.

The details were put to a Russian government meeting on Friday evening, 23 July. Boris Fyodorov, the finance minister, was away in the United States. His reformist colleagues, Anatoly Chubais and Sergei Shakhrai, said later they did not like what they were being told. Whatever their doubts, the extraordinary aspect of their behaviour was that neither had the political sense to telephone Fyodorov nor the authority to consult Yeltsin and urge him to stop or at least soften the measure before the Central Bank went public. Fyodorov only learnt of it from the American press on the Sunday morning, almost forty-eight hours after it was taken. Yeltsin never made clear when he was told. He was in a difficult position. If he knew in advance and did nothing, he would be blamed for condoning the move. If he was not told, his leadership would look weak.

On the Monday evening, some hours after his rival, Ruslan Khasbulatov, condemned it in a special nationwide television broadcast, Yeltsin issued a decree to extend the deadline and raise the amounts people could change. He did not reject the basic thrust of the measure, and at a summit meeting with the leaders of the

Central Asian republics two weeks later described it as a 'logical step'.

In spite of the fiasco, no minister or Central Bank official resigned or was sacked. The episode revealed that there were no clear lines of authority within the government, or between the government and the president. Every minister acted on his own. The cabinet had no collective discipline. Although Yeltsin frequently argued that Russia's crisis of authority was caused by the unresolved struggle between parliament and the president, the money fiasco showed that the Russian government itself was split into factions. It also demonstrated the weakness of the press. No newspaper attempted to find out which ministers knew what and when. Instead, they fell back on polemics. The pro-Yeltsin media tried to prove that Khasbulatov had privately supported the decision to withdraw the banknotes and that his public criticisms were hypocritical and opportunist. The pro-Khasbulatov papers claimed the president knew of the move from the beginning.

If in the Soviet period there was one source of propaganda, now the press was divided into two equally blinkered camps, 'the propaganda of the democrats and the propaganda of the anti-democrats', wrote Vitaly Tretyakov, the editor of *Nezavisimaya Gazeta*, on the second anniversary of the August coup. 'Once again, the public is deprived of objective information.' During the putsch his paper was forcibly closed, but along with other reformist editors who had been locked out of their presses he put out an underground news bulletin, called the 'General Paper'. In August 1993, Tretyakov was a deeply disillusioned man. He headlined his piece 'The Agony of the Political System is Obvious to All'. 'From top to bottom not one of the branches of power is working properly. Each one is fighting with the others, and very often among themselves. The parliament is split. The government is split. The president's staff is split ... No one can be sure that decisions taken today will not be reversed tomorrow.'

Tretyakov's jeremiad spelt out at length what many Russians were saying more pithily. The common phrase was devastatingly simple – 'Khozyaina nyet,' meaning 'There is no one in charge.' It was not that people wanted a return to authoritarianism. They could not accept the way Russia had slipped towards the other extreme: political and economic chaos in which the government appeared powerless and privatization became 'prikhvatisatsiya' (grabbing).

Yuri Afanasyev called it the 'capitalization of privilege'. After the collapse of the Soviet parliament, where his radical speeches frequently riled Gorbachev, Afanasyev became president of the Russian Humanitarian university, which aimed to be the first liberal arts college in Russia since 1917. By 1993 he too was an unhappy man, although as a historian he was not surprised by post-Communist Russia's failure to change quickly. In his words, Russia was 'a pre-modern society.'[2] He defined a modern society as one in which the emphasis was on the individual rather than the collective, the spirit of rational debate prevailed over emotion and myth, there was a legal contract between authority and the citizens, and a balance between private and the state economic spheres. 'The problems of our society have been present at least since Ivan the Terrible ... There never were any democratic forces, only people oriented towards democracy,' he argued. In spite of his awareness that changing Russia would take a long time, Afanasyev maintained a kind of morose optimism. 'There is no control, but Russia is free-wheeling towards the market,' he commented after a sustained pause when I asked him to name the best aspect of life in Russia two years after the coup.

The market system to which Russia was moving was characterized by growing inequalities of income and extraordinary opportunities for white-collar crime as state officials and directors of newly-privatized enterprises exported oil and metals abroad or swapped company roubles into dollars for themselves. A thin layer of new rich was enjoying wealth unknown in Soviet times – late-model foreign cars, privately-owned villas in the countryside around Moscow, and bank accounts abroad. The top levels of the Communist party nomenklatura had had access to enormous privileges denied to the rest of Soviet society, but it was not private property. An official who fell out of favour lost almost everything. Under the new system the Russian rich had nothing to fear – except from the professional criminals in their own income group. The new wealth spawned scores of protection rackets. Gangland shootings became a regular feature of urban life as different groups carved out their turf or targeted companies which failed to pay their debts. In 1994 contract killers murdered several bankers, two deputies of parliament and a journalist investigating corruption.

There were, of course, honest businessmen too. I visited Alexander Panikin at the textile factory he had set up in a Moscow back-street. A tall man with the broad shoulders of a former karate enthusiast, Panikin used to be the administrator of a theatre. When Gorbachev first allowed private businesses to get going, disguised by the ideologically safe alias of 'co-operatives', Panikin bought six ancient machines, and, with six workers in a small room, started making clothes. 'We sold them from tables in the street,' he recalls wistfully. Later he turned the firm, in the new jargon, into a 'joint venture', though his German partner was himself. He merely registered his company in Germany as well as in Russia so as to get loans from a German bank to buy Western machines. By ploughing his profits back into the business, he built it up over four years into a company with six hundred workers. They were producing a range of contemporary T-shirts, jogging suits, blouses, skirts, sweaters and other clothes. 'We still have no shop of our own, but we have built eight kiosks,' he explained. There was no genuine property market, and he did not have good enough connections with Moscow's mayor to be allocated a decent building with a ground-floor frontage on a busy street, he said. Panikin had other complaints. The tax system discouraged investment, inflation made it hard to get long-term loans, and bureaucracy still stifled initiative.

Mikhail Alexandrov was in a different line of business. A queue of people carrying their privatization vouchers was slowly advancing up the two flights of stairs outside his door when I dropped round. Aged twenty-six, he was already a director of Alfa-Kapital, one of

Moscow's fledgling investment funds, which advertised that it could help people to find the best home for their vouchers. The company exchanged them for shares in its own business. It then used the vouchers to buy a stake in state companies which were being privatized. The key element in any investments decision is information, and Alexandrov readily admitted that in Russia's chaotic market reliable data were almost impossible to get. It was precisely that sense of ignorance and impotence which was driving people up his stairs. They felt Alfa-Kapital had a better overview than any ordinary citizen could get.

Alexandrov spent his time checking on privatized companies, noting what percentage of shares they were selling on the open market and trying to evaluate their performance and investment plans. Then his company pounced. Pointing to a paperback book on his desk, called *The Predator's Ball* by Connie Bruck, he said he was learning almost as much from it as from the two years he spent with Western companies. 'I'm fascinated by the clash between owners and managers,' he smiled. He soon had a chance to put his interest into action. Alfa-Kapital found itself involved in Russia's first take-over bid after it bought 25 per cent of the shares in a Moscow cake and biscuit factory called Bolshevik. At a noisy and emotional thirteen-hour meeting, Alexandrov appealed to Bolshevik's workforce, the majority share-holders, to oust Oleg Shimanov, the managing director. Alfa argued, with the support of some of the other managers, that Shimanov was failing to bring in new machinery to develop the plant.

Beside these new businessmen there was a generation of young men who were making money from importing Western clothes and consumer goods. They were the most conspicuous layer of Russia's 'yuppies'. While this group was doing well out of the market economy, at the bottom of the social scale a huge swathe of people, including industrial workers, clerks, sales staff and urban professionals such as teachers and doctors were suffering. They had had a gradual increase in their incomes during perestroika but suffered a severe drop when the Gaidar reforms were launched and inflation outstripped wages. Taking 1990 as the base year with a value of 100, average real income (after discounting for inflation) moved from 75 in 1985 to a peak of 105 in the last quarter of 1991. By the spring of 1993 it had slumped to 55.³

Inflation and the failure of wages and pensions to keep pace with it hit large families and the elderly particularly hard. On the second anniversary of the coup the minimum pension was 14,000 roubles, well under the government's official poverty line of 19,200 roubles. The shortfall pushed thousands of old people into the most primitive kind of market activity. Alongside the thriving kiosks with their busy young sellers, a different generation lined the pavements, offering single items for sale, a bottle of vodka or Pepsi-Cola, a packet of cigarettes, a pair of hand-sewn woollen gloves. It was barely-disguised begging.

Homeless people began to throng Moscow's railway stations. Runaway children and orphans slept rough in underpasses. It was what Russians called 'diki' (wild) capitalism, as they began to realize that the model they were lurching towards was not the Western European or North American prosperity they aspired to but something closer to Brazil or the Philippines.

The reduction of government subsidies led to a crisis in public health and education. Glasnost under Gorbachev had shown that the Soviet health system was a long way behind the image which the government tried to present. Figures released in October 1992 by Alexei Yablokov, a presidential adviser on public health showed that 40 per cent of hospitals were without hot water, and 12 per cent had no water at all.⁴ But the pressure on the government to cut its spending in the transition to a market economy not only prevented improvements being made, it also caused a further decline. In an attempt to find new sources of funding the government sanctioned the introduction of fee-paying medicine. Hospitals and polyclinics were able to charge patients for service. The change was nothing less than an earthquake, yet it was not introduced after public consultation with doctors, administrators, or consumers. The government merely allowed each medical unit to act as it pleased.

The same happened in education. When I visited the headmistress of Middle School number 149 in a Moscow borough, I found a pile of cardboard boxes in her office full of cigarette cartons. Natalya Shmatova explained with some embarrassment that she was renting the school's basement to a commercial firm, and they had had their first goods delivered before it was ready. 'Under the latest Russian law, schools have the right to be independent with their own bank accounts,' she said. 'Money from renting the basement means I can pay teachers more, provide better lunches, and subsidize holiday travel for the children.' Her school also had new freedom to set its own syllabus. While the headmistress welcomed these changes, she pointed out the school was not fee-paying. Other schools in the borough had started to charge. 'I first want to see the results of the fee-paying schools,' she commented pragmatically. 'Maybe it will be bad for children if they think money can buy everything.'

The headmistress had no idea whether her views represented a common perception among parents and teachers. 'We're just not organized. We have no teachers' union,' she said. 'We still get summoned to old-style meetings where the education authorities simply announce the plans.' Her comment illustrated the weakness of the democratic process. Under Yeltsin, as much as under Gorbachev, it remained 'revolution from above'. Without self-organization and the development of horizontal structures, Russia's civil society would remain weak.

In spite of widespread unhappiness at the social and economic change since 1992, few Russians wanted to go back to the old Soviet system. It was accepted that the transition to the market was irreversible. Many felt nostalgia for aspects of the past – the stability, the low level of crime, and the welfare benefits – but they wanted to combine these with the market economy, not replace it altogether.

Signs of a new and more conservative mood appeared in the provinces earlier than in Moscow. Two weeks before the nationwide referendum in April 1993, the region of Oryol about 300 miles south of Moscow held an election for its governor. Yeltsin's candidate, Nikolai Yudin, was roundly defeated by Yegor Stroyev, a former member of the Soviet Communist party's Politburo. Stroyev still called himself a Communist, though he added cheerfully that it would be better to describe him as 'an intelligent pragmatist'. His ruddy, round face gleaming like a well-polished apple, he was sitting in his office celebrating his victory with a stream of friends who came round for a glass or two of cognac. 'People expected more from Yeltsin. Now the president tells them there is no alternative to his policies,' he said. Obviously enjoying the irony, he added, 'He urges people to be patient. Things will be better, but no one knows when – just like the old days.'

Although nominally a Communist, Stroyev was doing well out of the market economy himself. He had set up an agri-business in Oryol, called 'Reforma', which grouped together two dozen collective farms of which he and most of the farm chairmen became private directors. They had a virtual monopoly on the distribution of farm machinery in the region, and also earned money by selling their produce in Moscow, where prices were high, rather than locally, as they used to have to do in the Soviet system. 'I'm for the market, but not a spontaneous uncontrolled affair,' he asserted. Local analysts said he won the election because he managed to persuade voters that his gradualist policies would do more to protect jobs and the value of pensions. Similar elections in Penza and Lipetsk, two other small towns near Moscow, also produced victories for anti-Yeltsin candidates in April 1993. It was a foretaste of the referendum results, which showed a swing against Yeltsin's reforms in most of the central heartland of Russia, although the president won a national majority, thanks to heavy support in Moscow, St Petersburg and the Pacific Coast.

The issue was what kind of market economy Russia should have rather than whether there should be a market economy at all. The fierce arguments between Yeltsin and parliament over which side should control the government were in one sense artificial. Whatever cabinet Russia had, the policies would be the same. The retreat from monetarism which Gaidar had been forced to make in April

1992 would be a long-term policy, at least until the end of the century. The state's role in the economy would remain large. Towards the end of 1993 when the privatization of industry was nearly complete, Russian economists were beginning to point out that the pattern of ownership did not remove the basic dilemma. How could the government permit closure of a large number of major industries in one go, especially when they were 'town-creating enterprises', that is, factories which were the only major employer in a single town? The question was where the money would come from to keep them open. These plants might already be privately-owned, in the sense that their workers and other citizens held the shares, but new private capital would not be invested in loss-makers. In the end, therefore, government money would be needed to keep these newly-privatized companies going, just as it had always done. Once again, the message was that the transition to a more efficient economy would have to be gradual. Mass bankruptcies were not the answer.

In their attitude to foreign trade the consensus among Russian industrialists by the end of 1993 was moving towards what even Andrei Kozyrev, the radically pro-Western foreign minister was calling 'reasonable protectionism'. After two years of listening to Western advice about the need to open the economy, the government was having second thoughts. In August 1993, it tightened licence restrictions on the export of oil, metals and other raw materials for fear that too much was leaving the country without government control. There was also pressure for controls on imports and for protecting Russian industry. The government's agreement under strong American pressure to cancel the sales of rocket technology to India in the summer of 1993 was a watershed, which caused many Russians to re-evaluate their assumption that their country had a natural partnership with the West. Some saw it as proof that the West was hypocritical in saying it favoured open trade and Russian prosperity. Others believed the West's aim was to 'de-industrialize' Russia and reduce it to the level of a Third World raw materials exporter. Still others argued that the early-

1990s crisis in the world economy, marked by fierce competition between the United States, the European Community and Japan in conditions of no overall growth, showed that the global market was saturated. Russia could not expect to export manufactured goods. Instead, Russia should protect its home market and let Russian industry work for Russian consumers, albeit under new market disciplines. The outcome was that Russian economic policy seemed set to become one of moderate nationalism for the next few years.

At the psychological level, optimists detected a shift in public attitudes two years after the August coup. Nikita Vvedenskaya, a senior mathematician who stood guard outside the White House in the tension-charged nights of August 1991 said, 'People are changing. They are realizing you have to work to earn money. If their rights are affected, they go to court. That never happened before.' Anastasia Posadskaya, the head of Moscow's Gender Centre, was guardedly hopeful in spite of her many criticisms. 'We had big expectations. But the democrats don't seem able to get things right. They haven't formed a political party. Power still corrupts, and it may even be worse now that democrats are in high positions,' she told me. 'But,' she went on, 'in spite of everything, including the growing differentiation of income, there is no starvation. A middle layer is emerging, and creating some sort of market, at least on the surface. Secondly, the non-state and non-profit sector is growing. People are beginning to form associations and build up a civil society.' With extreme caution she concluded, 'It could be very optimistic, potentially.'

16

October 1993

I have a soft palm but a strong fist

BORIS YELTSIN, TV INTERVIEW, NOVEMBER 1993

As dawn broke on 4 October 1993, a line of T–80 tanks became visible on Moscow's Novy-Arbatsky Bridge, their gun turrets pointing at the Russian White House, the seat of parliament. The approach by which they had entered the Russian capital was the one Napoleon used when he occupied Moscow in 1812. The bridge on which they now waited, menacing and silent, connected the White House with Kutuzovsky Prospekt named after the gruff general who thwarted the French invader by retreating into the Russian interior and refusing to surrender.

But these were not foreign tanks. They were under the command of Boris Yeltsin, who had given an order a few hours earlier to prepare to storm the parliament and detain its occupants. According to accounts in the pro-presidential newspaper *Izvestiya*, General Pavel Grachev, the defence minister, had responded evasively to repeated telephone calls from the president the previous night to attack the building.[1] Only when the president assured the general that he would take full responsibility on himself for any consequences did the reluctant army commander agree to use his troops in a domestic political conflict.

The ironies could not have been lost on either man. In August 1991, during the failed pro-Soviet coup, Yeltsin had stood on a

371

tank outside the same building, that time to urge the army not to shoot on its fellow citizens. General Grachev, then the commander of airborne troops, had maintained a similar position of studied neutrality in 1991 before finally refusing an order from the pro-putsch defence minister to send his men into action.

This time it was different. At around 9 a.m. the first salvo of tank shells was launched at the massive building, perched like a marble fortress above the Moscow river. Pieces of shattered window glass crashed down. Papers from ruptured filing cabinets fluttered in the morning breeze. With armoured personnel carriers already in action on the other side of the building, and paratroopers blasting their way through the doors and ground-floor windows, some of the building's defenders fought back with machine-gun and automatic rifle fire. From every nearby balcony and roof people watched in excitement. Astonishingly, several hundred raced towards the firing close to the building for a better view.

It was indeed an extraordinary sight. Laser-guided shells from the top-of-the-line tanks unerringly penetrated the windows, leaving the masonry and marble overlay almost untouched. As the news of the fighting spread, more and more people hastened to the scene. Troops and police did nothing to drive them back out of harm's way. Many sat on walls or wandered about between the tanks and the building, occasionally ducking and running, before coming back to the fray, oblivious of danger even when people near them were hit by bullets. It was as though the fight going on around them was nothing but a spectator sport.

Yeltsin's and Grachev's reversal of roles between 1991 and 1993 was not the only irony of that amazing day. More striking were the echoes of a troubled Russian past. It was the third time that a Russian government had used force against an elected parliament. On 9 July 1906, only seventy-two days after Russia's first Duma had opened, Tsar Nicholas the Second sent troops to the building to close it down. The liberal-conservatives, his only supporters in the parliament, numbered about a third of the deputies, and even though the parliament's powers were limited, the Tsar saw it as a threat. As 9 July was a Sunday, no deputies were in session, and the troops had an easy task in nailing the Tsar's dissolution decree to the door and standing guard. After new elections, the next Duma fared little better. It lasted 105 days before being closed, this time without any need for force. The third one ran its full five-year term, though the Tsar frequently suspended it for several months when controversies arose so that he could rule in the interim without opposition and by decree.

In mid-November 1917, barely three weeks after the Bolshevik seizure of power, Russians voted for a Constituent Assembly. It was to be the first parliament of the post-monarchist era. In the large cities and industrial areas the Bolsheviks were the biggest winners, but nationwide their poll was 24 per cent. On 6 January 1918, the day after the Constituent Assembly opened, the commander of the guard, a sailor and well-known anarchist, mounted the tribune, and ordered the chairman to close the meeting because 'the guard is tired'.[2] As Bolshevik troops entered the hall, the chairman stubbornly kept it going for twenty minutes before adjourning until the next morning. The Assembly never re-opened.

Yeltsin's decision to dissolve the Congress of People's Deputies and the Supreme Soviet was a replay in slow motion of the earlier occasions of anti-parliamentary action by the executive this century. The basic framework – a leader able to rely on the support of only a quarter or a third of the deputies – was the same. Even the issues were uncannily similar. The first Duma in 1906 clashed with the Tsar's government on two main issues – control over the budget and the appointment of ministers. Deputies were annoyed that the Tsar exempted from their scrutiny payments on state debts, the expenses of the Imperial household, and all credits which he chose to define as 'extraordinary'. The Tsar would not give up the power to nominate his ministers, or allow parliament any form of supervision over the bureaucracy.

When, two generations later, Russia's infant parliamentarianism emerged again at the end of the Communist period, deputies continually clashed with Yeltsin on exactly the same points. The difference was only the speed of the process and its denouement.

Unlike Nicholas the Second in 1906 and the Bolsheviks in 1918, Yeltsin started in 1990 with a majority of the deputies on his side. He lost their support in 1992 and 1993 with his unpopular economic strategy and his inability to work for compromise with parliament. From October 1992 he started on a path of confrontation, repeatedly threatening to close parliament, and after the referendum of April 1993, using his control of the state broadcasting media to paint parliament in the worst possible light and advise it voluntarily to disband. He rejected the deputies' offer of simultaneous elections for parliament and president. In July, he infuriated deputies with a speech to the Constitutional Conference in which he said 'democracy and soviets (councils) are incompatiable'.

Yelstin's contempt for the Supreme Soviet and his refusal to work with it created a political stalemate, in which parliament's minority of hardliners gained the upper hand over the moderates. For almost a year Yeltsin had not appeared in the Supreme Soviet. He never consulted with the fourteen faction leaders. Parliament's centrists were gradually pushed aside by radicals who wanted nothing more than an out-and-out clash with the executive in the old Russian tradition. A row over the budget for 1993 was the last straw. The government proposed a budget of 10 trillion roubles, which was designed to cut the deficit to around 12 per cent of Gross Domestic Product. Deputies flatly turned it down, and proposed a budget of 21.7 trillions, leading to what the government said would be a colossal 25 per cent of GDP and hyperinflation. Government economists were horrified. Some deputies said they were merely implementing the promises of social welfare and wage increases which Yeltsin had made during the referendum campaign, totalling an estimated 7 trillions, and which the Finance Ministry now wanted to forget. Others insisted on new credits to state industries to prevent bankruptcies and unemployment. They also claimed government estimates understated the amount of tax revenue to be expected, and were therefore exaggerating the likely deficit.

By September 1993, when Yeltsin, in a provocative metaphor,

announced he was starting 'artillery preparations' against parliament, the chance for a truce, let alone a constructive new start by both sides, was minimal. His dissolution of parliament turned the verbal battle between executive and legislature into a physical confrontation. Deputies hurried to Moscow to hold an emergency session of the Congress of People's Deputies. After the Constitutional Court declared Yeltsin had violated the constitution (a charge which the president, claiming in his televised address that 'the security of Russia and its people is a higher value than formal observation of discrepant norms', implicity accepted was true) deputies nominated Vice-President Rutskoi as acting president. The White House was put under siege. The mayor of Moscow cut its electricity and phone lines. The building was surrounded by razor wire and thousands of Interior Ministry troops. Deputies could not get in or out, and even journalists were blocked for several days, and then allowed in only under escort.

The siege conditions intensified the process of radicalization. Armed groups led by notorious extremists who were not deputies, including General Albert Makashov, a defeated candidate in the 1991 presidential election, and Viktor Anpilov, the head of Working Russia, took the upper hand inside the building. Both men were hardliners who would have tried to install a military dictatorship had they ever come to power. In the crowd of several hundred supporters who camped round bonfires on the grass verge outside parliament an unsavoury collection of Stalinists and Fascists joined forces. There were young men in black uniforms with Swastika emblems from the Russian National Union, and elderly people with pictures of Stalin and the red flag.

In the first two days of the confrontation, Rutskoi and Khasbulatov had sought to maintain the moral high ground by confining themselves to a political reaction. If they had then left the building and tried to build political resistance in the regions, they might have created a counterweight to the president for a compromise on the lines of simultaneous elections for parliament and president – although, with control of TV and radio in Yeltsin's hands, they would have had difficulty in getting their message out. At least, it would have been politically dangerous for Yeltsin to arrest them. They would have remained as a focus of legitimate defiance.

But both men appeared to have been infected by memories of the defence of the White House in August 1991. They preferred to stay inside the building, turning a political chamber into a military fortress. They did nothing to evict the armed extremists and the undisciplined volunteers who had their own agenda in coming to the White House. A hard core of Communist and nationalist deputies, the so-called irreconcilable opposition, also believed the time had come for a showdown with a regime which in their view had destroyed the Soviet Union. Yeltsin, for his part, avoided the mistake which the coup plotters of 1991 had made. Instead of bringing tanks into Moscow early, he tried to strangle the White House slowly by a controlled process of isolation. It was like an anti-terrorist operation with the deputies cast in the role of hostage-takers.

Yet, by the end of the first week of the siege, the crisis was moving towards stalemate. More than half the country's regional councils stayed loyal to the parliament in Moscow, as did several republican leaders. The army was still proclaiming neutrality. To the president's annoyance, Patriarch Alexi, the head of the Russian Orthodox church, stepped in with an offer to mediate. Yeltsin could not refuse. The Patriarch took up a suggestion made by several regional leaders, as well as many deputies, that new elections be held simultaneously for the presidency and parliament.

In itself, the proposal was no threat to Yeltsin since he would easily have won re-election. The problem was that to accept the compromise would have been a political retreat. Yeltsin's men wanted victory, as indeed did the hardliners in parliament. The stage was set for another Russian tragedy in which two sides insisted on absolute control and neither was willing to do an honourable deal.

The initiative lay with Yeltsin. His problem was how to use it.

He needed to bring the crisis to a head either by forcing the parliament to surrender or else by taking the White House by storm. The difficulty was to find a political justification for military action, which would stop the army high command dithering and preserve Yeltin's reformist image abroad. On 3 October the pretext was found. Exactly what happened the day before the tanks moved in may never be known. Russia has no tradition of independent public inquiries. One by Alexei Kazannik, the prosecutor-general, stopped when he resigned. The new parliament cancelled plans for an investigation at the same time as they released Rutskoi and Khasbulatov in February 1994. Yeltsin's own version ignores many central questions but contains the improbable assertion 'During these days we never considered even a theoretical plan to take the building.'[3] What happened must therefore remain speculative, though there is strong circumstantial evidence that Yeltsin's men, perhaps without the president's knowledge, sprang a deadly trap.

The story started the day before, on 2 October, when an ultimatum was set demanding that the White House be evacuated within forty-eight hours. With tension mounting a crowd of about 1,000 erected barricades across Moscow's ring road near the Foreign Ministry about half a mile from the White House. According to eyewitnesses and reporters, it was a poorly organized mob, which included several drunks – what Russians call 'lumpen'. They let down the tyres of parked cars, lit bonfires, and prepared Molotov cocktails. Yet the police stood by and watched. For several hours traffic was diverted and the makeshift barricades were not removed until nightfall.

If the police action that day could be explained charitably as incompetence, what then of their behaviour on 3 October? The hardline group Working Russia had announced that it would hold a rally at its favourite spot in front of Moscow's biggest statue of Lenin on October Square. It needed no great intelligence to predict that these demonstrators would be more determined than the crowd the previous day. Their last meeting, on May Day, five months earlier, had turned into a violent clash when several dozen thugs at the head of the march attacked police lines, killing one officer. Yet this time, in spite of the turbulence on the previous day and in spite of Working Russia's tough reputation, the police presence was small. As the crowd left October Square and walked towards them, the police lines gave way. They fired some tear gas, flailed with their truncheons and fled.

It still took the crowd another forty minutes to reach the White House. But the police not only failed to bring up reinforcements, General Viktor Yerin, the interior minister, ordered the cordon round the White House to be lifted. 'The police did not disappear. They were relocated,' he told a press conference on 7 October. He justified the move by saying that the people in the White House had started firing. 'It was absurd to keep policemen under fire from sub-machine guns, grenade throwers and sniper rifles. I must tell you that it is not always the best option to stand up to the enemy bare-chested.' The minister's statement was baffling. Russian and foreign journalists heard some firing as the march approached the White House, but reported that it came from police ranks. 'Bullets shattered windows in the White House,' *Moscow News* reported. If there had been as much fire against the police as General Yerin claimed, how come not a single policeman was killed? Strangely, when the police departed, they left the keys in the ignition of several cars and lorries.

Whether this was also incompetence or something more sinister, the ingredients were in place for the people in the White House to do something stupid. After a week of siege, they were suddenly 'liberated' – the police had disappeared. Among the armed militants who had been preparing the building against attack, the mood of victory was strong. Egged on by Alexander Rutskoi, they decided to take the offensive. First they seized the mayor's office, just across the road. Then they moved five miles across the city, some by underground, some in the abandoned police vehicles, to the main television centre at Ostankino.

Police tactics now underwent an important change. The hard-liners' symbolic 'victory' must not become a real one. Lieutenant-

General Alexander Kulikov, deputy minister of the interior, who was later appointed to run the curfew ordered by Yeltsin, sent armoured personnel carriers and extra contingents of men to reinforce the police guards already in place. The new forces reached Ostankino at 5.30 p.m. just before the protesters arrived from the White House. Albert Makashov, a hardline general who was sacked from the army two years previously, demanded that the police let the protesters into the building. A lorry was driven into the glass doors of the foyer to try to force the issue. When the police refused, Makashov withdrew and waited for the number of his supporters to build up.

According to Lieutenant-General Kulikov, this allowed the police troops to secure all the TV station's buildings and prepare them for defence. 'Was the unit late? They had two hours or rather an hour and a half to prepare for battle, and thank God it happened that way. Fire was planned very carefully and defensive positions were taken. The unit was fully ready,' he told a press conference on 7 October.

At 7.10 someone in the Makashov crowd fired a grenade launcher at the front entrance, killing a guard. By then, according to the police, there were about 100 armed men with Makashov, and an unarmed crowd of 4,000. The grenade attack led to a volley of answering fire. The crowd was caught in the open in the dark with almost nowhere to hide. In the ensuing shooting dozens of people were killed, including four television cameramen. The carnage was made worse when another fifteen Interior Ministry armoured personnel carriers and an extra hundred troops arrived. Without waiting to get a clear picture, and apparently under the impression that anti-Yeltsin forces were inside the building, they started blazing away.

General Pavel Grachev, the defence minister told a press conference on 8 October, that the danger to the building lasted about ten minutes. There had been some discussion that the army should send reinforcements, but he decided it was unnecessary. In the defence minister's words, 'The Ministry of Internal Affairs ordered no first use of weapons and the employment of police methods only. The guards used their weapons only after the attackers had opened fire. Ten minutes later the crowd drew back. They say that they wanted to regroup and resume their assault, but this is only a bluff. An operational team went out there. The minister of internal affairs phoned me to say that he had enough forces there. We agreed that the attackers, having sustained losses, would not attempt another assault. This is what happened.'

Although the attack had been repulsed, the extraordinary thing is that the government side went on firing intermittently for another seven or eight hours. Government forces were in various parts of the huge Ostankino complex, and armoured personnel carriers were cruising around it. Eyewitnesses who watched the tracer bullets say they are convinced they all came from government forces. Makashov's armed people had melted away and returned to the White House.

It was an amazing spectacle, permeated with a heavy dose of Russian foolhardiness. The police had not blocked the roads, and joyriders and gawpers drove by to watch, scattering only when bullets hit their vehicles. Boys of fourteen and fifteen were making Molotov cocktails with petrol taken from abandoned cars. Maybe the young soldiers in the armoured personnel carriers genuinely felt frightened. Maybe the forces in the building were ill-disciplined victims of too many Rambo films, spraying blindly with their automatic weapons. The troops appeared to be under orders to fire whenever a group of people gathered. The shooting went on sporadically until around 4 a.m. The final death total reached between fifty and sixty.

Even if the troops themselves were unprofessional, why did no senior officer, or General Yerin himself, order them to stop firing early in the evening when the only real 'attack' had easily been repulsed? They could have used watercannon or tear gas to drive off the crowd, or wait until cold and the need for sleep dispersed them. It was as though the authorites wanted to keep the shooting going.

At no time after the first ten minutes was there any serious possibility of the crowd taking control of the TV station, yet its chairman, Vyacheslav Bragin, a Yeltsin appointee, ordered news broadcasting at Ostankino to shut down. It resumed later that evening from another TV centre. The dramatic disruption had the effect of magnifying the alleged threat to Ostankino to millions of Russians who were following events anxiously at home. The ensuing reports on government-controlled radio and television then gave distorted picture of what was going on, as though a knife-edge struggle for Ostankino was underway for hours.

It was this phoney battle which turned public sympathy away from the White House. Yeltsin himself was later to talk of an 'armed uprising', 'a parliamentary revolt' (as though the crowd consisted of MPs), and the threat of a civil war. If it was a provocation by the government side, it had achieved one goal. Blood had been spilt, and blame for it appeared to lie squarely on the supporters of the White House. The government-controlled media pumped home the message.

Yeltsin's second goal, that of persuading the army to join in the storming of the White House, had not yet been achieved. General Grachev brought some forces into Moscow on Sunday evening to guard his own buildings, the Defence Ministry and the headquarters of the General Staff. He was still not willing to go on the offensive against the parliament, apparently well aware that the armed actions by its supporters had fizzled out. In his initial view, they still did not justify an attack on the White House. It took President Yeltsin several phone calls and a personal visit to army staff headquarters after midnight to ensure Grachev's agreement to join in the attack on the building on the morning of 4 October. The president later criticized him publicly for his hesitation.

For those who are suspicious of conspiracy theories, the counter-argument boils down to two points. The police failure to stop the march on the White House and their decision to carry on shooting for most of the night around Ostankino were the results of pure incompetence. No doubt there were mistakes and stupidities by the police, but this alone does not explain their abandonment of the cordon round the White House. Lieutenant General Kulikov himself admitted it was a policy decision.

The second argument against the notion of a 'provocation' is that President Yeltsin had left Moscow on Saturday for his country house, and eyewitnesses who were in the Kremlin on Sunday evening when news of the attack on Ostankino was coming in reported a mood of panic. This, it is claimed, shows that Yeltsin and his team had not expected the 'break-out' by the White House supporters.

The argument is weak, since anyone running a 'dirty trick' of the kind which appears to have been perpetrated on 3 October would hardly bring more than a handful of senior people into the plot. Those who did not know of it would quite likely have panicked. As for Yeltsin's absence from Moscow during the early part of it (he flew back 'to take charge' that evening), this looks like an alibi. Or it may have been that the president himself was not told of the plans so that he could later deny involvement, if necessary. The radicals among his senior staff could have concocted the plot with General Yerin alone, although General Yerin seemed to give the lie to that at his 7 October press conference. Asked about his contact with the president during the events, he answered thus: 'During all these critical days and nights, I had permanent communication with the president. Sometimes we were in contact several times an hour.'

Many of the details of the assault on the White House are as obscure as what went on the day before. Endless arguments erupted afterwards over the casualty figures. The official death toll over the two days of shooting in Moscow was put at 147, though there were suspicions the figure was considerably higher. Government troops caused the vast majority of deaths. Deputies who surrendered were treated arbitrarily. Some were escorted out by government forces and allowed to go home unharmed. Others suffered beatings in a nearby stadium or in the entrances and darkened courtyards of ordinary blocks of flats. Oleg Rumyantsev, the young executive secretary of the Constitutional Commission (see Chapter Thirteen), had one of the worst ordeals. He was led by a group of men from the former KGB's Alpha unit to a nearby building. 'They left, but from the doorway an "Omonovets" – a member of the special police troops – jumped out with an automatic rifle and shouted "Lie down, you bastard,",' Rumyantsev recounted later. 'They pushed me into the entrance-hall. A drunken face grabbed me by the beard: "Come here, Jewish shit." They hit me three times in the face. Then they searched me. I had no money, only a small Sony radio. They hit me again in the ribs and the stomach. Then they pushed me out again. An officer whispered to me, "They're shooting in the yard. Run over to that entrance." We ran there. I was with an artist I had met in the White House. It was the same picture in the next entrance, the same hell, just a different group. The police were beating two young kids, not more than seventeen-year-olds, who were stripped to the waist for some reason. The police grabbed me and beat me several times in the testicles. For a week afterwards I was urinating blood. They used their rifle butts to push us into the courtyard. There was indeed shooting going on there. It was not clear who they were shooting at, but we heard single shots'.

Rumyantsev's fearful experience went on a further ten minutes. Another policeman accosted him. 'Imagine it. A drunken man with a rifle, his eyes with nothing human left in them, at his feet someone's corpse. "It's all over, you bastard, say goodbye to life," he told me. He spat twice in my face, then shouted, "Turn round." I turned round. "Kneel." Then he fired over my head. I lay there, without the strength to get up.' Eventually, he managed to run into another entrance, and dashed upstairs. He rang a doorbell, and told the woman who opened it, 'I'm a deputy, Rumyanstev.' 'We recognize you. Come in,' she said. It was a one-room flat with a family of three. Rumyantsev stayed there for several days, slowly recovering.

Flushed by victory, Yeltsin also allowed euphoria to overcome better judgement, just as it had overwhelmed the hardline defenders of parliament on the Sunday before the storming. At the human level, there were flashes of reconciliation. The wounded from different sides of the barricades shared the same hospital wards. The Orthodox Church held joint funerals, and the president decreed special payments to the families of the bereaved, regardless of which side their loved ones had been on. But at the political level, Yeltsin showed no mercy. Several newspapers were closed, and censorship was imposed on the rest. Those deputies who stayed in the White House until the last weekend were ordered to move out of their flats within three days. In his first television appearance, three days after the crisis came to its climax, the president claimed it was the result of a 'Communist-fascist' plot which had been 'carefully planned for months'. He denounced the Constitutional Court, and signed a decree to suspend it. He asked the councils in Russia's eighty-eight regions and republics to disband. They were to be replaced by smaller bodies with reduced powers after new elections. Federal elections were promised for 12 December to a new two-chamber parliament. Its Lower House would be called the State Duma like the one which Nicholas the Second had regularly closed. In the meantime the president and government would rule by decree.

On the evening of the assault on the White House I listened to the spectators lining the bridges and the river embankment as huge tongues of flame licked the top floors of the parliament. It was encouraging and a surprise to find that, even if parliament and president had long ago lost the ability to talk to each other, ordinary Russians had not. Two men and a woman sat in the first car I approached, parked on Borodinsky bridge with a prime view of the blazing building. One man supported the parliament, the other supported Yeltsin, but they were still friends and in the same car. A few yards away I stopped at one of the many knots of people peacefully arguing over the event. 'We Russians do not yet deserve to live like other nations. We are still not mature enough,' a middle-aged man was saying sadly. I climbed to the top of a block of flats just opposite the White House. A woman opened the door and let me on to the roof where about a hundred people were lining the parapet, watching tracer bullets flash through the darkening sky while tanks and armoured personnel carriers began to trundle away. By then Rutskoi and Khasbulatov had surrendered, and the siege was over. As I left the flat again, I asked the owner what she thought of Rutskoi. She made as if to spit on her hall floor. What then of Yeltsin? Was her opinion of him better or worse than it used to be? 'Worse,' she growled.

Her answer helped to explain the paradox of the relatively calm reaction among the White House spectators. People felt distanced from the events. The battle they were watching meant little to them. Many supported neither side, or if they did prefer one over the other, it was without enthusiasm. There seemed to be an overriding view that the bloody outcome brought shame on Russia, and showed how far Russia was from the politics of the 'civilized' countries which Russians so eagerly aimed at. Stanislav Govorukhin, whose nostaligc pseudo-documentary about Tsarist Russia, *The Russia We Lost*, had captivated audiences two years earlier (see Introduction) included strongly critical footage of the storming of the White House in a new film, called *The Great Criminal Revolution*.

In the days which followed the storming of the White House a mood of dull depression emerged, coupled with twinges of fear. If there was one thing which worried Russian liberals almost more than Communism, it was civil war. The strongest approval for Yeltsin's action came from the older intelligentsia, who remembered the Stalin period. They accepted the president's line that he had forestalled a Communist comeback. They were glad he had flouted democracy in the name of blocking Communism and Fascism. But even here the first signs of unease appeared. Writing in *Moscow News* after the dissolution of parliament but before the storming of the White House, Sergei Kovalev, the chairman of Yeltsin's human rights commission and a political prisoner from the Brezhnev era, commented: 'If the next parliament does not please the president, will he decree its dissolution? What will happen to Russia's fledgling parliamentarianism then? I hope this president does not become its grave-digger.'[4]

Many other intellectuals, particularly those with no record of political protest in the Communist era, took the president's side because it was the safest thing to do. Andrei Sinyavsky, a writer who was arrested in 1965 under Brezhnev and imprisoned after a notorious trial which demonstrated that Khrushchev's brief thaw was finished, published a scathing attack on Russian intellectuals' apparent need to go with winners. Since his release from prison Sinyavsky had lived for years in Paris. Life in Western Europe gave him a clarity and coolness of view which eluded most Russians. 'Why am I against Yeltsin?' he wrote in *Nezavisimaya Gazeta* on 13 October. 'Because in this clash of two forces, there must not be any winners. Both sides should leave the political scene, since the art of government consists of the mastery of compromise and the latent for co-operation. Victory for one side is a defeat for democracy, and victory at the cost of such bloodshed is a crime . . . The worst thing is that my old enemies are beginning to speak the truth, while my own tribe of Russian intellectuals, instead of offering some opposition to Yeltsin so as to correct the mistakes which he and his team are making, welcomes what the great leader is doing and once again starts calling for tough measures. It has all happened before. This is how Soviet power began.'

Among middle-aged and younger Russians the October events gave a new boost to the disillusionment with politics which had been growing all year, first marked by the drop in turnout for the April referendum. *Nezavisimaya Gazeta* captured it in a headline a few days after the storming. 'Free thinking: only in the kitchen,' it said in a reference to the old style of Soviet life, when people preferred not to talk about anything sensitive at work or in the office.[5] The president's men recognized it themselves. When the Kremlin published Yeltsin's decree on the rules for the December election in early October, the requirement of the 1989 and 1990 elections that at least fifty per cent of the electorate had to take part in any constituency for the poll to be valid had been changed. Under the new rules as long as only one in four voters turned out, the elections would be counted as legitimate. The Kremlin's precautions were justified, but even their pessimism was exceeded. Several local elections the following spring had to be annulled because less than 25 per cent of voters bothered to take part. It was a sign of how much things had changed since the exciting spring of 1989, when Russian voters had their first chance to take part in contested elections. Then they had turned out in huge numbers, celebrating a genuine moment of civic participation. Now they were tired and disappointed.

Conclusion

After the failed coup of August 1991 many people in the West understandably had high hopes for democracy in Russia. With the end of the Communist system, they wanted the country to become as quickly as possible like the West. Much of the Russian intelligentsia shared their dream.

I have argued in this book that those hopes were misplaced. Reform is relative, and no society can easily import other countries' solutions or escape its own traditions. The lesson of Russian history is that 'revolution from above' is insufficient, and that hasty changes in a society with no practice of law bring chaos. The crucial need is to encourage participatory democracy and a culture of tolerance and compromise over a period of decades.

The first two and a half years after the 1991 coup bore out how unrealistic the dream of quick democracy was. The tragic conflict between president and parliament which reached its climax in October 1993 was a direct result of the inability of the various factions in the Russian elite to find a civilized dialogue. Nevertheless, with the storming of the White House, a new wave of hope emerged among some foreign observers. Boris Yeltsin had slain another dragon on the road to democracy, and Russia was set for a fresh start. The elections which Yeltsin called for December 1993 would be a crucial mechanism for building a multi-party system and creating a parliament which would not stand in the way of reform, it was argued. Once again, the promise was aborted. Not only did the elections fail to strengthen the formation of parties, and produce a reformist majority in the new parliament, they allowed a sinister right-wing populist to burst on to the stage.

Russia clearly needed to form a multi-party system as one element in the building of democracy. But the context in which the elections were held showed how weak the understanding of democracy still was among Russian leaders, including the president. Yeltsin used the vacuum left after parliament's dissolution to make further unilateral and authoritarian changes in the draft Constitution which his team had been working on throughout the summer. Some increased the powers of the president, making them more formidable than those of either the French or American presidents. Others reinforced Moscow's rights vis-à-vis the republics by withdrawing the clause which described them as sovereign. Having promised to hold early presidential elections in June 1994, Yeltsin wrote a special 'transitional' codicil to the Constitution which put them off again.

After toying publicly with a plan to let the next parliament adopt the constitution, the president abandoned it for fear that even his supporters whom he expected to win a majority in the new body might insist on creating a more even balance between executive and legislature. Yeltsin announced he was putting the draft to a nationwide referendum in December 1993 on the same day as the elections. In the month leading up to the referendum Yeltsin's men used their monopoly control of Russia's two nationwide television channels to praise the document while limiting access to critics. Yeltsin's decree laying down the rules for the parliamentary elections allowed each block to have equal time for unpaid broadcasting. It said nothing about allowing equal time for opponents and supporters of the constitution. Worse still, half-way through the campaign, when some candidates used their free broadcasts to oppose the constitution as well as promoting their own parties, Yeltsin summoned the party leaders to the Kremlin and threatened to cut air time from anyone who criticized it. After an outcry in some of the Russian newspapers and most of the foreign press he modified his warnings, but the note of intimidation had already been sounded.

In these conditions it was hardly surprising that the referendum produced a result in the president's favour. But the victory was controversial. Before the voting Yeltsin issued a decree changing the rule that half the electorate must approve any constitutional issue. In future, a 50 per cent turn-out was sufficient. Of these a majority must support the proposal. In the event Nikolai Ryabov, Yeltsin's appointee as head of the Central Election Commission, declared that 54.8 per cent took part. Although close to a thousand international observers were invited for the elections, none was allowed into the counting centre in Moscow. A government commission later caused a sensation by saying the turn-out was only 49 million, roughly 46 per cent. Some independent analysts queried the commission's methodology, but agreed its findings were backed by internal government documents.

The parliamentary elections were conducted in a better atmosphere. The big difference was the time given to all competing blocks and parties to conduct unpaid political broadcasts. The opening was exploited skilfully by Vladimir Zhirinovsky, the leader of the far-right Liberal Democratic Party. He won 23 per cent of the vote, some 8 per cent more than the pro-government block, Russia's Choice.

Zhirinovsky's law-and-order populism had already shown its appeal in the presidential elections of June 1991. Trained in law and foreign languages, he had an obscure job in a publishing house for many years. It was widely assumed he had been plucked out of this niche and chosen to lead the party by the KGB after the Communist Party agreed to change the constitution in 1990 and allow a multi-party system. Because of the old Communist tradition of setting up controlled organizations to try to fill the space which genuine independents might otherwise occupy, the LDP was seen as artificial. Observers noted the generous television time it received and the fact that it was the first party registered after the Communist Party abandoned its monopoly.

Zhirinovsky was not a member of the Russian parliament, and after the 1991 election journalists and politicians largely forgot him. But Zhirinovsky continued to maintain his party organization, two regular newspapers, and groups of supporters around the country. When Yeltsin called the December 1993 elections, Zhirinovsky was better prepared than most other parties. This time his message was even stronger. He attacked Yeltsin's record as well as Gorbachev's. In 1991, his main targets had been the crumbling of the Soviet Union, the enforced Russian retreat from the Baltics, and rising crime. By the end of 1993, his range of fire was wider. Two years of economic shock therapy, the decline in most Russians' living standards, the havoc of short-time working and unemployment, and the emergence of a layer of aggressive new rich who flaunted what everyone assumed was ill-gotten wealth gave Zhirinovsky his chance. He projected himself as a 'third force' which could offer Russians hope where first the Communists and later the democrats had failed. He tapped into the well of resentment, despair, and confusion which had built up over the five years since perestroika had started to flounder. Although most Russians accepted the retreat from empire calmly at the time, it lingered under the surface as one factor in a wider feeling of a world turned upside down.

Zhirinovsky had once made an issue of having Jewish connections. Moscow Jews remembered him as an active director of a Jewish cultural organization founded in 1989. He reportedly described his father, Volf, as a Jew who married a Russian. Volf died in a car crash soon after Vladimir was born in 1946. He had moved to Kazakhstan from Poland. His son later blurred his father's ethnic background and in his autobiography merely describes Volf as a name 'not very familiar to a Russian ear'. Called Shalom, the cultural organization Zhirinovsky worked for was intended by the authorities to rival VAAD, an independent Jewish movement emerging under glasnost. But colleagues of that time say Zhirinovsky fought to steer it free of Soviet control by helping to expel several directors linked to a notorious Cold War front organization, the Anti-Zionist Committee.

Alexander Smukler, a leader of VAAD who later emigrated from Russia, told the *New York Times* that Moscow Jews had doubts about Zhirinovsky's motives. 'He always identified himself as a Jew but we thought he was a stranger in our movement. In 1990, when he was elected chairman of the Liberal Democratic Party, that was the end of our relationship,' he said. 'I know him well. I met him dozens of times. He's a brilliant politician. He makes talented speeches, but at the same time he's a populist, who will say anything to reach his goal, and his goal is power.'

Since those days Zhirinovsky has made frequent comments verging on anti-Semitism. At his first press conference after his December 1993 triumph, he called for Jewish television announcers to be replaced by 'pure Russians' and said Jews should be proud of Israel, 'the richest country in the world'. During the election campaign he posed as the only candidate who understood Russians' national humiliation, the plight of millions of refugees driven out of the Caucasus and Central Asia, and the anger of thousands of army officers hastily displaced from their flats in East Germany and the Baltic states and sent off to homelessness in Russia. Zhirinovsky said he had no plan to restore the empire by force, but he made millions of Russians feel good by claiming that the former Soviet republics would soon go down on their knees and beg to be taken back in. He even boasted that Russian troops would eventually move south beyond the old borders of the Tsars and wash their feet in the Indian ocean. Politically, it was absurd. Psychologically, it was powerful.

While Zhirinovsky's lurid sabre-rattling captured most of the international headlines, Russian commentators and politicians ascribed his success to his promises on domestic policy. Exit polls found that people voted for him because of anger over economic hardship and in protest at the government's indifference rather than because they supported the restoration of the Soviet system. Russia has no history of fascism, so that to call Zhirinovsky a 'fascist' made little sense. He is a populist, an extreme right-winger, and a nationalist.

Gennady Zyuganov, the leader of the revived Communist party, also strongly attacked Yeltsin's economic failings and appealed to nostalgia, though without Zhirinovsky's wild foreign policy predictions. He performed well in the polls by taking 12 per cent, only one point less than Yegor Gaidar's pro-government block, Russia's Choice. But Zyuganov had two disadvantages. In spite of repeated pledges to respect Russia's new political pluralism and his attempt to exploit nationalistic themes (he was a founder of the National Salvation Front which Yeltsin later banned), Zyuganov was tarred with the Communist brush. He spoke moderately and looked conventional.

Zhirinovsky, by contrast, thrived on unpredictability. When he strode on to the world stage at his first press conference after victory, he wore a dinner jacket and dark-grey silk bow-tie. 'Why a dinner-jacket?' a reporter asked. 'Why not a dinner-jacket?' he shot back. 'We're for pluralism of dress.' The clothes matched one side of his image as a fast-talking, deadpan music-hall entertainer. But the political content was deadly serious. To millions of Russians he seemed to be a down-to-earth, ordinary 'muzhik' (little man) who understood their anger. For those who had watched Yeltsin's growing challenge to Gorbachev three years earlier, there was a strange sense of roles reversed. Yeltsin's initial electoral appeal also rested in large part on his image as a plain-talking 'muzhik'. In his case it was enhanced by the aura of martyr and defector. He was a senior figure of the apparat who had dared to speak out against privilege and suffered punishment for it.

Zhirinovsky's career was different. It had always been humble, and in the December 1993 elections he used his 'muzhik' qualities to even better effect than Yeltsin. Whereas Yeltsin was slow and ponderous, a man of instinct more than intelligence, Zhirinovsky was bright and quick. His victory posed a fearful challenge to Yeltsin. A presidential contest between the two men would be the elephant against the gnat.

Zhirinovsky was greatly helped by Yeltsin's election rules. The president's advisers had spent part of the summer, arguing over the right scheme for choosing the Lower House of a new Russian parliament. The tactical requirement was for the reformists to win. The strategic one was to encourage the development of a multi-party system. The rules for the last three Russian elections had been based on the French system, in which candidates ran in constituencies, and a second round was held between the top two candidates if no one won over half the votes in the first round. Some experts whom Yeltsin's team consulted said there was no reason to change it. Running candidates in constituencies did not prevent parties from developing. On the contrary, it could help them to put down local roots by making sure they were spread throughout Russia. Other advisers said a list system with votes being distributed by proportional representation was better. It would give the embryonic parties more visibility through having a nationwide set of names, and ensure that several got into parliament. The sub-text was that the reformists were not well organized in the provinces, but had plenty of well-known people, including government ministers. The list system would turn the election into a kind of national beauty contest and minimize the need for local campaigning.

After lengthy argument a compromise was adopted with half the seats to be chosen by lists, and half in constituencies (though without the second-round run-off). For Zhirinovsky, the star system was perfect. Although he had organizers in many areas, he was the only well-known figure in the party. In the reformist camp, the star system backfired. It opened up splits, as the most ambitious men decided to form their own lists with themselves as number one, rather than unite. Four reformist lists emerged, only one of which was even called a party. Of the other nine groups which managed to pass the complex barrier for being registered four called themselves parties. Most preferred to be described as blocks or movements. Many were formed simply for the purpose of running in the poll, and would probably fade away afterwards. Even the more solid-looking ones were in reality fragile. Leaders of Russia's Choice, the best-known of the pro-government groups, openly quarrelled during the campaign, and in many constituencies candidates from the pro-Yeltsin grass-roots movement, Democratic Russia, broke from Russia's Choice and ran independently.

For Yeltsin the results of the election were a bitter blow. They left a parliament which was even less willing to do his bidding than the one he had dissolved. The forty members from Russia's Choice were the only ones he could rely on. In addition to Zhirinovsky's party (59 seats), the Communists (32) and their allies, the Agrarian Party (21), were against him on most issues. There were two centrist groups, Women of Russia (21) and the Democratic Party of Russia (14). Grigory Yavlinsky's block (20) and Sergei Shakhrai's Party of Russian Unity and Consensus (18) might sometimes support Yeltsin, but not always. On the surprise vote to amnesty Rutskoi and Khasbulatov, Shakhrai's group supported the majority, which went 252 to 67 in favour of the motion, giving Yeltsin a humiliating defeat. They also voted to make Ivan Rybkin, the head of the Communist faction in the last parliament, the new speaker.

The December poll, with its implicit rejection of economic shock therapy, since every party except Russia's Choice condemned it during the campaign, forced Yeltsin to change his government. Yegor Gaidar and Boris Fyodorov, the monetarist Finance Minister, were left out. Viktor Chernomyrdin, the Prime Minister, gained influence and made it clear he sided more with the new majority in parliament than with Yeltsin. It was another victory for the old economic nomenklatura, who wanted a more gradual shift to the market, a form of privatization which would maintain their control over industry, and a government more willing to provide factories with finance.

The third disaster for Yeltsin, making his October victory over the last parliament look Pyrrhic, was the new political influence of the army. Having 'saved' the President by agreeing to use tanks, they exacted a price. They would be consulted more frequently on foreign policy. The only consolation for the president was that he had his new constitution which gave him extra power over parliament. He could legislate by decree without reference to the deputies. But it soon became clear that the new constitution was as flexible – and ignorable – as the last one. The change was that this time parliament began to connive with the president in setting it aside. In the spring of 1994 the parliamentary leadership joined the president in discussions to overturn the requirements for new elections at the end of 1995 and for a presidential poll in 1996. Fear of another Zhirinovsky success and of further alienation by the public from politicians in general led to the argument that it would be better to postpone elections until the end of the century.

While the main reason for the difficulty of building democracy in Russia is the country's age-old culture of authoritarianism, the job was made worse after 1991 by the sharpening of the economic crisis. In the wake of the failed putsch some Western observers and most Western governments urged the Russian leadership to put the primacy on economic change. They argued that dismantling the state-dominated economic system was the priority, even if it meant taking unpopular decisions and a cut in living standards. The process of reform was bound to be painful and it was better to conduct the surgery quickly. It was also claimed that until there was a layer of wealthy entrepreneurs in parliament, backed by a society of middle-level property owners, there could be no democracy.

I have sought to show that the development of a political culture of peaceful conflict-resolution and mutual give-and-take must go hand-in-hand with economic change, if not precede it. Western advisers who pressed for rapid economic change claimed that reform would only work if done drastically and all at once. Many also had a barely veiled and destructive political agenda, the notion that, unless the old system was smashed, Communism could return. It was the 'Dracula Syndrome', the lurid belief that unless a stake was driven through the heart of the corpse, it might yet revive. I believe the idea was mistaken. The collapse of the August coup showed that, as a dominant system of organizing power in Russia, Communism was discredited and gone beyond recall. If opposition to market reforms were to grow, it would be the result of a new social and economic crisis, not the consequence of old institutions. The far right's victory in the December 1993 elections confirmed this. Zhirinovsky prided himself on never having been a member of the Communist party. He made it clear he had no wish to restore centralized control over the economy.

If Yeltsin and the Western governments which supported him had concentrated on creating a more conciliatory political atmosphere once Communist party rule had collapsed, as well as on encouraging a more gradual process of economic change, they could have cut some of the ground from under Zhirinovsky. The leadership of Russia's parliament and the deputies share some of the blame for the failure to find compromises, but Yeltsin as the man in charge had the prime responsibility to set the tone. For over a year before he dissolved it, he did not appear in the Supreme Soviet. He never invited the faction leaders to the Kremlin to consult or negotiate with him individually as an American or French president does. By treating parliament with growing contempt, which culminated in the storming of the building, Yeltsin created a climate of wilfulness. If Russia's elite could gamble so carelessly with power, why should the simple voter not do the same and cast a vote for an adventurer like Zhirinovsky? Yeltsin's desire for a democratic Russia might not be in doubt. What caught the eye was his methods.

I have also suggested in this book that the Yeltsin team was wrong to allow the ideology of privatization in Russian industry to take precedence over more important issues such as changing managers and financing the introduction of new technology. The type of privatization conducted by the Russian government, in a context of a society without law and or a sense of social responsibility among the elite, too often turned into corruption and the theft of state property without encouraging long-term investment, the development of a capital market, or management reform. On paper, the results were impressive. By early 1994 roughly a third of the 14,000 largest companies, employing 20 million workers, had become private. The change was often in name only. Workers now held pieces of paper called shares, and were told they were part-owners of the factory. But the managers were the same, and in many cases the plants still relied on state orders. There was no new investment for modernization.

In the pre-Gorbachev era Russia was sometimes labelled 'Upper

Volta with rockets'. It was an inaccurate phrase, suggesting that Russia was essentially an under-developed country except for its military sector. In fact, by 1985 Russia's civilian sector was more developed than most of the rest of the world with the exception of the advanced capitalist states. It had a working infrastructure of communications, energy, and transport superior to that of the typical Third World country, as well as a domestic consumer goods and engineering industry, producing everything from cars and refrigerators to passenger aircraft and computers. The quality of the products was not up to that of the advanced industrial countries, and the environmental damage caused by Soviet mines, chemical factories, and metal works was immense, but the level of economic development was high by world standards. The lifting of restrictions on civil liberty as the Soviet system ended left Russia with a good potential for evolving into an industrial democracy with a strong social consensus, unlike most of Africa or Latin America – mass literacy, an efficient and almost universal school system, a high degree of urbanization, and a relatively equal distribution of income. What was lacking was any practice of democracy, or the institutions which would encourage it to grow.

One reason why efforts to introduce IMF-style 'shock therapy' ran into such political resistance in the Russian parliament may seem paradoxical. In a sense, Russia was too democratic for it. The spirit of protest was strong. Governments in Egypt, Zambia, Ghana and General Pinochet's Chile were able to enforce it on submissive populations. Russia was in a different league. Although the country was not democratic enough to have a functioning and stable balance of power between the executive and legislature, or a system of competing parties, Russian politicians, journalists, and industrial managers were able to criticize and resist what they did not like. So too were Russian voters. The December 1993 election was not as free and fair as it should have been, since the government still exerted huge control over broadcasting, but it was much freer than elections in most Third World countries.

If Yuri Andropov, the first Soviet leader to make a cautious effort at reform after the stagnation of the Brezhnev period, had been able to return to Russia ten years after his death in early 1984, he would have found a country that was, at first blush, unrecognizable. It was not just that the country had shrunk in size, with the Kremlin now ruling over 150 rather than 300 million people, nor that the Communist party was out of power. The shift in people's attitudes was the major new factor. Conformity, the worst legacy of seventy years of totalitarian rule, had disappeared. The crushing anxiety about putting a foot wrong was gone.

Moscow was full of foreign advisers, journalists, and businessmen while Russians were able to get passports and travel abroad in huge numbers. There were no queues in the shops and the assortment of goods was unbelievably wide. Kiwi-fruit and avocado pears which Russians had never seen in their lives were being sold at roadside stalls. Bananas, which the authorities used to put out on public sale as a special treat only on important occasions like Communist Party Congresses or the 1980 Olympics, were in every fruit shop and market.

The new freedom allowed all the previously repressed groups in Russian society to emerge into the open. Priests could walk in the street in their robes and black hats instead of leaving them behind inside their churches. People on crutches or in wheelchairs appeared in public and Russians suddenly became aware of a whole category of people who had been shut up at home or in institutions because they undermined the image of a society of strong and healthy citizens. The laws that had made homosexual activity punishable by imprisonment were repealed. The one area where there was no advance, but rather a slight retreat, was in the public position of women. Russia remained a strongly patriarchal society. With the collapse of the quota system for women, the new parties and political institutions were more male-dominated than the old ones. Unemployment hit women first, and the closing of free kindergartens because of budget cuts also forced many mothers who wanted to work to stay at home. The emergence of porn magazines and sex clubs added to the degradation. In strong protest at these developments voters in the December 1993 elections propelled a new political entity, Women of Russia, into fourth place in the Lower House of parliament, ahead of three other pro-reform blocks.

On the positive side private business – once damned as 'speculation' – was legal, and any enterprising person was able to start a company. The freest men in Russia were indeed the businessmen, and not just those who began from nothing. The first laws on state enterprises in 1987 which had allowed them to become 'self-accounting' were followed by the slackening of 'state orders' so that managers had to find their own suppliers and customers. With the breakdown of economic ties which accompanied the collapse of the Soviet Union, managers were forced into total independence, a process which many were only too happy to exploit. They used their monopolistic position to make barter deals, rack up prices, or sell scarce raw materials and metals abroad without declaring their profits.

Even before the battle between parliament and president reached its bloody climax in October 1993 the cascade of changes left many Russians in despair. They complained that the lifting of the externally imposed constraints of totalitarianism had revealed a society without any form of self-discipline. People were enjoying freedom without responsibility. The removal of the pervasive ideology of Communism with its claim to be building a new structure of common values left a moral vacuum which could not easily be filled. The concept of a public interest was virtually abandoned. According to the prevailing new orthodoxy, the individual had to act on his own, for himself and his family. Coupled with the long absence of material plenty, this created a drive for satisfaction that became a race to get rich quick, regardless of the method.

The collapse of Soviet order uncovered a society without law. Accustomed to equality, many Russians resented the way the new rich had gained their wealth so crudely and so fast. The middle-aged and the elderly reverted to nostalgia, looking back to the Brezhnev era with fondness. The terror of Stalin's time had gone by then, and under Brezhnev life was at least predictable and economically secure. Zhirinovsky's campaign appealed to this longing for the past. At the other extreme were those who wanted the country to move even more rapidly to the market economy, partly, they said, so as to forestall any reimposition of central control.

In the anxiety of the mid-1990s, and still angry at their enforced ignorance and silence during the Stalinist period, most Russian analysts argued that the rampant crime, the absence of respect for law, the economic chaos, the cynicism, and the political mud-slinging showed that Soviet rule had damaged Russian society more deeply than anyone had expected. A few began to look back to pre-revolutionary Russian history. The fact that a totalitarian system had taken hold in Russia and survived for so long was not the malaise itself but the symptom of a deeper disease. Russia had never had the institutions of democracy, nor the inter-action of organized citizens and an accountable state which allow for civilized government.

Amid all the difficulties, the most encouraging feature of life in Russia as the Communist system imploded and in the years of radical change which followed was the lack of street violence. While ethnic conflict and war raged in many parts of the Commonwealth of Independent States, in Russia itself there was remarkable calm. Even the events round the White House in October 1993 remained localized. I commented earlier on the resigned popular reaction to the withdrawal of the pre-1993 banknotes and the dispassionate way most Russians accepted their loss of empire. On May Day 1993 a clash between anti-Yeltsin marchers and the militia left one policeman dead, crushed when demonstrators commandeered a lorry and reversed it into a group of policemen. The Russian press and politicians responded with alarm verging on hysteria. There was much talk of a new civil war, which started up again as a result of the October events. Russians were surprised when foreigners pointed out that demonstrations in the West frequently produced street clashes and that Western cities could tolerate sporadic bombings and urban terrorism without this meaning that all social controls had broken down.

Some Russians argued that their country's social peace was deceptive. The Russian people was unpredictable, and if its patience snapped, the bloodshed would be immeasurable. They were right that the absence of a civil society and the network of restraints which it creates can lead to extremism. The argument reinforced the need for the process of democratic reform not to be stopped.

Unfortunately, the second half of 1993 suggested that the trend was going the other way. There appeared to be a retreat towards authoritarianism. The December elections were the first multi-party poll since 1917 but they were not the first free and fair elections. In 1989 and 1990, and in the presidential poll of 1991, Russians had had a genuine choice of candidates. What made the 1993 poll less impressive than the 1991 race when Yeltsin swept into the presidency was the government's tighter control over television, and the way the administration frequently changed the rules.

Throughout its history Russia has suffered long stretches of immobility, punctuated by upheavals of sudden reform or revolution. The liberalization of Alexander the Second in the 1860s, Nicholas the Second's grudging concessions to parliament after the failed uprising of 1905, and the Bolshevik revolution of October 1917 were all followed by consolidation and reaction. In each case the same men who started the reforms later ended them. Would future historians see the Gorbachev/Yeltsin years of democratic change from 1985 to 1993 as part of a similar pattern – Russia's fourth period of aborted liberalization?

Even before the shock of Zhirinovsky's strong showing in the elections, the government had begun to re-assert control over investment decisions, industrial policy, and foreign trade. A more authoritarian kind of democracy was creeping in, with the president making it abundantly clear that he wanted greater power for the executive and a reduced role for parliament. By voting for the far right, a sizeable section of the population showed it wanted tough action. The love affair with the outside world was also fading, as Russians began to speak more loudly of the need to defend national interests.

These trends did not mean that Russia was reverting to the past, or was doomed to a new tyranny. Nor did they signify the sputtering out of another 'Westernizing' phase in Russian history. The enormous gains of the post-1985 period would not be reversed in their entirety. Thanks to modern communications and the television revolution Russia was too integrated into the outside world for a majority to want to return to cultural isolation. But for most Russians the false euphoria of 1991 was over.

Spurred by Zhirinovsky's victory and their growing awareness of Yeltsin's failings, some Western observers belatedly began to remember Russia's long history of authoritarianism before Communism. In 1991, they had expected a quick switch to democracy. Now they tended to give up. The new priority for Russia was said to be stability, even if that meant a certain amount of authoritarianism to keep the Russian beast in check. That is not my argument here. Russia has suffered a troubled and bloody past. It has had little chance to develop a civil society. But unless the process of democratic reform is carried forward, civil society will not be able to grow. The stability of repression is always more apparent than real, and eventually leads to social and political explosions.

While an elite alone cannot change a country, since political advance is a complicated process in which all layers of society have to be involved, an elite has a key responsibility. The example which it gives in upholding the law and peacefully resolving conflicts among its own members inevitably sets the tone for others. The tragedy of Russia's 'democrats' in the first years after the collapse of Communism was that they seemed unable to encourage pluralism, tolerance, and the search for compromise. Without these values, Russia would take a long time to evolve towards genuine democracy, if ever.

Notes

For full details of books cited, please see the Select Bibliography.

INTRODUCTION

1 Jane Burbank, *Intelligentsia and Revolution*, p.194.

1 FIRST SHOOTS OF A CIVIL SOCIETY

1 *Guardian*, 12 September 1987.
2 *Smena*, no.12, 1987, p.5.

2 THE LEADERS' LEGACY

1 Interview with author.
2 *Argumenty i Fakty*, 27 April 1993.
3 Tass, 11 July 1988.
4 Interview with author, July 1992.
5 Interview with author, December 1991.
6 Angus Roxburgh, *The Second Russian Revolution*, p.8. This book was based on the eight-part television series of the same name, produced by Norma Percy and made by Brian Lapping Associates for the British Broadcasting Corporation. I am grateful to Norma Percy and Brian Lapping for permission to read and quote from the transcripts (hereafter referred to as Lapping, TV series).
7 Interview with author, December 1992.
8 Alexander Yakovlev, *Predisloviye, Obval, Poslesloviye (Foreword, Collapse, Postscript)*, p.135.

9 Interview with author, July 1992.
10 Interview with author, December 1992.
11 Interview with author, October 1992.
12 Interview with author, January 1993.
13 Nikolai Ryzhkov, *Perestroika, Istoriya Predatel'stv* (*Perestroika, a Story of Betrayals*), p.82.
14 Ibid., p.114.
15 Boris Yeltsin, *The View from the Kremlin*, p.290.

3 THE ROOTS OF FAILURE

1 From the archives of the second Duma, quoted in E. Vasilievvskii, 'Sotsial' no-ekonomicheskoye soderzhaniye krest'yanskikh prigorov i nakazov' ('The Socio-economic Content of peasants' instructions and *mandates*'), *Uchenniye zapiski MGU*, 1956.
2 Richard Pipes, *Russia under the Old Regime*, p.155.
3 Teodor Shanin, *Russia as a 'Developing Society'*, p.81.
4 Teodor Shanin, *Russia, 1905–07, Revolution as a Moment of Truth*, p.122.
5 Yuri Tolstoy, *Perviye Sorok Let Snosheniii mezhdu Rossiyu i Angliyu, 1553–1593* (*First Forty Years of Relations Between Russia and England*), St Petersburg, 1875, quoted in Pipes, op.cit., p.77.
6 Teodor Shanin, *Russia as a 'Developing Society'*, p.119.
7 Jane Burbank, *Intelligentsia and Revolution*, p.120.
8 Ibid., p.198.
9 *Belinsky, Chernyshevsky, and Dobrolyubov: Selected Criticism*, edited by Ralph E. Matlaw, New York, 1962, pp.86–7.
10 Isaac Deutscher, *The Prophet Armed*, p.188.
11 *Listener*, 2 May 1968.
12 'Razmyshleniya o russkoi revolyutsii' ('Thoughts on the Russian Revolution'), in *Russkaya Mysl'*, January-February, 1921, p.20.
13 'Patriotica', in *Smena Vekh: sbornik statiei* (*Landmarks: Collection of Articles*), Prague, 1921, pp.52–3.

4 A VERY RUSSIAN COUP

1 *Pravda*, 6 November 1991.
2 Interview with *Moskovskaya Pravda*, 31 August 1991.
3 Interview in *Kuranty*, 12 December 1991.
4 Lapping, TV series, Programme Eight.

5 Interview with *Izvestiya*, 30 September 1991. Anatoly Chernyayev, Gorbachev's aide, was also imprisoned at Foros with the president.
6 Interview with author, *Guardian*, 29 September 1991.
7 Interview with author, 9 December 1992.
8 Mikhail Gorbachev, *Augustovski Putsch* (*August Coup*), p.11.
9 Vadim Bakatin, *Izbavlyeniye ot Illyuzii* (*Escaping from Illusions*), p.162.
10 Interview with author, January 1993.
11 Interview with author, January 1993.
12 *Nezayisimaya Gazeta*, 5 September 1991.
13 *Komsomolskaya Pravda*, 24 August 1991.
14 *Argumenty i Fakty*, no.33, 1991.
15 Lapping, TV series, Programme Eight.
16 Interview with author, January 1993.

5 CHALLENGE TO THE PARTY

1 Vadim Bakatin. *Izbavlyeniye ot Illyuzii*, p. 88.
2 Interview with author, January 1993.
3 Nikolai Ryzhkov, *Perestroika, Istoriya Predatel'stv*, p. 275.
4 Interview with author, December 1992.
5 Alexander Rahr, 'Turnover in the Soviet Nomenklatura?', Radio Liberty Research Bulletin, Munich, 15 June 1988.
6 Reuters, 8 December 1987.
7 Interview with author, January 1993.
8 Angus Roxburgh, *The Second Russian Revolution*, p. 86.
9 Interview with author, 28 July 1992.
10 Interview with author, 19 August 1992.
11 Alexander Yakovlev, *Predisloviye, Obval, Poslesloviye*, p. 128.
12 Yegor Ligachev, *Zagadka Gorbacheva* (*Riddle of Gorbachev*), p. 141.
13 Speech to representatives of the mass media, 14 July 1987, published by Novosti, Moscow.
14 *Pravda*, 19 March 1989.
15 Lev Sukhanov, *Tri Goda s Yeltsinym*, (*Three Years with Yeltsin*), p. 240.
16 *Pravda*, 11 November 1988.
17 Interview with author, January 1993.
18 Nikolai Ryzhkov, op.cit., p. 284.
19 Interview with author, January 1993.

6 THE FAILURE OF REFORM

1 Central Television, 16 February 1989.
2 *Pravda*, 9 May 1990.
3 Interview with author, 15 August 1991.
4 Interview with author, January 1993.
5 Interview with author, October 1992.
6 Interview with author, October 1992.
7 Manuscript of book by Shakhnazarov, shown to author.
8 Interview with author, 19 August 1992.
9 Interview with author, 15 August 1991.
10 Interview with author, 21 December 1992.

7 THE IMPERIAL RINGS

1 *Polnoye sobraniye sochinenii (Complete Works)*, St Petersburg, 1896, p. 523.
2 Alexander Solzhenitsyn, 'How to reconstitute Russia?', *Komsomolskaya Pravda*, 18 September 1990.
3 *Observer*, 5 July 1992.
4 Nikolai Ryzhkov, *Perestroika, Istoriya Predatel'stv*, p. 200.
5 Evan Mawdsley, *The Russian Civil War*, p. 282.
6 *Izvestiya Tsk KPSS*, Moscow, no. 9, 1989. pp. 191–218.
7 *Washington Post*, 16 November 1992.
8 Interview with author, January 1993.
9 Cordovez interview with author, 29 January 1985.
10 *Washington Post*, 16 November 1992.
11 *Trud*, 24 October 1991.
12 The cables were published in the Moscow paper, *Sovershenno Sekretno*, no. 9 (40), 1992.
13 *Literaturnaya Gazeta*, 17 February 1988.
14 Tass, 25 April 1987.
15 Interview with author, 19 August 1992.
16 Interview with author, 21 December 1992.
17 Tass, 11 March 1985.
18 Interview with author, 19 August 1992.
19 Interview with author, September 1992.
20 *Guardian*, 12 June 1989.
21 *Izvestiya*, 20 August 1989.

22 Archives of the general department of the central committee of the CPSU, Folio 89, List 9, Document 33, 28 September 1989.
23 *Guardian*, 18 May 1989.
24 *Izvestiya*, 21 August 1989.
25 Lapping, TV series, Programme Five.
26 Ibid.
27 Eduard Shevardnadze, *Moi Vybor* (*My Choice*), Novosti, Moscow, 1991, p. 225.

8   THE SOVIET DISUNION

1 *La Stampa*, Milan, 1 September 1988.
2 Interview with Japanese TV company NHK, published in *New Times*, Moscow, no. 12, 1992.
3 Dzintra Bungs, 'Migration to and from Latvia', Radio Liberty, Report on the USSR, Munich, 14 September 1990.
4 Associated Press, 14 January 1991.
5 Interview with author, January 1993.
6 Interview with Japanese TV company NHK, op. cit.
7 Archives of the general department of the central committee of the CPSU, Folio 89, List 9, Document 28, 30 August 1989.
8 Interview with author, January 1993.
9 *Izvestiya Tsk KPSS*, no. 6, 1990.
10 Radio Vilnius, monitored in BBC Summary of World Broadcasts, 15 January 1990.
11 Quoted by Bohdan Krawchenko, *Social Change and National Consciousness in Twentieth-Century Ukraine*, p.40. His book is by far the best recent analysis of Ukrainian society before perestroika. Lenin's 1914 speech was dropped from the Soviet editions of his works because it advocated the independence of Ukraine.
12 Ibid., p.24.
13 Interview with author, December 1991.

9   RUSSIA *v.* THE USSR; YELTSIN *v.* GORBACHEV

1 Transcript supplied by Tass, 12 December 1991.
2 Mikhail Gorbachev, *Dekabr'-91*, p.120.
3 Interview with author, 15 January 1993.
4 Boris Yeltsin, *Against the Grain*, p.143.

5 Interview with author, January 1993.
6 Boris Yeltsin op. cit., p.154.
7 Lev Sukhanov, *Tri Goda s Yeltsinym*, p.40.
8 Interview with author, January 1993.
9 Interview with author, December 1992.
10 Interview with author, January 1993.
11 Lev Sukhanov, op. cit., p.150.
12 Andrei Grachev, an advance excerpt from his book, *Gorbachev's Shipwreck*, published in *Moscow News*, no. 45, 1992.
13 Ibid.

10 PARLIAMENT, SOVIET-STYLE

1 *Guardian*, 24 June 1989.
2 *Guardian*, 2 June 1989.
3 Radio Moscow, 4 August 1989.
4 Radio Moscow, 23 October 1989.
5 *Guardian*, 28 February 1990.
6 Radio Moscow, 21 September 1990.
7 *Los Angeles Times*, 20 June 1991.

11 LURE OF THE STRONG HAND

1 *'Neopublikovannaya Stat'ya, Zven'iya* (Unpublished Article), Moscow, 1934, vol. III/IV, p.380.
2 *Literaturnaya Gazeta*, 16 August 1989.
3 Richard Pipes, *Russia under the Old Regime*, p.271.
4 Interview with author, *Guardian*, 24 December 1992.
5 A. Sobyanin, E. Gelman, Ekspertnaya informatsionno-analiticheskaya gruppa, *Degree of Support among Deputies for the Course of Radical Political and Economic Reforms*, Moscow, December 1992.
6 *Guardian*, 19 October 1992.
7 Findings published in *Partinform*, no. 2, 1993, published by Informatsionno-izdatel'sky Komplex 'Delo'.
8 *Moscow Times*, 28 January 1993.

12 BIG SHOCK, LITTLE THERAPY

1 *Nezavisimaya Gazeta*, 27 February 1992.
2 Interview with Independent Television News, 14 February 1992.
3 Russian Television News, 28 October 1991.
4 Michael Ellman, 'Shock Therapy in Russia: Failure or partial success?', Radio Free Europe/Radio Liberty Research Report, Munich, 28 August 1992.
5 Reuters, 27 January 1993.
6 *Ekonomika i Zhizn*, no. 10, 1992.
7 Philip Hanson, 'The Russian Budget Crisis', Radio Free Europe/Radio Liberty Research Report, 3 April 1992.
8 *Ekonomika i Zhizn*, no. 26, 1992.
9 *Guardian*, 28 April 1992.
10 *Nezavisimaya Gazeta*, 28 November 1992.
11 *Guardian*, 28 April 1992.
12 Michael Ellman, op. cit.
13 *Pravda*, 13 January 1988.
14 *Moscow Times*, 27 January 1993.
15 *Nezavisimaya Gazeta*, 28 November 1992.
16 Meeting with Foreign Correspondents' Association, October 1992.
17 *Assessment of the food situation and outlook in the republics of the former USSR in 1992–93*, UN Food and Agriculture Organization, Rome, 15 September 1992.
18 *Rossiiskaya Gazeta*, 25 July 1992.
19 Lapping, TV series, Programme Four.
20 Ibid.
21 *Results of a Sociological Inquiry*, Centre for Sociological Research, Belovo, October 1992.

13 NATIONALISM AT A LOW LEVEL

1 *Guardian*, 30 March 1991.
2 *Guardian*, 4 April 1991.
3 Alexander Rahr, 'Rutskoi challenges Yeltsin', Radio Free Europe/Radio Liberty Research Reports, 28 February 1992.

14   A LAW-BASED STATE

1 Nikolai Ryzhkov, *Perestroika, Istoriya Predatel'stv*, p.124.
2 Interview with Judge Ernest Ametistov, *Sevodnya*, 2 March 1993.
3 *Newsweek*, 31 August 1992.
4 *Moscow Times*, 4 December 1992.
5 Tass, 12 February 1993.
6 Ibid.
7 *Moscow Times*, 17 May 1994.
8 Ibid.

15   THE 'NEW RUSSIA'

1 From 'Rules for a Ruler' in *The History of a Certain Town*, 1869.
2 Yuri Afanasyev quoted in Stephen Handelman, 'A Pre-Modern Society', *Moscow Times*, 12 May 1993.
3 *Sevodnya*, 23 April 1993.
4 *Guardian*, 8 October 1992.

16   OCTOBER 1993

1 *Izvestiya*, 5 October 1993.
2 Richard Pipes, *The Russian Revolution*, p.553.
3 Boris Yeltsin, *The View from the Kremlin*, p.269.
4 *Moscow News*, 3 October 1993.
5 *Nezavisimaya Gazeta*, 8 October 1993.

Select Bibliography

Abalkin, Leonid, *Neispol'zovanny Shans, Politizdat* (*Missed Chance*), Moscow, 1991.

Afanasyev, Yuri, *Ya Dolzhen Eto Skazat'* (*I Must Say*), Pik, Moscow, 1991.

Ali, Tariq, *Revolution from Above*, Hutchinson, London, 1988.

Bakatin, Vadim, *Izbavlyeniye ot Illyuzii* (*Escaping from Illusions*), Kemerovo, 1992.

Barnett, Anthony, *Soviet Freedom*, Picador, London, 1988.

Beschloss, Michael and Talbott, Strobe, *At the Highest Levels*, Little, Brown and Company, London, 1993.

Blackburn, Robin (editor), *After the Fall*, Verso, London, 1991.

Burbank, Jane, *Intelligentsia and Revolution, Russian Views of Bolshevism, 1917–22*, Oxford University Press, 1986.

Cohen, Stephen, *Rethinking the Soviet Experience*, Oxford University Press, 1985.

Cohen, Stephen and van den Heuvel, Katrina, *Voices of Glasnost*, W.W. Norton, New York, 1989.

Custine, Marquis de, *Letters from Russia*, Penguin, London, 1991.

Danilov, V.P., *Rural Russia under the New Regime*, Hutchinson, London, 1988.

Davies, R.W., *Soviet History in the Gorbachev Revolution*, Macmillan, London, 1989.

Deutscher, Isaac, *The Prophet Armed*, Oxford University Press, 1987.

Doder, Dusko and Branson, Louise, *Gorbachev, Heretic in the Kremlin*, Macdonald, London, 1990.

Glebov, Oleg and Crowfoot, John (editors), *The Soviet Empire: Its Nations Speak Out*, Harwood, London, 1989.

Gorbachev, Mikhail, *Perestroika*, Collins, London, 1987.

———*Augustovsky Putsch* (*August Coup*), Novosti, Moscow, 1991.

———*Dekabr'*–*91* (*December*–*91*), Novosti, Moscow, 1992.

Hosking, Geoffrey, Aves, Jonathan and Duncan, Peter, *The Road to Post-Communism*, Pinter, London, 1992.

Kagarlitsky, Boris, *Farewell Perestroika: A Soviet Chronicle*, Verso, London, 1990.

Kotkin, Stephen, *Steeltown, USSR: Soviet Society in the Gorbachev Era*, University of California Press, Berkeley, 1991.

Krawchenko, Bohdan, *Social Change and National Consciousness in Twentieth-Century Ukraine*, Macmillan, London, 1985.

Lewin, Moshe, *The Gorbachev Phenomenon*, University of California Press, Berkeley, 1988.

Ligachev, Yegor, *Zagadka Gorbacheva* (*The Riddle of Gorbachev*). Interbuk, Novosibiirsk, 1992.

Mandel, Ernest, *Beyond Perestroika*, Verso, London, 1989.

Mawdsley, Evan, *The Russian Civil War*, Allen and Unwin, Boston, 1987.

Medvedev, Roy, *Let History Judge*, Macmillan, London, 1972.

Medvedev, Zhores, *Gorbachev*, Blackwell, Oxford, 1986.

Morrison, John, *Boris Yeltsin: From Bolshevik to Democrat*, Penguin, London, 1991.

Murarka, Dev, *Gorbachev, The Limits of Power*, Hutchinson, London, 1988.

Nove, Alec, *Glasnost in Action: Cultural Renaissance in Russia*, Unwin Hyman, Boston, 1989.

O'Clery, Conor, *Melting Snow: An Irishman in Moscow*, Appletree Press, Belfast, 1991.

Pipes, Richard, *Russia under the Old Regime*, Penguin, London, 1974.

———*The Russian Revolution, 1899–1919*, Fontana, London, 1990.

Reddaway, Peter (ed.), *Uncensored Russia:Protest and Dissent in the Soviet Union*, American Heritage Press, New York, 1972.

Roxburgh, Angus, *The Second Russian Revolution*, BBC Books, London, 1991.

Ryzhkov, Nikolai, *Perestroika, Istoriya Predatel'stv*, (*Perestroika, A Story of Betrayals*), Novosti, Moscow, 1992.

Shanin, Teodor, *Russia as a 'Developing Society'*, Macmillan, London, 1985.

———*Russia, 1905–07: Revolution as a Moment of Truth*, Macmillan, London, 1986.

Shevardnadze, Eduard, *Moi Vybor* (*My choice*), Novosti, Moscow, 1991.

SELECT BIBLIOGRAPHY

Simonia, Nodari, *Chto My Postroili* (*What We Have Built*), Progress, Moscow, 1991.

Sixsmith, Martin, *Moscow Coup*, Simon and Schuster, London, 1991.

Sobchak, Anatoly, *For a New Russia*, HarperCollins, New York, 1992.

Sukhanov, Lev, *Tri Goda s Yeltsinym* (*Three Years with Yeltsin*), Vaga, Riga, 1992.

Taheri, Amir, *Crescent in a Red Sky*, Hutchinson, London, 1989.

White, Stephen, *Gorbachev and After*, Cambridge University Press, Cambridge, 1992.

Wilson, Andrew and Bachkatov, Nina, *Living with Glasnost: Youth and Society in a Changing Russia*, Penguin, London, 1988.

Yakovlev, Alexander, *Predisloviye, Obval, Poslesloviye* (*Foreword, Collapse, Afterword*), Novosti, Moscow, 1992.

Yeltsin, Boris, *Against the Grain*, Cape, London, 1991.

——*The View from the Kremlin*, HarperCollins, London, 1994.

415

Chronology

1985   March: Gorbachev becomes general secretary of CPSU.

1986   January: Yeltsin becomes Moscow party secretary.
December: Sakharov released from internal exile.

1987   January: Gorbachev puts political reform on agenda of Central
Committee of party.
November: Gorbachev calls for re-evaluation of party history
on seventieth anniversary of revolution.
December: Yeltsin resigns as Moscow party secretary.

1988   July: Gorbachev proposes contested elections to a new
Congress of People's Deputics (Parliament).
October: Popular Fronts set up in Baltic republics.

1989   March: Elections to new Congress of People's Deputies.
June: Lithuanian Communist Party proposes break from
CPSU.
July: Miners' strikes.
December: Sakharov dies.

1990   February: Central Committee votes to end one-party rule.
March: Gorbachev elected by Congress as first executive
President of the USSR.
March: Lithuania declares independence.
March: Elections to new Russian Parliament.
June: Yeltsin elected chair of Russian Parliament; Parliament
adopts Russian declaration of sovereignty.

July: Last congress of CPSU; conflict between conservatives and reformers; Yeltsin resigns from party.

1991 January: Cabinet of Ministers appointed, with conservative Valentin Pavlov as Prime Minister.
January: Soviet troops storm TV tower in Lithuania and public buildings in Latvia in attempt to overthrow governments.
March: Referendum on changing nature of USSR.
June: Yeltsin's landslide victory in poll for Russian presidency.
August: Failed coup by hard-liners against Gorbachev. Yeltsin defends White House, Russian parliament building; CPSU dissolved.
September: Baltic states acquire independence.
December: Yeltsin, Kravchuk, and Shushkevich sign pact to end USSR. Gorbachev resigns. USSR dissolves.

1992 January: Yegor Gaidar ends price control, starts economic 'shock therapy'.
May: Russian parliament annuls 1954 transfer of Crimea to Ukraine.
October: Russian government starts 'voucher' privatization.
December: Russian Congress of People's Deputies withdraws Yeltsin's special powers; Chernomyrdin replaces Gaidar.

1993 March: Yeltsin survives impeachment attempt in Congress.
April: Yeltsin wins referendum on economic reforms.
September: Yeltsin's Decree number 1400 dissolves Congress. MPs remain in White House; constitutional court condemns President.
October: Storming of White House.
December: Elections to new Parliament: strong showing by Zhirinovsky, weak performance by Yeltsin's team.

1994 February: Parliament amnesties Rutskoi and Khasbulatov.
May: Solzhenitsyn returns to Russia.
June: Russia joins NATO's 'Partnership for Peace'.

Index

Bakatin, Vadim: August coup, 65–6, 68–9, 72; Lithuania issue, 201; presidential election, 125; quoted, 83; sacked by Gorbachev, 199
Baklanov, Oleg, 69, 70, 72
Baltic republics: elections, 209, 212; history, 154; independence vote, 32; nationalism, 31; Russian settlers, 155, 192; secession, 247, 265; Soviet troops, 148; Supreme Soviet legislation, 260; Yeltsin's attitude to independence, 189, 244, 328
Baltic Shipping Company, 130
banknote crisis, 359–62
Barannikov, Viktor, 40
Bardakov, Vladimir, 315
barter, 16, 47
Bartsov, Alexander, 314
Bashkin, Major General Gennady, 69
Bashkortostan, 339
Beda, Lieut-General A., 61
Beijing, 28, 180, 182
Belarus, 154, 228, 230–1, 248
Belinsky, Vissarion, 53
Belov, Vasily, 326
Berdyayev, Nikolai, xiv, xvi, 52–3
Berezov, Vladimir, 208
Berlin, Isaiah, 56
Berlin Wall, 28, 184, 186
Bessarabia, 159
Bessmertnykh, Alexander, 70, 137
Black Hundreds, 332
Blinikov, Nikolai, 101–2
Blokhin, Yuri, 266
Bogomolov, Oleg, 95
Bokarev, Aleksei, 318–19
Boldin, Valery, 69–70
Boldyrev, Yuri, 353–8
Bolsheviks: attitude to judges, 342; attitude to Kerensky government, 325; attitude to Soviet republics, 149, 159; 'dual power' concept, 283; internationalism, xiv; media presentation, xiii; neo-Bolshevism, 43, 271, 286; party membership, 86–7; Russian dictatorship, 272–3; slogans, 93
Bondarev, Yuri, 85, 122
Bonner, Yelena, 277
Brazauskas, Algirdas, 141, 206–7, 211–12
Brest agreement, 228–9, 231–2, 247, 248
Brezhnev, Leonid: Afghan intervention, 164;

165; attitude to demonstrations, 10; corruption, 350; death, 293; doctrine, 179; Gorbachev's criticisms, 270, 271; imprisonment of journalists, 8; industrial personnel, 24; personality, 33; Politburo, 84; regime, xvi, 110, 122, 286; Vysotsky's ballads, 11; Yeltsin appointment, 239
Bruck, Connie, 365
Bukhara, Emirate of, 208
Bukharin, Nikolai, 6
Bulgaria, 152, 176
Burbulis, Gennady: attitude to Congress, 285–8; Brest agreement, 231–2, 248; career, 230–1; Gaidar collaboration, 294; 'neo-Bolshevik', 286; relationship with Yeltsin, 230, 239, 243, 285–8; Rutskoi's distrust of, 335; sacked by Yeltsin, 288; views on Union treaty, 230
Bush, George, 61, 228, 241
Buzgalin, Alexander, 127, 129–30
Byelorussia, 126, 159, 160, 205–6, 209

Canadian Broadcasting Corporation, 351
cash: banknote crisis, 359–62; shortage, 302
Castro, Fidel, 150
Catherine the Great, 217
Ceausescu, Nicolae, 133, 185
Cekuolis, Algimantas, 206
Central Asia, 155, 161–2, 213, 311
Central Bank, 284, 296, 300, 302, 361–2
Central Economic Mathematical Institute, 293
Centre for Studying Public Opinion 76
Chaadayev, Peter, 267
Change – New Politics, 280, 289
Chechens, 333
Chekhov, Anton, 55
Chernobyl nuclear disaster, 13, 220, 221–2, 331
Chernomyrdin, Viktor, 38, 305
Chernyayev, Anatoly, 20, 24–5, 86–7, 97, 138
Chernyshev, Lieut-Colonel Vladimir, 213–14
China: reforms, 23, 94–5; response to Gorbachev, 28–9; Tienanmen Square, 180
Chornovil, Vyacheslav, 224
Christian Democratic Party, 277
Chubais, Anatoly: banknote crisis, 361; foreign correspondents' dinner, 285; privatization minister, 285, 293, 306, 310, 354–5; relationship with Gaidar, 293, 306

Jakes, Milos, 182–3
Jarmalavicius, Juozas, 198–9
Jaruzelski, General Wojciech, 180
Jews, 156, 332, *see also* anti-Semitism
judges, 342, 347–8, 350

Kagarlitsky, Boris, 8–9
Kalashnikov, Vladimir, 121, 123, 257
Karmal, Babrak, 165, 168–70
Kashpirovsky, Anatoly, 53
Kazakhstan: Brest agreement, 228, 247; Fifteen plus Zero proposal, 247; nationalism, 157; nuclear weapons, 231; Russian border threat, 248; Russian population, 155, 157
Kazakov, Ivan, 311–12
Kazannik, Alexei, 377
Kerensky, Alexander, 325
KGB: Afghanistan exhibition, 164–5; August coup, 60–1, 65, 72, 78; control of, 6; dismantled, xv; economic reports, 20; headquarters, 15, 133; Memorial demonstration, 15; phone tapping, 11; Yeltsin's plans, 116, 229, 245–6, 344
Khasbulatov, Ruslan: background, 37, 282; banknote crisis, 361–2; compromise meeting, 349; coup rumours, 285; economic policies, 305; October 1993 siege, 375–85; opposition to Yeltsin, 37, 288, 290; powers, 282
Khatuntsev, Boris, 155–6
Khodyrev, Vladimir, 113
Khomeini, Ayatollah, 169
khozyaistvenniki (economic managers), 24
Khronopulo, Admiral, 66
Khrushchev, Nikita: attitude to demonstrations, 10; Gorbachev comparison, 77; overthrow, 79, 113; political thaw, 3, 5, 94, 97; rehabilitations, 15; Warsaw Pact, 151
Khrustalov, Alexander, 311–12
Kiev elections, 221
Kirgizia, 155
Kirilenko, Andrei, 110
Kirillov, Yuri, 102–4
Kiselev, Alexander, 121–2
Kislyuk, Mikhail, 317, 320
Kissinger, Henry, 151
Klyamkin, Igor, 268, 269
Kogan, Yevgeni, 266
Kohl, Helmut, 185, 186

Kommunist, 293
Komsomol, *see* Young Communist League
Kosygin, Alexei, 94
Kovalev, Sergei, 385–6
Kozhukovsky, Igor, 322
Kozyrev, Andrei, 38, 285, 369
Krasnodar 'mafia', 340
Kravchuk, Leonid: August coup, 79, 219; Brest agreement, 231; Gorbachev's Union treaty, 226, 248; Ukrainian nationalism, 219–20, 223, 248; Ukrainian referendum, 225, 226; Yeltsin discussions, 215
Krawchenko, Bohdan, 226
Kremlin, 229
Krenz, Egon, 186
Kryuchkov, General Vladimir: Afghan talks, 170; August coup, 61, 62, 67–8, 69, 78, 135, 139; cabinet appeal, 265; Polish policy, 181
Kudryavtsev, Vladimir, 125
Kudryavtsev, Yuri, 218
Kulikov, Lieut-General Alexander, 379, 382
Kuptsov, Valentin, 345
Kurds, 161
Kuzmin, Colonel-General Fyodor, 195
Kuznetsov, Alexander, 352
Kyrgyzstan, 155

land: private allotments, 315–16; reform, 50, 312
Landsbergis, Vytautas, 191, 211–12
languages, 161, 162, 217, 220, 327
Latvia: deputies, 125; independence from Tsarist empire, 159; independence movement, 189–200, 269, 324; nationalism, 212; Russian population, 148, 155, 197, 210–11, 212; Soviet use of force, 197, 209; Supreme Soviet delegate, 252; Yeltsin's approach, 190
leadership, 272–3
Lebedev, Boris, 323
Left-Centre, 280, 281
Lenin, Vladimir Ilyich: congress of deputies plan, 92; death, 161; federation plan, 160; Gorbachev on, 22, 271; Leninists, 21; mausoleum, 31; Peace of Brest, 228; prohibition of factions, 86; Selyunin's criticisms, 41–2; slogans, 93, 100, 283; Stalin warnings, 3; status, 12, 14, 224, 273; Ukraine policy, 216
Leningradskaya Pravda, 111

INDEX

press: Gorbachev's relationship, 99–100; official and unofficial 8, 13, 16; response to reforms, 95–6
price de-control, 295–6, 297, 299–301, 305, 335–6
Primakov, Yevgeni, 68, 201
privatization: buildings, 354; Chinese model, 94; commercialization, 296; consequences, 17, 369; Gaidar's approach, 296, 306; kiosks, 309–10; mines, 321, 322; strategies, 280, 306–10; worker-shareholders, 306–9
Problems of Peace and Socialism, 25
Prokhanov, Alexander, 173–4, 326–31
protection rackets, 309, 364
publishing, 14
Pugachev, Yemelian, 43
Pugo, Boris, 78, 192–3, 199–200, 201–2, 265
Pushkin, Alexander, 324
Pushkin Square, Moscow, 85

racism, 150, 332
Radical Democrats, 280
radio, 108, 287
Razin, Stepan, 43
Reagan, Ronald, 19, 84, 151
Red Proletariat machine-tool plant, 101–4
Red Proletariat publishing, 14
Red Square, 10, 352
religion, 53–4, 130, 216, 327, *see also* Islam, Russian Orthodox church
Renewal party, 338
Republican party, 289
republics, autonomy, 16, 79
Revenko, Grigory, 227
Revolution, Russian, *see* October Revolution
Revolution (1905–7), 43, 46, 56
Romanenko, Major-General V., 66
Romania, 152, 159, 176
Rubiks, Alfred, 190–1, 196, 202
Rukh, 220, 222–5, 226
Rumyantsev, Oleg, 8, 245, 336–7, 348, 382–3
Rus Society, 218
Russia faction, 279
Russian Communist Workers' party, 142
Russian Federation, 62, 245, 264, 279, 331, 339–40
Russian Humanitarian University, 363
Russian National Legion, 332

Russian Orthodox Church, xiv, 5, 52–4, 326, 329, 339
Russian Party of Communists, 142
Russian Soviet Federation of Socialist Republics (RSFSR), 160
Russian Union of Industrialists and Entrepreneurs, 338
Russian Unity, 279
Russia's Choice, 391, 395
Rust, Matthias, xi
Rutskoi, Alexander: acting president, 375; agricultural report, 316; attitude to economic reformers, 292; August coup, 61, 62, 67–8; background, 334–5; criticisms of Yeltsin, 288, 290, 335–6; imprisonment, 333; October 1993 siege, 375–85; on crime and corruption, 353; patriotism, 336–7; People's Party of Free Russia, 277, 280, 333, 335; personality, 334; policies, 333–4, 335–6; White House, 335; Yeltsin's treatment, 38, 39
Ruutel, Arnold, 209
Ryabov, Nikolai, 391
Ryzhkov, Nikolai: attitude to Congress, 93; attitude to reforms, 94–5; Communist party ban hearings, 343; economic reform strategy, 263–4, 271, 297, 307; Lithuanian strategy, 199; memoirs, 273; miners' strike, 317–18; ministerial appointments, 257; on Kazakh nationalism, 157; presidential elections, 247; quoted, 342; relationship with Gorbachev, 32, 33, 34, 140, 168; relationship with Yeltsin, 237, 246

Saburov, Yevgeni, 294
Sachs, Jeffrey, 298
Sajudis, 203, 205
Sakha, 339
Sakharov, Andrei: Article Six, 35, 116–17; Congress election, 92, 107, 108, 116; Congress speech, 253; Gorbachev's attitude, 35–6; Inter-regional Group, 240; memorial meeting, 123; relationship with Yeltsin, 240, 241, 242; release from exile, 24–5
Saltykov-Shchedrin, Mikhail, 359
Scientific and Industrial Union, 338
Second World War, xiv
Security Council, 284–5
Selyunin, Vasily, 41–2, 48, 50, 51